What It Will Take

REJECTING DEAD-ENDS AND FALSE FRIENDS IN THE FIGHT FOR THE EARTH

• • •

Carol Dansereau

ISBN: 1523897007
ISBN 13: 9781523897001
Library of Congress Control Number: 2016902613
CreateSpace Independent Publishing Platform
North Charleston, South Carolina

For
Emily and Corey
Sammy, Gabriel, and Ruben
Julia, Sean, Sophie, Gen, Gabe and Ryan

And for
Brucie

[W]e must honestly face the fact that the movement must address itself to the question of restructuring the whole of American society. There are forty million poor people here, and one day we must ask the question, "Why are there forty million poor people in America?" And when you begin to ask that question, you are raising a question about the economic system, about a broader distribution of wealth. When you ask that question, you begin to question the capitalistic economy. And I'm simply saying that more and more, we've got to begin to ask questions about the whole society. We are called upon to help the discouraged beggars in life's marketplace. But one day we must come to see that an edifice which produces beggars needs restructuring. It means that questions must be raised. And you see, my friends, when you deal with this you begin to ask the question, "Who owns the oil?" You begin to ask the question, "Who owns the iron ore?" You begin to ask the question, "Why is it that people have to pay water bills in a world that's two-thirds water?"

Martin Luther King, August 16, 1967

Table of Contents

PART I

Starting Points

• • •

CHAPTER 1

Urgent Questions

● ● ●

IN THE FALL OF 2011, after 28 years as an environmental organizer and attorney, I found myself plagued by monumental questions:

- Are we losing the struggle for the Earth, dooming our children and grandchildren to horrible environmental conditions and possibly even extinction?
- If we are losing, why is that so? What stands between us and the reforms we want?
- Might the environmental groups we rely on to lead the way forward be part of the problem?
- Is there hope? Do we have the power to turn things around in time?
- What should we do?

As cries of "We are the 99%" resounded from Occupy Wall Street encampments around the world, I embarked on a journey to find answers to these questions. I reviewed my experiences as an activist, researched environmental trends and the forces that influence policies, spoke with other activists, and took the time to think.

The result is this book, a labor of love, offered to everyone who wants to create a just world that ensures our descendants' survival.

Yes, we are losing. The situation is dire and climate change is only one of many threats to our children's happiness and survival.

But yes, there is hope. We have ample natural resources, wealth, and technical know-how to solve every environmental problem and meet the needs of every person on Earth.

And yes, we do have the power to turn things around. In fact, when we look carefully at what we're up against and how we've been fighting, the path forward becomes remarkably clear. The only reason we're losing is that we are continually diverted into dead ends that squander our power.

This book provides the big-picture analysis we desperately need at this pivotal point in history:

Part I shares tales from my decades as a staff person at environmental organizations. These tales illustrate how topics examined later in the book play out in the context of specific nitty-gritty battles for environmental justice. The obstacles we face are insidious, pervasive, and constant. They keep us from even fostering meaningful discussions of environmental problems, let alone winning actual solutions.

Part II looks at how we are doing on environmental issues overall. Despite the illusion of progress fostered by incremental victories and misleading statistics, we are hurtling towards the point of no return on multiple environmental fronts. We must understand the breadth and severity of the environmental crisis we face if we are to address it.

Part III examines the first reason we're losing on environmental issues: the current economic set-up makes it impossible for us to win. Capitalism creates a Big Money giant that calls the shots. We must fully understand this giant, where it comes from, and how it disempowers us, if we are to forge effective strategies for saving our planet.

Big Money control over elections is only a tiny part of why we can't win. Current campaigns for getting money out of politics, though well-intentioned, will not work and could well make matters worse. These campaigns focus on symptoms rather than on the roots of our disempowerment. "Deregulated" capitalism is not the problem. Capitalism is.

Part IV examines the other reason we are losing: we are not fighting back effectively. The environmental groups we've been relying on to save the day are not delivering. They are shaped and influenced by Big Money, and they engage in numerous self-defeating behaviors that keep us running in place or even drag us backwards. These behaviors range from pretending the deck isn't stacked against us to supporting the Democratic Party instead of building a party of our own committed to economic democracy.

Part IV shows that the same dynamics at play regarding environmental issues permeate other social justice issues as well, and it uses health care as an example. It discusses the din created by countless groups waging resource-intensive campaigns in isolation from one another and challenges common assumptions about how to bring about change.

Part V connects the dots from what's detailed in earlier chapters to what we need to do to save our children's world. It lays out the principles we need to follow, the economic democracy agenda we must advance, and specific steps we must take to turn things around. Part V also explains why there is ample reason for optimism despite the dire nature of our situation.

Another question plagued me in the fall of 2011 as I began to work on this book. What was I supposed to do for a living? I had come out of law school decades earlier believing one could make a career out of saving the Earth. But funding for the work I did with farm worker families exposed to pesticides had always been tough to come by, and by 2011 it had dried up completely. I searched for environmental advocacy positions that would allow me to do the work that was most needed, but these positions did not exist.

Thus I faced a choice. I either had to give my time, energy, and passion to an environmental advocacy job I did not believe in, or I needed to separate my activism from my income. The final chapter of this book shares the decision I made. It speaks to the countless young people today who are preparing for environmental careers they hope will help save the world.

It takes courage to examine the facts about where the world is headed, the huge forces undermining democracy, and the ineffectiveness of the groups and strategies we've been relying on. Resist the urge to look away, however. We must understand what's going on around us if we are to choose the right course in these do-or-die times.

Moreover, by gazing unflinchingly into our seeming powerlessness, we ultimately discover that it is actually a mirage. We realize that control over our world and our destiny has been ours for the taking all along. The time has come to use our power to create a just and sustainable world.

CHAPTER 2

Tales from the Trenches

• • •

MANY PEOPLE ROMANTICIZE ENVIRONMENTAL ACTIVISM. They imagine public interest champions presenting compelling arguments for reform and responding to rebuttals in important forums. The going may be tough, but eventually with dogged persistence, these champions win victories for the Earth.

In the real world, things aren't like that at all. There is no grand debate underway. More often than not, environmental activists find themselves locked out of important forums, denied vital information, unable to get real problems and real solutions on the agenda for discussion, and otherwise disempowered.

The stories below provide glimpses of this reality. Each showcases powerful barriers that stand between us and obvious solutions to the world's environmental problems.

Together they provide an important backdrop for the analyses provided later in the book regarding what we're up against, how we're fighting back, and what we need to do differently. While the stories relate to the particular issues I worked on, the barriers they illuminate permeate all environmental activism.

Most of the stories shared here are from my experiences working with farm worker families fighting for the right to no longer be exposed to pesticides. This is a classic "environmental justice" struggle. As members of a low-income community of color, these farm worker families experience disproportionate environmental harm. Language barriers and the threat of deportation make for a particularly egregious situation. Very toxic chemicals are intentionally released into the environment in large volumes near farm workers' homes, daycare centers, schools, and workplaces. Children as well as adults come in regular contact with chemicals associated with cancer, neurological damage, reproductive problems, respiratory disease, and other serious health problems. Acute poisonings of individuals and groups of people are common.

The first story, however, took place before I began working with farm workers. It relates to the famous "Battle of Seattle" at the very end of the twentieth century, when the World Trade Organization (WTO) met in Seattle. I start with this story because the trade agreements we protested at that time have been so instrumental in undercutting environmental, labor, and human rights. They have been a key factor contributing to mass migrations, including the migration to Washington State of people who became the farm workers I worked with. And the protests we mounted in 1999 were harbingers of the protests happening around the world today that offer real hope for humankind turning things around.

Tale Number 1: The WTO Comes to Town

It was 1999 and the WTO was about to meet in Seattle. The Clinton Administration was hurriedly engaging in eleventh-hour outreach to environmentalists and other social justice activists. Administration officials had heard that we were angry and planning to take to the streets in huge numbers. This worried them because there was a chance that the protests might derail the Administration's trade agenda, at least for a while.

We were indeed angry, and justifiably so. Representatives of big corporations had been working hand in glove with the U.S. Trade Representative (USTR) via their membership on 20 large advisory committees that had access to key documents and information. The "Chemical and Allied Products Advisory Committee," for example, included representatives of Dow Chemical, Union Carbide, Amoco, and dozens of other chemical corporations.[1]

Public interest groups, on the other hand, were explicitly excluded from participating in these committees.[2] We had no access to key documents and no influence over what was in them. My organization at the time, the Seattle-based Washington Toxics Coalition (WTC), was suing the Clinton Administration in an attempt to force inclusion of a single public-interest representative on the chemical advisory committee. Similar lawsuits had been filed challenging corporate exclusivity on other committees.

As the result of heavy corporate influence, trade agreements had become a treasure trove of tools corporations could use to block and derail the policies we want. This was the case even with respect to policies that have nothing to do with trade. Corporations had given themselves the power to use international forums to attack local, state, provincial, and national laws they dislike even when these laws apply equally to domestic and foreign products.

As WTC's director, I attended a private meeting that Clinton Administration officials organized with environmental leaders in Seattle. When it was my turn to speak, I pointed to a leaked document in my possession, showing how the USTR had used WTO trade provisions to pressure the European Union (EU) to back off on banning lead in electronic products. The EU requirement was needed to prevent lead exposures for workers and for those who use and dispose of electronic products. It applied equally to electronics produced locally and those imported from other countries. *Why in the world are you fighting against such an important health and safety measure?* I asked Clinton Administration officials at the meeting, pointing out that they were undermining our work as well as that of European activists. *Oh, we were just passing on the position of the American Electronics Association*, they replied, as if that somehow made it okay. The American Electronics Association represented the technology industry.

The basic message delivered to environmentalists in the meeting was this: *Darn. It really is too bad that you weren't included before, but the president cares about you, and from now on, we're going to try to hear from you, too.* When some of us pointed out that the harm had already been done and the only way to remedy the situation was to amend existing agreements, we were told that this was not going to happen. There were thousands of pages of trade agreement provisions on the books that aggressively undermined the public interest, but we were supposed to treat that as water under the bridge and shut up.

The Clinton Administration had another eleventh-hour event planned to appease environmentalists. In the waning days before the WTO would descend on Seattle to finalize yet more outrageous trade provisions, the Environmental Protection Agency (EPA) would at last hold a public meeting on trade and environmental issues. We didn't hear about this via a notice from EPA. Instead we received a call from Kathy Becker, the program officer for our grant from the Bullitt Foundation. EPA had asked the foundation to help organize the meeting, and she wanted me to serve on a planning committee.

Our funders had always had a lot of leverage over us by virtue of determining whether we had money for our work or not. Now, Bullitt was taking things to a new level by acting as gatekeepers for the government. The foundation was deciding who would be at the table to provide input on a government event. Moreover, as a facilitator for the planning process, Bullitt would directly observe and interact with groups for which it held the purse strings, and it would steer how discussions proceeded.

EPA would likely have certain expectations of the Bullitt Foundation regarding how things should proceed. Asking one of the most important environmental funders in the Pacific Northwest to be its helper was a clever move on the Agency's part.

It's hard to say *no* to your major funder, no matter how busy you are. So I found myself on the planning committee for the meeting along with two other environmental activists, a representative of the Chamber of Commerce, and others. Bullitt facilitated the meetings, which were held by phone. Right away it became obvious that EPA had no intention of actually holding a *public* meeting—one in which, at long last, the public would get to provide input to EPA and the USTR on trade. When the committee was asked about the appropriate format for the meeting, I proposed that after a brief opening statement by EPA Administrator Carol Browner, people be allowed to line up at microphones to speak. Others had a different idea. *How about we have EPA and other Administration officials speak, and then we have a panel that includes an environmental group representative? After all that, we'll have someone read a limited number of questions selected from written submissions from the audience.* The committee discussed these options briefly and did not reach agreement. The first item on the agenda for the next meeting was continued discussion of this topic.

Instead, when the next meeting began, Kathy Becker announced that EPA had told her that it would accept no format other than one with pre-screened questions. Therefore, there would be no further discussion on the topic. As Becker amiably moved on to issues like whether to serve donuts, I listened in frustration. After a few minutes, I spoke up, saying that we needed to talk further about the meeting format. *No, Carol, EPA has made it clear. Screened questions read by someone else is a condition it is imposing, so there's nothing to discuss.*

Given how important Bullitt funding was to us, my heart was pounding, but I replied that this sort of condition should not be imposed in a democracy. It was clear that EPA's intent, with the Bullitt Foundation's assistance, was to stage an EPA propaganda meeting, using environmental groups on the planning committee as cover. I noted that I could no longer serve on the committee, excused myself, and left the call. Afterwards, I stared at the phone for a long time, wondering about our future funding.

Later that day, Kathy Becker and Bullitt President Denis Hayes called me. They explained that there is a time and place for the sorts of issues I was raising, but that planning for the meeting was not it. They noted that another local funder of ours and other individuals they described as very "pro-democracy" had agreed to screen audience members' questions, implying that my concerns were therefore unfounded. Screening would assure better coverage of diverse issues, they asserted. I disagreed, noting that lack of a public voice—lack of democracy—was precisely the issue of the day. People needed to speak for themselves. Moreover, a format in which someone reads other people's questions is bound to cause problems. What if Carol Browner misunderstood or evaded a question, for example. No one would be at the mike to point that out. Our funders were not moved by my arguments, however.

As a bone, EPA told the Bullitt Foundation that a couple of us could submit questions in advance. They promised that Browner would respond to these in her opening remarks. So, we put energy into submitting specific, detailed questions. Then we got to work preparing for the public meeting. We sent out an alert to Toxics Coalition supporters and allies, urging people to attend and summarizing our concerns about the WTO agreements. We noted that there would be no opportunity to speak and suggested that people bring signs stating their views.

Soon I received another phone call from Kathy Becker. An unnamed person had seen our alert and contacted her with concerns about "the tone." I wondered who had complained to our funder and whether Becker had even read the alert herself. I took a deep breath and asked her to clarify what she was saying. Becker replied that we should have just given the time and place for the meeting and not included our organization's concerns about the WTO agreements.

But what really seemed to upset her was the alert's suggestion that people bring signs. There was great concern that things could get violent, Becker said, strongly implying that I should be ashamed of promoting violence. She equated encouraging signs with encouraging violence, apparently because people could use sticks as weapons. I was flabbergasted and longed to tell Becker that she was way out of line, but I was dealing with our major funder. I maintained a professional tone and explained that no one was advocating violence. I mentioned the First

Amendment and suggested that people could be encouraged to bring signs that were not on sticks.

Later in the day, Becker called back with Denis Hayes on the line. It seemed he had talked to her about how alerts work, and perhaps she had finally seen what we had written. In any case, our grant program officer no longer criticized us for listing concerns about the WTO on our alert. Becker noted that she'd confirmed that signs without sticks would be allowed at the EPA meeting.

Pause for a moment and consider. After excluding voices of dissent up to the eleventh hour, EPA had enlisted the help of a major funder for regional environmental groups to organize a "public" meeting that promised to actually be a public relations spectacle promoting corporate-serving trade agreements. At the forum, dissent would still be censored and muted, and we had had to fight for even the basic democratic right to express an opinion by holding up a sign.

When the public meeting took place, everything we'd warned about came to pass. Carol Browner gave a lengthy stump speech for President Clinton. She and other Administration officials lauded his supposed commitment to democracy, neatly overlooking the grotesquely undemocratic provisions he had placed in the WTO agreements and his outright exclusion of anyone but corporate officials in the development of those provisions. Browner did not mention or respond to any of the questions we had been urged to submit in advance. Not a one.

The "public" question portion of the evening was torturous to sit through. My own question was among those selected to be read by Washington's secretary of state, Ralph Munro. Although I had had a colleague with impeccable handwriting write my submission to make sure it was very legible, Munro butchered it. He claimed it was hard to read and stumbled on the words, altering their meaning. I scribbled a note to a colleague: "Help! I'm being channeled by Ralph Munro!" Browner did not answer my question. She didn't even talk about the topic I had raised. Instead, she jumped to one of her unrelated talking points. Other questions were similarly destroyed by Munro and evaded by Browner.

Though it was what we'd expected, the event was terrible to experience. It was thoroughly frustrating to have no way to even ask a question, let alone offer a comment, particularly as the event was held up as evidence of President Clinton's keen interest in hearing from someone other than the polluting corporations on his advisory committees. Toward the end of the meeting some members of the audience resorted to heckling Browner.

After the meeting, the Toxics Coalition and allies held an impromptu news conference, but there was no coverage of our perspective in the news media in the following days. Reporters and editorial boards didn't pick up on what we said at our impromptu news conference, nor did they have a chance to hear from extremely knowledgeable activists present in the audience for the "public" meeting, since they had not been allowed to speak. The only thing those who attended the meeting heard from environmentalists was the very brief commentary offered by the lone environmental panelist allowed on stage.

Thus, yet again, there was no media coverage of the issues environmentalists and others were urgently trying to raise. Even worse, *The Seattle Times* ran an editorial chastising environmentalists. *The Times* focused on the heckling that occurred late in the meeting. It claimed that by interrupting Browner, people allowed her to get away with not explaining or defending Administration actions on a particular gasoline issue the paper felt was important. "The administration should be held to account on this matter," the paper intoned. "That means requiring—and permitting—administration officials to make the best case they can for their actions. Only then can informed judgments be made by the citizenry. This is how democracy is meant to function." In short, the public was gagged at the public meeting, as we had been throughout years of corporate-dominated trade negotiations, yet *we* were described by *The Times* as the ones undercutting democracy.

Shortly thereafter, the WTO arrived in Seattle. Despite the Clinton Administration's eleventh-hour attempts at appeasement, tens of thousands of people took to the streets to protest. Our actions, combined with divisions inside the trade meeting, kept the WTO from achieving its goals. WTO participants left town without finalizing various corporate-friendly agreements.

This was only a temporary victory, but it shows the power we can bring to bear. The energy that pulsed through Seattle in 1999 would later infuse Occupy Wall Street and other future uprisings. Kindling that energy remains our greatest hope.

We'll look more at protest as a strategy later in the book. We'll also explore important barriers to environmental progress showcased by this tale, such as policy processes that put private profiteers in the driver's seat and exclude the public, funders pressuring those they fund to adopt certain perspectives, difficulties in securing good media coverage, Democratic Party leaders claiming to serve the public but serving private interests instead, and corporate use of international forums to do end-runs around policies we adopt within our nations, states, and localities.

TALE NUMBER 2: HOW DARE YOU PUBLICIZE OUR STUDY!

It was late January 2004, and I was now working with the Farm Worker Pesticide Project (FWPP). At last, scientists at Fred Hutchinson Cancer Research Center (Fred Hutch) were meeting with me to talk about an important new study of theirs that was going to be published in the February issue of *Environmental Health Perspectives*.

In December, in the course of tracking studies for FWPP, I had come across the pre-publication posting of this study online. Its importance to farm worker families had been immediately obvious. The study documented widespread pesticide exposures among workers who do not handle pesticides as well as those who do, and among workers' children. Community members, policymakers, and the general public needed to know about these new findings as soon as possible. They were highly relevant to upcoming legislative debates and agency rulemakings. FWPP planned to do a news release as soon as the study appeared in print, directing reporters to it and discussing the implications for imminent policy discussions. Media coverage was a critical part of how we would publicize the study.

Ferreting out scientific data that would otherwise sit unseen on library shelves was an important part of the work FWPP was doing. We naively assumed this kind of work would be easy and noncontroversial.

As my meeting with the two scientists who did the research began, however, their hostility towards me was palpable. *How dare you plan on publicizing our study!*

Did Fred Hutch intend to do a news release of its own? No. Why not? In the past, members of their Community Advisory Board (CAB) had expressed concern about being caught off guard by media calls. The CAB was also worried about the public being "unduly alarmed" by news stories. If in the future the CAB wanted a release, the scientists might do one then, but media publicity wasn't going to happen any time soon. The scientists urged me to not contact reporters about their study.

I brought up the importance of the findings for imminent policy discussions. The scientists replied that working together with growers on pesticide issues was a better approach. Oddly, they considered publicizing their own study as somehow incompatible with working with growers.

If a good relationship was maintained with growers, the scientists informed me, there was a chance that someday they might "put information about how to reduce pesticide exposures right on workers' paycheck stubs." *This would be the most effective way to protect workers and their families*, they said. I asked the scientists whether growers would publicize upcoming rulemaking hearings and other policy forums affecting farm workers on pay stubs. *No, of course not*, the scientists replied. *Information would be limited to things like advising workers to remove work shoes before entering their homes.*

Leaving shoes outside was one of the "interventions" Fred Hutch and others were encouraging in an attempt to reduce pesticide exposures. Other "interventions" included things like families regularly washing their floors and vacuuming their cars, i.e., menial tasks that place the burden of dealing with pollution on victims rather than on polluters. Fred Hutch was studying the effectiveness of these interventions.

The scientists believed that they were acting in the community's best interests. It was a desire to honor the CAB's wishes that motivated them, they said. They saw the CAB as the vehicle through which they served and empowered the community they studied. And they reiterated that CAB members didn't want to be caught off guard by reporters calling. Caught off guard? I'd been in contact with the scientists for weeks discussing our planned February release. More importantly, hadn't the scientists been briefing the CAB about the study for years?

Who was on the CAB? The scientists wouldn't tell me. Later I pieced together that, at a minimum, the CAB included a farm worker community member as well as representatives from EPA, the state health department, the state agriculture department, a Spanish language radio station, a legal services organization, Washington State University, and the Growers' League.

The Growers' League represents people who *employ* farm workers. By allowing the League to serve, and by embracing a consensus approach, the Fred Hutch scientists created a dynamic that undercut the interests of working families. The Growers' League had substantial resources at its disposal to steer the CAB toward its priorities. More important, the League and other pro-pesticide participants could block consensus on anything they didn't like. Farm workers serving on the CAB were in a vulnerable position because what they said could get back to employers, affecting their job prospects.

There is little doubt that it was the Growers' League that discouraged Fred Hutch scientists' communications with reporters without prior CAB review. The Growers League called for the same sort of restrictions on University of Washington (UW) scientists when they served on a UW research advisory committee (on which I also served) around this time.

But it didn't really matter who had persuaded the scientists to not publicize their studies and to discourage groups like ours from talking to reporters. Something is very wrong when an advisory committee limits public access to important scientific information.

And the problem runs deeper than this. Doing research for this book, I learned something I did not know in 2004. I came across an article in which the Fred Hutch scientists described how they formed the CAB.[3] They had made sure to select only "moderates" from each constituency. They had also insisted that their research project was to have "a nurturing rather than punitive approach," by which they meant that it "needed to make clear to all concerned that there would be no attempt to eliminate pesticides." Unquestioning acceptance of air blast spraying of drift-prone neurotoxic chemicals near homes, daycare centers, schools, and workplaces was apparently classified as "nurturing."

This framing of the issues and of who might serve on the CAB was outrageous. Using organophosphates and other highly toxic pesticides to control insects on apples and other crops is by no means the only option available to farmers. Lots of farmers use effective organic alternatives that prevent environmental contamination and toxic exposures altogether. Yet, the CAB was not allowed to talk about this fact or to propose studies that did things like compare exposures for families of workers at organic orchards to those of workers at non-organic orchards. Indeed, the carefully selected moderates serving on the CAB wouldn't have dreamed of raising the concept of alternatives to pesticides. And the Fred Hutch scientists limited their research accordingly, all under the guise of serving the public interest.

Putting blinders on with respect to important options that greatly affect health does a disservice to the community scientists claim to serve. It is also profoundly unscientific.

But let's get back to my meeting in 2004 with the Fred Hutch scientists. I told them that I would think about their request that we not do our news release and I would talk with them the next day. After the meeting I sent them an email: "Please, help me make sure I understand your desires correctly. I know that you dislike the idea of a news release. Are you also asking me to not alert individual reporters by phone that a new study has been published? What about reporters with whom I have built relationships who call me periodically to ask what's new?"

Before I could contact the scientists the next day, they emailed to say they were doing a news release of their own after all. If we could hold off on ours, they would appreciate it. I agreed to do that and asked for advance notice before they sent out their release so we could get ours out in a timely manner. Ultimately, the Fred Hutch scientists gave us no advance notice and sent their release out late in the afternoon on a Thursday, a time that tends to minimize news coverage. We hurriedly got our release out shortly thereafter.

As the result of our work, a very important study that would other-wise have been hidden from public view was widely publicized via various newspapers and at least one radio station. It was cited in legislative discussions and in a *Seattle Post-Intelligencer* editorial opposing legislation that would have undercut a program that protects farm workers from pesticides. We counted shining the spotlight on this study as a small victory.

In May of 2008, a review of the impact of Fred Hutch's "interventions" was published in *Environmental Health Perspectives*.[4] The news was not good. Fred Hutch's efforts had not decreased concentrations of pesticide residues found in the dust in people's homes and vehicles. Nor had they decreased concentrations of pesticide metabolites—chemicals that pesticides break down into—measured in the urine of people in intervention homes as compared to those in non-intervention homes. Moreover, in all the households, intervention and non-intervention alike, there had been a significant increase in the median concentrations of particular metabolites found in urine by Year 4 as compared to Year 1 of the study.

There were, however, decreases in the detection rates and median concentrations of one particular pesticide, Guthion, in the dust samples.

EPA had announced an impending ban on this pesticide and had imposed tougher restrictions on workers re-entering Guthion-treated orchards in the meantime. In other words, regulatory action banning pesticides works, while teaching people to take off their shoes, mop floors, and engage in other menial chores does not.[5]

With time, it became harder and harder to get media coverage on our issues. Newspapers like the *Seattle Post-Intelligencer* went under, and with them we lost access to reporters and editors who had shown an interest in the information we had to share. In general, we found fewer and fewer reporters each year who were able and eager to cover the health and justice issues we addressed.

Gathering and sharing information about pesticide exposures and health effects was supposed to be the easy part of our work at FWPP. But even this task felt like pulling teeth. We faced scientists like those at Fred Hutch who inappropriately limited their research and were openly hostile to broad dissemination of results. We also found it difficult to obtain basic information that should have been readily available if there was to be an informed public discussion about the life-and-death issues farm workers and others in agricultural areas face. For example:

- We did not have easy access to most scientific studies because the charge for downloading them was too high for a nonprofit organization. *Environmental Health Perspective's* policy of making all of its studies available free of charge is an exception.
- In most states, those who apply farm pesticides are not required to publicly report their applications.
- Except for rare short-term testing as part of limited studies, there is no monitoring of pesticides in the air.
- Farmers don't have to notify neighbors before spraying next to them.
- Systems for tracking pesticide poisoning cases are inadequate.
- There is very little tracking of other health effects associated with pesticides.

Those who manufacture and sell pesticides benefit when the public can't get basic information. They claim that the burden of proof is on us to establish harm from their products before action can be taken against those products. Then, because we lack the information they've kept hidden, they argue that we haven't met this burden of proof. When, despite the informational barriers they have erected, we *do* assemble compelling cases against their products, they have additional aces up their sleeves to block reform, as we'll see shortly.

Later we'll return to the barriers to environmental progress showcased in this tale. Lack of environmental monitoring, difficulties accessing scientific data, polluter influence over research, exclusion of public interest voices and ideas, and other problems revealed here dominate issues beyond the ones addressed by FWPP.

Tale Number 3: The Department of Royal Run-Arounds

Not long after these adventures with Fred Hutch, I found myself serving on a Washington State Department of Agriculture (WSDA) workgroup. After ignoring 100% of the suggestions that the Farm Worker Pesticide Project had made in written comments submitted during an earlier pesticide rulemaking process, WSDA had at least formed this workgroup. Ostensibly we would discuss pesticide drift, thereby helping WSDA decide what to do about it.

It was obvious from the outset, however, that the workgroup wouldn't lead to real protections for farm workers and others exposed to pesticides.[6] At the beginning of our first meeting, WSDA staffer Ann Wick looked pointedly at me and announced that we wouldn't need to review studies and other data in this workgroup. She knew my propensity to try to foster fact-based discussions and apparently wanted to nip that in the bud. Wick also made it clear that WSDA would not invite an organic farmer to speak to the group, let alone serve on it. Nor would experts on drift or the health effects of pesticide exposures be invited to speak to us.

Another important thing WSDA made clear was that it wouldn't take any action against drift unless there was consensus for that action. The workgroup, as usual, was dominated by those associated with the manufacture, sale, and use of pesticides. Any one of these individuals would be able to block consensus. We were defeated before we began.

Inane. That's really the best word to describe the discussions in our workgroup. Here's what happened on a couple of topics the workgroup considered, for example:

Is drift even a problem at all? Despite Ann Wick's admonitions, FWPP and others provided the group with extensive data documenting that drift was a very serious problem in Washington State and beyond. This information languished unreviewed by WSDA and the workgroup.

Meanwhile, pro-pesticide participants asserted, without evidence, that drift isn't anything to worry about. Some argued that it doesn't occur much because it wastes an expensive product and growers wouldn't want that. Others emphasized that drift creates public relations problems for manufacturers and growers, and therefore they wouldn't let it happen. This is the sort of "analysis" that took place while actual data was kept off the table by WSDA.

At other times, and without any sense of irony, pesticide promoters argued that it was inappropriate to discuss anti-drift measures because drift happens all the time! Drift is to be expected when pesticides are used! That this statement directly contradicted prior claims that drift occurs only *rarely* did not even raise an eyebrow on the part of the WSDA facilitator. Contradictions like these were glossed over as the facilitator smiled and moved us forward in our discussions.

It was also asserted that if drift does occur, it's silly to worry about it because EPA ensures pesticide safety. When I attempted to point to health studies casting doubt on this assertion, discussion was cut off. Perhaps the most Orwellian moment was when pesticide users labeled our attempt to force discussion of scientific studies as an "emotional appeal."

Oh well, there's no consensus on whether drift happens or is a problem. Time to move on, the moderator said. WSDA acted as if it had no duty to try to discern the actual truth. As long as some workgroup members felt that everything was okay, the Agency believed it had no duty to change its policies and programs.

What about promoting safer alternatives to drift-prone pesticides? In previous written comments to WSDA, FWPP had urged the Agency to begin phasing out "bad actor" pesticides with an emphasis on those that are drift-prone. As part of that effort, we called for WSDA to develop and implement a program to help growers transition and thrive via significant educational, technical, and financial assistance.

Our attempts to bring up this topic in the workgroup ran into a brick wall of opposition from those favoring pesticides. Organic growers spray pesticides and engage in inappropriate practices too, it was asserted. No facts were offered to support this. Non-organic farmers have invested in equipment and therefore cannot change, it was argued, again without documentation.

Programs to promote alternatives to highly toxic pesticides are inappropriate for discussion, we were told, because the market system already ensures movement to the least toxic ways of growing food.

Or does it? Again missing the irony, pesticide interests on the workgroup also argued that organic agriculture is doomed and therefore not worthy of discussion because the market system will not allow it to take off. The biggest problem with organic farming, someone said, is that growers can produce more organic product than the market can handle.

Thus the market system was held up as a reason to not discuss programs to transition growers to drift-free agriculture, both because the market was supposedly causing transitions to happen already, and also because the market wouldn't allow them to happen! This shallow, self-contradictory discussion of the topic occurred without a single organic grower present to share his or her knowledge.

At times, statements made by pro-pesticide participants arguing against new drift regulations inadvertently painted a shocking portrait of why such action was so urgently needed. One day, for example, we discussed the idea of requiring growers to notify schools prior to spraying drift-prone pesticides near them. One of the pesticide users on the workgroup argued against this using the following analysis: There are often four or five properties abutting a school. In May each grower may apply pesticides five times a week. Four growers next to a school times five applications per week adds up to 20 applications next to the school per week. On top of all this, 60 to 70 different pesticides may be sprayed. How much paperwork did we want to result from requiring notification to neighbors, the man asked. Meanwhile, I was wondering why we tolerate 20 pesticide applications a week of 60 to 70 pesticides near children.

Periodically, as the free-for-all progressed over the months, the meeting facilitator asked whether consensus had emerged on any issues. Not surprisingly, it hadn't. Also not surprisingly, WSDA blocked discussion of most of the measures to protect people from drift that we had tried to put on the table.

Suddenly, one day, the Agency disbanded our workgroup and announced that it was going to propose a rule requiring certain pesticide users to warn certain neighbors (like schools) before spraying certain pesticides. Woohoo! The Agency might actually take a tiny step forward! At least the few institutions receiving notification would be able to take precautions like shutting off intake vents.

But no. After a lengthy process of drafting the rule, putting it out for public comment, and holding several public hearings, WSDA quietly rescinded its proposed rule on December 30th, 2005. FWPP had worked hard commenting on drafts of the rule, providing the studies Ann Wick eschewed, and mobilizing others to get involved. The record for the rulemaking showed overwhelming support for notification, with most people wanting the rule to be made stronger. (The count was 277 for the rule, 25 opposed, according to the Wenatchee World.)[7]

But WSDA decided to do nothing. The rule was dead. We were back to ground zero.

WSDA gave two outrageous reasons for its retreat. First, it couldn't adopt the rule because there was no consensus. Second, the rule would put schools at risk of liability. *What if a school knows spraying is going to occur and doesn't take adequate steps to protect people, and then someone sues the school?* It's better to keep schools and other farm neighbors in the dark about impending applications of highly toxic chemicals next door, WSDA concluded.

We mobilized an impressive array of groups and individuals who contacted the governor to urge her to force WSDA Director Loveland to adopt the notification rule. Previously, Governor Gregoire had ignored our request to appoint someone other than Loveland to head WSDA and she held true to her policy of ignoring us with respect to the notification rule. Gregoire knew there would be no price to pay for these and other anti-environmental actions. Indeed, in the 2008 election, other environmental groups praised her as an eco-hero.[8]

We had all sorts of other adventures with the Department of Royal Run-Arounds. For example:

* When labor organizations nominated me to serve as the labor rep on WSDA's Pesticide Advisory Board (PAB), WSDA ignored them. That position was unfilled in February 2005 when the PAB voted on whether WSDA should suspend the workgroup discussed above (without it having examined proposals put forth by pesticide exposure victims). The agency then had the audacity to point me to the PAB vote as evidence of the wisdom of the suspension.[9] (Note that even with labor represented, the PAB is

heavily stacked in favor of pesticide interests.) Finally one day when I called the agency yet again to find out what was going on, an administrative assistant cheerfully informed me that the labor position had been filled. "Might I ask who's been appointed so labor organizations can have some idea as to who is representing us?" I inquired. The assistant missed the irony of my question.

◆ WSDA inspector David Zamora did a good job of enforcing drift and other pesticide regulations. So farmers and the Farm Bureau got state legislators to pressure WSDA to remove him from his position, accusing him of wrongdoing. WSDA complied. Even after an independent investigation fully exonerated Zamora, WSDA refused to reinstate him. Enforcement rates dropped precipitously after Zamora's removal.[10]

◆ Through a public disclosure act request, we obtained a letter sent by WSDA to a state legislator assuring her that she needn't worry about WSDA enforcing against drift. The letter openly acknowledged that "drift occurs in almost every pesticide application." It thoroughly contradicted what WSDA said publicly, which was that drift is rare and the Agency takes strong enforcement action when it happens.

◆ Six farm workers were tending grapes when a helicopter sprayed a neurotoxic pesticide called malathion on an adjacent orchard. They felt the pesticide hit them and immediately became violently ill. They were taken to the hospital via ambulances. Years later, some still suffered health effects.

WSDA inspectors tried to do the right thing. They levied a $7500 fine and suspended the pilot's license for 120 days in this clear-cut case. The applicator appealed, however, and WSDA's director sided with him. The farm workers had to go to court. More than five years after the workers were poisoned, WSDA's director was finally forced by the courts to reinstate penalties. She did so, but decreased the fine to $5600 and the suspension to 84 days.

Top managers at WSDA enjoyed an extremely cozy relationship with pesticide corporations and farm organizations committed to on-going pesticide use. Their disdain for anyone concerned about the impacts of pesticides on health and the environment was obvious.

As we'll see later in the book, undue private influence over agencies in charge of implementing and enforcing environmental laws extends far beyond pesticide issues. Agencies everywhere empower the parties they're supposed to regulate by declaring that consensus must be reached with them before regulatory action can be taken. They fail to adopt rules that fulfill the protective goals of statutes adopted by legislatures. They also fail to enforce laws and regulations, and they undercut inspectors who try to do the right thing. These realities are central to why we are losing the fight for our environment. They must be addressed if we want to win that fight.

TALE NUMBER 4: WE TEST THE AIR, WIN A VICTORY, AND PAY THE PRICE

By 2006, we'd wasted years trying to get the state agriculture department to protect people from pesticide drift. They would neither acknowledge that drift was a problem nor gather air samples to assess the situation. It was time for us to take matters into our own hands.

We decided to test the air ourselves. Our goals were to obtain scientifically useful results and to shame the state into doing its own testing. If we documented that highly toxic pesticides were drifting into the air that workers and their families breathed, surely this would help us win the protections we needed.

The environmental group Pesticide Action Network provided us with "Drift Catchers" and training, and we held workshops to identify and train families who wanted to participate. Adhering to strict scientific protocols, two families gathered air samples in their yards for three weeks during the chlorpyrifos spray season. Chlorpyrifos is strongly linked to neurological impairment and other chronic health problems, especially in children. It can also trigger acute poisonings.

We published our results in a report entitled *Poisons on the Wind* and got some news coverage. We had found chlorpyrifos in the air in both families' yards every single day of the three-week test period. Concentrations frequently exceeded the so-called Reference Exposure Level (REL). We'll talk about RELs in more depth later, but for now a brief description: they supposedly mark the dividing line between concentrations of a pollutant that are safe and those that are cause for concern. The basis for declaring sub-REL exposures safe is highly flawed, however, as will be documented later.

Our air monitoring work succeeded in changing the terms of the debate. We were invited to speak to the state's Pesticide Incident Reporting and Tracking (PIRT) Panel, which then adopted a resolution calling on the state to monitor the air for pesticides. PIRT's resolution helped us persuade the state legislature to allocate money for a two-year pesticide air-monitoring program, to be administered by the State Department of Health (DOH). DOH engaged the University of Washington to collect the chlorpyrifos air samples.

Years after we tested the air, UW published results that reinforced our own. UW found near-field concentrations of chlorpyrifos that were comparable to what we'd found. They also showed that chlorpyrifos was drifting throughout the entire region in which it was sprayed. It was present in the air every day of the spray season, even far from the fields.[11]

Was action taken to curtail drift as the result of both FWPP and the state proving that drift was real and constant? The next tale will answer that question. Before going there, however, we will look at the ugly consequences of our "radical" action of demanding and obtaining information about what people are forced to breathe. The veil that hides pesticide drift had been pulled back and pesticide interests made sure that heads rolled as a consequence.

An all-out attack was launched against PIRT; the DOH program that facilitated PIRT meetings; the director of that program; and Dr.

Steven Gilbert, the toxicologist on PIRT who encouraged it to support state air testing. Key perpetrators of the attack included:

* Washington Friends of Farms and Forests (WFFF). Its board included representatives of Bayer CropScience (the manufacturer of one of the pesticides for which we wanted air testing); Wilbur-Ellis Company (an international marketer and distributor of agricultural products with sales exceeding $2 billion in 2007); Weyerhaeuser-Regeneration (one of the largest pulp and paper companies in the world, which applied pesticides on forest lands and battled neighbors over drift); the Royal Flying Services (which sprayed pesticides from airplanes); and others with a financial stake in encouraging ongoing pesticide use.[12] One wouldn't know WFFF's true allegiance from its name.

* Consultant Jim Jesernig, a former director of the state agriculture department, who was a classic beneficiary of the revolving door between industry and government. Jesernig's clients included Croplife (which represented pesticide developers, manufacturers, formulators, and distributors and counted among its members Dow and Bayer, the manufacturers of particular pesticides we wanted tested), Responsible Industry for a Sound Environment (which represented producers and suppliers of specialty pesticides and fertilizers),[13] and the Potato Commission (which was concerned about potential air testing of a pesticide widely used on potatoes).

These groups and the farm organizations that regularly ally with them carried out a coordinated offensive.[14] Through a flurry of letters, other written communications, and meetings with state officials, they claimed that PIRT was acting beyond its jurisdiction—an absurd accusation that conflicted with clear language in the statute that established PIRT. (The Panel's mission included "identifying inadequacies in state and/or federal law that result in insufficient protection of public health and safety," for example.)[15] Dr. Gilbert was absurdly denounced as prioritizing his own personal agenda and career. Gilbert and PIRT were even chastised for the new "Science Corner" item on PIRT's monthly agenda, a 10- to 15-minute slot used to discuss the latest scientific studies related to pesticide exposures and health effects. FWPP and Pesticide Action Network were slammed as "fear-mongers."

The industry groups didn't hesitate to fabricate things out of thin air to undercut us. They invented a story about one of PIRT's monthly meetings, claiming that environmental and labor groups rudely interrupted speakers and otherwise disrupted the meeting. In truth, the meeting was dull and ordinary. There were no interruptions or disruptions whatsoever. Nonetheless this lie was widely repeated.

Behind the scenes, WFFF and Jesernig led the pressure on Democratic Governor Chris Gregoire to remove Dr. Gilbert from the panel. We know the details because of documents we obtained through a public disclosure request.

We and an impressive array of public interest allies defended PIRT, DOH, and Dr. Gilbert. We urged the governor not to cave to pesticide industry pressure. But she did. Here is the unfortunate chronology:

* Gregoire refused to reappoint Gilbert, leaving the toxicologist position on PIRT unfilled for an extended period.
* Gregoire then appointed Dr. Charles Timchalk, a toxicologist who had worked for Dow from 1986 to 1997 and still received funding from them regularly. Dow manufactures chlorpyrifos, which was a primary subject of air monitoring and was the cause of acute poisonings tracked by PIRT. Documents we received through our public disclosure request indicated that Jim Jesernig and the governor's office had to work hard to persuade Timchalk to agree to be appointed.[16]
* We discovered the Dow connection and told reporters, thereby causing a newspaper story that exposed what the governor was doing.

* The governor refused to back down but the Dow-funded appointee resigned. The Toxicologist position was again unfilled, as Dr. Gilbert regularly attended meetings as an audience member and reiterated his desire to serve.

* As we prepared to give reporters additional documentation of the influence the pesticide industry had over Gregoire and to further expose her anti-environmental positions, we were approached by a staff person from a leading state environmental organization. She advocated that we pull back. In particular, she discouraged us from using our most effective tool—news coverage that exposed and criticized the governor's actions and positions. *What's the value of beating up on her further?* she asked.

  The value of continued news coverage was obvious. We were finally getting some traction. Besides, shouldn't people know what the governor was up to on these issues?

  It was an election year. Environmental activists didn't want the Democratic governor to look bad—even if she *was* bad—because that might help her Republican opponent. Around this time, in a separate discussion with an environmental activist about the upcoming election, I complained that it was hard to imagine anyone worse than Gregoire on pesticide issues. *Oh no it isn't* came the immediate reply. *Her Republican opponent is worse.* We needed to buck up and support Gregoire no matter how horrible she was on major environmental issues, according to this activist.

* A committee that reviewed candidates for the unfilled toxicologist position on PIRT continued to urge reappointment of Gilbert and offered another candidate as well, but the Governor appointed neither.

* We tried to get the *Seattle Post-Intelligencer* to follow up on its earlier hard-hitting reporting but instead they pulled back. They even issued an editorial asserting that Gregoire's failure to appoint Gilbert wasn't motivated by pressure from pesticide

interests. Shortly thereafter, the *Post-Intelligencer* predictably endorsed Gregoire for governor.

- Under the laughable guise of budgetary necessity, the governor proposed that PIRT be eliminated. It cost almost nothing for PIRT to meet. We fought off PIRT's demise for a year, and then lost. PIRT was erased, and with it we lost a forum in which we had at last been engaging in meaningful public discussions about farm pesticide issues.
- The governor's budget also gutted the Department of Health's pesticide program. The program was forced to get by with half as many people and half as much money.
- The governor refused to clarify what her policy was with respect to government appointments and conflicts of interest.
- State air monitoring was not renewed.

In short, through herculean efforts we had won a legislative victory and the state had monitored the air. But the program was not renewed, we lost PIRT, and DOH's pesticide program was crippled.

The forces that slammed into us in response to our simple desire to have the air tested for pesticides are the same forces that slam into environmental activists everywhere when they try to make progress. Later in the book we'll dig deeper into concepts highlighted by this tale, such as behind-the-scenes pressure on government officials, private interests hiding behind public-interest-mimicking front groups, personal attacks on scientists and activists who start to get somewhere, environmental groups and newspapers holding punches for Democrats, and elected officials appointing people who have obvious financial conflicts of interest to important positions.

But first, another tale from the trenches. After all, our intrepid community-based environmental group had secured clear proof that highly toxic pesticides do, in fact, drift. We had shown that chlorpyrifos is in the air everywhere in agricultural regions, every day of the lengthy spray season. Surely we would get some action to protect people now.

Tale Number 5: Risk Assessment: A Magical Tool for Declaring Toxic Exposures Okay

It turned out that pesticide corporations have another ace up their sleeve. They can compare concentrations of pesticides found in the environment to "Reference Exposure Levels" (RELs).[17] If concentrations are below those levels: Presto! They're not a problem, and anyone who's worried about them, well, we are obviously emotional and anti-science.

It works best for pesticide profiteers when academics make comparisons to RELs for them. This adds an undeserved aura of independent scientific validity to declarations of safety. And that's what happened when UW scientists finally released the results of the air tests they did for the state DOH under the program we had forced. The University was only supposed to collect the samples, leaving analysis of health implications to DOH. But they made a point of using RELs to dismiss their findings as nothing to worry about.

There were three RELs that UW scientists could have used: two identical ones from EPA and a California government agency, and a third more conservative REL which we had used in our *Poisons on the Wind* report that analyzed our own air test results. UW scientist Dr. Richard Fenske had specifically reviewed our REL when our report came out, declaring it scientifically valid. But now he acted as if it didn't exist. Comparing what UW found in the air to the EPA/California REL, the UW scientists declared that "it does not appear that the agricultural spraying we monitored posed a health hazard to nearby residents and communities." Because the chlorpyrifos concentrations they measured were below their chosen RELs, the scientists announced that "no health impacts are anticipated."[18] They never mentioned the more protective REL and the fact that concentrations they had measured exceeded it.

With RELs being used to declare that ongoing daily exposures to chlorpyrifos are A-OK, we decided to get a better understanding of what underlay these numbers.

RELs are the product of a three-step process:

- First, researchers do laboratory studies in which they expose animals to a particular pesticide and watch for certain adverse effects. The effects they look for, the design of the study, and how it is carried out are each important.
- Second, EPA or some other agency or institution looks at these studies and determines what the No Observable Adverse Effect Level (NOAEL) is.
- Finally, EPA, other regulatory agencies, or non-governmental scientists use the NOAEL as the base number in a calculation to determine a "safe" level of exposure for people. They can choose to multiply the NOAEL by various safety or uncertainty factors if they want. They might multiply it by 10 or some other factor to account for potentially greater human vulnerability as compared to lab animals, for example. They might also multiply it by some factor to account for children's greater susceptibility as compared to adults. Each step in the calculation involves a policy decision regarding how cautious to be. In any case, the number that comes out of this calculation is the REL, which purportedly delineates the line between safety and cause for concern regarding people's exposures to toxic chemicals.

All three of the RELs UW had to choose from—including the more protective one they ignored, which used a safety factor that reflected children's greater susceptibility to harm—were based on the very same NOAEL. We set about finding out where that NOAEL came from.

Our quest was long and arduous. Ultimately we learned two things: i) RELs for chlorpyrifos are based on garbage, and ii) the system is set up to keep that hidden.

The first part of our quest involved identifying the studies from which the NOAELs were derived. This was not an easy task, but eventually we figured it out. Two producers of chlorpyrifos—Dow and

Makhteshim-Agan—had given EPA a total of seven studies. Two of these studies were used to determine the NOAEL for short and intermediate periods of inhaling chlorpyrifos. The other five were used to come up with the NOAEL for longer exposure periods.

We finally knew which studies underpinned the RELs. We wanted to read them, so we searched EPA's website. They were not there. We searched the internet, and still they didn't show up. DOH's toxicologist was on the trail, too, and also could not find the studies.

Eventually, I found someone at EPA who knew where, in the bowels of the Agency, the studies were hidden. EPA required me to complete an "Affirmation of Non-Multinational Status" form to obtain them. This form, and its accompanying materials, made it clear that FWPP would risk being sued if we made it easier for others to read these important studies by, for example, posting them on our website, as had been our plan. "You may…wish to take steps to avoid inadvertent disclosure of the data by keeping it in a secure place," the fact sheet for the form said. "Before publishing it or deliberately disclosing it to others, you may wish to seek legal advice." This was all supposed to ensure that competitors of Dow and Makhteshim-Agan didn't see the studies. Those competitors had probably figured out a way to get them long ago.

Let me make sure you understand how warped this all was. RELs were used to tell people not to worry about inhaling chlorpyrifos and to justify government inaction regarding drift. But to get the studies on which the RELs were based, we needed to search for a long time, file an information request, and promise to not make it easier for other people to see the studies.

I signed the damn form, submitted it, and waited. Finally, a disk with the studies on it arrived in the mail. After one last challenge—finding someone whose computer could open the files—I had the actual printouts on my desk and could read them.

Several things were striking about the studies on which everything hinged:

- They had never been published. That meant they had never been peer-reviewed, a process that is supposed to ensure scientific quality.
- They were very old. When I tracked down the studies underpinning the RELs used to dismiss our concerns about chlorpyrifos in the air, it was 2009. EPA, the UW scientists, and others were relying on numbers based on studies done in 1971, 1985, 1989, and 1990.
- There were so few of them. Who would have thought that such grand pronouncements of safety were all balanced on a handful of studies?
- The scope of what was studied was quite limited. The exquisite sensitivities and capacities of human brains are worlds apart from those of rats and dogs, yet measurements on changes in those animals determined what was considered safe for humans.
- The studies were all done by manufacturers of chlorpyrifos who had obvious financial conflicts of interest.

Around this time I obtained a copy of an analysis done by a team of neuroscientists at Stanford University that specifically examined the scientific quality of Dow's *published* chlorpyrifos research. The team had found rampant scientific errors in the Dow studies. Significantly, whenever any error affected determinations as to risks posed by chlorpyrifos, the studies served to understate those risks.[19]

The RELs used by UW and FWPP rested on a small stack of pathetic, old, unpublished corporate studies. Meanwhile, they ignored all sorts of important independent research, including human studies, with decidedly different implications than those of the manufacturers' research. The UW scientists surely knew about these studies, as we had communicated with them about this topic. Nonetheless they made no mention of the fact that the RELs they were using failed to incorporate significant scientific research. They simply indicated that the RELs they'd chosen were not exceeded and therefore people really didn't need to worry. They pretended that RELs are based on sound science rather than hidden, unpublished corporate-funded studies from decades ago. And in 2010, when a California agency adopted a more conservative REL equivalent to the one FWPP had used, the UW scientists declined to amend their report to make use of it. Nor did they mention that their results included exceedances of that new California REL.

It was also obvious that we had a "tails you win, heads we lose" situation with the UW scientists regarding community pesticide exposures. In previously reviewing FWPP's results and the fact that they frequently exceeded the protective REL we used, Dr. Fenske had declared that an REL is "not a clear dividing line between 'safety' and 'danger'." He had said that "findings above the level indicate that there may be a concern regarding risk, and that further investigations are needed."[20] In other words, when pesticides in the air are *below* RELs, everyone is safe, and pesticide exposures can continue unabated. And when pesticides in the air are *above* RELs, well even then exposures can continue while scientists like Dr. Fenske and his colleagues do more studies.

Throughout our struggle for environmental justice, Dr. Fenske played a role of soothingly implying that action to stop drift and associated exposures was premature. Newspapers quoted not only his assurances that the REL exceedances we documented simply meant that more studies would be good, but also included other statements he made that were dismissive of our concerns. Dr. Fenske criticized FWPP for testing the air at homes that were 50 or 60 feet from orchards because they reflected *high* exposures rather than *average* exposures, for example.[21] Of course we tested the air of families living next to and within orchards. Our goal was to protect those families, but Dr. Fenske's criticisms undercut us.

When exactly *can* we get action to stop toxic exposures? That's unclear. There are no standards declaring certain pesticide levels in the air illegal. There are only RELs, benchmarks based on hidden industry data. When concentrations of a pesticide in the air are below the RELs, exposures will continue unabated. When concentrations exceed the RELs, exposures will still continue unabated as scientists take a few more years to propose, fund, and carry out more studies. Who knows what they have to find before they'll suggest ending exposures.

Reporters should have asked Dr. Fenske what levels of chlorpyrifos in the air *would* warrant action to stop the exposures. The answer appears to be that the sky's the limit.

Still, we held tight and submitted all sorts of written comments to the state DOH, urging that agency to propose policy reforms to better protect health as promised. But it was too late. By the time UW finally made its air testing results public, DOH's pesticide program had already been gutted, as detailed in the last tale. From the run-around we now got from DOH management, it was clear that this agency had become as unhelpful to those exposed to pesticides as WSDA was.

For years, we contacted DOH and urged it to act, to no avail. While writing this book I made another stab at getting the agency to move. I got back a bizarre letter indicating that DOH had acted long ago. They just hadn't thought to mention this to FWPP and others who had worked so hard on these issues. What DOH had done was punt to EPA. Instead of evaluating the health implications of constant widespread chlorpyrifos drift—a phenomenon that could no longer be ignored due to the testing we had forced—and recommending policy reforms as planned, DOH had simply sent the air testing results on to EPA. That Agency had already received this information years earlier.

So now the only hope we had was EPA. That was sobering because EPA and its predecessor agency had approved and reapproved chlorpyrifos since 1965. We were approaching half a century of people being exposed to a toxic chemical strongly linked by substantial research to neurological impairment and other health problems.

In 2000, EPA had announced that Dow and other manufacturers had agreed to voluntarily cancel *residential* uses of chlorpyrifos. The impact on Dow had been limited. (Only an estimated 15% of its $350 million annual sales in the U.S. at that point were affected.) With 10.5 million acres of cropland sprayed with chlorpyrifos in the U.S., Dow could continue to rake in profits. While expanding farm sales in the U.S., it could push residential as well as farm sales abroad. Meanwhile, the Clinton Administration had been able to sound tough on pollution. EPA Administrator Carol Browner had denounced chlorpyrifos as "part of a class of older, riskier pesticides..." that could cause neurological effects. She had said "it is clear the time has come to take action to protect our children from exposure to this chemical."

Well, certain children that is. EPA condemned farm worker children and others who live and work in agricultural areas to ongoing chlorpyrifos exposures. These exposures continue today as I write these words.

RELs are not only used to downplay air testing results. They are also small but important pieces in the giant Risk Assessment process used to justify ongoing approvals of pesticides. Slipshod numbers are plugged into larger analyses, producing flimsy conclusions. Those conclusions become faulty assumptions for the next level of calculations, replete with its own additional, questionable data and protocols. And so it proceeds onward and upward. There are so many variables and steps involved in a major EPA Risk Assessment—such as the ones it is doing in its current review of chlorpyrifos—that each completed assessment can be said to provide, at best, highly uncertain conclusions. Add in the pesticide industry's influence and one can only conclude that Risk Assessment is a charade. Those who malign communities reluctant to trust their lives and health to it are supremely arrogant and misguided.

Dow is a primary provider of the studies and data on which EPA is relying, as it decides whether to reapprove chlorpyrifos once again. Meanwhile, the Agency is ignoring other data, such as important studies by independent scientists and large numbers of acute poisoning cases involving chlorpyrifos. In EPA's machinations to determine whether chlorpyrifos might hurt people's health, it pretends, for example, that 10 Washington State farm workers did not experience vomiting, stomach cramps, diarrhea, headaches, and other extreme symptoms as the result of chlorpyrifos drift in a Washington State orchard in the spring of 2010. No, the Agency has found a way to file that case and others like it in a drawer somewhere, while claiming to be dedicated to ensuring that people aren't hurt by chlorpyrifos.

If somehow EPA's risk calculations do conclude that chlorpyrifos can't be used without creating risks the Agency considers too high, it can still re-approve it. The federal pesticide law requires EPA to compare costs to benefits in ultimately deciding what to do.[22] Again relying primarily on industry information, the Agency tends to conclude that the costs of banning a pesticide outweigh the benefits of protecting people. EPA allowed ongoing used of the pesticide Guthion for years after its own Risk Assessments produced outcomes that should have triggered a ban, for example. Workers were forced to enter Guthion-laden fields after only 14 days even though EPA's calculations indicated they were unsafe for 102 days.

The Risk Assessment approach that rules at EPA and state agencies is one that allows pesticide companies to spread their toxic chemicals throughout the world. Contamination and exposures continue unless and until people prove that we're being harmed, which is nearly impossible given the dynamics of Risk Assessment, including the obvious power that pesticide corporations have to manipulate it. Risk Assessment stands in sharp contrast to a precaution-based approach, which requires proof of safety before toxic chemicals are used.

For 50 years, the federal government has allowed ongoing agricultural use of chlorpyrifos, even though crops can be grown sustainably without it. In a rational society, we would grow food without exposing pregnant women, other adults, and children to highly toxic chemicals. Risk Assessment is used to create the Orwellian impression that those who want to end toxic exposures are irrational while those who perpetuate those exposures are reasonable and wise.

Risk Assessment is used to justify not just ongoing production, sales, and use of pesticides, but also all sorts of other environmentally destructive products. Later in the book, we'll explore where this huge obstacle to sane environmental policies comes from. It is just one of several frameworks big corporations manipulate to get their way, and only one of the avenues through which the imprimatur of "sound science" is falsely applied to profit-serving analyses that are the antithesis of sound science.

OTHER TALES FROM THE TRENCHES

"Too Much" Organic. A person who worked for the Washington State University Center for Sustaining Agriculture and Natural Resources (CSANR) attended one of the farm worker pesticide tours FWPP organized. He was kind enough to bring handouts[23] that showed that organic apple acreage was up more than 60% in 2008 as compared to 2007. Even with that growth, most orchards were not organic. Only 8% of the state's apple acres were farmed organically.

When I asked how we could increase that number, the Washington State University (WSU) staffer discouraged the whole idea. Putting more acres into organic production would reduce organic apple prices, he explained. And organic growers need that price premium to survive. In other words, someone who was supposed to be promoting sustainable agriculture was discouraging it. The barriers were not biological or physical. They were strictly political—an outcome of our economic system.

These same market barriers undermine us on environmental issues beyond pesticides, such as the need to substitute renewable energy for fossil fuels. A more rational approach that empowers us to implement the changes we need will be discussed later in the book.

Goodbye Guthion. Hello Whatever. In 2007 and 2008 I served on an advisory committee providing advice to EPA regarding the phase-out of the pesticide Guthion. This organophosphate pesticide was to finally be fully banned six years later and EPA wanted input on handling the transition. It was the usual set-up, with two farm worker representatives outrageously outnumbered by pesticide corporations and those who enjoy a cozy relationship with the pesticide industry.

I and the other farm worker representative gamely put forth a commonsense premise: any strategies and materials that EPA produced related to growers transitioning away from Guthion should analyze the health and environmental impacts of what they could transition to. *Let's get all of that information on the table and then help growers move to the most sustainable alternatives available, including non-chemical methods of controlling pests*, we said.

EPA staffers never actually refused to do what we suggested. *Oh yes, good idea. That information should be examined. We'll get to it later*, they replied. They just never did. *How's never? Does never work for you?*

Matrices were produced without columns for health and environmental information, let alone the information itself. EPA's list of alternatives to Guthion included options that raised major red flags, such as other organophosphates. The list included "neonicitinoid" pesticides, which hurt bees and other pollinators.

The other farm worker rep on the committee volunteered to be part of a three-person team to produce a transition case study for apples. I was to assist her. But the two other team members quickly produced a case study, which they sent to EPA without including the farm worker rep at all. They then attacked me at the next meeting for having the gall to object to this unacceptable process. EPA acted as if ignoring the agreed-upon process and excluding farm worker representatives in the preparation of the case study was no problem whatsoever.

We kept providing information and trying to get EPA to engage in the rational review we'd requested, to no avail. Eventually, the meetings became less frequent and then they stopped altogether. EPA later referred proudly to having worked with "stakeholders" to develop draft Guthion transition strategies, without mentioning that farm worker perspectives were not reflected at all in their transition strategies.

Our experience with this workgroup is typical of what goes on with workgroups and committees across the spectrum of environmental issues. We gained nothing, at the same time enabling EPA to falsely claim that it had listened to public interest perspectives in making its decisions.

My Alma Mater Deepens Its Relationship with Dow Chemical. I received a cheerful message in 2012 from my alma mater, the University of Michigan (UM). I and other alums were invited to the Westin Book Cadillac Hotel in Detroit to hear a fabulous announcement. Dow Chemical Company CEO Andrew Liveris and UM President Mary Sue Coleman were going to unveil an innovative new collaboration.

As I waited on the appointed day to listen to the announcement online, I was treated to a repeating loop of ads depicting Dow Chemical as a sustainability leader. Dioxin, napalm, chlorpyrifos, and other dramatically unsustainable Dow products and byproducts were not mentioned.

Finally the lovefest began. Liveris and Coleman gushed over each other and their partnership. Dow was going to give UM $10 million over six years. It would fund paid fellowships for 300 masters, doctoral, and postdoctoral students, enabling them to engage in research, discussions, and strategizing on sustainability issues. A grateful student talked about how grad students have debts and would welcome fellowships like these. Liveris mentioned that Dow's intellectual property rights would have to be protected, but Coleman and he had worked that all out. Neither Coleman nor Liveris acknowledged the disconnect between letting Dow own ideas and technologies emerging from the school and claiming that the partnership was all about "sharing."

A copy of the Dow-UM contract, obtained by a local environmental group, stated that Dow would get to embed an employee at the university to monitor and be involved in the programs it was funding. According to the contract, Dow would play a key role in determining which individuals were selected as fellows and which would be honored with Dow awards. The university was required to produce an annual report for Dow and get the corporation's pre-approval for films, books, and other materials.

Comprehensive policy stances and materials were expected to be produced as the result of the UM-Dow collaboration. In other words, this private corporation with a financial stake in policy outcomes will get to influence those outcomes via financial ties to an academic institution.

Dow's mega donation to my alma mater is just the tip of the iceberg regarding how corporations use academic institutions to serve their private interests. All sorts of huge corporations—not just chemical corporations like Dow—give huge amounts of money to universities and to K through 12 schools, as we'll see later. This dramatically undermines our ability to create the world we want.

State Farm Isn't There. FWPP was required to get office insurance by our landlord. But State Farm refused to sell it to us. Why? Higher-ups felt that some of the company's customers might not agree with our work. It turns out that the "good neighbor" thing doesn't apply if you do something radical like promote alternatives to pesticides.

This tale illustrates the insidious ways in which the tentacles of those who profit from the environmental status quo undercut activists fighting for change. Bizarre episodes like this are not limited to pesticide issues.

The Class Ceiling and Turning Off the Lights. For years I was known as the "grant queen" because of my high success rate in obtaining grants. When I decided to work with farm worker families, we naïvely believed that we'd be able to use my contacts and skills to deliver much-needed funding for taking on one of the biggest environmental problems in America.

But that didn't happen. Our organization struggled. We learned that in general, foundation lip service to helping low-income communities of color is just that: lip service.

FWPP did wonderful work. We worked hard and strategically, and we rapidly changed the debate on agricultural pesticide issues. Our work had national as well as regional and local impacts.

Despite this great record and the energy we put into fundraising, FWPP was never able to gain a real funding foothold. We got numerous grants but most were quite small, meaning we had to track lots of pots of money with different grant years and reporting requirements. And we didn't have enough money in the bank at any given time to confidently offer long-term employment to people. We were grateful for the foundation assistance we did receive, but longed to pull in a big grant or two to get the footing we needed to move forward.

Much of the time I worked for FWPP, I earned part-time wages to ensure funds for employing a staff person from the farm worker community. In the best of times, we were able to employ a total of two part-time staffers, including me.

We were in a real catch-22. Our small size was a sticking point, particularly for bigger foundations we approached that could have easily transformed our organization with what to them was pocket change. Farm worker pesticide issues had been ignored for a very long time, and we were pulling ourselves up by our bootstraps from nothing. Yet, we were denied funding because we lacked funding. *We need you to increase your staffing and funding before we can support you*, foundations told us. But how could we increase our staffing and funding without getting some nice grants that gave us the stability and security that we needed? The Great Recession made things even worse.

We held fundraising events and solicited help from small and major donors. But it takes money to really make much money in these endeavors.

Over the years I saw a transformation in the foundation world. They started demanding things like business plans more and more. Our experiences with the Kresge Foundation are illustrative. We had great hopes that this large foundation would be our ticket to the big leagues because our plans and accomplishments meshed so well with its stated priorities. Our letter of inquiry prompted an encouraging reply from a program officer who understood the issues we faced. She asked us to supply her with information to use in educating others at the foundation about why they should take on farm worker pesticide issues. For years we were in a mode of sending materials and waiting, hoping that our ship would ultimately come in.

Finally, the day came when our request moved on to the next step. The program officer introduced us by phone to a businessperson at the foundation who would handle things from then on. The discussions changed radically. This new person had no discernable awareness of or interest in the issues we addressed. She had no understanding whatsoever of organizing, particularly in a low-income community plagued with challenges like the constant threat of deportation. *What's your business plan?* she asked. *What return will Kresge get on a financial investment in your organization?* I adopted her lingo and couched our work in the business terms she craved. But ultimately, as an underfunded organization representing a community long-abandoned by the funding world, we could not give Kresge the investment return assurances they wanted. Eventually it was clear that we would not get a dime of Kresge money, after chasing after a grant from that foundation for years.

We tried everything we could think of to get the funding we needed, including attempting to coordinate approaches to foundations with other organizations. But ultimately we fell short and our intrepid, much-needed organization went under. To our knowledge, FWPP had been the only nonprofit in the U.S. focused solely on the enormous issue of agricultural pesticides and their impacts on farm worker families. We played a vital role on these issues locally, regionally, and nationally, despite extremely limited resources. But the funding we needed to survive and grow never came through.

FWPP shined a light on farm worker pesticide issues for a while, but now that light has been extinguished. No one is testing the air to create pressure for change or urging the state to renew its air monitoring program. No one is systematically tracking new pesticide studies in order to share them with the community and inject them into relevant policy forums. No one from Washington State has submitted comments based on farm worker families' perspectives on various important recent EPA proposals affecting those families. No one has responded to incredibly misleading reports issued by pesticide industry front groups in the Northwest.

The silence on agricultural pesticide issues has deepened. There are now even fewer voices challenging the script that the pesticide industry has so long pushed as the only script that can be used.

The funding issues we experienced are the same ones activists face on every environmental issue. We'll return to this topic shortly.

Looking Back

When I think of the extraordinary people I've worked with over the decades, I feel admiration, amazement, and love. Nonprofit staffers and community members fighting for justice affirm my faith in people's compassion, selflessness, and desire to create a just world.

But looking back, I also feel frustration. We were dedicated, strategic, and tenacious in our struggle for obviously needed reforms, but we couldn't make headway. Over and over again, against all odds, we pulled ourselves up to the tops of towering peaks, only to find that they were false summits. Somehow another higher peak needing to be scaled always appeared in front of us. We were up against something invisible and enormous that always had another ace up its sleeve.

Everyone's talking these days about the need for campaign finance reform. "We've got to get money out of politics! That Citizens United case is the problem...we've got to amend the Constitution and reclaim democracy," an acquaintance told me recently. His analysis is typical.

But "money in politics" was only a tiny part of what undermined us in the trenches of environmental activism. Democracy was subverted all right, but the buying of elections by Big Money wasn't the half of it.

Take the concept of financial conflicts of interest, for instance. It used to be understood that those who stand to make or lose money as the result of a policy must not be in a position of power shaping that policy. That principle has been completely obliterated. Governor Gregoire had no qualms about appointing a Dow-funded scientist to a state panel discussing policies affecting Dow's products. Those representing pesticide manufacturers, sellers, and users sat on agency workgroups and scientists' advisory committees, enjoying de facto veto power over policies and research that affected their profits.

Often, nice-sounding words like "collaboration" and "partnership" were used to mask the ceding of power to those with financial conflicts of interest. We were supposedly all "partners" collaboratively coming up with solutions for today's problems. Certain parties at the table were causing the problems we discussed. They profited from the status quo and would never agree to real change. But it was considered inappropriate to mention these facts.

On other occasions, there was no pretense of partnership. Only those who worked for chemical corporations were allowed to serve on the Clinton Administration's chemical trade advisory committee, for example. Having a major financial conflict had literally become a prerequisite for a seat at the table, as opposed to a barrier to it.

As those with private financial gains at stake dominated every forum, we often found ourselves completely excluded or silenced. Not only were there no seats for us on Clinton's trade advisory committees, we were also not allowed to speak at his "public" meeting on trade issues held in Seattle shortly before the WTO's arrival. People who weren't "moderates" were not welcome on the Fred Hutchinson Community Advisory Board. Individuals nominated by labor groups to represent them on the state Pesticide Advisory Board were not appointed.

It wasn't just individuals who were excluded from important forums. Vital ideas and information were also excluded, even when we did manage to get a seat at the table. Regularly, the most essential concepts of all—the ones we should have been discussing as a priority—were declared off-limits. WSDA would not consider alternatives to pesticides, scientific data about pesticide drift, or even tiny steps forward like air monitoring. Fred Hutch researchers made sure to never study or even mention alternatives to pesticides, even though these could eliminate people's toxic exposures altogether. EPA refused to identify and compare the environmental and health impacts of the various pest control options available to growers as a substitute for Guthion.

Even our own allies within the environmental movement undercut discourse about the critical issues of our day. They urged us to stop providing reporters with information about the governor's despicable behaviors propping up the pesticide industry at the expense of public health. And they endorsed her for reelection, carefully avoiding honest discussion of her actual record.

The funding world contributed mightily to the silencing of public interest voices. FWPP had a very hard time getting funding, and we were pretty much the only group in the U.S. focusing solely on the huge issue of farm worker family pesticide exposures. Meanwhile, the agribusiness perspective had resources aplenty. And ultimately, even FWPP folded due to lack of funds.

Forces undermining democracy made sure that even the most basic environmental information was not collected or was not publicly accessible. Dr. Gilbert's success in persuading PIRT to call for pesticide air monitoring triggered vicious attacks that led to his banishment and ultimately the demise of the panel itself. Dow Chemical's shoddy studies underlay major government decisions, but it was extremely difficult for members of the public to obtain those studies. And Fred Hutch scientists consciously downplayed their own studies for fear of alienating their pesticide-friendly partners.

And there's more. The news media covered our issues less and less over the years. Our group had to struggle with petty things, like being denied office insurance, because the tentacles of the pesticide industry were everywhere. Dow gained an undeserved aura of scientific respectability and environmental sustainability by giving a huge donation to the University of Michigan. This donation also allowed it to impact policy debates by influencing large numbers of students and the materials they produce. The list goes on and on.

These were the insidious and constant barriers we faced in the nitty-gritty world of environmental activism. They made it nearly impossible to get the necessary discussions going, let alone to achieve our ultimate goals. To forge an effective path forward, we must examine these realities. In Part III of this book we'll do just that. We'll explore what we're up against and where debilitating frameworks, structures, mindsets, and perceptions come from.

First, however, we need to take a moment to assess how we are doing overall. Are we making progress despite the challenges we face?

Looking honestly at the long-term impacts of the campaigns I was involved in over the years, I am forced to conclude that we failed to achieve our goals. Victories like the 1999 derailment of the WTO and getting Washington State to test the air for pesticides were short-lived.

The trade agreements we protested in 1999 have not been rescinded or reformed. Indeed, they have been followed by equally abhorrent agreements, pushed through via equally undemocratic processes.

As for farm worker pesticide issues, we did not halt the spraying of chlorpyrifos and other pesticides we targeted. Nor did we win policies that move growers to sustainable alternatives. We did not spare farm worker families and others in agricultural areas further toxic exposures. The truth is that we lost, despite the extraordinarily compelling case we made for change.

Moreover, trade agreements and other policies have continued to spur mass migrations, fostering an underclass of people who lack even the most basic rights. There has been no real immigration reform, and Barack Obama has earned the title "Deporter-in-Chief" by deporting more immigrants than any of his predecessors. Thus, farm workers face an even greater risk now when they speak up about pesticide exposures or other abuses on the job than they did years ago.

In short, we have moved backward on the farm worker pesticide issues my colleagues and I worked so hard to address, not forward.

But surely on the whole, the environmental movement has made progress, right? Overall, despite outcomes like the ones detailed in these tales from the trenches, we're moving forward, aren't we?

If only that were the case.

PART II

How Are We Doing?

• • •

*"Whatever you do, don't talk much about how
things are going on environmental issues.
It's too depressing and people's eyes will glaze over."*

Multiple friends advising me about this book.

CHAPTER 3

Can We Talk?

• • •

Once upon a time..........

A group of people lived together in a large house.

"Um, I hate to mention it but does anybody notice that we live on the railroad tracks and a giant train is barreling towards us?" Adrian asked.

"Why are you so negative?" replied Chris. "Can't you see the progress we've made improving the environment here? We've ended carbon monoxide emissions from the heater, added green plants to every room, and put solar panels on the roof."

"That's how we make our home beautiful and life-sustaining," added Jamie. "With each step forward we are closer to our vision of how we want to be. That's how change happens, bit by bit."

"I kind of heard a train whistle getting closer," admitted Pat. "But I'm sure the people in charge are on top of it, so I'm not worried."

"I think we're in trouble," insisted Adrian. "We really need to talk about that train."

"That's a big mistake," chimed all of Adrian's friends together. "You'll make people feel hopeless! Stick to the positive, like the big gains we're making with the garden and the new wall insulation!"

"Bravo!" "Yay!" "Congratulations!" we shouted into the conference call from our respective locations across the U.S. and Canada. One of the groups in our environmental alliance had won a small victory in a local pesticide battle. "When one group wins, all boats rise," our wonderful conference moderator reminded us. "This is how we change things, step by step."

Did anyone else on that conference call have the same doubts as me?

What the moderator said had long been taken as an article of faith by most of us. We kept each other's spirits up and we kept our organizations' members inspired and involved by identifying and celebrating victories whenever we could. We let ourselves believe that somehow, altogether these small advances were adding up to progress, moving us all steadily towards a world in which pesticide exposures and contamination would no longer occur.

The problem with hanging out in an echo chamber is that it becomes hard to separate reality from the upbeat statements resounding all around you. That's why stopping to sort things out from time to time is critical. If we don't, we could be spinning our wheels in a deeper and deeper rut, dooming ourselves to ultimate failure without realizing it. If we don't assess how we're doing overall, how can we be sure we're being effective?

Moreover, if things are going downhill fast but we promote the impression that they're not, might our assurances themselves be a problem? Might we be engaging in a dangerous deceit that undercuts the movements and people we're trying to serve?

Some are leery of examining negative environmental trends. They conflate shattering people's misplaced faith in current strategies with fostering hopelessness. But there is no better way to create real hope than being honest about how things are going and figuring out what we need to do to win. Indeed, as we examine what's going on around us, we learn that we have more power than most people realize. If we use that power strategically, we can rapidly change our world.

This book is about being truthful with ourselves and thereby creating real opportunity for saving our environment. As a starting point, we need to stop and look at how we're doing overall.

The next several chapters examine our progress on a wide range of environmental problems. First we'll look at the matter of pesticides going beyond the farm worker issues already discussed. Then we'll look at the world of toxic chemicals beyond pesticides. Finally, we'll examine a wide range of issues ranging from biodiversity to fisheries to global warming.

There are multiple threats to our survival. Focusing on only one can lead to strategies that rob Peter to pay Paul, staving off disaster on one front only to hasten it on another. It is important to engage in the broad review that follows.

CHAPTER 4

Pesticides

● ● ●

DESPITE GIVING IT OUR ALL, the Farm Worker Pesticide Project and our allies did not win the policies and programs we need. Could our experiences on *farm worker* pesticide issues be an anomaly? Might those fighting to protect public health and the environment from other pesticides be turning the tide despite the barriers we encountered in our particular battles? Unfortunately the answer is no.

ONGOING PESTICIDE USE AND CONTAMINATION

It is hard to get complete information on the volumes of pesticides used each year, but the numbers are clearly staggering. The most recent global figure available is 5.2 billion pounds in 2007. The figure for the United States alone that year was 1.1 billion pounds.[24] World expenditures on pesticides totaled more than $39.4 billion in 2007, with $12.5 billion of that spent in the U.S.[25]

It is true that organic product sales in the U.S. grew by 9.5% in 2011 as compared to 4.7% growth for non-organic foods. And the organic food sector grew by 2.5 billion U.S. dollars that year, passing the $30 billion mark for the first time. But these impressive-sounding figures mask a starkly unimpressive reality. Even after all that growth, organic food sales still represent only 4.2% of U.S. food sales.[26] Out of approximately 2 million farms in the United States, only about 13,000 are organic.[27]

Increases in organic acreage are often used to infer that pesticide use has declined. Worldwide in 2013, however, there were still only 43.1 million hectares of land cultivated organically. That represents 0.98% of all agricultural land. [28]

Washington State is often touted as an environmental leader. Yet in 2011, only 1.9% of the farms, 0.7% of farmland, and 1.5% of harvested cropland in our state were organic.[29] Only 8.5% of apple acreage and 4.3% of farm-gate sales were organic.

These statistics are pathetic. Decades ago, when I started working on environmental issues, I certainly expected to see a lot more progress than this by now. Today pesticides are still used on most farms and to grow most food. The overwhelming majority of food that is sold is not organic.

Pesticide contamination all around us drives home the point that we are not winning. Pesticides are typically present throughout the year in most streams in agricultural and urban areas in the U.S. More than 50% of agricultural streams and more than 80% of urban streams have concentrations of at least one pesticide that exceed supposedly acceptable reference doses for aquatic life. As discussed earlier, those benchmarks are almost certainly not adequately protective. Moreover, pesticides in our waterways typically exist in complex mixtures that may increase the damage caused as compared to single chemicals.[30]

The contamination of rivers and streams mirrors contamination in our own bodies. The Center for Disease Control has found 18 different pesticides, or the chemicals they break down into, in the blood or urine of at least half of all Americans sampled. Some, like TCP, a breakdown product of chlorpyrifos, are present in the blood or urine of most Americans.[31]

An average American is exposed to 10 or more pesticides per day simply from eating food and drinking water. Pesticides have been found in the body fat of every human tested.[32]

ENDLESS EPA ALLEGIANCE TO COUNTLESS PESTICIDES

For pesticide after pesticide, the story is the same one we endured for chlorpyrifos. EPA and state agencies approve it, relying on limited data provided primarily by the manufacturers. Those manufacturers then move into high gear, aggressively marketing their product. Soon it is used widely. Contamination and exposures become ubiquitous.

The sheer number of approved pesticides, combined with the lack of programs tracking impacts, means that most pesticides are never challenged. In some cases, however, environmental groups connect the dots between a pesticide and damage to health or the environment. We launch big campaigns to restrict or ban the pesticide. If we win—something that is very hard to do—it invariably takes years. Meanwhile, contamination and exposures continue.

Take the weed-killer atrazine as just one example. Registered for use way back in 1959, it is now used on half of the U.S. corn acres and 90% of our sugarcane acres. These and other uses add up to some 80 million pounds applied in the U.S. each year.[33] As a result, atrazine is now widely detected in surface and drinking water samples throughout the U.S., including at levels exceeding "reference doses."[34] Meanwhile, as people and wildlife have been exposed to this chemical, evidence has accumulated linking it to birth defects, other reproductive problems, and cancer.[35]

Large amounts of time and energy are being invested in the uphill battle of cancelling atrazine's registration. Even if activists eventually win, irreparable damage will already have been done to our ecosystem, various species, and countless individuals. Damage from ubiquitous atrazine contamination will continue.

Few if any pesticides exist in a vacuum, acting alone. They circulate in our environment and in our bodies in the company of a slew of other chemicals. Chlorpyrifos and atrazine are often found in combination with one another, for example. It turns out that the damage each can do increases when living things are exposed to the other concurrently.[36]

Pesticides can also exacerbate other threats to living things. Both atrazine and chlorpyrifos increased salamanders' susceptibility to a viral pathogen in laboratory experiments, for instance. The concentrations that were studied mimicked real-world concentrations.[37]

Chlorpyrifos and atrazine are just two of thousands of pesticides in use.

SOMETIMES WE WIN. OR DO WE?

Once in a while, a particular pesticide or class of pesticides finally does get removed from use. The manufacturers withdraw it voluntarily, perhaps because pests have become resistant. More rarely, EPA cancels a pesticide over industry objections.

But even when a nasty pesticide is no longer used, have we really won? Not really. Not in the long run.

In making pest control decisions, growers rely first and foremost on advisors from pesticide companies.[38] These "field men" have all sorts of ideas for new pesticides growers can buy to replace the ones that are no longer available. This has been the reality for decades, rendering our "victories" short-lived, as growers switch to the next pesticide promoted by manufacturers.

For example, when DDT and other organochlorine pesticides were banned, growers switched to organophosphates (OPs). We've already examined the multiple ways in which chlorpyrifos and other OPs wreak havoc in our world.

Chlorpyrifos is still used in massive quantities, but some organophosphates have indeed been phased out. Guthion is now finally illegal, for example.

Even so, we cannot truly celebrate. As Guthion use has declined, the use of "neonicitinoids" (neonics) has skyrocketed. Bayer has moved seamlessly from making big profits selling Guthion to making big profits selling neonics. In 2010, it took in over $1 billion in revenue from two neonic products alone: imidacloprid and clothian-idin. [39]

In a news story in March of 2012 Bayer was cited as saying that neonics are used on 90% of the corn grown in the U.S.[40] Substantial portions of the soy, wheat, cotton, sorghum, and peanut seed markets now rely on neonic-soaked seeds. In 2010, neonic-treated seeds were used on at least 142 million acres, a landmass equal to the footprints of California and Washington State combined.[41]

All of this has major implications for bees and other pollinators. Pollinator populations have been declining rapidly for many years, and neonic pesticides are strongly implicated in these declines. [42] Beekeepers warn, "We're facing the extinction of a species."[43]

Neonics are not the only factor implicated in pollinator loss, but there is ample reason to believe they are a significant one. Substantial research indicates that neonics can be immediately lethal to pollinators in certain circumstances. They can also cause subtle changes that undermine survival. Exposures to neonics can reduce the ability of bees and other pollinators to fly and navigate properly, taste, learn new tasks, resist infection, and resist pathogens and parasites.[44]

All of this is extremely important to the future of life on Earth. The UN Food and Agriculture Organization estimates that of the 100 crop species that provide 90% of the world's food, 71 are pollinated by bees.[45] About one of every three mouthfuls in our diets directly or indirectly benefits from honey bee pollination.[46]

In chapter 2, I described the frustrating experience of serving on a committee advising EPA and USDA about the phaseout of Guthion that was underway. These agencies and others refused to evaluate alternatives to Guthion in terms of their potential impacts on health and the environment. EPA's list of substitutes for Guthion included neonics such as imidacloprid, which is made by Bayer, the same company that produced Guthion. The Agency made no comment about environmental implications, even though France and Germany had already banned certain neonics.

And now we fight neonics. We are in the same place we're always in, pouring energy into trying to persuade EPA to ban a class of pesticides. We are circulating petitions, sending out action alerts, filing lawsuits, and doing all sorts of other things to try to get neonics off the market.

EPA has made it clear that it will not act against neonics any time soon. As usual, it will allow contamination, exposures, and harm to continue for years, if not decades, despite warning bells going off all around us about the folly of this approach.

And neonics are just one category of pesticides disseminated into our environment.

The pesticide merry-go-round keeps turning even though effective, non-chemical means of controlling pests exist. A rational society would ensure financial security for growers and provide them with technical and financial aid as they transition to alternatives. Research would focus not on new chemicals to broadcast in the environment in order to make profits for manufacturers and sellers, but instead on pest control measures that don't contaminate our world and don't put people at risk.

Environmental activists advocate common sense and precaution, including pest control measures that don't involve broadcasting chemicals in our environment. But the pesticide industry remains in charge of what happens next. Their marketing pitches determine which new chemical will contaminate our world next in order to make them profits.

LOSING GROUND

How are we doing overall on pesticide issues? We are losing. Pesticide corporations are able to register their products and sell them for years, regardless of the impacts on health and the environment. Our victories take a long time and are short-lived. We are constantly jumping from one toxic catastrophe to another because pesticide manufacturers rather than common sense rule the day.

Things are getting worse as pesticide corporations tighten their grip on agriculture with each passing year. Three giant agrichemical corporations—Monsanto, DuPont, and Syngenta—now control 53% of the global commercial seed market, for example. The top 10 seed firms account for 73%.[47] The vast majority of the four major commodity crops in the U.S. are now genetically engineered: soybeans (93% transgenic in 2010), cotton (88%), corn (86%), and canola (64%).[48]

Falsely touted as something that would *reduce* pesticide use, genetic engineering is greatly increasing pesticide use.[49] Both GMO organisms themselves and the increased reliance on pesticides associated with them threaten ecosystems.[50]

By patenting genetically modified seeds, pesticide corporations also deny growers the power to cultivate and save their own seeds. This makes those who grow our food more and more subservient to large agribusiness corporations.

Growers are at the mercy of those who sell them seeds and other inputs and those who offer them contracts for selling crops. They are in competition with massive, vertically organized corporations that own and control everything from the seeds and the ground in which they are sown to food distribution systems. High costs, little return, and stress among farmers are contributing to rapid loss of farmland as long-time farms are sold to developers. Land that remains agricultural is being consolidated into fewer and fewer hands.

The face of farming is changing for the worse. Giant GMO mono-cultures that are heavily dependent on toxic chemicals are becoming the norm. Frightening as it is to acknowledge, when it comes to pesticides and associated agricultural policies we are losing the war. We are losing it resoundingly.

CHAPTER 5

Broader Toxic Pollution Issues

• • •

Pesticides are just one part of a broader toxic pollution problem on Planet Earth. Even if we are losing on pesticides, are we perhaps winning on toxics issues overall?

Again, the answer is a resounding No. What is happening on pesticides is not an exception within the realm of toxic pollution issues.

A Golden Age of Chemical Manufacturing

When Congress passed the Toxic Substance Control Act in the 1970s, supposedly to protect people from toxic chemicals, it "grandfathered" 62,000 chemicals already in commerce. Those chemicals didn't need to be tested or to meet safety standards. Since the Act was adopted, EPA has approved another 22,000 chemicals, most with little or no data on risks to health or the environment.[51]

Thus, there are more than 80,000 chemicals in use today in the U.S., most of which have not been independently tested for safety.[52] EPA adds an average of 700 new chemicals per year to this list.[53]

The situation in the United States is mirrored elsewhere in the world. An estimated 140,000 chemicals are on the market in the European Union, for example.[54]

Chemical sales in the U.S. exceeded $318 billion in 2011. Exxon Mobil's sales alone were $41.9 billion. DuPont's were $34.7 billion.[55]

Globally, there was an estimated $3.7 trillion (U.S. dollars) in chemical sales in 2008, and sales were growing at a rate of 3.5% per year.[56]

According to the United Nations chemical production and use is expanding more rapidly in countries that are "developing or in economic transition" as compared to developed countries. Developing and transitioning countries also bear a disproportionate burden of chemical industry wastes.[57]

The method of extraction known as "fracking" is making natural gas abundant and cheap. This is helping to spur chemical industry growth. Cal Dooley, president and chief executive of the American Chemistry Council, has declared that natural gas development is ushering in "a golden age in chemical manufacturing in the United States."[58]

WIDESPREAD CONTAMINATION AND EXPOSURE

People are exposed on a regular basis to dangerous chemicals in household products. There are over 5000 children's products used in Washington State alone that contain chemicals linked to cancer, hormone disruption, and reproductive problems.[59]

Production and disposal of toxic chemicals also contaminates our environment, leading to exposures for humans and for other species. In 2010, industrial facilities dumped 226 million pounds of toxic chemicals into U.S. waterways. Approximately 1.5 million pounds of these chemicals were linked to cancer. "The Clean Water Act's original objective was to clean up all of America's waterways by 1985—27 years ago," said Rob Kerth, co-author of a report on this topic. "Many people born in 1985 have kids of their own now, yet still millions of pounds of toxic chemicals are being dumped into our waterways," he noted.[60]

A recent federal study of the Columbia River found 112 toxic chemicals, including flame retardants, pharmaceuticals, pesticides, personal-care products, mercury, and cleaning products. "Science is having a hard time keeping up with all the new compounds being constantly introduced," said Jennifer Morace, the lead investigator.

While there are no toxicity standards for the materials found, "it is not hard to imagine they may have some sort of impact on aquatic life as well as people," she said.[61] The Columbia River likely mirrors the situation in other great rivers around the world. It is probably cleaner than many rivers.

According to EPA data, more than half of rivers and streams in the U.S. are in such bad shape that they cannot adequately support aquatic life. EPA found more than 55% of tested U.S. waterways to be in poor condition, compared to only 21% in good condition. Human activity was the most widespread cause of problems, with high levels of phosphorus found in 40% of rivers and streams. Phosphorus is a component in fertilizers, pesticides, and detergents.[62]

Contaminated waterways are a subset of millions of toxic contamination sites throughout the world. There are an estimated two million toxic contamination sites in Europe, the U.S., and the Russian Federation alone.[63]

Toxic contamination is so widespread that there is now no place on Earth that is free from it. Even remote areas like the Arctic and Antarctic are contaminated with toxic chemicals.[64]

What happens to our environment happens to us. The chemicals that contaminate the world around us also contaminate our own bodies. Certain toxic chemicals are found in most or all people on Earth. National human exposure studies have found flame retardants known as polybrominated diphenyl ethers (PBDEs) in the blood of almost everyone tested. Similarly, more than 90% of those tested have Bisphenol A (BPA)—a chemical associated with plastics and resins—in their urine. Most people tested have perfluorinated chemicals associated with nonstick coatings in their bodies.[65]

In fact, most humans carry *hundreds* of toxic chemicals around in our bodies. Even blood tests on babies routinely find more than 200 synthetic chemicals, such as flame retardants, lead, stain removers, and pesticides, including some chemicals banned long ago.[66] Exposures to an array of pollutants *before* birth are also well documented.[67]

Sobering Implications for Human Health

As a staff person at the Washington Toxics Coalition I gave presentations to diverse audiences about the fact that many widespread pollutants have turned out to be "hormone disruptors." This means that they can block or mimic hormones in our bodies, setting into motion an array of adverse impacts on health. My presentations highlighted hormonal abnormalities showing up in wildlife, such as polar bears with both male and female sex organs. It then outlined various hormone-connected human diseases and birth defects on the rise and referred to laboratory studies providing supportive evidence that exposures to hormone-disrupting pollutants could well be contributing to these conditions.

Way back in 1991, scientists from around the world signed a joint statement about hormone-disrupting pollutants at the Wingspread Conference Center in Wisconsin. The "Wingspread Statement" warned that the concentrations of a number of hormone-disrupting chemicals measured in the U.S. human population were already at that time "well within the range and dosages at which effects are seen in wildlife populations." In fact, the statement warned, "experimental results are being seen at the low end of current environmental conditions."[68]

In 2013, the UN Environmental Programme (UNEP) and the World Health Organization (WHO) issued a report emphasizing how serious the problem of hormone-disrupting pollution is. Close to 800 common chemical pollutants are now known to interfere with hormones, and human and wildlife populations all over the world are exposed. There is ample reason for concern about this, including the high incidence of hormone-related disorders in humans, similar effects observed in wildlife, and laboratory studies linking hormone-disruptors to the sorts of problems we're seeing. Examples of human health problems on the rise include genital malformations in baby boys, neurobehavioral disorders associated with thyroid disruption, and hormone-related cancers such as breast, prostate, and ovarian cancers.[69]

Interfering with hormones is only one way that pollutants can cause harm. They can also interfere with the central nervous system through a variety of other biological mechanisms, for example.

According to the Mount Sinai Children's Environmental Health Center, autism spectrum disorder (ASD) now affects 1 out of every 88 American children—a 23% increase from 2006 and a 78% increase from 2002. Attention Deficit Hyperactivity Disorder (ADHD) now affects 14% of American children. The Center has provided a list of 10 categories of chemicals found in consumer products that are suspected to contribute to autism and learning disabilities, including lead, methyl mercury, PCBs, organophosphate pesticides, organochlorine pesticides, endocrine disruptors, automotive exhaust, polycyclic aromatic hydrocarbons, brominated flame retardants, and perfluorinated compounds.[70]

A Stanford University study with 192 pairs of twins, where one twin is autistic and one is not concluded that genetics accounts for 38% of the risk for autism. Environmental factors account for 62%. Physician Brian Moench pointed to this study and others and connected the dots to what is happening to bees and other pollinators. One impact of toxic exposures is a kind of "bee autism" he posited, making the bees unable to find their way home. Sure, bees are insects and humans are not, but our nerve cells share the same basic biologic infrastructure, Moench explained. And yes, humans are bigger than bees, but early in the first trimester a human fetus is indeed no bigger than an insect. The average newborn has already been in contact with over 200 different toxic chemicals and heavy metals before it is born. "Little wonder that rates of autism, attention deficit and behavioral disorders are all on the rise," Moench said.[71]

The National Academy of Science has reported that scientists generally agree that about 3% of all developmental defects in children are attributable to exposure to toxic chemicals and physical agents, including environmental factors, and another 25% may be due to a combination of genetic and environmental factors, for a total of 28% or nearly a third of developmental defects potentially influenced by environmental factors.[72]

Cancer is another health problem linked to toxic chemicals in our environment. Hormone disruption is one of the mechanisms that can trigger it. In its 2008-2009 report and cover letter, President Obama's Cancer Panel concluded that the true burden of environmentally induced cancer has been grossly underestimated. With nearly 80,000 chemicals on the market, exposure to potential environmental carcinogens (cancer-causing chemicals) is widespread, the Panel said. Exposures occur before birth, and babies are born "pre-polluted," it noted. "Grievous harm" from environmental carcinogens has not been addressed adequately by the National Cancer Program.[73]

JUST LIKE WITH PESTICIDES: VICTORIES THAT AREN'T VICTORIES

Periodically, environmental activists celebrate the end of some toxic chemical that has been harming people for a long time. Unfortunately, however, when one toxic chemical bites the dust another one rises up to takes its place, just like with pesticides.

Flame retardants provide a classic example. The Chicago Tribune put together an excellent chart showing the history of flame retardants and how the chemical industry went from one to the next. After causing widespread contamination of ecosystems and human bodies with one chemical, the corporations moved effortlessly on to the next chemical as the damage from the first one became apparent. The new chemicals were touted as safe, despite a complete absence of proof. Later, oops, the replacement turned out to be harmful as well.[74]

The Washington Toxics Coalition boasted in 2012 about winning a first-in-the-nation ban on the flame retardant deca-PBDE.[75] Later, the organization was forced to send an alert to supporters that began, "We've all been duped! A few years ago Washington State told the chemical industry to stop using PBDEs....Instead of using safer chemicals, they switched to cancer-causing Tris Flame Retardants. A recent study found Toxic Tris Flame Retardants in 80% of children's products tested, like car seats, nursing pillows and changing pads!"[76]

The story is always the same. With explicit or tacit governmental approval, a chemical corporation pushes its chemical product, claiming it is safe to use. Widespread use leads to widespread exposures and harm. Only after damage has been done for years is there a chance that the chemical will be banned. But then the next "safe" chemical is marketed in its stead.

Professors David Rosner and Gerald Markowitz provide chilling examples in their aptly named article, "You and Your Family Are Guinea Pigs for the Chemical Corporations." They describe how the lead industry successfully portrayed lead as safe despite clear evidence to the contrary, issuing coloring books that encouraged children to paint their rooms with lead-based paint, for instance.[77] The article provides useful context for the toxic chemical realities we face today.

In conversations with toxics activists, I asked whether their groups had won any meaningful victories in the last five years or so. The answer was consistently, *No, not really*. People could only point to nebulous achievements like "building momentum" and "laying the groundwork for reform."

To keep supporters' spirits up, environmental groups working on toxics issues regularly claim that we're making progress. But the reality is that, on the broad and important issue of toxic pollution, we are quite clearly losing.

CHAPTER 6

The Global Environmental Meltdown

• • •

THINGS ARE NOT GOING WELL in our struggles pertaining to pesticides and other toxic chemicals. Now it's time step back further and look at the full range of environmental problems our planet faces.

Surely we must be faring better on other environmental issues, you might be thinking. Despite the bad news on pesticides and other toxic chemicals, overall we're making progress, aren't we?

Unfortunately, the answer is again *No*. Despite humankind's overwhelming desire to protect the environment that sustains us, we are in a downward spiral, hurtling toward the point of no return on multiple fronts, ranging from biodiversity to global warming.

TWO DECADES AFTER THE 1992 RIO EARTH SUMMIT: WHERE DID WE STAND?

In 1992, the United Nations hosted an important summit on environmental issues in Rio de Janeiro, Brazil. Assembled nations reviewed the environmental threats facing the planet and agreed upon many different goals and strategies. Treaties on biodiversity and climate change were endorsed.

Twenty years later, in June of 2012, leaders from over 100 countries met at the UN's "Rio+20" summit to review how things were going. The news was not good.

Progress had been made on only four of the 90 critical environmental goals set in 1992: getting lead out of gasoline, increasing access to improved water supplies, boosting research on how to reduce marine pollution, and eliminating substances that deplete the ozone layer in our atmosphere. Ironically, ozone depleters were replaced with hydrofluorocarbons (HFCs), which contribute to global warming.[78]

"World Remains on Unsustainable Track Despite Hundreds of Internationally Agreed Goals and Objectives," read the UN Environment Program news release.[79] UNEP Executive Director Achim Steiner told world leaders that they had to show more commitment now than they had 20 years earlier, "[b]ecause 20 years after Rio 1992, on virtually all the megatrends that we described, we cannot stand before our either elders or children [sic] and claim that the last 20 years have succeeded in turning these trends around."[80] Steiner also said that "[t]he moment has come to put away the paralysis of indecision, acknowledge the facts and face up to the common humanity that unites all people."

According to a UNEP report, "[t]he currently observed changes to the Earth System are unprecedented in human history. Efforts to slow the rate or extent of change—including enhanced resource efficiency and mitigation measures—have resulted in moderate successes but have not succeeded in reversing adverse environmental changes. Neither the scope of these nor their speed has abated in the past five years." The report notes that "[a]s human pressures on the earth accelerate, several critical global, regional and local thresholds are close or have been exceeded. Once these have been passed, abrupt and possibly irreversible changes to the life-support functions of the planet are likely to occur, with significant adverse implications for human well-being."[81]

As the world prepared for the Rio+20 summit, 22 scientists from three continents published a paper in the journal *Nature*.[82] The biologists, ecologists, geologists, and paleontologists compared the biological impact of past episodes of global change with what is happening today. They warned that a "tipping point" in which the biosphere goes into swift and irreversible change, with potentially cataclysmic impacts for humans, could occur as early as this century. In other words, we could be within just a few generations of collapse.

Here are a few examples of disturbing environmental trends noted in UN reports issued at the time of the Rio+20 Summit:

* Competing demands for food, feed, fuel, fiber, and raw materials were intensifying pressures on land, helping to drive deforestation. The rate of annual forest loss had decreased as compared to the year 2000, but remained alarmingly high, with 13 million hectares of land deforested each year.[83] Since 1990, primary forest area had shrunk by 300 million hectares, an area larger than Argentina.[84]

* The world had failed to reach its goal of a significant reduction in biodiversity loss by 2010. Approximately 20% of vertebrate species were threatened and coral reefs had declined by 38% since 1980.[85]

* The previous two decades had seen unprecedented deterioration in fish stocks. Commercial fisheries and overfishing were the main threat.[86] For a chilling review of what is happening with fish stocks around the world, see the film "The End of the Line." It documents collapses of major fisheries that have already occurred and the course we are on for a massive fish crisis within 40 or 50 years. One of the people interviewed in the film reminisces about the good old days for bluefin fishing. "But then bluefin tuna became big business. I mean really big business," he says. After describing the overfishing that is going on he notes, "What is at stake here is an infamous minority of people making millions and millions and millions by decimating a species. Is that right? Is that moral?"[87]

* Little or no progress had been achieved in preventing, reducing, or controlling pollution of the marine environment.[88] The number of coastal dead zones had increased dramatically. Of 169 coastal dead zones worldwide, only 13 were recovering, and

415 coastal areas suffered from eutrophication—excess nutrients in water leading to excess plant growth and oxygen depletion.[89]

UN reports in 2012 also discussed at length the world's failure to make progress on climate change issues. Annual global carbon dioxide (CO_2) emissions had increased by 36% between 1992 and 2008, from about 22,000 million tons to just over 30,000 million tons. In underdeveloped countries, there had been a 64% increase in total annual CO_2 emissions and a 29% increase on a per-person basis. Total emissions of CO_2 in developed countries had increased by nearly 8%. Per-person emissions in those countries, though down by 18%, were still 10 times higher than those of underdeveloped countries. CO_2 emissions in developed countries would have been higher if so much manufacturing and other production hadn't moved overseas to poorer nations.[90]

According to the UN data, there had been a steady mean increase of CO_2 in the atmosphere from 357 parts per million by volume (ppmv) in 1992 to 389 ppmv in 2011.[91]

The UN 2012 reports laid out disturbing facts related to global warming. The 10 hottest years ever measured had all occurred since 1998. The clear long-term trend was one of global warming. Northern latitudes were seeing the most extreme changes in temperature. Consequences of this warming included melting ice sheets and thawing permafrost.

As global temperatures had risen, so had the average ocean temperature. And global sea levels had been rising at an average rate of about 2.5 millimeters per year between 1992 and 2011.

The acidity of the ocean's surface had also been increasing because of growing concentrations of CO_2 in the air. This could have significant consequences for marine organisms, could disrupt marine food webs and ecosystems, and could damage fishing and other human activities. For example, if the acidification trend continues, coral reefs will likely be threatened by mid-century, with 75% facing high to critical threat levels. Massive numbers of people depend upon seafood as a key part of their diets, and acidification threatens that food supply.

Meanwhile, most mountain glaciers around the world were diminishing rapidly, with severe impacts on the environment and human well-being. Diminishing glaciers and ice caps not only affect sea levels but also threaten the well-being of the one-sixth of the world's population who depend on glacial ice and seasonal snow for water during dry seasons. The speed of glacier loss had been increasing in recent decades. This trend could lead to deglaciation of large parts of many mountain ranges on Earth by the end of this century. The Arctic could be virtually ice-free in Septembers as soon as 2040 if multiple feedback processes speed up the loss.[92]

The UN report sharing these disturbing statistics offered this understatement: "Global efforts since 1992 to slow the growth of, and ultimately reduce the total level of CO2 emissions, have not yet fully succeeded. These efforts must be strengthened; otherwise, it is very unlikely that the target of limiting temperature increase to 2°C by 2100 to reduce global warming, as agreed by global leaders in Cancun in 2010, will be met."[93]

At various major meetings prior to Rio+20, the nations of the world had failed to commit to real action to stop global warming. At the climate summit in Copenhagen in 2009, for example, neither the U.S. nor China, the two countries responsible for 40% of the world's carbon emissions, was prepared to offer major concessions. On the final day, world leaders, including President Obama, flew in and adopted a face-saving "Copenhagen Accord." This purely voluntary agreement established no real commitments and no means for enforcing goals. A December 2011 climate change summit in Durban, South Africa, was equally unproductive."[94]

How Have We Been Doing Since 2012?

Despite the dire warnings issued by UN agencies and others leading up to the Rio+20 Summit in 2012, the countries attending it did not take meaningful action. The word "encourage" appeared 50 times in the key draft agreement they discussed and the word "support" appeared 99 times. In contrast, "must" appeared only 3 times and "we will" only 5. The upshot was a final agreement that was weak and ineffective.

The 2012 summit showed that "the world's leaders are not able to come together and lead for the sake of humanity,"[95] lamented Severn Cullis-Suzuki, who, as a child at the 1992 Summit, had delivered a passionate plea for action. Journalist and climate change activist George Monbiot was more biting in his analysis: "The paranoid, petty, unilateralist sabotage of international agreements continues uninterrupted. To see Obama backtracking on the commitments made by Bush the elder 20 years ago is to see the extent to which a tiny group of plutocrats has asserted its grip on policy."[96]

International summits since Rio+20 have also not produced meaningful commitments.[97] In fact, by and large, governments around the world are advancing the profits of the corporations they serve ever more aggressively despite the dire consequences for humankind. This is the case on the full array of environmental crises we face from toxic chemical pollution to fisheries to biodiversity.

FULL THROTTLE IN THE WRONG DIRECTION: GLOBAL WARMING AS AN EXAMPLE

HUGE INCREASES IN FOSSIL-FUEL PRODUCTION

The extraction and burning of fossil fuels is being ramped up precisely when we should be phasing out these activities.

In the U.S., for example, oil production is skyrocketing. An energy expert told a U.S. Senate Committee in 2013 that by 2020 "the United States will become the largest producer of hydrocarbons in the world, surpassing Russia." He spoke as if that was a good thing and never mentioned global warming. "Indeed, the oil and gas industry in this country has attracted tens of billions of dollars of investment capital," another expert said in written testimony. "In the United States, spending to develop oil and gas fields rose 37% from 2009 to 2010—from $50.6 billion to $69.4 billion. Spending increased further in 2011," he added. Yet another expert forecast 20% growth in U.S. crude production over the next decade.[98]

At the time of that Senate hearing, U.S. oil production exceeded 7 million barrels a day for the first time since March of 1993. Production had grown at the fastest pace in U.S. history in 2012 and was predicted to accelerate thereafter. The International Energy Agency had noted in November of 2012 that U.S. oil production was on track to surpass Saudi Arabia's by 2020.

The Obama Administration brags about increased oil production in the U.S., as if global warming were not a problem. According to an Administration website, as of 2011 American oil production was at an eight-year high. Domestic crude oil production had increased by an average of more than 720,000 barrels per day since 2008.[99] We'll examine the Obama Administration's all-out promotion of oil and gas in more detail in a later chapter.

While it is true that new coal power plants are not being built in the U.S., corporations are as busy as ever taking coal out of the ground. They just export more of it now than they did before.[100]

Coal corporations are preparing to ship even more coal overseas. As of this writing, for example, five separate proposals for coal terminals are under consideration for the Pacific Northwest.[101] If all five are built, they will be used to ship nearly 150 million tons of coal to China and other Asian countries. By 2026, an estimated 18 daily coal train trips (9 round trips) will occur in Seattle, meaning approximately one coal train will pass through the city every 1.3 hours. Coal trains will be 7000 feet long in 2015, increasing to 8500 feet shortly thereafter.[102]

New infrastructure is being built to accommodate more oil and gas production as well. "We've added enough new oil and gas pipeline to encircle the Earth and then some," President Obama bragged in a speech in 2012.[103] New oil terminals (which would greatly increase rail shipments of oil) are being proposed in many different locations,[104] despite recent disasters such as a Quebec derailment in 2013 that killed 47 people and a derailment in Virginia in 2014 that contaminated the James River.[105]

Ever More Extreme Measures to Get Fossil Fuels

In the frenzy to maximize fossil-fuel production precisely when we should be eliminating it, corporations are going to new extremes.

Mountain-Top Removal. To get at coal, they routinely blow off the tops of mountains, for example. It is hard to imagine a more destructive way to get coal out of the ground.

Offshore Drilling. Similarly, deepwater drilling poses extreme risks for our oceans, but it has become rampant. Deepwater production "was barely on our radar screen 10 years ago, and is expected to more than double," an ExxonMobil executive cheerfully exclaimed in December of 2012.[106] He did not mention the Deepwater Horizon disaster in the Gulf of Mexico that had occurred just two and a half years earlier. In that disaster, a BP oil rig exploded and sank, killing 11 people and seriously injuring 17 more. Over the course of 86 days, two hundred million gallons of crude oil gushed into the Gulf, devastating fisheries, wildlife, tourism, and communities.[107] The disaster created an oil sheen spreading hundreds of square miles.

The Obama Administration imposed a moratorium on *new* drilling permits in the Gulf after the BP disaster but lifted that moratorium within a year. Since then the Administration has been opening up more and more offshore areas for drilling. The Interior Department has endorsed seismic exploration for oil and gas in the Atlantic, for instance. This is considered a crucial step toward allowing drilling off the coasts of the Carolinas, Virginia, and possibly Florida.[108]

The Obama Administration has even approved drilling in the Arctic Ocean.[109] A spill there would be very hard to clean up. Ironically, fossil-fuel companies have expanded their plans for the Arctic because melting ice has made more oil and gas accessible.[110]

<u>Fracking.</u> And then there's "fracking." This is short-hand for "hydraulic fracturing" and "horizontal drilling" used to reach deeply buried oil and gas that was previously inaccessible. "Fracking" directs a high-pressure jet of sand, water, and chemicals underground to crack open shale formations. While fracking has been around for a while, the newest technologies are much more dangerous. They employ 50 to 100 times more water and chemicals than wells that don't involve fracking.[111]

A report prepared for the fossil-fuel industry by the consulting firm Control Risks includes an extraordinary map showing where gas can be fracked around the planet. Vast swaths of land on every continent but Greenland are highlighted as places to consider fracking.[112]

Extreme fracking techniques have spurred dramatic increases in estimates of how much natural gas is available. In the U.S. alone as of the end of 2012, over 2300 trillion cubic feet of natural gas were considered technically recoverable.[113] A veritable frenzy of activity is now underway as drillers buy or lease land for fracking. In 2011, shale mergers and acquisitions accounted for $46.5 billion in deals and became one of the largest profit centers for some Wall Street investment banks.[114]

Natural gas has been portrayed by some as a climate-friendly "bridge" between coal and oil on the one hand, and renewable non-fossil-fuel alternatives on the other. But burning natural gas releases climate-warming pollutants into the air. Shale gas obtained by fracking may even leave a greenhouse gas footprint that is greater than that for conventional gas or oil. This is because fracking results in emissions of methane, which is a more potent greenhouse gas than carbon dioxide, especially in the first decades after it enters the atmosphere.[115]

The International Energy Agency (IEA) projects that global reliance on natural gas for one-quarter of the world's energy supply by 2035 would lead to a 3.5 C degree increase in temperature and out-of-control global warming.[116] "While natural gas is the cleanest fossil fuel, it is still a fossil fuel," said Nobuo Tanaka, IEA's executive director.

A study by the National Center for Atmospheric Research (NCAR) published in the fall of 2011 looked at global warming emissions associated with natural gas in more detail. The report states that "[i]n summary, our results show that the substitution of gas for coal as an energy source results in increased rather than decreased global warming for many decades.[117]

Global warming is only one of the environmental downsides of fracking. Fracking also disrupts rural areas, uses huge quantities of water, contaminates air and water, and poses other dangers to communities.

Tar Sands Extraction. A discussion of the extreme extraction measures now used by fossil-fuel corporations would be incomplete without talking about obtaining oil from tar sands—areas where solid or semi-solid oil is mixed with sand under the ground. Tar sands oils are much dirtier to burn than conventional oils. Getting them out of the ground and separating the oil from the sand requires a lot of water and energy while it devastates large sections of the landscape.[118]

Beneath the Boreal forests of Alberta, Canada, for example, lie 141,000 square kilometers of tar sand deposits and about 1.7 trillion barrels worth of oil. Scientists have warned that taking this oil out of the ground and burning it represents "game over" for the climate.[119] Nonetheless, massive extraction and sales of Alberta tar sands oil are proceeding apace. Open pits spread as far as the eye can see. Leachate ponds threaten adjacent rivers.[120] The devastation left behind by tar sands extraction in Alberta has been compared to Mordor in the *Lord of the Rings*.[121]

While the "northern leg" of the KXL pipeline (connecting Hardisty, Alberta, to Steele City, Nebraska) was rejected in November of 2015, oil corporations have been aggressively expanding other ways to transport tar sands oil from Alberta. The KXL system itself includes a different "northern leg" connecting Hardisty to Steele City. From there oil can flow to refineries in Illinois, or through the "southern leg" of the KXL system (approved by Obama in 2012) to the Gulf Coast. As of April 2012, more than 10,000 miles of new, tar sands pipelines were planned. These were slated to carry an additional 3.1 million barrels of oil from Alberta to export markets each day.[122]

The use of railroads to transport Canadian oil increased by over 7000% annually between 2007 and 2011. The number of crude oil-carrying rail cars in North America tripled to more than 200,000 between 2011 and 2012 and is expected to continue to grow in the foreseeable future. According to the U.S. State Department, with modest expansion and upgrades to existing infrastructure, railroad networks in the U.S. could handle all new oil produced in Western Canada through 2030.[123]

In fact, North American energy companies are starting to invest more in railroad terminals than the railroad companies themselves are investing. In January of 2013, oil and gas pipeline operators announced plans to spend about $1 billion on rail depot projects to help move more crude oil from inland fields to coastal refineries. This surpassed expenditures by the largest U.S. railroad, Burlington Northern Santa Fe (BNSF), which spent $400 million on terminals in 2012.[124]

Alberta is not the only region where fossil-fuel corporations want to destroy the land to get at shale and tar sands oil. Up to three trillion barrels of shale and tar sands oil could be recovered in the state of Utah, for example. That's more oil than has been used so far in human history.[125]

THE GLOBAL WARMING MELTDOWN ALL AROUND US

As fossil-fuel extraction and burning accelerates, the consequences of global warming are becoming more dire and more apparent every day. In the years since the Rio+20 reports laid out the distressing details of what global warming was already doing to the planet, we have witnessed all sorts of additional firsts associated with climate change. These include:

* Record high temperatures.[126] In the spring of 2015 hundreds died in India as temperatures neared 122 degrees Fahrenheit in some regions, literally melting roads.[127] A report commissioned by the World Bank released in December of 2012 warned

that temperatures could rise by 4 degrees Celsius (7.2 degrees Fahrenheit) by the end of the century, even if countries meet their current pledges to reduce emissions. If they fail to meet those pledges, the increase could happen even sooner.[128]

* Major droughts and wildfires.[129]
* Extreme weather such as "Frankenstorm" Sandy, a storm of historic proportions spanning 520 miles from its eye.[130] Typhoon Haiyan, one of the strongest typhoons in world history, which devastated the Philippines in 2013.[131] And, extreme winter conditions in the Eastern and Midwestern United States in early 2014.[132]
* Indications that ocean acidification may be doing damage far earlier than predicted, such as causing tiny snail-like creatures called pteropods to dissolve.[133]

In the Arctic in 2012, the first atmospheric concentration of carbon dioxide above 400 parts per million (ppm) was measured. That same grim threshold was exceeded in Hawaii in 2013. And in May of 2015, the National Oceanic and Atmospheric Administration (NOAA) reported that the monthly global average concentration of greenhouse gas has surpassed 400 parts per million for the first time.[134] A far lower concentration of 350 ppm has long been considered the CO2 atmospheric level threshold above which severe impacts are likely to occur.

In the fall of 2013 and the first part of 2014, the United Nations' Intergovernmental Panel on Climate Change (IPCC) issued three reports providing the most definitive review of climate change issues done to date. The first report showed that climate change was "unequivocally" caused by human activity. The second warned that global warming's impacts—from extreme weather to reduced food production—pose a grave threat to humanity and could lead to wars and mass migration. The third noted that clean energy needs to triple its output and dominate world energy supplies by 2050 to avoid catastrophic climate change. So far efforts have failed to stop spiraling emissions of greenhouse gases, which have risen to "unprecedented levels" in the past decade, the report noted. If no action is taken, global temperatures will rise by up to 4.7C (8.5 F) by the end of the century, which scientists believe will trigger dramatic and irreversible damage to the planet. Moreover, if we don't take serious steps within the next 15 years, controlling climate change will become much harder and more expensive.[135]

OUR GLOBAL SITUATION: A RECAP

On a wide range of pressing environmental issues facing our planet, we are losing ground. From loss of biodiversity, to crashing fish stocks, to ubiquitous agricultural and environmental poisons, to a rapidly heating planet, we are failing abysmally to make essential changes. In fact, on key issues we are moving in the wrong direction, at an ever-increasing pace.

The threats confronting us are so severe that we absolutely must gain control over them without delay. There is no time to waste. Survival of our species is on the line.

CHAPTER 7

A Different Call to Action

● ● ●

How ARE WE DOING IN our efforts to protect the environment that gives us life? Terribly. There are no two ways about it. We are losing, and time is running out to turn things around.

Global warming gets a fair amount of attention these days. Many refer to it as *the* environmental issue of our day. But that is misleading. Global warming is only one of many intertwining extremely important environmental crises we face. Crashing fisheries, declining pollinator populations, deforestation, widespread toxic contamination, and other environmental problems all demand our immediate attention as well.

It is sobering to talk about this big picture, but we must. The fact that we are losing is obscured by the messages that bombard us each day. We hear impressive-sounding statistics about organic agriculture and renewable energy without realizing how miniscule each remains. We hear about victories but not about what happens next: another toxic chemical takes the place of one we banned or a hard-won regulation is quietly rescinded. Most of all, we hear that tiny steps forward are adding up to progress, when in truth that's not what's happening. Instead, we are hurtling backwards.

The time for pretending is over. The wolves are at the door. Playing pinochle at a table inside, as if everything is okay, is suicidal. We must acknowledge the severity of the crises we face and the impotence of the approach we've been taking so we can forge an effective strategy to turn things around.

Others have written articles and books calling on us to redouble our efforts to protect the environment. Often the general message is: *Care more! Change your personal lifestyle and find some environmental campaign to support! If we all try harder and have faith, things will work out in the end.*
My call to action is different.

We do *not* need to care more, work harder, and have more faith. We do *not* need to keep on keeping on. These things will not be enough. Plenty of people have cared enormously about environmental issues for a long time, and we've dutifully plugged along working as hard as we can to win reforms. Look at where that's gotten us.

No, what we need to do first and foremost is think. We need a new strategy. The way we've been fighting hasn't been working. Indeed, our disempowerment grows by the day.

So far we've looked unflinchingly at how we are doing, discovering that time is short and the water is rising. Now we need to look just as unflinchingly at the question of *why*. Why are we losing? Why does it feel like the deck is stacked against us? Why does it seem like there is an impenetrable wall between us and the world we must create?

Only by answering these questions will we be able to find the way forward.

PART III

What We Are Up Against

• • •

WHY ARE WE LOSING THE struggle to protect our environment? The answer is staring us in the face.

First and foremost, we are losing because the deck really *is* stacked against us. The resources of the world have become more and more concentrated in the hands of a few individuals and corporations. This has transferred power to them that should belong to us all. We have created an enormous giant that blocks our way forward. That giant grows bigger each day, rendering us less and less in control of our individual lives and joint destiny.

The next chapter describes the gap between rich and poor in our world today, a topic we need to thoroughly understand if we are to win the environmental battles we are fighting, or any social justice battles for that matter. The remaining chapters in this part of the book explore the consequences of that gap. They lay out the many ways in which those who accumulate wealth and resources exert control over the rest of us.

Taking in the full breadth of the forces aligned against us, it would be easy to become discouraged. Nonetheless, resist the urge to skip ahead. To undo our disempowerment, we need to fully understand it.

Many of the strategies promoted today are based on an incomplete grasp of what we're dealing with. As a result they treat symptoms rather than the real problem. They keep us spinning our wheels and going nowhere as time runs out. Only by scrutinizing what we're up against can we overcome it.

CHAPTER 8

The Rich and the Non-Rich

• • •

THERE IS AN IMMENSE GAP between the rich and poor in our world. It is getting bigger every day.

THE GAP IN THE UNITED STATES

INCOME AND ASSETS[136]
In 2009 the statistics about earnings and ownership in the U.S. were already shocking:

- The top 1% of households received more than a fifth of the nation's income.
- That top 1% owned over 35% of the nation's private wealth, which was more than the combined wealth of the entire bottom 90%.
- The wealthiest 20% of the population controlled 87.2% of all wealth, while the bottom 80% controlled only 12.8%
- An unsettling 37.1% of U.S. households had net worths less than $12,000. In other words, more than a third of U.S. households had such minimal savings and assets that they were extremely vulnerable should any special needs or problems arise.
- Even worse, approximately one in four U.S. households had *zero* or *negative* net worth, up from 18.6% in 2007. A shocking 40% of all

black households had zero or negative net worth.[137]   The median net worth for black households was $2200, the lowest ever recorded.

⚬ The net worth of the wealthiest 1% of U.S. households was 225 times greater than the net worth of median households.[138] This was the highest ratio on record.[139]

But 2009 was the "good old days." Since then, the imbalance has become even more pronounced.

The median net worth of U.S. families plunged from $126,000 in 2007 to $77,300 in 2010, which was approximately the same as the median net worth of families way back in 1992. In other words, we lost nearly two decades of wealth in a few years. The middle class bore the brunt of that loss, while the wealthiest families saw their median net worth rise slightly over this time period. The collapse of the housing market was key, with home values dropping 42% between 2007 and 2010.[140]

The Great Recession[141] destroyed wealth across classes, but unevenly. From 2007 to 2009, average annual household wealth declined 25% for the poorest four-fifths of Americans and only 16% for the richest one-fifth. That richest fifth increased their share of wealth by 2.2%, giving them 87.2% of the total wealth. Meanwhile, the poorest four-fifths lost that 2.2% and held onto just 12.8% of the total.[142]

The 400 richest Americans listed by Forbes magazine in 2010 have a net worth of $1.37 trillion, up from $507 billion in 1995.[143] The six Walton family heirs to the Walmart Empire have a combined wealth of $69.7 billion. That's equivalent to the wealth owned by the entire bottom 30% of the U.S. population.[144]

POVERTY AND LOW INCOMES

By 2010, 49.1 million Americans were living below the poverty line,[145] while another 97.3 million were considered "low-income." In other words, nearly half of the U.S. population (48%; 146.4 million people) had fallen into poverty or were scraping by on low incomes.[146]

While the precise numbers fluctuate from year to year, nearly one out of every two Americans today is low-income or poor.

Between 2009 and 2010 an additional one million children joined the ranks of those living in poverty. That brought the total number of poor children in the U.S. to 15.7 million in 2010, an increase of 2.6 million since 2007. Of these children, 5.9 million were under the age of 6. Nationwide, 24.8% of young children (under age 6) were poor in 2010, which is 1.9% more than the year before.[147,148]

Child poverty increased significantly in 38 states between 2007 and 2010. No rural or central city locations had estimated child poverty rates below 10% as of 2010.[149]

Deep Poverty

There are now 20 million people who live in what is known as *deep* poverty—getting by on half of the poverty level or less. That means less than $9000 per year for a family of three. Attacks on safety net programs for the poor are one of the causes of deep poverty. President Clinton signed a "welfare reform" bill in 1996, for example, which prompted his assistant secretary of Health and Human Services, Peter Edelman, to resign. According to Edelman, "basically, right now, welfare is gone." Given inadequacies in welfare and other programs, six million people in the U.S. now rely on food stamps as their sole source of income—an income that amounts to one third of the poverty line.

The 1996 welfare law gave states the authority to handle welfare as they see fit. Nineteen states serve less than 10% of their poor children. In Wyoming, only 4% of poor children receive Temporary Assistance to Needy Families (TANF).[150]

A Multi-Decade Trend

The gap between rich and poor has been steadily growing for several decades as numerous stunning statistics attest:

* In 1976, the top 1% of households received 8.9% of all pre-tax income. As of 2008, their share was 21.0%, following a peak of 23.5% in 2007. Between 1979 and 2009, the top 5% of American families saw their real incomes increase 72.7%. During the same period, the lowest-income fifth saw a decrease of 7.4%.[151]

* In 1980, the top 10% in the U.S. received a bit more than one-third of the nation's reported income, including capital gains. By 2007, they received nearly half (49.7%). Meanwhile the top 1% doubled the percent of income it receives from 10% in 1980 to 20% in 2010.[152]

* Average wealth for the Forbes 400 increased by 633% from 1982 to 2000, from $509 million to $3.7 billion. In 2009, wealth of the Forbes 400 averaged $3.2 billion—up 523% from 1982.[153]

* Since 1983, the richest 5% have consistently held more than 50% of all wealth, but the share increased from 56.1% in 1983 to 63.5% in 2009. The bottom 80% of wealth holders have consistently held less than 20% of all wealth, but the share declined from 18.7% in 1983 to 12.8% in 2009.[154]

* In 1962, the wealthiest 1% of households averaged 125 times the wealth of the median household. In 2009, the wealthiest 1% of households averaged 225 times the wealth of the median household.[155]

* According to 2010 census data, inflation-adjusted average earnings for the bottom 20% of families fell from $16,788 in 1979 to less than $15,000 in 2010. Earnings for the next 20% remained flat at $37,000. In contrast, earnings of the top 5% of families climbed 64% to more than $313,000. [156]

Census data show that the wealthiest Americans received most of the benefits from the economic recovery that began in June of 2009. As Robert Greenstein of the Center on Budget and Policy Priorities put it, "The gains from economic growth in 2011 were quite unevenly shared as household income fell in the middle and rose at the top." Average incomes fell for the bottom 80% of those earning money and rose for the top 20%. The top 1% of households had a 6% increase in income.[157]

Data released by the Pew Research Center in April of 2013 confirmed this finding. According to Pew's analysis, the top 7% of U.S. households saw their incomes rise 28% during the two-year recovery period following the Great Recession. For the remaining 93% of households, income declined. The wealth gap dividing the top 7% from the bottom 93% reached 24 to 1 in 2011 as compared to 18 to 1 in 2009.[158]

In other words, the Obama Administration has presided over a dramatic further redistribution of wealth upward to the wealthy.

Ever More Disparate Wages

One thing driving the growing gap between rich and poor has been wage stagnation for most working people. Workers have been more productive than ever, and they have created more profits than ever, but wages do not reflect this. Between 1947 and 1972, the average hourly wage for workers, adjusted for inflation, rose 76%. But since 1972, it has risen only 4%.[159] If the minimum wage had kept up with growth in worker productivity, it would be over $16.50 an hour today according to some experts.[160] Others say it would be $21.72.[161]

Vast numbers of Americans now work for the minimum wage. Many even work for less. A recent survey of domestic workers, for example, such as nannies, caregivers, and housecleaners found that nearly a quarter earned less than their state's minimum wage. Domestic workers received almost no benefits.[162]

Because wages are so low, people are working more hours than ever. Many have taken on second jobs to make ends meet. Elderly people are retiring late or coming out of retirement to get by or to help their grown children. Low wages and high debt are causing widespread stress.[163] In the majority of two-parent families, both parents have paid jobs as well as the unpaid vital job of raising children.[164]

Meanwhile, salaries and other income of the 1% have skyrocketed. In 2009 CEOs of major U.S. corporations averaged 263 times the average compensation of American workers. Those who cut payrolls most did particularly well, taking home 42% more compensation than the average for CEOs of the 500 corporations on the Standard and Poor list of top corporations.[165]

In 2011, the median pay for the nation's 200 top-paid CEOs at public companies was $14.5 million. The median pay raise for these CEOs was 5%. These figures do not include many billions of dollars earned by top hedge fund managers and private-equity dealmakers. Even so, in 2011, for the first time ever, not one, but two executives earned nine-figures.[166] The average Fortune 500 chief executive now makes 380 times more than the average worker.[167]

Abby Zimet of Common Dreams did the math to compare oil corporations' profits to working people's incomes. Every hour in 2012, the five biggest oil companies made $14,400,000 in profits, or more per minute than what 96% of American households earn in a year. Each hour they also received more than $270,000 in federal tax breaks, for a total of $2.4 billion per year.[168]

The New York Times reported in March of 2013 that we are in "a golden age for corporate profits," which are at record highs. These profits have not led to more jobs in the U.S., and corporations don't feel the need to raise salaries since millions are out of work. Corporate profits stood at 14.2% in the third quarter of 2012, the largest share at any time since 1950, but the portion of that income that went to employees was 61.7%, near its lowest point since 1966. "There hasn't been a period in the last 50 years where these trends have been so pronounced," remarked Dean Maki of the financial institution Barclays.[169]

If You Think the 1% Has Made Out Well, Take a Look at the 0.1%

While the term "the 1%" is used as a handy way to refer to the massive divide between the rich and the rest of us, the gap is even more extreme when looking at the ultra rich at the very top. The gap between the least and most wealthy individuals *within* the top 1% is quite large. People just a few tenths of a percentile above the cash income cutoff at the bottom of the 1% ($506,553) make much more than that amount. A family at the 99.5[th] percentile, for example, makes $815,868. Another family at the 99.9[th] percentile makes more than twice that amount, at $2,075,574 a year. In other words there is increasing inequality among the wealthy, as America's very richest people pull further and further away from everyone else.[170]

By 2007, the top one-hundredth of the top 1% (less than 25,000 households) earned more than 6% of all national income in the U.S.—nearly $1 trillion.[171]

UNEMPLOYMENT

The recession of 2007-2009 left behind the largest number of long-term unemployed people since records were first kept in 1948.[172] As of August 2011, the U.S. unemployment rate was still 9.1%, and that number did not include people who had given up on finding work, people working for fewer hours than they want, or people who are overqualified for their jobs.[173]

Since 2011, the *official* unemployment rate has declined, but it is difficult to know what the *real* rate is. In early 2012 the official rate was still over 8%, but best estimates of *real* unemployment ranged upward from 12%.[174]

Asked for U.S. unemployment statistics in May of 2012, economist Paul Krugman gave the official number of 13 million people, but noted difficulties in coming up with an accurate figure. According to Krugman, if we count the underemployed and people who have given up on looking for work "something like a third of the American population either are themselves, or someone close to them is suffering, from this economy in a very direct way. So, it's a huge number." Krugman also noted that almost 4 million people have been out of work for more than a year, saying you have to go back to the 1930s to find anything like that. "That destroys lives. That destroys families," he said.[175]

Reviewing supposed gains in employment in January of 2014, economist Paul Craig Roberts expressed grave doubts about the official rates: 7.0% dropping with holiday hiring to 6.7%. "Clearly, this decline in unemployment was not caused by the reported 74,000 jobs gain. The unemployment rate fell, because Americans unable to find jobs ceased looking for employment and, thereby, ceased to be counted as unemployed," Roberts said. "In America the unemployment rate is a deception just like everything else. The rate of American unemployment fell, because people can't find jobs. The fewer the jobs, the lower the unemployment rate," he added.[176]

Home Ownership and Foreclosures

In 2009, for the first time on record, the percent of home value that homeowners own outright dropped below 50%. That meant that banks now owned more of the nation's housing stock than people did.[177]

Lots of mortgage holders are "underwater," meaning they owe more on their house than what the house is worth. As of the third quarter of 2010, 10.8 million mortgages, representing 22.5% of homeowners with mortgages, had zero or negative equity. Nearly 10% of those mortgages were underwater by 25% or more.[178]

More than 2 million homes were foreclosed upon in the U.S. in 2011.[179]

There are no reliable numbers, but observers say that America's homeless population is clearly rising fast.[180] The number of people living in city shelters in New York City alone reached an all-time high of more than 43,000 in the spring of 2012.[181]

A new feature of the national homeless population is young adults, many with college credits and work histories, who cannot find jobs or whose jobs do not pay well enough for them to afford a place to live. While many young adults are living with their parents as part of the "boomerang set," others end up on the streets and in homeless shelters.[182]

DEBT

With wages stagnating, Americans have had to borrow more and more money. As of 2011 total U.S. consumer debt was $11.4 trillion and 75% of Americans owed money.[183] We are a nation of debtors.

Middle income and poor households spend a much higher percentage of their incomes paying down debt than the richest households do. In 2010, for example, the 10% of U.S. households earning the most money spent 9.4% of their income servicing debt, while the average for the bottom 90% was 19.6%. The bottom one-fifth of households spent a whopping 23.5% of their incomes for debt payments. These ratios do not capture additional costs borne by low-income families dependent on things like pawn shops and payday lenders. Those entities often charge very high fees for their loans.[184]

Spending over 23% of your income each year on debt instead of food and other necessities strikes me as difficult. But the generally accepted definition of economic "hardship" for debt payments is spending more than 40% of your income on them. In 2010, only 2.9% of households in the top 10% crossed that line. Meanwhile 15.4% of the middle fifth of households—nearly one out of every six middle-income families—did so. What was the economic hardship percentage for families in the bottom fifth? A disturbing 26.1%. More than a quarter of all of those lowest income households had to give more than 40% of their income to debt payments.[185]

Despite a new law making it harder to declare bankruptcy, 6.1 adults per every 1000 declared personal bankruptcy in 2011.[186]

One major source of debt is borrowing money to get a college education. On April 25, 2012, U.S. student debt reached $1 trillion, an all-time high.[187] According to the Pew Research Center, the number of households with college debt doubled from 1989 to 2010 and jumped 15% over just the last three of those years—2007 to 2010.

The poor are the most burdened by this type of debt, with student loans taking nearly a quarter of household income for the poorest 20% of Americans. Nearly one in five households now have debt from college loans in the U.S.[188]

According to a Federal Reserve report released in June of 2012, nearly 11% of families surveyed about college debt were at least 60 days late paying a bill, up from 7% in 2007.[189]

There are huge numbers of *student* borrowers in financial distress, but vast numbers of *parents* who have taken out loans to pay for their children's college educations are also highly stressed. In the first three months of 2012, 2.2 million borrowers of student loans were over 60 years old, a figure that had tripled since 2005. These borrowers jointly owed $43 billion, up from $8 billion seven years earlier. Nearly 10% of the borrowers over 60 were 90 days or more behind on their payments during the first quarter of 2012 as compared to 6% in 2005.[190]

Food Stamps and Other Public Assistance

The USDA reports that an average of 44 million people were on public assistance in 2011, up from 17 million in 2000.[191] The number of people with graduate degrees (masters and doctorates) who have applied for food stamps, unemployment, or other assistance more than tripled between 2007 and 2010, according to a report by the Chronicle of Higher Education. In 2010, 360,000 of the 22 million Americans with graduate degrees received some sort of public assistance.[192]

The number of people using food stamps has jumped to 18 million, a 70% increase, since the recession began.[193] As mentioned above, there are six million people in the U.S. whose only income is food stamps, an income which is the equivalent of one-third of the poverty line. As of early 2015 more than 16 million children in the U.S. lived in families receiving food stamps.[194]

The number of low-income Americans who consistently lack adequate food increased by 800,000 in 2011. According to the U.S. Department of Agriculture, 5.5% of the U.S. population—nearly 17 million people—suffered "very low food security," meaning they had to skip meals or go without food for a full day.[195]

RETIREMENT

Few workers in the U.S. receive pensions from private employers to use in retirement. These remaining private pensions, along with public employees' pensions, are in jeopardy. At the same time with a huge percentage of U.S. government funds going to military expenditures, programs like Social Security have been chronically underfunded for years. Thus, more and more people must rely on their own savings to supplement Social Security, which alone is inadequate to fully support people in retirement.

Unfortunately, most people are not able to save much towards retirement. Professor Teresa Ghilarducci of the New School for Social Research estimates that 75% of Americans nearing retirement in 2010 had less than $30,000 in their retirement accounts.[196] Thus a majority of senior Americans will either live without adequate resources in old age, keep working whether they want to or not, or depend upon family and friends for support, thereby adding to others' financial burdens.

INEQUALITY AROUND THE WORLD

THE GAP BETWEEN RICH AND POOR

The same imbalance that exists in the U.S. exists throughout the world. The following statistics provide a snapshot of this imbalance:

* In 1960, the 20% of the world's people in the richest countries had 30 times the income of the poorest 20%. In 1997, the number was 74 times as much.[197]
* According to a *Forbes Magazine* tally in March of 2011, the world's 1210 billionaires at the time held a combined wealth equal to half of the total wealth of the 3.01 billion adults around the world with net worths of less than $10,000 each.[198]
* In 2006, when there were about 6.5 billion people in the world, global gross domestic product was about $48.2 trillion.

The world's wealthiest countries (approximately 1 billion people) accounted for $36.6 trillion (76%) of this. The world's billionaires (497 people representing just 0.000008% of the world's population) were worth $3.5 trillion, which was over 7% of the global GDP. Low-income countries (2.4 billion people) accounted for $1.6 trillion (3.3%). Middle-income countries (3 billion people) accounted for just over $10 trillion (20.7%).[199]

⊛ In 2005, the world's wealthiest 20% accounted for 76.6% of total private consumption, while the poorest fifth accounted for 1.5%. The poorest 10% accounted for only 0.5% and the wealthiest 10% for 59% of all private consumption.[200]

⊛ The United Nations estimates that $30 billion per year could eradicate hunger. Several individuals have more than this amount in personal wealth.[201]

⊛ Eighty individuals now own as much wealth as the bottom half of the global population. The top 1% now own 48% of the world's wealth and are on course to own more than 50% by 2016.[202]

Poverty

Almost half the world—over three billion people—live on less than $2.50 a day. At least 80% live on less than $10 a day.[203] One billion of the world's 2.2 billion children live in poverty.[204] About 22,000 children die each day due to poverty.[205]

Even in the world's richest countries, tens of millions of children live in poverty. Some 13 million children in the European Union, Norway, and Iceland lack basic items necessary for their development, for example. "The data reinforce that far too many children continue to go without the basics in countries that have the means to provide," said Gordon Alexander, Director of UNICEF's Office of Research.[206]

Hunger

Nearly 870 million people, or one in eight people in the world, suffered from chronic undernourishment in 2010 to 2012. Most lived in developing countries, where 15% of the population is hungry.[207] Poor nutrition plays a role in at least half of the 10.9 million child deaths that occur each year. It magnifies the effects of every disease. Stunting due to malnutrition affects 32.5% of children in developing countries—one in three children.[208]

In the last decades of the 20th century, the number of hungry and malnourished people in the world was shrinking. Then it started to rise, slowly at first, then more rapidly, as grain was diverted for use as fuel in cars.[209] Droughts associated with global warming and other factors are also contributing to high food prices.[210] "A new norm of high prices seems to be consolidating," noted Otaviano Canuto of the World Bank in November of 2012.[211] As a world hunger summit got underway in London, Prime Minister David Cameron noted that "[t]he figures are truly shocking. One in three child deaths are linked to malnutrition, and 171 million children are so malnourished by the age of two that they can never physically recover."[212]

Unemployment

High rates of unemployment exist in many parts of the world. In the nations most hit by the European debt crisis, for example, unemployment is very high. By early 2012 the unemployment rates in Spain, Portugal, Ireland, and Greece were 23, 12, 14, and 22%, respectively. Unemployment figures do not capture economic hardship endured by those who are employed. In Greece teachers and university professors have suffered pay cuts of 30% or more, for instance.

Corporations

A look at the distribution of wealth in the world would be incomplete without a reference to corporations. The riches of the 1% and the 0.1%

are directly linked to the major corporations with which they are involved as CEOs, board members, major shareholders, and owners. Wealth is sequestered not only in individual bank accounts but also in the private companies that enrich individuals with high salaries, dividends, pensions, bonuses, and other payments. Author Charles Ferguson reported in his 2012 book *Predator Nation* that U.S. companies are sitting on two trillion dollars in cash.[213] A consulting firm for corporations noted in a report that U.S. companies had up to $5 trillion in liquid assets globally as of mid-2012.[214]

In fact, of the 100 largest economies in the world, 51 are corporations, and only 49 are countries. This conclusion is based on a comparison of corporate sales and countries' gross domestic products.[215] In other words, many corporations have more resources than whole nations.

Corporations have grown wealthier and wealthier by pocketing rising profits produced by workers while keeping the wages of those workers stagnant, and through an ongoing frenzy of mergers and acquisitions. With each passing year, society's wealth is controlled by fewer and fewer corporations and the individuals who own them.

The last decade has been financially trying for most people in the world, but not for major corporations and their leaders and owners. Since 2000, for example, America's four largest oil companies have accumulated more than $300 billion in *excess* profits, which are profits over and above the profit rate in the prior decade. Investment banking bonuses were similarly gigantic—an estimated $150 billion over the decade. The *average* annual salary of New York bankers stayed steady at about $390,000, even after the financial sector's collapse in 2008.[216]

Oil and gas corporations account for eight of the top ten largest global corporations.[217] They are profiting handsomely and growing through those profits as well as through mergers and acquisitions. Exxon's fourth-quarter profits surged in 2011 "thanks to gas production," a January 2012 news article explains.[218] Energy Transfer Partners has acquired Sunoco, valued at $5.3 billion, merging the two companies' vast holdings of pipelines and other oil and gas resources, according to an industry journal.[219]

As previously noted, every hour in 2012, the five biggest oil companies (Shell, ExxonMobil, BP, Chevron, and ConocoPhillips) made $14,400,000 in profits, or more in one minute than what 96% of American households earn in one year. The average salary per minute for the CEOs of the three U.S. oil companies was $40. That's per *minute*, not per hour. In one day, the five biggest oil companies reap $342 million in profits and each CEO receives $60,000 in salary.[220]

To begin to understand how just a few corporations control things, take a look at some of the online documents showing who owns what. One fascinating chart shows how only 10 multinational corporations control a huge number of product brands. Did you know, for example, that Nestle owns Clairol, Gerber, Ralph Lauren, and Purina, among many other brands?[221]

Gaps Related to Gender, Race, and Color

African Americans, Latinos, and Native Americans are significantly more likely to live below the poverty line than white non-Latinos.[222] As noted earlier, 40% of all black households in 2009 had zero or negative worth, as compared to one in four for U.S. households overall. Nearly one in four (24%) Latino households are food insecure while the rate in Caucasian households is one in 10 (11%).[223]

As of 2013,[224] white families were more than twice as likely as Hispanic[225] and black families to have wealth above the median U.S. level. As of 2013, the median wealth levels of Hispanic and black families were about 90% lower than those of whites, and median family income levels were 40% lower. Disparities persist even after accounting for age and education levels.

There are many more statistics like these.

Gaps also exist between women and men. In the U.S., on average, a woman working full-time year-round earns $39,157, while a man working the same amount of time earns $50,033. In other words, women overall receive 78 cents for every dollar a man receives. This gap persists regardless of industry and educational level.[226]

Things are even worse for women of color. African American women earn 64 cents and Latinas earn 56 cents for each dollar earned by white, non-Hispanic men.

CITIGROUP'S VIEW OF THE WORLD: THE RICH AND THE "NON-RICH"

Those who advise the wealthy on how to invest their money have come up with a new term for the type of society we live in: *plutonomy*. A strategist for Citigroup coined the term in a memo he wrote in 2005. That memo and two follow-up memos were leaked to outsiders and ended up being featured in Michael Moore's movie *Capitalism, A Love Story*.

The memos make for extraordinary reading. The authors observe that "[t]he World is dividing into two blocs—the Plutonomy and the rest....The U.S., UK and Canada are the key Plutonomies—economies powered by the wealthy." They discuss the disproportionate income, wealth, and consumption of the 1% and especially of the 0.1%, using terms like "The Managerial Aristocracy" to describe the wealthy few. The authors' main point is that wise investors will "buy shares in the companies that make the toys that the Plutonomists enjoy."[227] In other words, money should be pumped into companies that produce goods and services pleasing to the ultra rich rather than those wanted and needed by the rest of us.

The memos' warnings to investors about what could go wrong and upset the plutonomy—i.e., "societies demanding a more equitable share of wealth"—provide good advice to those of us who *want* things to "go wrong."[228] Here are a few choice paragraphs from the Citigroup memos bearing on the state of the world we inhabit. The emphasis is mine.

In a plutonomy there is no such animal as "the U.S. consumer" or the "the UK consumer", or indeed the "Russian consumer". There are rich consumers, few in number, but disproportionate in the gigantic slice of income and consumption they take. *There are the rest, the "non-rich," the multitudinous many, but only accounting for surprisingly small bites of the national pie.*[229]

Asset booms, a rising profit share and favorable treatment by market-friendly governments have allowed the rich to prosper and become a greater share of the economy in the plutonomy countries. Also, new media dissemination technologies like internet downloading, cable and satellite TV, have disproportionately increased the audiences, and hence gains to 'superstars'....These 'content' providers, the tech whizzes who own the pipes and distribution, the lawyers and bankers who intermediate globalization and productivity, the CEOs who lead the charge in converting globalization and technology to increase the profit share of the economy *at the expense of labor,* all contribute to plutonomy.[230]

Despite being in great shape, we think that *global capitalists are going to be getting an even greater share of the wealth pie over the next few years, as capitalists benefit disproportionately from globalization and the productivity boom, at the relative expense of labor.*[231]

...in the plutonomy countries, the rich are such a massive part of the economy, that their relative insensitivity to rising oil prices makes US$60 oil something of an irrelevance. *For the poorest in society, high gas and petrol prices are a problem. But while they are many in number, they are few in spending power, and their economic influence is just not important enough to offset the economic confidence, well-being and spending of the rich.*[232]

...we believe that *the rich are going to keep getting richer* in coming years, as capitalists (the rich) get an even bigger share of GDP as a result, principally of globalization. *We expect the global pool of labor in developing economies to keep wage inflation in check, and profit margins rising—good for the wealth of capitalists, relatively bad for developed market unskilled/outsource-able labor.* This bodes well for companies selling to or servicing the rich.[233]

Who Calls the Shots?

A very small number of corporations and individuals own much of the world's resources and wealth. Their assets grow by leaps and bounds as they pull in jaw-dropping revenues every day. Meanwhile, billions endure grinding poverty. Even in the United States, the wealthiest country on Earth, nearly half the population is low-income or poor. Debt is rampant. People lack savings for a rainy day, let alone for retirement. Vast numbers struggle to get by, working hard for low pay if they're able to find jobs at all.

In and of itself this situation demands our attention. As a matter of basic morality and justice, it is unacceptable. But this situation also demands our attention because it is the reason we are unable to address the environmental crises that threaten human survival.

Political scientists have documented what we all know to be true. The gap between rich and poor translates into power for the affluent and lack of power for the have-nots. Professor Martin Gilens, for example, reviewed policies adopted between 1964 and 2006 in the United States, comparing what the public wanted to what we got. Gilens concluded that "American citizens are vastly unequal in their influence over policymaking, and that inequality is growing. In most circumstances, affluent Americans exert substantial influence over the policies adopted by the federal government, and less well off Americans exert virtually none. Even when Democrats control Congress and the White House, the less well off are no more influential."[234]

Gilens warned that, "[a] democracy that ignores most of the public most of the time has a tenuous claim to legitimacy."

Inequity is the biggest environmental issue of our day. It enables an elite minority to call the shots, blocking essential plans and programs desired by the majority. The remaining chapters in this part of the book explain how.

Big Money's use of accumulated wealth to influence elections and legislation are examined first. But these expenditures are only a small part of how the 1% undermines us. Read on to explore other ways in which the wealthy few use money and their control over major resources to determine what happens next in our world, regardless of what makes sense for our planet and our survival.

CHAPTER 9

Influencing Elections

● ● ●

EVERYONE KNOWS THAT BIG MONEY is corrupting elections. Many mistakenly believe, however, that the problem relates primarily to the Republican Party. They cling to the illusion that the Democrats, and individual candidates like Barack Obama, rise above Big Money and its influence. It is important to dispel this illusion. Thus the first part of this chapter reviews the Democratic Party's funding record, using Barack Obama as an example.

Discussions about money influencing elections also generally focus on contributions to candidates and parties during campaigns. But Big Money shapes election outcomes through other avenues as well, as detailed below.

CAMPAIGN CONTRIBUTIONS

OBAMA'S FUNDERS
Lots of people believe that small donations from working people propelled Barack Obama into office, and that Obama didn't take money from big corporations and from lobbyists. This perception was actively promoted by Obama and his staff.[235]

Here's the reality. In both 2008 and 2012, the bulk of Obama's funding came from big contributions. Small donations ($200 or less) accounted for only 34% in 2008[236] and approximately 33% in 2012[237] of money received from individuals. When other sources of funding beyond individual donations are considered, small donations represent an even smaller percent of the funds that put Obama in the White House.

Like other candidates, Obama did not accept money directly from corporations, which would have been illegal. He also placed some voluntary limits on accepting donations from corporate PACs (Political Action Committees). But Obama still raked in huge piles of money from big corporations. Most important, he had top executives at these corporations "bundle" donations from corporate colleagues and family members. According to the Center for Responsible Politics, bundlers are "people with friends in high places, who, after bumping against personal contribution limits, turn to those friends, associates, and well, anyone who's willing to give, and deliver the checks to the candidate in one big 'bundle.'"[238] In 2008, 558 bundlers delivered at least $76,250,000 to Obama.[239] In 2012, 769 bundlers gave him at least $186,500,000.[240]

Obama's bundlers included executives from major oil corporations. In 2012, funding from individuals associated with Exxon, BP, Chevron, and Shell exceeded $102,000; $59,000, $96,000 and $68,000, respectively.[241]

Obama also pulled in huge amounts of money from Wall Street interests. In 2008, money flowed to his election coffers from Goldman Sachs ($1,034,615), JPMorgan Chase ($847,895), Citigroup ($736,771), Morgan Stanley ($528,182), and other financial giants.[242] In fact, Obama took more money from Wall Street in 2008 than any other presidential candidate in that election. His total from the "Hedge Funds & Private Equity" sector was over $3.4 million.[243]

In 2012, Obama took in less Wall Street money than Mitt Romney, his Republican opponent; and some Wall Street donors gave only to the Republican this time around. But Wall Street remained a major source of funding for Obama. For example, Obama got money from donors associated with Goldman Sachs ($135,343), JPMorgan Chase ($148,826), and Citigroup $101,091.[244] His campaign received over $43 million from the "Finance, Insurance, and Real Estate" industry.

Prominent investment bankers, hedge-fund managers, and private equity executives all pulled together cash for Obama's 2012 campaign.[245]

Health care industry executives also poured money into Obama's bid for the White House. Obama took in a staggering $20,175,303 from the health care industry in 2008.[246]

Obama's bundlers included higher-ups from communications corporations, a billionaire casino developer, the director of military supplier General Dynamics, partners at top law firms, and other wealthy contributors.[247] Agribusiness donors gave Obama over $2.5 million in 2008 and over $2 million in 2012.[248]

It is wrong to claim that corporate interests didn't pour money into electing Barack Obama. They did.

Some Obama bundlers were made to feel part of the campaign's inner workings as members of a "national finance committee." At weekly conference calls and quarterly meetings, Obama's 2008 bundlers could quiz the candidate or his strategists. Bundlers got advance copies of speeches. They got to meet with Obama's policy advisers.[249]

What about Obama's claim that he did not accept money from "lobbyists"? This too was highly misleading. Many of the big corporations at which money was bundled for Obama—corporations like Goldman Sachs, Citigroup, and Google, for instance—have a major lobbying presence in Washington, D.C.[250] Their "in-house" lobbyists were ignored because those firms were not formed specifically to lobby. Similarly, individuals who had lobbied heavily in the past and would again in the future simply stopped being lobbyists for a short time while they were donors. Scott Blake Harris, a Washington telecommunications lawyer, for instance, avoided Obama's ban on accepting money from federal lobbyists by cutting off his work for companies like Microsoft, Cisco, and Sprint Nextel at the end of 2006.[251]

Obama included lobbyists among his informal advisors, such as Broderick Johnson, head of the Washington lobbying practice Bryan Cave, which represented Shell Oil. He also accepted money from *state* lobbyists and from the spouses of federal lobbyists.[252] Obama repeatedly held fundraisers at law firms that lobby in Washington, such at the of-fices of Greenberg Traurig, whose lobby clients included gambling and handgun interests.

Obama's campaigns have been bankrolled not just by wealthy people in general, but by some of the wealthiest of the wealthy.[253] Events aimed at ultra-rich individuals were a core activity of the Obama fundraising machine.[254]

A *New York Times* article described fundraisers Obama attended in March of 2012 in New York, and how he raised $5 million in just one night. It mentioned a dessert event in New York City's Upper East Side as "his 100th major fund-raiser of the campaign."[255] That was in March, with over eight months left before Election Day.[256]

Obama and the Democrats are certainly not alone in receiving major financial assistance from wealthy corporate donors. That the Republican Party and its candidates depend on the largesse of big cor-porations and the ultra rich for a substantial portion of their funding goes without saying.

CONVENTIONS AND INAUGURATIONS: MORE OPPORTUNITIES FOR BIG DONORS

Large corporations and wealthy individuals also influence elections by funding the Democratic and Republican Party nominating conventions. These carefully orchestrated theatrical extravaganzas are important to each party's strategy for winning the White House. So, both major parties are eager to attract big sponsors for them.

In 2008 there were 141 business sponsors for the Democratic Convention and 91 for the Republican Convention.[257] Each party had a very long list of corporations donating $100,000 or more. Sixty-eight corporations gave $100,000 or more to *both* parties' conventions. BP, Dow Chemical, Pepsi, Citigroup, Goldman Sachs, Pfizer, Eli Lilly, Verizon, JPMorgan Chase, and Ford, for instance, were all "double givers."

The two convention host committees raised $118 million dollars from private sources in 2008: $61 million for the Democratic Convention and $57 million for the Republican one. Eighty percent of the funds raised came in as donations ranging from $250,000 to $3 million.[258]

It's sobering to read the brochures soliciting corporate donations for the conventions in 2008. "As a corporate sponsor, you will be invited to exclusive forums and special events where you will interact with our state's and nation's government and business leaders," a brochure for the Democratic Convention noted. Apparently oblivious to the implications, it explained that, "[f]or all of us, what we get in life and in business is often in direct proportion to what we give. In financial terms, your sponsorship is an investment in the future." The brochure then spelled out who donors would get to rub shoulders with for each giving level, such as the "Presidential Level" at $1 million.

In 2012, the Democratic Party announced a self-imposed ban on corporate contributions for its convention. It got a lot of great press from this announcement and repeatedly claimed that regular folks were footing the bill.[259]

In reality, the Democratic Party still depended primarily on wealthy individuals and corporations to fund its convention, as did the Republicans. The Party allowed individual donations to the Host Committee of up to $100,000. It allowed in-kind donations from corporations. And it set up a separate entity called New American City, which *did* accept monetary corporate contributions.[260] In other words, as we shall see time and again, the Democratic Party embraced the tried and true, though disingenuous, technique of "let's not and say we did." In this case: let's *not* refuse huge donations from giant corporations and the ultra rich, and pretend that we did.

Convention sponsors in 2012 included AT&T, Bank of America, Duke Energy, Time Warner Cable, Coca Cola, Wells Fargo, UnitedHealth Group, Piedmont National Gas, US Airways, and the law/lobby firm McGuireWoods.[261]

The official host committee for the convention was co-chaired by Duke Energy CEO Jim Rogers. He got to hobnob with co-chairs who were elected officials—a Governor, a Senator, and a Mayor. Rogers secured 10 to 11 million dollars from local corporations for the convention.[262] Duke Energy is the nation's largest utility. It relies overwhelmingly on nuclear power and burning coal, including coal obtained through mountain top removal.[263]

In 2012, a private entity called Conventions 2012.com and its subgroups—GOP 2012 Convention Strategies and DNC 2012 Convention Strategies—handled the task of bringing Big Money interests together with elected officials.[264] LeeAnn Petersen, a staffperson with Conventions 2012 was quite clear about what her corporation was offering. "The name of the game is access and exposure to Members of Congress," she said. "It's like shooting fish in a barrel."[265]

The 2012 Inauguration offered an additional opportunity for corporations and their top employees to give big bucks to Obama and the Democrats. Obama allowed unlimited corporate contributions to his Inaugural Committee. ExxonMobil gave over $260,000, for example: $250,000 from the company itself and $10,750 from an ExxonMobil attorney.[266]

BEYOND PRESIDENTIAL RACES

Mega corporations and ultra-wealthy individuals don't limit their electoral spending to presidential races alone, of course. In fact, the percentage of funding from small donors is even lower for other races than it is for presidential races. In the 2010 election cycle, the average Congressional campaign got 84% of its money from donations of $200 or more.[267] Incumbent members of Congress typically raise less than 10% of their campaign funds from small donors, as do candidates for governor and for state legislatures.[268]

The ultra-rich implement national electoral strategies to ensure that their interests are advanced. Oil and gas industries gave more than

$22.6 million to members of Congress in the 2010 election cycle, for example. This included donations to 88% of the members of the House of Representatives—387 individuals. It also included donations to 89 of the 100 Senators.[269] As of July 2012, the industry had already contributed $17.8 million in the 2012 cycle.

Wealthy interests target those serving on key committees in Congress. According to a report released in November of 2011, agribusiness had contributed $27 million to members of U.S. House and Senate agriculture committees over the prior decade. The American Crystal Sugar Company had given $984,998 to Agriculture Committee members, for example. The Dairy Farmers of America had given $550,100. The National Cotton Council had given $332,718.[270]

As members of Congress gain power and seniority over time, the industries they are supposed to be regulating steer more and more money into their campaign coffers. Just before senators or representatives become ranking members of Congress or chairs of key committees, increases in donations to them are particularly large.[271]

These statistics are just a tiny slice of the huge donations from the super rich that flood our electoral system at all levels from local races on up to national ones.[272] Ultra-wealthy individuals talk unapologetically about "investing" enormous amounts of money in elections.[273]

GROOMING CANDIDATES: THE RICH DECIDE WHO GETS TO RUN

So far we've been talking only about contributions to candidates and parties *during* electoral campaigns. Large corporations and wealthy individuals influence elections in another very important way, however. They play a lead role in determining who is visible and who is financially able to run for office.

Take Barack Obama's successful presidential bid in 2008, for example. It's as if he came out of nowhere. How did an Illinois state legislator, not well known in his own state let alone the nation, rise in the course of a few years to the U.S. Senate and then to the Presidency before he was even done with his first Senate term?

Well before he announced in February of 2007 that he was running for President, Obama began assembling his bundlers.[274] Money from major donors enabled him to gain name recognition, be considered a contender, and start pulling in other donations.[275]

But long before that, big money paved the way for Obama by helping him get elected as a state legislator and then as the U.S. Senator for Illinois. Wealthy interests brought his name to prominence and allowed him to be seen as legitimate.

They also funded his formidable small donor fundraising machine. List maintenance, direct mail, phone banking, and other aspects of securing small donations all require significant upfront investments. Branded products given to donors as incentives also cost a lot of money. In short, it takes money to make money, and early big donors determine who will be contenders.[276]

Early money from wealthy interests also gives a savvy candidate cash to buy allies. Obama used some of the money raised by his Political Action Committee in the 2005-2006 election cycle to build support for his presidential run by making donations to Democratic Party organizations and candidates around the country. That pile of money included thousands from defense contractors, law firms, and the securities and insurance industries.[277]

Becoming a viable candidate has everything to do with impressing the "right people," i.e., those with lots of money and connections. Barack Obama did just that. Investment bankers, real estate moguls, and other ultra-wealthy corporate leaders organized meetings for Obama when he was a little-known candidate for the U.S. Senate. They introduced him to other big donors and power brokers who introduced him to still more wealthy individuals. The details were chronicled late in 2006 by investigative journalist Ken Silverstein in an article that appeared in *Harper's Magazine*.[278] Mike Williams, vice president for legislative affairs of the Bond Market Association, for example, set up a conference call for

Obama with financial industry lobbyists and organized a fundraiser for him at the Bond Market Association. That event was attended by 200 people, including many highly influential people who donated money and connected Obama to even more wealthy and powerful patrons.[279]

Obama got early funding from an array of big corporations via their PACs and their staffs. Between 2001 and 2006, he received over $1.5 million from the securities and exchange industry, $330,000 from commercial banks, $456,000 from miscellaneous financial institutions, and $195,465 from the insurance industry, for example. His list of top 100 contributors included Goldman Sachs ($59,500), JPMorgan Chase ($52,600), Citigroup ($27,600), Bank of America ($31,500), and Comcast ($24,566).[280]

Obama pleased major corporations early on and thus enjoyed their steady financial support throughout his career. He got funding from insurance companies and their lobbyists for his state senate campaign and for his successful bid for the U.S. Senate in 2004.[281]

Over the course of his career, Obama has taken staggering aggregate sums from different sectors. He received over $57 million from the finance, insurance, and real estate sector between 1989 and 2012, for instance.[282]

Obama has a long and lucrative relationship with the nuclear industry. As of November 2006, Exelon, a leading U.S. nuclear power corporation, was Obama's fourth largest donor, having contributed $74,350 to his campaigns.[283] In February 2008, the *New York Times* reported that since 2003, executives and employees of Exelon had contributed a minimum of $227,000 to Obama's campaigns for the U.S. Senate and the presidency.[284]

Obama did not garner support from the insurance, nuclear, financial, communications, and other industries because he planned on subordinating their needs to those of the public. On the contrary, they could count on him to uphold their private interests. Exelon was surely pleased, for example, when Obama helped vote down an amendment to a 2005 energy bill that would have killed huge loan guarantees for power-plant operators developing new energy projects. The Bond Market Association was likely happy that he helped pass a Republican-driven bill that undercut the ability of people to bring class action lawsuits against the association's members. He also pleased the association by opposing bill amendments that would have capped credit-card interest rates at 30%, a change consumer advocates had sought.[285]

The wealthy individuals and corporations that lifted Obama up did so because they knew he would represent their interests. They promoted him not because he would bring radical change, but because they were confident he would prevent it. As one major donor and Obama promoter put it, "There's a reasonableness about him...I don't see him as being on the liberal fringe."[286]

What made Obama particularly appealing? His ability to sound populist while supporting policies that advanced the interests of wealthy corporations and individuals. As one Washington lobbyist put it, "What's the dollar value of a starry-eyed idealist?"[287]

THE BIG MONEY PARTIES SHUT OUT THIRD PARTIES

Gigantic sums of money donated to Democrats and Republicans give them an extreme advantage over less well-funded third parties. But the Democratic and Republican Parties aren't satisfied with that advantage. They also systematically exclude third parties from public forums that should be open to all.

Take the presidential and vice-presidential candidate debates as a key example. These are run by something called "The Commission on Presidential Debates." The name makes it sound like a governmental body, but the Commission is actually a private corporation financed by Anheuser-Busch and other major companies. It was created by the Republican and Democratic parties to seize control of the debates from The League of Women Voters, the non-partisan organization that had previously run them. Every four years, the Republican and Democratic Parties meet behind closed doors and agree upon a contract that sets the terms of the debate. They exclude parties that have the support of less than 15% of people in a poll—a threshold that is extremely difficult to meet since the U.S. public rarely sees anyone but Democratic and Republican candidates via the news, ads, mailings, and the like. As a result, with rare exceptions, only Democrats and Republicans are showcased in the nationally televised debates. Only candidates approved and lifted up by the super-wealthy get to be heard.[288]

A description of one of the "debates" in 2012, billed as having a "town hall" feel, reminds me of the World Trade Organization meeting I attended years ago that I described in chapter 2. Questions for the candidates had to be submitted in advance for scrutiny just as the questions posed to EPA in Seattle years ago were screened. But for the presidential debates, "town hall" audiences were also pre-vetted and handpicked by the event organizers. Audience members actually had to participate in a rehearsal with the moderators.[289]

Asked why the League of Women Voters decided to no longer sponsor the presidential debates, a League spokeswoman explained that Democratic and Republican Party officials had been exerting huge pressure on the League. Those officials insisted on total control of items ranging from the debate format to the choice of moderator and the selection of questions that would be asked. The League issued a statement in 1987 that said:

> Between themselves, the campaigns had determined what the television cameras could take pictures of. They had determined how they would select those who would pose questions to their candidates...They had determined that they would pack the hall with their supporters. And they had determined the format. The campaigns' agreement was a closed-door masterpiece. The agreement was a done deal, they told us. We were supposed to sign it and agree to all of its conditions. If we did not, we were told we would lose the debate....In Winston-Salem, they went so far as to insist on reviewing the moderator's opening

comments. It turned out that the League had two choices. We could sign their closed-door agreement and hope the event would rise above their manipulations. Or we could refuse to lend our trusted name to this charade. The League of Women Voters is announcing today that we have no intention of becoming an accessory to the hoodwinking of the American public.[290]

BIG MONEY'S INFLUENCE OVER ELECTIONS IS GROWING

Recent court decisions have made Big Money's dominance of elections worse than ever. In particular, the Supreme Court's ruling in 2010 in the Citizens United case allows Super Political Action Committees (Super PACs) to accept and use unlimited amounts of money from individuals and corporations to support or oppose candidates, as long as they don't coordinate directly with candidates. Nearly 80% of the money raised by Super PACs in 2011 came from donations of $100,000 or more. In addition, any donor can now give an unlimited amount of money to an organization that has 501(c)(4) status under the federal tax code. These organizations can use the money to influence elections, and the donors can remain anonymous.[291]

Others have written about how Citizens United and related court decisions have "opened the floodgates" for Big Money control over elections. [292,293,294] The 1% had elections locked up long before these court decisions, but the decisions certainly have made matters even worse.

As the wealthy few have poured more and more money into elections over the years, the cost of running for office has skyrocketed. This makes it even harder for regular people, relying on small donations, to run.

The amount of money spent on campaigns is truly staggering. Parties, candidates, and other organizations spent about $7 billion in the 2012 presidential election, for example.[295] U.S. Senators, on average, each raised $10,476,451 to win their seats in Congress in 2012, an average of $14,351 every day during the 2012 election cycle![296] Scott Walker, the Wisconsin Republican Governor, raised more than $30 million for his recall election. He received sums as high as $500,000 from single individuals.[297]

Increasingly, those elected to office are themselves very wealthy. Roughly 11% of Congress (27 members) have a personal net worth that exceeds $9 million, according to a *USA Today* analysis of 2010 financial disclosures. That puts them in the nation's top 1%. Two hundred and fifty members of Congress are millionaires. The median net worth in Congress is $891,506—almost nine times the typical U.S. household's wealth.[298]

Party leaders in the House of Representatives are particularly wealthy. House Minority Leader Nancy Pelosi and her husband jointly reported financial assets of $40 million to $187 million, according to a 2012 news story.[299] Majority Leader Eric Cantor listed financial assets, including stocks and real-estate holdings, valued at $4 million to $9.6 million on his annual disclosure statements. House Speaker John Boehner reported unearned income of at least $10,116 and as much as $46,700 from mutual fund dividends or capital gains distributions, which together greatly exceed what most Americans earn from actual work.

One hundred and thirty members of Congress have traded stocks collectively worth hundreds of millions of dollars in companies lobbying on bills that have come before their committees. The lawmakers bought and sold a total of $85 million to $218 million in 323 companies registered to lobby on legislation that appeared before them. Almost one in every eight trades intersected with legislation. The party affiliation of those making the trades was almost evenly split: 68 Democrats and 62 Republicans.[300]

The economic experiences and financial interests of a high percentage of our federal elected officials stand in sharp contrast to those of most Americans. Even leaving aside the influence exerted by corporations and wealthy individuals via donations, the *personal* wealth of our elected officials tips them decisively towards the interests of the 1%.

Recap: Big Money Unduly Influences Who Gets Elected

Those who control the world's wealth have long dominated electoral politics from the presidency down to city councils. Recent Supreme Court decisions have made the situation worse, but things were plenty bad before those decisions. And wealthy interests have deftly gotten around any and all attempts to meaningfully control campaign spending. Bundling, funding party conventions, limiting who gets to participate in debates, grooming, and elevating future candidates and other measures are all part of how the ultra rich heavily influence who is elected to public office. Big Money dominates not only the Republican Party but also the Democratic Party, despite claims to the contrary.

But elections are only a tiny part of the picture. As the next chapters document, there are myriad other ways in which wealth concentrated in the hands of a few prevents us from creating the world we want.

CHAPTER 10

Influencing Legislation

• • •

ULTRA-WEALTHY INDIVIDUALS AND CORPORATIONS ARE adept at using their vast fortunes to influence legislation. So extreme is the influence they exert that public interest organizations and members of the general public are hard-pressed to make even modest impacts on the laws that affect us. Even if we work hard on the legislative front, we generally come up short.

Often we don't even try because we know we won't get anywhere. Several years ago I attended a national meeting of groups fighting the widespread use of agricultural pesticides. Someone proposed mounting a lobbying effort to influence the U.S. Farm Bill that greatly affects farming practices across the nation. Ultimately we concluded that such an effort was pointless because the lobbying resources of the agrichemical industry would be too big to overcome.

HUGE EXPENDITURES ON LOBBYING

Corporations spend huge amounts on in-house lobbyists and outside lobbying firms. In 2012 alone, Dow Chemical spent $11,570,000 on federal lobbying.[301] That same year, Exxon Mobil spent $12,970,000 and the nuclear power corporation Exelon spent $7,779,350. Koch Industries spent $10,550,000 and Duke Energy $7,250,000.

These are just some of countless examples, and these figures only encompass lobbying at the federal level. The same mega corporations heavily influence legislation at the state and local level as well.

The aggregate lobbying expenditures for different industrial sectors are truly mind-boggling. Total reported federal lobbying expenditures for the chemical industry in 2012 exceeded $56 million, for example. That seems small compared to the figures for agribusiness and the oil and gas industry: over $139 million and $143 million, respectively.

Major Financial Support for Other Entities That Lobby

In addition to paying people to lobby directly on their behalf, large corporations also support trade associations and other organizations that weigh in on legislative matters.

The U.S. Chamber of Commerce, for example, is a huge lobbying force in Washington, D.C. It spent over $136 million on federal lobbying in 2012 alone. Its funders have included Dow Chemical, Chevron Texaco, Goldman Sachs, and other major corporations. As of 2008, nearly half of its $140 million in contributions came from just 45 donors.[302] The Chamber has long promoted oil and gas extraction, opposed clean energy alternatives bills, and opposed other legislation that would protect the environment.[303]

Here are just a few examples of other organizations that lobby on behalf of industry:

* The American Chemistry Council, which represents chemical corporations' interests and reported over $9 million in federal lobbying expenditures in 2012.

* The American Petroleum Institute, which bills itself as "the only national trade association that represents all aspects of America's oil and natural gas industry" and spent over $7 million on federal lobbying in 2012.

* CropLife America, which represents developers, manufacturers, and distributors of pesticides and spent over $2.4 million on federal lobbying in 2012

Revolving Doors and Other Corporate Access[304]

Wealthy interests also solidify their influence over legislation by sending people back and forth through the "revolving door." Elected officials and legislative staffers who previously worked for an industry have been steeped in that industry's perspective. They're easy for corporate lobbyists to approach. In addition, elected officials and staffers working on bills that affect an industry know that if they play their cards right, a lucrative position may await them in the future.

Of the 49 lobbyists representing Dow Chemical in 2012, 37 had gone through the revolving door. That's 75.5%! Dow's lobbyists included various former members of Congress.

Of 549 lobbyists for the chemical industry in 2012, 340 (61.9%) had come from government. That same year, 484 of 804 (60.2 %) of oil and gas industry lobbyists had previously worked for the government. Industry reliance on lobbyists who previously served as elected officials or staffers for elected officials is rampant.

There are other direct connections between legislators and the industries that are affected by the legislation they consider. Sixteen members of Congress, including House Minority Leader Nancy Pelosi, own shares in Dow Chemical, for example.[305]

Hidden Influence

Some lobbying by wealthy individuals and large corporations is fairly visible, at least for those who have time to consult lobbying records filed under federal and state law. But other activities that influence legislation are hidden from view because they are not covered by reporting requirements.

Encounters that occur under the auspices of the American Legislative Exchange Council (ALEC) are a prime example. Because its mission is ostensibly educational, ALEC does not file lobbying reports, even as it very directly influences legislation across the United States.[306]

Here's how ALEC works.[307] It brings thousands of state legislators together with corporations, right-wing think tanks, conservative foundations, corporate law firms, and lobbying firms. The legislators are wined and dined. They engage in fun free activities, like shooting events sponsored by the National Rifle Association. They also attend "educational" seminars where they hear industry perspectives and receive talking points to use when confronting others who might challenge that perspective. In August 2011, ALEC hosted a seminar entitled "Warming Up to Climate Change: The Many Benefits of Increased Atmospheric CO2," for example. According to a reporter who managed to attend, speaker Craig Idso argued that we "should let CO2 rise unrestricted, without government intervention." According to Idso, "CO2 is definitely not a pollutant." Idso is founder and former chair of the ExxonMobil-funded Center for Study of Carbon Dioxide and Climate Change. ExxonMobil's list of "Worldwide Contributions and Community Investments" for 2011 indicates a donation of $86,500 to ALEC under the category "Public Information and Policy Research."

But the most important business happens in task forces that ALEC operates, on issues ranging from health and safety to the environment to taxation. Task force meetings occur behind closed doors. Legislators and corporate representatives jointly produce and approve bills that are then introduced throughout the United States by legislators who belong to ALEC. The list of major corporations serving on ALEC task forces as of mid-2011 was extensive. It included Anheuser-Busch, AT&T, Bank of America, Bayer, BP, Chevron, Duke Energy, Eli Lilly, ExxonMobil, General Electric, General Motors, Koch Companies Public Sector, Occidental, Philip Morris, Shell, Walmart, and many others.[308] ALEC churns out hundreds of these boilerplate laws to be introduced concurrently in state capitals across the nation.

Although bills introduced in state legislatures are remarkably similar or even virtually identical to ALEC's original language, legislators rarely mention ALEC and the corporations that produced their bills. Governor Tommy Thompson, an ALEC alum, put it this way, "I always loved going to those meetings because I always found new ideas. Then I'd take them back to Wisconsin, disguise them a little bit, and declare that's mine."

BALLOT MEASURES

Most laws are passed by Congress and other legislative bodies, but people can also bypass elected representatives and put proposed laws on the ballot for direct voter approval. Naturally, Big Money has its hands all over this process as well. A Washington State ballot initiative to require GMO labeling lost in 2013 after major corporations and out-of-state organizations spent more than $22 million to defeat it. Monsanto spent more than $5 million. Dupont spent almost $4 million. Pepsi, Coca-Cola, and Nestle each spent more than $1.5 million.[309]

INFLUENCING LEGISLATION: A RECAP

Wealthy individuals and corporations have amassed so much wealth that they now largely determine which laws are passed and which are not. They accomplish this through direct lobbying, supporting others who lobby, funding groups like ALEC, and spending millions of dollars to defeat ballot measures.

CHAPTER 11

Influencing How Laws Are Implemented

• • •

Even if we manage to pass a good law, that doesn't mean we've won. Often laws require government agencies to adopt rules that spell out the details of what happens next. They leave crucial matters in the hands of these agencies, like whether to lease coal deposits to a mining corporation or whether to approve a particular pesticide. Moreover, laws and rules don't do much good if they're not enforced.

The rich use the enormous wealth at their disposal to influence whether and how laws are carried out. One thing they do is make sure that there are lots of friendly faces at the agencies that are supposed to implement the laws. The Revolving Door operates as effectively between industry and government agencies as it does between industry and legislative bodies.

Former Dow Chemical executive Elin Miller, who became Administrator of EPA Region 10, is one of countless examples. Islam Siddiqui, a senior executive at the pesticide trade association CropLife America, who was appointed by President Obama to lead U.S. trade negotiations on agricultural issues, is another. Ernest Moniz, whom Obama selected to head the Department of Energy despite his close ties with fossil-fuel and nuclear corporations, is yet another.

But that's just part of the story.

REGULATION IN THE PRIVATE INTEREST

Private Interests Dominate Rulemaking Forums. When agencies put proposed rules out for public comment, those concerned about their private profits almost always dominate the comment process. A study of 90 hazardous air pollution rules proposed by EPA, for example, found that, on average, industry comments comprised over 81% of those submitted. By contrast, public interest group submissions averaged 4% of the comments. Industries commented on *all* of the rules, while public interest groups commented on only 46% of them.[310]

Even before rules are formally proposed, wealthy corporations influence government agencies. With respect to the air pollution rules mentioned above, EPA had an average of 178 contacts with interest groups before officially proposing rules and seeking public input. This rule development period "was almost completely monopolized by regulated parties."

Wealthy interests participate in agency workshops and advisory committees to shape future rules. Pesticide corporations dominated the EPA advisory committee on the pesticide Guthion on which I served, as you may recall. EPA panels examining fracking are mainly composed of oil and gas industry representatives along with agency personnel, many of whom have worked for the oil and gas industry.[311]

Frameworks That Favor Private Interests. Over the years, wealthy private interests have managed to embed within various laws, and within the cultures of government agencies, a series of frameworks that serve them well. They use these to keep agencies from protecting the environment.

Risk Assessment is a prime example. Remember our futile attempts to get EPA to protect people from the neurotoxic pesticide chlorpyrifos? None of the compelling information we and others shared with EPA moved the agency at all. Relying steadfastly on Risk Assessment calculations, based heavily on shoddy, inaccessible manufacturer data, EPA has relentlessly approved chlorpyrifos over and over again.

Chaining EPA and other agencies to the hoax of Risk Assessment is one of the most effective coups ever accomplished by polluting corporations. Among other things, they've placed provisions in trade agreements that require signatory nations to choose Risk Assessment over precaution, as we'll see in the next chapter. Almost certainly public relations expenditures—a topic examined in another future chapter—have fostered the "sound science" image Risk Assessment undeservedly enjoys, facilitating its spread throughout environmental agencies.

"Cost-benefit analysis" is another now-ubiquitous framework pushed by corporations that undermines the public interest as laws are implemented. Even when Risk Assessments establish what agencies consider problematic threats to health and the environment, those agencies will still likely approve the polluting chemical or activity in question. Their justification? The costs of protecting health and the environment outweigh the benefits. Where does much of the data used in cost-benefit analyses come from? From the regulated industries, of course.

Discussions about assumptions to use in cost-benefit analyses can be incredibly heartless. Cost-benefit gurus have debated the dollar value to assign to each IQ point a child loses when exposed to neurotoxic pollutants, for example. Is it any wonder we're having such difficulty winning rational environmental policies when the dominant mindset is one that considers this approach acceptable?

There is no need to spray neurotoxic pesticides. Safe sustainable alternatives for protecting crops abound. Nonetheless, the cost-benefit framework plugs damage to children's brains into a monetary formula that—surprise!—almost always produces an answer that perpetuates toxic exposures and associated corporate profits.

Risk Assessment and cost-benefit analysis aren't the only frameworks that steer environmental agencies away from actions that protect the environment. A commitment to "collaboration" and "seeking consensus" is also pervasive. Our experiences with the stakeholder group formed by the Washington State Department of Agriculture (WSDA) are typical. WSDA refused to adopt any new pesticide rules unless all "stakeholders" agreed. In other words, pesticide proponents had virtual veto power over any and all of the reforms we sought.

As we battled chlorpyrifos in Washington State, six unions, representing thousands of EPA employees, sent a letter to the head of EPA, objecting to Agency managers' close alignment with the pesticide industry. The employee letter decried "the belief among managers in the Pesticide and Toxics Programs that regulatory decisions should only be made after reaching full consensus with the regulated pesticide and chemicals industry."[312] The consensus model is prevalent throughout U.S. environmental agencies and beyond.[313]

Risk Assessment, cost-benefit analysis, and stakeholder-consensus mindsets are just some of the many tools wealthy interests use to prevent agencies from protecting the environment. For an overview of how the chemical industry keeps EPA tied up in knots, check out a useful report published by Natural Resources Defense Council in 2011 entitled, "The Delay Game: How the Chemical Industry Ducks Regulation of the Most Toxic Substances."[314] Industry actions described in the report include attacking early drafts of health assessments, holding workshops populated with industry-funded panelists, releasing new industry-funded studies, forcing reviews, enlisting political interference from elected officials, and other tactics.

White House End Runs Around Agencies. In the rare event that federal environmental agencies decide to do something regulated industries don't like, those industries have yet another ace up their sleeves: the Office of Information and Regulatory Affairs (OIRA, pronounced oh-EYE-ra).

OIRA exists within the Office of Management and Budget (OMB), inside the White House. It is directly connected to the president, who, as detailed in chapter 9, spends a good deal of time seeking campaign donations from executives at corporations affected by rules under review. This is the case whether it is a Democrat or a Republican who sits in the Oval Office.

Each year, OIRA drags hundreds of draft agency rules into a nightmare of external review. Between 2001 and 2011, it ensnared 6,194 draft regulatory actions from EPA, the Food and Drug Administration, the Occupational Safety and Health Administration, and other agencies for cost-benefit reviews.[315] Even though agencies engage in multi-year technical analyses, including reviews of extensive public input, OIRA does not hesitate to substitute its own judgment for an agency's, altering rules to suit corporate priorities.

Input to OIRA is overwhelmingly dominated by industries whose profits are affected by potential rules. Between 2001 and 2011, 65% of the 5,759 people who met with OIRA represented regulated industries—about five times the number of people participating on behalf of public interest groups. Even under Barack Obama, who promised to end undue influence of industry on government and to ensure transparency, industry visits outnumbered public interest visits four to one. Seventy-three percent of the rule reviews OIRA undertook had participation from industry alone.[316] These statistics only provide a glimpse of what has been going on due to the highly secretive nature of the OIRA review process.

Obama's OIRA changed 76% of the rules submitted to it for review, compared to 64% changed under George W. Bush. "The sad reality here is that the president appointed strong leaders to the environmental, health and safety agencies, but has undermined them over and over by allowing OIRA to substitute its judgment for the expertise of the agencies," lamented Rena Steinzor of the Center for Progressive Reform.[317]

Lists of those who took part in meetings with OIRA include the corporations and trade associations you'd expect to see. The American Chemistry Council was OIRA's most frequent visitor for the period of 2001 to 2011, with 39 meetings. ExxonMobil, the American Petroleum Industry, the U.S. Chamber of Commerce, Mortgage Bankers Association, National Cattlemen's Beef Association, American Forest and Paper Association, and others representing industry all met with OIRA. A few public interest groups are also included on lists of those attending OIRA meetings, but their participation is dwarfed by that of regulated parties.[318]

Under the Obama Administration, as of June 1, 2011, OIRA had looked at far more rules from EPA than from other agencies and had altered EPA rules a stunning 84% of the time. This compares with a rule alteration rate of 65% between 2001 and 2011. These changes rarely, if ever, lead to greater protection of the public. Instead, they weaken rules, making OIRA a "one-way ratchet"[319] used to undercut the public interest on behalf of private interests.[320]

Obama issued an executive order on January 18, 2011, to make White House end runs around agencies even more prevalent. The order required a comprehensive review of all *existing* government regulations.[321] Within a day, the American Chemistry Council, the National Association of Manufacturers, and other industry trade groups pounced on the new executive order, using it to attack EPA rules.[322]

Most of the White House's actions undermining agency rules have been hidden from view. A few have been briefly visible, however. The White House forced EPA to rescind a smog rule it had promulgated, for example, even though the rule had already been weakened at the request of the White House. In its stead, EPA was forced to confirm a Bush-era smog rule that Administrator Lisa Jackson had previously described as "not legally defensible given the scientific evidence."[323]

As another example, days after a March 2011 meeting with nuclear corporation Exelon executives, a White House official instructed EPA to rewrite major portions of a draft rule affecting water intake at nuclear power plants. The rule had sought to protect fish and other aquatic life. "You are disappointed, but you can't work at the agency without understanding you are not the decision maker," offered EPA official Mary T. Smith.[324]

In 2009 Exelon lobbyist Elizabeth Moler declared, "We are proud to be the president's utility."[325] The company delivers power to Obama's house in Chicago, but its connection to Obama is much deeper than that. "It's nice for John to be able to go to the White House and they know his name," Moler commented, referring to then-Exelon chief executive John Rowe.[326]

ENFORCEMENT IN THE PRIVATE INTEREST

If somehow, despite all odds, useful environmental policies emerge from legislatures and agencies and they are not gutted or killed by OIRA, there's still the matter of enforcement. The very entities from which agencies are supposed to protect us have undue influence over those agencies' enforcement policies.

Good Ole Boy Enforcement. Our experiences with the Washington State Department of Agriculture illustrate how things work. WSDA is supposed to enforce state and federal pesticide laws, thereby protecting health and the environment. But Agency management has a chummy relationship with pesticide interests. It is more than happy to turn a blind eye to violations and to undercut its own inspectors.

Lax enforcement by state agencies is not just limited to Washington State, nor is it limited to pesticide issues and agriculture agencies. The Office of Inspector General concluded in 2011 that "[s]tate enforcement programs frequently do not meet national goals and states do not always take necessary enforcement actions." According to the Office, "[s] tate enforcement programs are underperforming: EPA data indicate that noncompliance is high and the level of enforcement is low." The Office reached these conclusions based on a review of enforcement of the Clean Air Act, the Clean Water Act, and the Resource Conservation and Recovery Act (RCRA), which deals with hazardous wastes.[327]

An analysis of six states (Colorado, New Mexico, New York, Ohio, Pennsylvania, and Texas) revealed serious problems regarding enforcement of laws governing oil and gas fracking.[328] It concluded that "[o]verall, and without exception, inspection capacity for each of the six states examined is egregiously lacking." In 2010, 54 to 91% of the nearly 350,000 *active* wells in these states operated without inspectors checking on compliance with state laws. Inspectors were rarely provided with equipment necessary to identify problems, and when they did uncover violations, these were often not formally recorded. Penalties were scarce and poorly tracked, and they provided little incentive to not violate again. The value of the gas from a single average

Marcellus Shale gas well was $2.9 million, an amount greater than the total penalties collected by any state in 2010.[329]

There was a bias at state agencies towards permitting drilling. Some reviews for drilling permits lasted only 35 minutes.

The analysis of state oil and gas enforcement found that there was often a distinctly cozy relationship between oil and gas agency staff and the industry they regulated. In some states, agency employees were even allowed to receive small gifts from oil and gas companies. Moreover, many agency employees had opted to leave government for higher-paying industry jobs.

Lack of enforcement is also a problem when *federal* agencies are in charge of enforcement. Consider the record of the federal Occupational Health and Safety Administration (OSHA) with respect to oil field accidents. A *Houston Chronicle* exposé published in March of 2014 revealed that nearly 663 workers in oil field-related industries were killed on the job in the U.S. between 2007 and 2012. About 40% of those workers died in Texas, where the death toll reached 65 in 2012 alone. In Texas oil fields in 2012, 79 workers lost limbs, 82 were crushed, 92 suffered burns, and 675 broke bones in work-related accidents reported to insurance companies.

The *Chronicle*'s investigation analyzed 18,000 injury and illness claims and data on hundreds of oil field accidents in Texas since 2007. OSHA has investigated only 150 of those 18,000 claims. There are only 95 inspectors to oversee safety rules for all Texas work sites, ranging from fast-food restaurants, to construction sites, to oil fields. Few inspectors have oil- and gas-related experience or training.[330]

When OSHA did investigate, it found safety violations in 78% of Texas oil and gas accidents, concluding that many could have been prevented with safer procedures and equipment.

The list of known instances where enforcement has been scant to non-existent goes on and on. Freedom Industries, the company that leaked toxic chemicals used in coal extraction into a major river in West Virginia in January of 2014 had reportedly not been inspected since 1991, for example. The leak resulted in dozens of hospitalizations, toxic exposures for countless individuals, and lack of water for hundreds of thousands for a significant period of time.[331] Who knows how many other environmental provisions exist in law but are not enforced, leading to contamination and toxic exposures that go unnoticed and unreported?

Attacks on Agency Directors Who Do Try to Enforce Laws. We've heard about agency managers serving the interests of the private corporations they're supposed to regulate by failing to enforce the law against them, or failing to inspect them on a regular basis. What happens when agency heads insist upon rigorously enforcing the law? Often they are attacked for doing so.

Here's a case in point. Al Armendariz indicated upon his appointment as head of EPA Region 6 that he would fully enforce environmental laws in that region. True to his word, he launched efforts to address air pollution and to investigate reports of water contaminated by Range Resources, a top U.S. gas drilling company. Oklahoma Senator James Inhofe immediately went on the offensive. "I have been made aware of a number of actions initiated by the EPA Region 6 Administrator... which have alarmed state and local officials and regulated industries," Inhofe wrote in a letter in 2010. Inhofe had received $1.39 million in campaign contributions from the oil and gas industry. Inhofe and others in Congress increased their pressure on Armendariz as he further articulated his intent to enforce laws applying to the oil and gas industry. Eventually, Armendariz was forced to resign.[332]

Getting Worse by the Minute. Claiming they lack resources for basic public programs, governments are cutting back enforcement even more these days. EPA noted in a draft strategic plan in December of 2013 that it intended to carry out 30% fewer inspections and evaluations than it had over the prior five years. It would initiate 40% fewer civil cases and keep its criminal goals the same as they were in 2012.[333]

There has been a steady decline in EPA's Criminal Enforcement Division investigations since 2001. In fiscal year 2013, only 297 investigations happened as compared to close to 320 in 2012 and nearly 500 in 2001. With just 38 prosecutors for the Department of Justice Crimes Section and 200 agents in EPA's Criminal Enforcement Division, the federal government has limited capacity to pursue criminal cases, particularly given the vast resources corporations have to drag out legal cases for years.[334]

Recap: Interfering With Implementation Is Another Arena for Big Money Control

In short, when a law is passed at the federal or state level, activists often declare victory and celebrate the change they believe will now occur. But even a cursory look at what happens as laws are implemented reveals that real victory is hardly assured by passage of a law. The 1% use the wealth at their disposal to influence implementation in multiple ways. Even though a law may talk about protecting the public, that protection may never be provided.

CHAPTER 12

Wielding Power Internationally

• • •

THE SUPER RICH USE THEIR wealth to influence public policy at the international level. The resulting harm to humankind cannot be overstated.

TRADE AGREEMENTS

The World Trade Organization (WTO) agreements we protested in Seattle in 1999 were heavily shaped by cadres of lawyers and other professionals working for big corporations. As a result, they are chock full of provisions that served corporate interests. The same is true of other so-called "free" trade agreements like the North American Free Trade Agreement (NAFTA), which had been adopted prior to 1999.

WTO and NAFTA agreements include environmentally destructive trade-related provisions, such as prohibitions on preferences for "buying local." They also include provisions that have nothing to do with trade. As you may recall, I objected in a meeting with trade officials to their use of WTO agreements to challenge a draft European Union ban on lead in electronic products—a ban that applied equally to foreign and domestic products.

The agreements establish outrageous procedures to ensure enforcement of corporate-serving trade provisions. Any nation participating in the WTO, for example, can challenge any other participating nation's laws, claiming they violate trade rules. A panel of three bureaucrats decides cases behind closed doors.

Only national governments appear before WTO panels, even if a state law has been challenged. Other parties affected by or knowledgeable about the matter in question—public interest groups, for instance—are shut out. There is an internal appeals process, but no way to foster review of decisions in a publicly accountable system of justice.

When a final WTO ruling has been issued, declaring that a policy violates trade rules, a losing country faces three unpleasant options. It can rescind its policy, pay compensation to the winning country, or face severe trade sanctions.

Corporations can have governments bring trade cases on their behalf. They can also file suits themselves using "investor-state" provisions in trade agreements. These appalling provisions enable corporations to directly challenge laws adopted by nations, states, provinces, or municipalities, claiming that these laws interfere with their profits. The corporations can demand compensation for the loss of money they *could have made* if a policy prioritizing human needs over profits had not been put in place.[335] In other words, corporations can force the public to fork over funds from our public treasuries as punishment for denying them the right to pollute.

In 2012, for example, Lone Pine Resources sued the Canadian government under the North American Free Trade Agreement (NAFTA), challenging Quebec's moratorium on fracking. It sought $250 million as compensation for "lost profits" because it was prevented from fracking in the Saint Lawrence Valley.[336]

Corporations like Chevron, Dow Chemical, and ExxonMobil are all joining the "investor-state" lawsuit game. By the end of 2011, over 450 of these suits had been filed against 89 governments, including the U.S. Over $700 million had been paid to corporations under U.S. free trade and bilateral investment treaties, with about 70% of the cases involving challenges to environmental policies.[337]

A 2008 report by the social justice group Public Citizen outlined multiple ways in which WTO requirements undermine our ability to address global warming. According to the report, the climate policy proposals mentioned by presidential candidates that year could not have been implemented without changes to WTO rules.[338]

The trade agreements we protested in 1999 played a major role in triggering the Great Recession by requiring signatory nations to deregulate financial institutions. The WTO's General Agreement on Trade in Services, for example, requires countries to get rid of size limits on banks, firewalls between banking and investment services, and bans on risky financial services.

Even now, knowing that deregulation sets the stage for reckless financial behaviors, U.S. trade reps are reportedly pressuring other countries to more deeply commit to WTO financial deregulation requirements. In the face of this, five consumer and financial reform groups sent a joint letter in 2011 urging trade reps to work for stronger financial regulation instead of promoting further deregulation.[339]

Proponents of the trade agreements we protested in the late twentieth century described them as tools to help American workers and improve conditions in impoverished lands. These promised benefits have not materialized. Instead, the adverse impacts predicted by opponents have come true.

In 2010, while serving as a United Nations envoy to Haiti, Bill Clinton actually publicly apologized to Haiti for the devastating impacts his trade policies had had on Haitian agriculture and self-sufficiency. Forced to lower tariffs on rice imports, Haiti could not compete with cheap subsidized U.S. rice. Haitian farmers lost their livelihoods and the nation became dependent on imports.[340] "Since 1981, the United States has followed a policy…that we rich countries that produce a lot of food should sell it to poor countries and relieve them of the burden of producing their own food, so… they can leap directly into the industrial era," Clinton said. "It has not worked. It was a mistake that I was party to."[341] Clinton has not demanded that the trade agreements he pushed through be repealed or amended, however. Nor has he opposed new agreements.

Haitian farmers are by no means the only people in other countries who have been harmed by trade agreements with the U.S. Mexico, for example, amended its constitution in the 1990s as a prerequisite for joining NAFTA. It privatized farmland that had previously been community-owned. These changes, along with tariff reductions and other reforms, have devastated Mexican farmers. In less than 15 years, approximately one-third of the country's rural population migrated away, searching for work. Those who moved to the cities became part of masses struggling there, a cheap labor pool for foreign investors to exploit. Border areas are now home to large numbers of "maquiladoras"—low-wage factories with poor working conditions that assemble imported materials for export to other countries. Similarly, in the early 1990s, Walmart did not exist in Mexico. Today it is Mexico's largest employer.

Many Mexicans migrated to other countries, including especially the U.S. Here they labor as farm workers on other people's land or engage in other forms of low paid labor, generally without basic rights. In other words they form an underclass of individuals subject to exploitation.[342]

The flip side of the displacement of workers in Mexico and other countries is the harm done to workers in the U.S. According to an analysis published in 2011 by the Economic Policy Institute, the U.S. lost nearly 700,000 jobs because of NAFTA.[343] Those with capital find it lucrative to invest in developing countries. Corporations outsource in order to take advantage of low wages and weak environmental and labor laws.

In short, trade agreements adopted in the latter part of the twentieth century have slammed working people. And they have given the ultra wealthy additional tools for blocking policies that serve our interests and promoting those that serve their own.

What's happened on trade issues since the 1999 WTO protests? Things have gotten even worse.

Instead of reforming or repealing existing trade agreements, political leaders are pushing through new agreements that are just as bad or worse. There are now over three thousand trade and investment agreements between two or more countries.[344] In the U.S., leaders of both the Democratic and Republican Parties aggressively support new agreements shaped by corporations and replete with corporate-friendly provisions.

As of this writing, for example, President Obama is vigorously advancing the Trans-Pacific Partnership (TPP), a new agreement with eleven other Pacific Rim countries.[345] Hundreds of corporate representatives have regular access to the negotiators and to the draft documents. Meanwhile, journalists, public interest groups, and even members of Congress have had to rely on leaks to get a glimpse of what is going on.

In fact, in 2010 the countries working on the TPP agreed to not release negotiating texts until four years after a deal is done or abandoned. This process is even more secretive than the WTO's process was. When challenged about this secrecy, the U.S. Trade Representative reportedly noted that a previous trade deal, called the "Free Trade Area of the Americas (FTAA)" agreement, could not be completed after the documents were released to the public. In other words, the only way to successfully adopt agreements that undermine the public interest is to keep the public in the dark about them, and that's what the Obama Administration is doing. Leaked documents reveal that the TPP is packed with provisions corporations can use to challenge everything from bans on fracking to laws requiring the labeling of genetically modified crops.[346]

The Trans-Atlantic Trade and Investment Partnership (known as TTIP or TAFTA) is also swiftly advancing, and corporations are in the driver's seat regarding what's in the agreement. Agribusiness giants CropLife America and the European Crop Protection Association have jointly proposed that the agreement mandate a "more harmonious risk assessment framework for pesticide regulations."[347] As we've seen, Risk Assessment promotes ongoing pesticide sales and use, regardless of the damage done to our environment and our health, in contrast to a precaution-based approach. "Harmonious" is code for TTIP countries with stronger pesticide standards weakening them to achieve "harmony" with weaker standards in other countries.

A concurrent chemical industry TTIP proposal calls upon European countries to abandon the "precautionary principle" in favor of Risk Assessment.[348] As you may recall from chapter 2, under the precautionary principle, chemical corporations must prove their products are safe before they can be dispersed into our environment. Risk Assessment, on the other hand, is highly manipulable. It allows massive sales of chemical products and widespread environmental contamination and damage before action is taken to protect health.

Presidential Assistance to Corporations That Interact With Other Countries

Obama and other presidents regularly invite corporate leaders to meetings with foreign officials to discuss trade. These corporate leaders use the meetings to secure lucrative new business contracts. Why do they get personal assistance from the president in maximizing their private financial gains? They're the ones who decide which goods and services are available for trading. (Production decisions greatly affect working people's lives and our society as a whole, but we have no real say in them.) Campaign contributions may also grease the skids for invitations to meetings with foreign officials.

When Chinese President Hu Jintao visited the White House in January of 2011, for example, he met not only with President Obama but also with 14 American CEOs. Obama announced $45 billion in new business contracts with China just before the meeting took place.[349] Similarly, when Obama went to India in 2010, approximately 200 top U.S. business leaders went with him, including the CEOs of Pepsico, Honeywell, and DuPont.

Including those who stand to make huge amounts of money in meetings with foreign leaders is always couched in terms of helping working people. The President talks about creating jobs in the U.S. Promises of increased U.S. employment ring hollow, however, given the history of trade agreements that delivered nothing but massive off-shoring. Facts included in various articles about presidentially mediated CEO access to foreign governments sow further doubt about whether there will be an overall benefit to U.S. workers. "India is still only number 12 in the list of U.S. trade partners," says one article. "But that untapped potential is drawing U.S. investors to India, especially in undeveloped areas such as infrastructure, transport and technology. GE, for instance, is investing $200 million in India over the next five years, and it already employs more than 12,000 people in the country."[350]

As a backdrop to his meetings with foreign leaders, Obama formed a job creation panel in 2011 to advise him. It was composed of the CEOs of corporations, many of which have been shipping jobs overseas despite rhetoric about maximizing jobs in the U.S.[351] Experts have estimated that another 40 million jobs will be transferred from the U.S. to other countries in the next two decades.[352]

Presidential assistance to large corporations doesn't stop at facilitating contracts that make them money. Consider what a top Obama assistant said to a top Indian official in an email that found its way to reporters at the time of Obama's visit to India. The Indian government had been working on a petition demanding additional money from Dow Chemical to compensate victims of the horrendous Bhopal chemical poisoning disaster of 1984.[353] In the email, Obama's assistant said, "...we are hearing a lot of noise about the Dow Chemical issue. I trust that you are monitoring it carefully. I am not familiar with the details, but I think we want to avoid developments which put a chilling effect on our investment relationship." Other sentences in the short email appear to imply that U.S. support for India on a matter before the World Bank would be adversely affected if India were to push too hard with respect to Dow's obligations to the Bhopal victims. The U.S. denies that any quid pro quo was intended. [354]

The U.S. State Department: Corporate America's Best Friend

In a documentary linking oil corporations to violence against environmental activists in Nigeria, a spokesperson for the U.S. Embassy in

Lagos explained how U.S. ambassadors view their role vis-à-vis corporations. "It's, generally speaking, the policy for all embassies overseas to support American companies and their operations abroad and to as far as possible support American exports overseas," the spokesperson said. "That applies in Nigeria and almost every embassy overseas."[355]

U.S. Embassy cables made public by Wikileaks illuminate just how much U.S. ambassadors and their staffs do for private corporations. They have become de facto corporate lobbyists, aggressively undercutting the public will in foreign lands and ignoring the environmental and human rights impacts of their advocacy. The corporations that hoard society's wealth use it to communicate regularly with State Department officials, enlisting their help in expanding corporate control in the world.

The U.S. State Department relentlessly promotes agriculture based on Genetically Modified Organisms (GMOs) on behalf of Monsanto and other corporations, for example. In country after country, diplomats pressure local officials, write op-eds, and request funds to fly local journalists back to the U.S. for tours promoting GMOs.[356] Embassy cables casually mention public opposition to GMOs and they refer to laws reflecting that opposition as if these mean nothing.

Embassies move into a full-court press if national leaders don't succumb to pressure. U.S. diplomats have called for all-out "retaliation" against France, for instance, including possible WTO trade sanctions, in response to the French President's insistence on honoring public opposition to GMOs.[357]

As another example, U.S. diplomats are undercutting the precautionary principle around the world.[358]

State Department advocacy on behalf of GMO and chemical corporations is just the tip of the iceberg. U.S. diplomatic staff go to bat for Big Pharma and other industries as well. They see this as a major part of their job. They closely track how well multinationals are doing in penetrating each country, remaining ever at the ready to give corporations an extra boost if needed to overcome reluctant communities or intransigent local leaders.[359]

U.S. diplomats are not alone in carrying water for the world's biggest corporations. Canadian diplomats have aggressively pressured other countries to not adopt policies that interfere with the profits of oil corporations active in Canada, for example, such as those pulling tar sands oil out of the ground in Alberta.

RECAP: GLOBALIZATION AND INTERNATIONAL FORUMS ARE POWERFUL TOOLS FOR THE WEALTHY FEW

In short, ultra-rich corporations use their wealth to enlist the help of presidents, trade representatives, and diplomats in international forums. They use these forums to circumvent public will and democratically adopted policies in countries, states, and municipalities around the world.

The Citigroup memo introduced in chapter 8 nicely sums things up:

"Despite being in great shape, we think that global capitalists are going to be getting an even greater share of the wealth pie over the next few years, as capitalists benefit disproportionately from globalization and the productivity boom, at the relative expense of labor."[360]

CHAPTER 13

Influencing Scientific Evidence and Public Access to It

• • •

WEALTHY INDIVIDUALS AND CORPORATIONS GREATLY influence what scientific information exists and whether it is publicly accessible. Despite claiming to be champions of "sound science" they regularly undercut it in a variety of ways.

WEALTHY INTERESTS BLOCK COLLECTION AND SHARING OF BASIC DATA

Chapter 2 provided a glimpse of what's happening with respect to scientific data related to farm pesticide issues. Air sampling, pesticide use reporting, tracking toxic exposures, monitoring impacts on health—none of these occur on more than a sporadic basis. The Farm Worker Pesticide Project and others fought hard for basic data collection to no avail. Indeed, we are in worse shape now than in the past because Washington State's nationally acclaimed Department of Health pesticide program has been gutted and its Pesticide Incident Reporting and Tracking Panel has been eliminated.[361]

We also lack vital information on other toxic chemicals that flow into our air, water, food, and bodies from manufacturing facilities, energy plants, and consumer products. When information does exist, it is difficult to access. What's the environmental and human impact of the Fukushima nuclear disaster? Testing has been limited, and the

U.S. Nuclear Regulatory Commission has actively kept information unfavorable to nuclear power away from investigative journalists.[362]

Product labels don't give us much information about what is in the things we buy. Manufacturers keep key ingredients secret as "proprietary information," even though the use and disposal of their products affects the environment that sustains us all.[363]

Public attempts to force disclosure meet with fierce, well-funded opposition from those whose profits could be affected. Monsanto and other corporate giants spend tens of millions of dollars to defeat ballot measures requiring the labeling of GMO foods, for example, as was mentioned earlier.[364]

Similarly, people throughout the U.S. have battled unsuccessfully to force oil and gas companies to divulge the chemicals they inject into the ground during fracking operations. In Pennsylvania, a law does require companies to disclose ingredients to doctors whose patients are experiencing health problems associated with exposures. But those doctors have to sign confidentiality agreements, promising to only use the information for the patients' treatments. They can't speak to the community about what they're being exposed to or the possible health implications.[365]

WEALTHY INTERESTS FUND RESEARCH, THEREBY ENSURING RESULTS FAVORABLE TO THEM

Funding from private corporations that stand to gain or lose depending on study results has become a dominant force shaping scientific research. Corporations with a financial stake in study outcomes fund front groups that carry out research. They fund universities, as will be discussed in greater detail shortly. They also do in-house research.

Limits on Research Topics. One of the most important impacts of corporations funding research is that they determine which topics will be studied. The experience of one PhD student at a large land-grant university provides a glimpse of the problem. When she approached her professors about studying organic agriculture and farmer's markets, they discouraged her. "My academic adviser told me my best bet was to write a grant for Monsanto or the Department of Homeland Security to fund my research on why farmer's markets were stocked with 'black market vegetables' that 'are a bioterrorism threat waiting to happen,'" the student said. "It was communicated to me on more than one occasion throughout my education that I should just study something Monsanto would fund rather than ideas to which I was deeply committed."[366]

Similarly, a survey of University of Wisconsin land-grant universities found that the amount of grant and contract money generated by agricultural science professors significantly influenced their salary and tenure status. This encourages academic research favored by corporations that offer grants and contracts, while discouraging research topics not in favor with big funders, such as studies of small-scale organic agriculture.[367]

As another example, scientists whose research might adversely affect the nuclear industry's financial interests have been pressured to downplay or not publish their findings. Some cannot get funds or university support for their work. Professors say they have been obstructed or told to steer clear of data that might raise public concern about nuclear power. "Getting involved in this sort of research [exposing risks from nuclear power] is dangerous politically," said Joji Ptaki, a Japanese biologist whose findings suggest that radioactivity from Fukushima has triggered inherited deformities in a species of butterfly.[368]

Thus, from the get-go, research topics reflect the interests of private corporations seeking to profit from the sale of products and services. Topics that would advance the public interest are discouraged and starved financially.

The Funding Effect. The impact of corporate funding on research goes well beyond censoring research topics, however. Of key importance is the so-called "funding effect." This is the name given to the tendency for study outcomes to align with the results funders want.[369]

Dow Chemical's research on its pesticide chlorpyrifos provides a clear illustration. As discussed in chapter 2, Dow has churned out vast numbers of studies that downplay the risks posed by chlorpyrifos. A team of neuroscientists from Stanford that reviewed Dow studies reported rampant errors in how the studies were done. The neuroscientists noted that errors bearing on chlorpyrifos's potential health impacts always understated those risks.

Even when studies in scientific journals are technically above reproach, those funded by corporations with a financial stake in the outcome tend to produce findings favorable to those corporations.

Numerous analyses have documented the funding effect. A review of studies investigating whether low doses of the chemical bisphenol A (BPA) cause harm, for instance, found that 92% of government-funded studies reported adverse effects, whereas 100% of the industry-funded studies found *no* adverse effects.[370] Another review concluded that "[i]ndustry funding of nutrition-related scientific articles may bias conclusions in favor of sponsors' products, with potentially significant implications for public health." Studies funded entirely by industry were about four to six times more likely to be favorable to industry interests than those without industry funding. None of the studies with all industry support reached conclusions unfavorable to the sponsors.[371]

Many other reviews also document the funding effect.[372] It exists across a wide range of research areas where corporations provide funding.

What factors may contribute to the remarkable correlation between industry funding and results that serve industry interests? The authors of the study reviewing nutrition research list several possibilities:

* Industries fund only those studies they believe will present their products favorably or their competitors' poorly.
* Investigators formulate hypotheses, design studies, and analyze data in ways consistent with corporate sponsors' interests.
* Industries delay or prevent publication of unfavorable studies.

* Authors of scientific reviews search and interpret the scientific literature selectively in ways consistent with their sponsors' interests.
* Scientific reviews arising from industry-supported symposia under-represent certain viewpoints—i.e., those of individuals not invited to participate—and over-represent others, particularly those of invited corporations.[373]

A former editor of the *British Medical Journal* said that it took him "almost a quarter of a century editing...to wake up to what was happening" with respect to the funding effect in the area of pharmaceutical studies. "The companies seem to get the results they want not by fiddling the results, which would be far too crude and possibly detectable by peer review," he said, "but rather by asking the 'right' questions—and there are many ways to do this."[374]

Now and then, principled scientists publicly object to corporate funders' strictures. In 1996, for example, four researchers quit in protest after their sponsor, the pharmaceutical company Sandoz, removed language in a draft manuscript highlighting a drug's potential dangers. But for every researcher who stands up, unknown numbers keep their heads down. A study of major engineering research centers found that 35% would allow corporate sponsors to delete information in papers prior to publication.[375] More than 15% of university scientists acknowledge having "changed the design, methodology or results of a study in response to pressure from a funding source."[376]

In short, corporate funding yields corporate-friendly results that don't interfere with continued sales and profits.

GOVERNMENTS RELY ON INDUSTRY-FUNDED STUDIES

Government agencies rely heavily on industry-funded studies as they develop laws and regulations, as the Farm Worker Pesticide Project's experiences with EPA attest. EPA relied on biased and scientifically flawed data from the manufacturers of chlorpyrifos, including studies that hadn't even been published. Meanwhile, high-quality independent published studies with different conclusions were ignored.

The same story is repeated over and over again with respect to other environmental issues. For example, EPA and other agencies relied on industry data as the basis for declining to protect the public from BPA, a chemical widely used in plastics and other products. As noted above, a review of BPA research showed that 100% of industry-funded studies found no adverse effects at low exposure levels.[377] Meanwhile, EPA has ignored over 100 other studies that *do* find adverse effects at low exposure levels, some at levels 2 million times beneath those producing effects in industry-sponsored studies. Renowned independent scientists have strongly criticized EPA, noting that "[t]he wealth of data from many independent laboratories, along with biomonitoring data from the CDC [Center for Disease Control], show clearly that most Americans are exposed to BPA at levels well within the range that is biologically active."[378]

WEALTHY INTERESTS UNDERCUT INDEPENDENT RESEARCH

There are scientists who engage in research without accepting funding from corporations whose profits might be affected by the study findings. But even here, the rich and powerful have ways of affecting the research.

WITHHOLDING INFORMATION AND ESSENTIAL MATERIALS

Corporate-funded researchers may fail to publish results adverse to their funders' interests and they may otherwise limit access to their data. This denies independent researchers important *information*.

Corporations also withhold *materials* essential to research. Take GMOs, for example. Seed licensing agreements can specifically bar research on GM seeds without the approval of the corporation that owns them. Thus, scientists cannot independently evaluate patented GM seeds to explore potential adverse environmental impacts.[379]   When an Ohio State University professor's research questioned the safety of biotech sunflowers, Dow AgroSciences and Pioneer Hi-Bred blocked her access to their seeds, preventing her from conducting additional research. When other Pioneer Hi-Bred-funded professors found adverse biological effects from a new GM corn variety, the company barred them from publishing the results. The company then hired new scientists who came up with the results they wanted, which helped secure regulatory approval. Another university investigator anonymously informed the journal *Nature* that a Dow AgroScience employee told him that Dow could sue if he published data adverse to Dow's interests.[380]

The use of patent law to prevent independent research on their GM products allows GM corporations to greatly limit the information entering the public record as regulatory decisions are made. In one policy forum, 26 university scientists from 16 states anonymously submitted a letter to EPA making this point. The scientists did not identify themselves because they feared reprisals, such as being blacklisted and losing private-sector research funding.[381] Their letter read in part:

> Technology/stewardship agreements required for the purchase of genetically modified seed explicitly prohibit research. These agreements inhibit public scientists from pursuing their mandated role on behalf of the public good unless the research is approved by industry. As a result of restricted access, no truly independent research can be legally conducted on many critical questions, regarding the technology, its performance, its management implications, IRM [insecticide resistance management], and its interactions with insect biology. Consequently, data flowing to an EPA Scientific Advisory Panel from the public sector is unduly limited.[382]

In 1955, when Jonas Salk was asked who holds the patent on the polio vaccine, he replied, "Well, the people. There is no patent. Could you patent the sun?" How different things are today. Genetically modified crops and other agricultural products aren't the only things that can be considered private and patentable. As of early 2013, for example, nearly 20% of the human genome[383]—more than 4000 genes—were covered by at least one U.S. patent.

Myriad Genetics held the patent on breast cancer-linked genes, for instance. Anyone who conducted experiments on those genes without a license could be sued by Myriad for infringement of its patent rights. Thus, Myriad was able to decide what research could took place, who could do it, and what any resulting medications and therapies would cost.[384]

An important U.S Supreme Court decision in June of 2013 ended Myriad's monopoly. But Myriad still retains control over all the information it generated during its 15-year monopoly. Unfortunately, other patents still stand, including some related to human genetics, because of the narrow wording of the decision.[385]

Scientists who perform industry-sponsored research routinely sign agreements requiring them to keep their methods and results secret for a period of time. A 1994 survey of 210 life science companies found that 58% of those sponsoring academic research required delays of more than six months before publication.[386] A 1997 survey of 2,167 university scientists revealed that nearly one in five were willing to admit they had delayed publication for more than six months in order to protect proprietary information. "As biotech and pharmaceutical companies have become more involved in funding research, there's been a shift toward confidentiality that is severely inhibiting the interchange of information," noted Steven Rosenberg of the National Cancer Institute in a 2000 exposé in *The Atlantic*.[387]

INTERFERING WITH INDEPENDENT RESEARCH IN OTHER WAYS

Corporations can influence independent research in other ways beyond controlling access to information and materials. They can serve on advisory committees for independent researchers. Government grants now regularly require that grantees establish "partnerships" with "stakeholders," including the very industries whose profits may be affected by unfavorable study results. Private funders are also increasingly demanding this "collaborative" approach, which allows those with a financial conflict of interest to influence research and control access to results.

As described in chapter 2, the "collaborative" process of working with a multi-stakeholder Community Advisory Board led researchers with Fred Hutchinson Cancer Research Center to reject the study of organic agriculture as a method for reducing toxic exposures. That same framework was used to justify failing to publicize their own studies and chastising others who wanted to publicize them.[388] When I served on an advisory committee for University of Washington research, suggestions for studies focusing on organic farmers, alternatives to pesticide use, prenatal exposures, and the like were quickly dismissed. Meanwhile, researchers listened with rapt attention to suggestions from agribusiness representatives.

This attitude on the part of researchers is likely related to the power that business interests bring to the table. They can allow researchers easy access to workers, or they can make access difficult. They can permit or deny access by researchers to their land or property for the purposes of data collection.

Researchers must consider not only the current study they are designing, but others they may want to do down the road. Will they have access to people and places they need? Will corporate interests label them as uncooperative, thereby making it harder for them to receive grants?

And of course, corporations can use their enormous lobbying power to demand reductions in funding for public institutions and the research they carry out. The ever-present threat posed by agribusiness interests to the funding for university researchers hung over many of the issues I worked on in Washington State.

On top of all of this, many scientists engaged in studies that are not directly tainted by industry funding have consulting arrangements with affected industries on the side. Or they may want to explore such options later in their careers. They may want to be in the running to serve as a director on an industry board and enjoy all of the praise, respect, and financial perks that go with that. In 2005, nearly one-third of land-grant university agricultural scientists reported consulting for private industry.[389]

Recap: Public Access to Unbiased Scientific Evidence Is Important Yet Denied

Without access to unbiased scientific evidence, we cannot make informed decisions. Nor can we make our strongest case for environmental reforms. We lack even the capacity to choose products and services that reduce our toxic exposures and are consistent with treading lightly on the Earth.

Big corporations and the groups they influence undermine the scientific evidence that exists in our world and restrict public access to that data. Despite the well-documented impact that funding has on study outcomes, a large percentage of studies are funded by those whose profits could be affected by the research findings. Money affects independent research too, by treating information, seeds, genes, and other materials as private property under the control of those holding patents and purse strings. Wealth is also used to block collection and sharing of basic data, as we found out in our struggles in Washington State for pesticide air monitoring and neighbor notifications prior to pesticide applications.

Despite all of this, some information unfavorable to business practices does manage to get past the censors. In chapter 14 we'll see how corporations use their power to discredit and silence scientists who *do* manage to publish results that make companies look bad.

Thomas Jefferson said, "Information is the currency of democracy." The literal currency of money has accumulated in the hands of a very few wealthy individuals and corporations. As a result, these same interests control the figurative currency of information. This gives them extraordinary power. It undermines democracy.

CHAPTER 14

Public Relations: Influencing Perceptions

● ● ●

WEALTHY INDIVIDUALS AND CORPORATIONS ALSO exert control in our society by developing and implementing public relations (PR) strategies.
These inundate society with messages and information that serve private interests while not necessarily appearing to do so.

One obvious result of PR strategies is the tsunami of political advertisements that inundate us each election season. In 2012, for example, by early September, nearly one million local television ads related
to the election had aired across the U.S.[390] In just one 10-day period
in the fall of that year there was a $77 million ad purchase by the
Obama campaign, another $30 million purchase by the Obama Super
PAC, and a $25 million purchase by the conservative organization
Americans for Prosperity, for a total of $132 million.

Huge amounts of money are spent on non-electoral PR campaigns
as well. An amount like $132 million is less than what a single major
automaker spends on advertising in two months. It is less than what the
auto insurance industry as a whole spends in two weeks.[391] A professor
of agricultural economics had this to say about Dow Chemical's PR expenditures: "My guess is that their marketing budgets are close to their
R&D budgets. That's how important they are."[392]

It is impossible to know just how much money is being spent
on public relations in total. In the late 1990s, the PR firm Burson-
Marsteller pulled in more than a quarter of a billion dollars in net
fees from its clients per year, and it employed 2200 public relations

practitioners.[393] As of this writing, hundreds of PR firms, including previously independent powerhouses like Burson-Marsteller, Hill+Knowlton, and others, have been bought by WPP, an immense international holding company based in London.[394] WPP says it has a workforce of 158,000 in 107 countries and that its billings in 2011 reached $72.3 billion. Other conglomerates and independent firms exist as well, and on top of that there are in-house PR specialists at countless corporations and organizations.

In short, billions—maybe trillions—of dollars are spent each year on PR around the world. The rich spend this much money because it is so effective in advancing their interests.

In this chapter we'll look at several important aspects of PR strategies: the creation of messages, dissemination of these and other information via front groups and experts who pretend to be independent, marginalization of opponents, infiltration of education, and control of the news media.

CREATING MESSAGES

One of the most important things public relations experts do for wealthy corporations and individuals is help them develop the most effective messages for selling whatever it is they are selling. The item to be promoted could be a product, a service, a technology, a whole industry, a particular corporation, a candidate, a piece of legislation, or practically anything else.

PR firms conduct surveys, convene focus groups, and engage in other research to figure out how to most effectively make their pitches. They then launch huge campaigns that disseminate chosen messages far and wide, making sure that all materials and statements under their control are "on message." Multiple corporations can and do engage in joint PR strategies, broadcasting a common message which enhances their common interests.

The Mantle of Public Service. PR strategies advance the private profits of the wealthy entities funding them, but the most effective messages hide that fact. They wrap environmentally destructive products and practices in words that make them appear noble and in the public interest. They studiously avoid mentioning any contrary views.

Dow's sales pitch for its "Enlist Weed Control System" provides an excellent example. That system includes the herbicide 2,4-D and genetically modified seeds that produce 2,4-D-resistant crops. Public health advocates, farmers, and others have long urged USDA to not approve Dow's Enlist products. They are concerned about 2,4-D's links to health problems like non-Hodgkin's lymphoma, damage to crops like tomatoes and grapes from 2,4-D drift, farmers losing the ability to save seeds, and the other dangers associated with genetic engineering.

Dow's PR pieces ignore these profit-threatening concerns and pump out messages linking the Enlist System to humanity-serving concepts and images. An Enlist promotion video never even mentions 2,4-D or genetic modification. As piano music plays in the background, a soothing voice talks about preserving the farming way of life, feeding the hungry world, and being in touch with the land.[395]

Other agribusiness corporations and trade associations use these same messages to promote a wide range of farm pesticides. If you examine industry websites, farming journals, and agribusiness comments to EPA you will encounter much of the same rhetoric as that used in Dow's Enlist video. When I served on agency workgroups with farmers and agribusiness representatives, I regularly heard these same talking points.

Similar misleading messages are developed for all sorts of environmentally destructive products and technologies. Ads by chemical manufacturers depict dioxin and other organochlorine pollutants as "natural." Proposed controls over the discharge of such chemicals are portrayed as an obstacle to water treatment, feeding the hungry, and other good things. They're declared an affront to science itself. Ads by coal companies feign concern for the poor who, they say, will have to pay more for electricity if action is taken to rein in coal. They warn about the loss of coal industry jobs, without mentioning the safer jobs that come with renewable energy development.

PR firms do not hesitate to co-opt language that sells well, even if that means completely distorting the original meaning of the words. By misusing environmental terminology, they kill two birds with one stone: first, they create a positive image for their clients' products and services. Second, they devalue a term that has been used to rally opposition.

The word "sustainable," for example, has become quite popular in PR messages selling all sorts of decidedly non-sustainable things. In several ads, Dow Chemical describes itself as a leader of sustainability, even as its dioxins contaminate rivers, its pesticides sicken farm workers, and the long-term impacts of its notorious Vietnam-era defoliant, Agent Orange, continue to unfold.[396] A consulting firm for the tar sands oil industry had the audacity to describe the industry as "on the threshold of a long-term commitment that will be instrumental in developing all sources of sustainable energy in the future."[397] The message blithely refers to tar sands mining as part of Canada's "profile and influence as a world leader in socially and environmentally responsible resource development."[398]

Unrefuted Inundation. Messages produced by PR firms are effective not only because they are crafted by experts in manipulation, but also because they are broadcast far and wide.

The Dow video mentioned above, for instance, is part of a much larger Dow PR blitz in support of its Enlist products. The broader strategy includes TV commercials, a dedicated website, an Enlist Twitter account, a YouTube channel, display ads in trade publications, and other communications.

We are inundated with PR messages every day. Often, PR versions of reality are accepted reflexively by government agency staffers, reporters, the public, and even some environmental activists. The propaganda is repeated so often that it is taken as indisputable truth.

Meanwhile, the voices of those who do not profit from toxic products and technologies are drowned out. UN reports conclude that sustainable agriculture rather than pesticide-dependent agriculture is better able to feed the world's hungry,[399] but that information falls by the wayside. Abundant studies link pesticides to human health problems and adverse impacts on wildlife. But these too go unnoticed. In fact, anyone who attempts to dispute ingrained PR messages is labeled as "out there" because the facts we wish to share conflict with common "knowledge."

Increasingly it is salespeople who "educate" us about important matters affecting our environment and survival. Farmers rely heavily on pesticide salespeople for information about how to grow food and whether pesticides are hazardous, for example. Pesticide corporation "fieldmen" are always there to share information: out in the fields, at meetings, and wherever growers are. A survey in North Central Washington State confirmed that the top source of information apple growers use in making pest management decisions is chemical company fieldmen.[400]

Agribusiness corporations hold regular "educational" events and they then visit growers who couldn't attend. "Years ago university Extension offered these events, but with cutbacks in funding it's become a service we can provide to the industry," the representative of one agribusiness corporation explained. [401] In other words, growers rely on information that is presented as neutral and as serving the public interest but which is actually designed to maximize pesticide corporations' sales no matter what.

Charitable Donations. Corporations use charitable donations to enhance their noble images. Dow Chemical was a sponsor of the 2012 Olympics in London. Exelon, the nuclear power corporation, creates a compassionate image for itself by donating to schools, Habitat for Humanity, the arts, programs for at-risk youth, and other charities. Charitable donations to environmental, health, and other public-interest groups can also influence the actions of those groups, reducing the threat they pose to corporate profits, as will be discussed later.

Messages About How Decisions Should Be Made. PR campaigns go beyond simply promoting favorable images for corporations and their products. They also promote false perceptions about how people are supposed to behave as issues are discussed and how governments are supposed to make decisions. These perceptions increase the power of the 1% enormously.

The notion of replacing the precautionary principle with industry-friendly "Risk Assessment" didn't come out of nowhere. Nor did the idea that "partnership," "collaboration," and "consensus" should dominate how decisions are made with regard to research and government policies, thereby actually putting corporate stakeholders in the driver's seat. These concepts and others that undermine democracy and weaken environmental protection are promoted by PR experts on behalf of wealthy clients.

Front Groups and "Independent" Experts

The most effective PR strategies hide the profit-hungry businesses that are actually pulling the strings. One effective way to do this is to fund organizations and "experts" who pretend to be independent even as they advance private profit agendas.

The "Third-Party Defense." Proceedings from a 1984 corporate conference spotlight early thinking about this concept. Introducing a panel of public relations staffers, Alan Miller of Philip Morris Tobacco explained the need for what he called the "third-party defense," noting that corporations "can't be self-serving." Miller said corporations should find seemingly independent third parties "to give us clout, to give us power, to give us credibility, to give us leverage, to give us access where we don't ordinarily have access ourselves." (The term "third party" here is not to be confused with third parties in the electoral sense.)

Miller explained that "[i]f you're not going to be willing to create vehicles to ride on, to put things together, in fact to invent things that didn't exist before, coalitions, associations, institutes, seminars, meetings, all kinds of things like that, you cannot be successful." He discussed at length how to pick people who might help the corporation down the road and how to painstakingly "cultivate" them, "gently bringing them along about what our problems are and how our problems impinge upon their livelihood."[402]

Other speakers agreed whole-heartedly about the need to cultivate third parties to ultimately promote corporate interests. George Woodward, of Miller Beer, noted that "when it comes time to testify before a particular government body or some type of other group of civic leaders.....[a]s talented and as professional as our people are, we prefer that they do not do the testifying. They are representatives of a multi-million company that is owned by a multi-billion operation. It's obvious that we have a vested interest." Woodward emphasized that Miller was "contributing thousands upon thousands of dollars to organizations who promote the reasonableness in the use and enjoyment of alcoholic beverages."[403]

Panelists described the big pay-off from cozying up to African American communities, women's groups, inner city housing advocates, and others, who then put a non-corporate face on a corporate message. Another Philip Morris representative bragged about how Philip Morris had become "pretty much a household word" among women's groups. She noted with pride that she had pioneered the cultivation of women's groups for corporate interests and then other corporations had quickly followed suit. "I mean [women's groups] have more sponsors than they know what to do with," she said.

Today: Front Groups Everywhere. The idea of "third parties" carrying the water for private corporations has really taken hold. Corporations regularly fund front groups that appear to be independent but can nonetheless be counted on to advocate corporate-friendly policies. They hide their tracks well, but countless examples have nonetheless been exposed.

In California in 2011, for instance, testimony on behalf of the "Citizens for Fire Safety Institute" from David Heimbach, a former president of the American Burn Association, was key to the demise of a bill that would have reduced the use of flame-retardants in furniture.[404] Heimbach told legislators that the Institute was "made up of many people like me who have no particular interest in the chemical companies: numerous fire departments, numerous firefighters and many, many burn docs." This sounded good, but the Citizens for Fire Safety Institute was actually a trade association for chemical companies.

The Institute's mission was to "promote common business interests of members involved with the chemical manufacturing industry." Its only sources of funding—about $17 million between 2008 and 2010—were "membership dues and assessments" and the interest that money accrued. The group had only three members: Albemarle, ICL Industrial Products, and Chemtura, the three largest manufacturers of flame-retardants.[405]

California is not the only state where Citizens for Fire Safety has testified in favor of flame retardants and against measures manufacturers opposed.[406] Nor is this organization the only flame retardant manufacturer front group.[407]

These flame retardant examples are just the tip of the front group iceberg. "Experts" with the American Council on Science and Health (ACSH), for example, have staunchly defended the pesticide atrazine without mentioning that ACSH is funded by Syngenta, the manufacturer of atrazine. How do we know about the ACSH-Syngenta funding connection? From memos obtained when an Illinois Sanitary District sued Syngenta over atrazine in its water supply.[408]

Other documents obtained by the sanitary district reveal multi-million dollar efforts by Syngenta to influence the public's perception of atrazine, and to stave off regulatory and legal action. Syngenta had plans to investigate reporters, "rattle cages" at EPA, and pay media pundits and third party defenders, among other things. A Syngenta Request for Proposal (RFP)[409] sought an organization for "public relations, issues management and possibly paid media, as appropriate, for support in connection with atrazine…." It included a whole paragraph on "Third-party spokesperson development." Syngenta was seeking a PR organization that had "a network of general, everyday, 'go to' sources comprising civic and opinion leaders, community-based organizations, nonprofits, advocacy groups, and others" who would act as spokespeople for Syngenta's interests.

The preliminary project budget listed in the RFP was $300,000 to $500,000 for 2010. Given the "investment of more than $2.6 million-a-day in research and development" noted in the RFP, this PR cost was a drop in the bucket for Syngenta. Yet it exceeded the entire annual budgets for groups like the Farm Worker Pesticide Project. And it could fund activities that would create huge obstacles for public interest advocates working to protect ecosystems from atrazine.

This Syngenta-proposed contract budget was small compared to other contracts and PR budgets at play in our world. With money spent on PR strategies easily dwarfing the funding available to public interest organizations, is it any wonder we can't get anywhere in our struggles?

Everywhere you turn, private interests are funding groups and individuals that advocate on their behalf but couch their advocacy in terms of noble public interest motivations. In our struggles for rational farm pesticide policies in Washington State, we regularly faced organizations and individuals with close connections to the pesticide industry who spoke as if they represented farmers. A coalition opposed to a California ballot measure that would have required labeling of GMO foods claimed to be fighting for consumers, but it was really a front for Monsanto, Dow, Syngenta, and other corporations.[410] A group called the Consumer Energy Alliance (CEA) opposes low-carbon fuel legislation and claims to be a grassroots "voice for consumers," but it's actually funded by BP, Chevron, ExxonMobil, Marathon, Shell, and Statoil.[411] There are countless more examples and these are only the front groups that have been exposed.

"Third-party defense" has become so sophisticated that wealthy corporations can purchase more than just organizations to speak on their behalf. They can also buy the appearance of independent, spontaneous, grassroots support for positions that bolster their profits. This is known as *astroturfing*. Oil and gas corporations have funded pro-fracking groups that organize rallies seemingly overnight, for example.

Industry-funded buses deliver crowds to these rallies. Speakers stick to industry-serving talking points. Participants wear brightly colored matching T-shirts.[412]

Global Warming Front Groups. In 1998, representatives of the American Petroleum Institute, Chevron, Exxon, and others hashed out a draft "Global Climate Science Communications Plan."[413] They set an explicit goal of ensuring that "[a] majority of the American public, including industry leadership, recognizes that significant uncertainties exist in climate science, and therefore raises questions among those (e.g., Congress) who chart the future U.S. course in global climate change."

The action plan said that

"Victory will be achieved when:

* Average citizens 'understand' uncertainties in climate science; recognition of uncertainties becomes part of the 'conventional wisdom'
* Media 'understands' uncertainties in climate science
* Media coverage reflects balance on climate science and recognition of the validity of viewpoints that challenge the current 'conventional wisdom'
* Industry senior leadership understands uncertainties in climate science, making them stronger ambassadors to those who shape climate policy
* Those promoting the Kyoto treaty appear to be out of touch with reality"

The plan then laid out what would be done to achieve these goals, including a national media relations program (budget $600,000), global climate science information tactics ($5 million, spread over two or more years), and national direct outreach and education activities ($300,000). Potential funding sources were identified as the American Petroleum Institute and its members, Business Round Table, and others. Potential fund allocators included the American

Legislative Exchange Council (ALEC), the Competitive Enterprise Institute, and others. The plan discussed recruiting and training "independent" scientists to be part of aggressive media outreach, heavy-duty contacts with news media, and producing and distributing a steady stream of climate science information to science writers around the country. Front groups would be used extensively, including establishing a new global climate science data center in Washington, D.C., which would be a "non-profit educational foundation with an advisory board of respected climate scientists."

We know all this because someone leaked a copy of the plan. It provides rare documentation of the sorts of PR strategies being proposed and carried out by those wishing to continue extracting, selling, and burning fossil fuels. Even without such a document, however, it's clear that sowing doubt about climate science is a well-funded, highly coordinated industry strategy.

The Union of Concerned Scientists (UCS) did an in-depth review of the role played by oil and gas corporations in the national conversation about climate change.[414] UCS found that several companies have been responsible for much of the misinformation on climate science that is being circulated. Many companies "made statements in support of climate science and policy in some public spaces while simultaneously spreading misinformation on climate science or hindering science-based policy in others." UCS identified the funding of other groups as "an important pathway through which corporations influence the national climate conversation without accountability."[415]

Have fossil-fuel industry PR tactics been effective? Harris polling in 2007 found that 71% of Americans believed that the continued burning of fossil fuels would cause the climate to change. By 2009, the figure was 51%. In June of 2011, it had dropped to 44%. According to the director of the Pew Research Center for People and the Press this is "among the largest shifts over a short period of time seen in recent public opinion history."[416] But industry PR was not the only factor in play. Later we'll examine the misguided decision by many environmental organizations to refrain from talking about global warming at the request of President Obama.

Sowing Doubt. Ninety-eight percent of actively publishing climate scientists now say that climate change is undeniable. How do climate deniers succeed in raising doubt? "They play up smaller debates," says Francesca Grifo of the Union of Concerned Scientists. Finer points remain unsettled, and climate deniers grasp those to imply much broader disagreement about the overall problem.[417] The news media has dutifully featured deniers' voices alongside others.

"It's that false balance thing," says paleoclimatologist Michael Mann. "You're a reporter and you understand there's an overwhelming consensus that evidence supports a particular hypothesis—let's say, the Earth is an oblate spheroid. But you've got to get a comment from a holdout at the Flat Earth Society. People see the story and think there's a serious scientific debate about the shape of the Earth."[418]

Manufacturing "doubt" has become a major service provided by PR firms in general for corporations whose products and services cause harm which spurs public activism. David Michaels' book *Doubt Is Their Product* (2008) lays out the details of industry's assault on science and how it threatens public health.

MARGINALIZING PEOPLE WHO THREATEN PROFITS

Another common PR tactic is to attack and marginalize anyone who might undercut corporate profits. As we saw, the 1998 oil and gas industry PR plan called for making supporters of the Kyoto Protocol appear to be "out of touch with reality," for example.

Similarly, people advocating policies that reduce toxic exposures are labeled chemophobes or the like. I recall being personally labeled a "fear-monger" on more than one occasion.

Indeed, throughout my years as an activist, the impact of PR strategies demonizing environmental and labor activists has always been palpable. On occasion, farmers who had never met me or heard me speak angrily demanded that I "go back to California." I was accused of "trying to shut down agriculture." These were bizarre sentiments since I wasn't from California, and farm workers who depend on agriculture for their livelihood want to sustain agriculture, not destroy it. But the pesticide industry PR machine is very powerful, and often people had made up their mind in advance to distrust anything a pesticide critic might say.

These sorts of experiences pale in comparison to what happens to scientists who publish studies against the wishes of large corporations. Take Professor Tyrone Hayes, for example.[419] He was funded by agribusiness giant Syngenta to study the impact of its pesticide atrazine on frogs. When Hayes started finding evidence that atrazine impedes frogs' sexual development, his relationship with Syngenta became strained. He ended that relationship in order to keep doing the research and ensure that it was published.

For years, Hayes told people that Syngenta was implementing a campaign to destroy his reputation. His claims of being watched, followed, and targeted by Syngenta led even sympathetic colleagues to wonder if he was paranoid.

As mentioned earlier, in 2012, hundreds of Syngenta's internal memos, notes, and emails became publicly available as the result of a lawsuit. These documents make it clear that Hayes's fears were well founded. Syngenta public relations staffers strategized about how to deal with him. They set an explicit goal of discrediting him and discussed how doing so would stop others from citing his data. They committed themselves to identifying and exploiting his psychological weaknesses.

Syngenta discussed purchasing "Tyrone Hayes" as a search word on the internet to ensure that searches would lead people first to Syngenta's material discrediting him. When I searched for his name as I worked on this book, an article entitled "Tyrone Hayes Not Credible" appeared at the top of the list.

The Syngenta PR team considered other nefarious means of discrediting Hayes as well. The documents refer to techniques like, "ask journals to retract," "set trap to entice him to sue," "investigate funding," and "investigate wife." At several PR team meetings, the concept of orchestrating systematic rebuttals at all of Hayes's appearances was considered.

The Syngenta team had a detailed plan for using third parties to do the dirty work of discrediting Hayes. The phrase "have his work audited by 3rd party" appears in a list of useful actions. Company emails indicate that the PR team compiled a database of more than one hundred "supportive third party stakeholders" including 25 professors. These individuals could be counted on to defend atrazine or act as "spokespeople on Hayes."

Syngenta's third-party defenders include Elizabeth Whelan, the president of the American Council on Science and Health, which receives funding from Syngenta, as noted earlier. Syngenta's PR team wrote opinion pieces praising atrazine and attacking scientific studies that raised concerns about it. They then sent these to third parties to submit to various newspapers as their own. When a few of the resulting articles came across as too aggressive, a Syngenta consultant warned that, "some of the language of these pieces is suggestive of their source, which suggestion should be avoided at all costs."[420]

An article in the *New Yorker* about Hayes' ordeal[421] quoted other scientists who have also felt targeted by chemical companies. The article then quoted a Syngenta spokeswoman, who claimed to be troubled by the suggestion that Syngenta would try to discredit anyone, despite the clear documentation of such activity in Syngenta's own internal communications. Syngenta just tries to set the record straight, she claimed, and "virtually every well-known brand, or even well-known issue, has a communications program behind it. Atrazine is no different." Indeed. And that's a big part of the problem we face. Big Money buys big PR, which insidiously skews the public debate in favor of private interests.

CONTROLLING HIGHER EDUCATION

Earlier we examined how wealthy interests fund research by scientists at universities. This gives them control over scientific evidence that guides policy decisions. But that's only one part of how Big Money influences education.

<u>Corporate Donations to Universities.</u> The $10 million grant from Dow Chemical to my alma mater, the University of Michigan, mentioned in chapter 2, is just one example of the enormous donations corporations are making to universities around the world. As you may recall, the Dow-UM grant created hundreds of advanced-degree fellowships for students. Moreover, Dow and the employee it embeds at UM will be actively involved at the university well beyond just footing the bill for the fellowship program.

This grant from Dow is certainly not its first to UM. An October 2011 UM news release, for example, celebrated Dow awards to professors in the College of Engineering and the College of Pharmacy adding up to $3.7 million over five years.[422]

Nor is UM the only university Dow funds. In 2012, Dow and the University of California Berkeley announced their own "sustainability" partnership, for instance.[423] In 2011, Dow awarded UC Santa Barbara $15 million to establish a "collaborative research initiative."[424]

This latest Dow donation to UM is part of President Obama's Advanced Manufacturing Partnership (AMP) initiative, a national effort bringing together industry, universities, and the federal government to invest in emerging technologies. Dow's CEO Andrew Liveris co-leads this new effort with MIT President Susan Hockfield. Numerous other corporations "invest" in academic institutions and participate in this new partnership, such as Honeywell, Procter and Gamble, Northrop Grumman, Johnson and Johnson, and Ford. The initial list of universities entering "partnerships" with for-profit corporations as part of AMP includes not only the University of Michigan, but also MIT, Carnegie Mellon, Georgia Institute of Technology, Stanford, and the University of California-Berkeley.

Through the AMP, other government-sponsored "partnerships", and grants not mediated by the government, private corporations are major donors to universities throughout the U.S. and the world. They directly influence research, curricula, individual students, and other aspects of the academic world to suit their private interests. These corporations' extraordinary disregard for academic independence and their unapologetic promotion of financial conflicts of interest deepens each year and is now regarded as normal.

Land-Grant Universities. The federal government created "land-grant universities" in 1862 by deeding tracts of land in every state for agricultural research to help farmers. Information and agricultural advances resulting from this research were shared freely, including via county extension agents working with farmers.

In recent decades, however, this public mission of the land-grant universities has been compromised. Government funding has dropped substantially and private funding has become pervasive.[425] By the early 1990s, these universities received more money from industry than from the U.S. Department of Agriculture (USDA). In 2009, corporations, trade associations, and foundations gave $822 million to land-grant schools for agricultural research compared to USDA's $645 million.

Agricultural research in the U.S is carried out mainly by three entities: the federal government, largely through USDA; academia, almost entirely through land-grant universities; and the private sector. Between 1970 and 2006, total private agricultural research expenditures (both in-house research and donations to land-grant universities) nearly tripled from $2.6 billion to $7.4 billion in inflation-adjusted 2010 dollars. During that period, total public funding to land-grant schools and USDA grew less quickly, rising from $2.9 billion to $5.7 billion.[426]

These changes were facilitated by the Bayh-Dole Act passed by Congress in 1980. That law encouraged universities to collaborate with private corporations.[427] A primary goal was to develop products such as seeds to sell to farmers under an increasingly aggressive patent regime.[428] With more and more agricultural research privately funded, farmers must now pay for knowledge and assistance that once was considered public and disseminated for free.

So Many Ways to Give. Corporate support for universities comes in many forms. Millions of dollars fund research, of course. But corporations also fund laboratories, buildings, student fellowships, curricula, course materials, and so forth. Monsanto, Walmart, Tyson, and others all have their names emblazoned on buildings, auditoriums, and other major campus structures they funded.

Corporate sponsors enjoy seats on academic research boards from which they influence academic agendas. The University of Georgia's Center for Food Safety, for instance, sells seats on its board of advisors to industry sponsors for $20,000. Advisory board members have included representatives of Coca-Cola, McDonald's, Con-Agra, Cargill, General Mills, and other corporations.[429]

And we mustn't forget corporate donations that pay for specific professors. Corporations pay substantial sums to endow faculty chairs. In 2011, as just one example, Monsanto gave $500,000 to Iowa State University to fund a soybean-breeding faculty chair.[430]

Many professors depend heavily on industry funding for research. Nearly half of land-grant agricultural scientists surveyed in 2005 acknowledged receiving research funding from a private company. Texas A & M Animal Science Professor Jeffrey Savell took 100% of his research grants from industry groups between 2006 and 2010, including more than $1 million from groups like the National Beef Association and Swift and Company.[431]

Frackademia. Oil and gas corporations have heavily funded academic research and analysis related to fracking. News stories have provided glimpses of what some call "Frackademia." The University of Texas (UT), for example, faced a public relations crisis in 2012 when it became known that Professor Chip Groat, author of a report downplaying environmental risks from fracking, had major undisclosed ties to the oil and gas industry.[432] The University stopped disseminating the report, the head of the Center where Groat worked resigned, and Groat himself left the University. This story had a satisfying ending, but it is sobering to realize that the facts only came to light because a nonprofit watchdog exposed them. Most of Frackademia likely remains hidden from view.

Moreover, a UT statement declared that "[t]he university and the Board of Regents embrace business collaborations and investments in university research, and they aspire to be a national model with public/private partnerships."[433] In other words, UT has no plans to stop seeking and accepting corporate funding. In 2012 the university accepted $1 million from ExxonMobil and GE—two corporations with a major stake in oil and gas extraction—for a program to train regulators and policymakers on the ins and outs of fracking. This parallels similar corporate-funded programs at Penn State University and the Colorado School of Mines.[434]

What Corporations Buy When They Fund Universities. Donations to universities generally are just a drop in the bucket compared to the full revenues and assets of the wealthy corporations who make them. But they deliver invaluable benefits to those corporations. These include:

* Direct influence over studies and analyses produced by universities. Research topics, how studies are framed, interpretation of results, whether results are published, and more can all be affected.

* Direct influence over the perspectives and career paths of large numbers of students. Consider the university student who wanted to study organic agriculture but was repeatedly advised to choose an area of study that Monsanto would want to fund. Subtly and not so subtly, students are funneled into corporate-serving areas of study. This affects their mindsets, knowledge, and direction as they enter the world after college.

* Use of vast public resources for private gain. Grant agreements with universities generally ensure that corporations will be able to treat inventions and discoveries made in conjunction with grants as corporate private property. They will profit from these inventions and discoveries even though the public resources of

the university played a large part in making them possible. A Dow announcement about the new Dow-UM collaboration notes that it will "leverage U-M's nearly $1.25 billion research portfolio," for example.[435] In other words, by investing $10 million, Dow benefits from nearly $1.25 billion.

⁂ An improved public image. Corporations are able to wrap themselves in the respectability of the universities they fund. Their representatives are honored and invited to speak at school events, regardless of the corporation's record on environmental, labor, and human rights issues. Corporations are praised, not just as generous donors, but also as visionary leaders on the great issues of the day. It doesn't matter if the corporation's history or fundamental purposes are at odds with society's needs. Dow Chemical, for example, is transformed from being the purveyor of organophosphates, dioxins, napalm, and Agent Orange into being a leader on sustainability. Despite the very low marks its studies received for scientific quality when reviewed by Stanford neuroscientists (see chapter 2), Dow gets to portray itself as a paragon of sound science.

⁂ Brand recognition. People see the corporate name and logo over and over again on school buildings, course materials, and university publications. This fosters familiarity and trust, which enhance the corporation's credibility in public policy debates and make people more likely to buy the corporation's products.

⁂ Tax breaks associated with making donations.

University, Inc. Meanwhile, our universities themselves have started to resemble private corporations. Their public educational mission, an important aspect of a functioning democracy, is being destroyed bit by bit. In the past, free exchange of information ruled the day, to the benefit of all. Now, most universities operate technology-licensing offices to manage their patent portfolios, often guarding "intellectual property" as vigorously as private corporations do.[436]

Far from promoting new discoveries and inventions, corporatized education stifles creativity. In a 2000 article about university funding and patent issues, intellectual property law expert James Boyle noted that if current trends continue, "creators will be prevented from creating" as the public domain is "converted into a fallow landscape of walled private plots."[437]

Beyond Environmental Issues. These examples of business influence over universities have focused on environmentally destructive corporations. But other corporations engage in the same behaviors. The University of Chicago business school has received large contributions from Citibank, JPMorgan Chase, Goldman Sachs, Pfizer, and numerous other mega corporations whose interests are directly affected by the economic policies espoused by the schools' professors and graduates, for instance. The Yale School of Medicine accepted funding from Pepsi for research on nutrition that focuses on problems like diabetes and obesity. A Yale dean declared that, "PepsiCo's commitment to improving health through proper nutrition is of great importance to the well-being of people in this country and throughout the world." Thus, a company whose products contribute to diabetes and obesity was transformed in one fell swoop into a purveyor of health by none other than the Yale School of Medicine.

Controlling K through 12 Education

Corporations do not only target universities. They are also busy infiltrating K through12 education. Wealthy interests gain access to schools by donating money, creating curricula, and offering personnel.

These offerings give donors the same benefits they get from funding universities. Their brands get a visibility boost as students, teachers, and parents are exposed to their message and logo. They gain influence over what students are taught, affecting how they will behave as consumers and as citizens. And, the companies gain an aura of philanthropic nobility.

Corporate involvement at the K through 12 level is even more insidious than at the university level. Children are more likely than adults to accept propaganda without question. They can also affect their parents by demanding products that corporations have marketed to them blatantly or subtly at school.

Fossil-Fuel-Funded Education. The Global Climate Science Communications Plan adopted by oil and gas corporations in 1998, examined earlier, specifically recognized the value of targeting K through 12 teachers and students. It called for a "direct outreach program to inform and educate…..school teachers/students about uncertainties in climate science." Telling teachers and students about "uncertainties in climate science" would "begin to erect a barrier against further efforts to impose Kyoto-like measures in the future," the Plan noted.

The Plan talked about organizing a "Science Education Task Group" to "serve as the point of outreach to the National Science Teachers Association (NSTA) and other influential science education organizations." It also discussed working with NSTA to develop school materials on climate science for use in classrooms nationwide. Educational materials were to be distributed directly to schools and "through grassroots organizations of climate science partners (companies, organizations that participate in this effort)." Measurements of plan success were to include the "[n]umber of school teachers/students reached with our information on climate science."[438]

As the result of this and other PR strategies, oil and gas corporations have their hands all over K through 12 education. A full accounting is difficult to come by, but we can catch glimpses of massive donations via various corporate websites.

ExxonMobil's list of contributions for 2011 includes over $55 million given to pre-college education, including over $44 million in the United States, for example. On an education webpage, the corporation brags about giving $125 million to the National Math & Science Initiative that provides professional development for current teachers and new recruits. On another website it boasts of donating $2 million to the

National Science Teachers Association and supporting the Mickelson ExxonMobil Teachers Academy, which is attended each summer by 600 third-through-fifth-grade teachers from across the U.S.[439]

These are just examples of ExxonMobil's funding related to K through 12 education. Chevron, BP, and other fossil-fuel giants are all playing the game too.

Beyond Fossil-Fuel Issues. The fossil-fuel industry is by no means the only environmentally injurious industry funding schools. Pesticide giant Syngenta, for example, runs a school garden grant program.[440] Grant recipients must teach students about "integrated pest management" (IPM). Syngenta makes sure that teachers won't steer children away from its toxic products, however. "Make No Mistake—IPM is not Organic Agriculture," their website declares. It clarifies further that "[s]ome recent definitions state that pesticides are only used as a last resort in IPM, but that is not true and would prevent the evaluation of all effective tools in an integrated approach."[441]

Syngenta, Monsanto, DuPont, Dow, Bayer, and other pesticide corporations all give major donations to the National FFA Organization (formerly Future Farmers of America). Money goes to lots of things, including programs to recruit, retain, and recognize teachers in agricultural science.[442] Asked about the benefits of sponsoring FFA's annual convention in 2012, a Syngenta spokesperson noted that students "….get to see the products that we make, the technology we have, and they can take back home and actually use on their own farms."[443]

Monsanto gives grants of $10,000 to $25,000 to rural school districts.[444] Bayer (which manufactures pesticides among other things) sponsors an initiative "to improve science education and advance science literacy across America"[445] and is part of the U.S. government-sponsored "Change the Equation" program influencing STEM (science, technology, engineering, and math) education.[446] There are countless other examples.

DuPont runs an essay contest for middle and high school students which leads contestants to web pages that present a rose-colored view of DuPont's environmental record.[447] "Together, we can protect people and the environment" DuPont declares, deftly sidestepping its actual record. "Together we can feed the world" was an essay topic in 2013, and DuPont suggested things essay-writers might explore, like reducing food waste and helping farmers produce more. What do you think the chances were of someone winning the contest with an essay on increasing productivity via organic agriculture and reforming our economic system to equitably distribute food?

Corporate influence can be subtle but powerful. Dow Chemical provides a high school curriculum entitled "The Balanced Equation,"[448] that purports to "help teach students about global sustainability and the role chemistry can play in developing long-lasting solutions." It is masterfully designed to set up straw men for students to tear down, creating the impression that arguments against Dow and its products are ridiculous.

Instead of hearing information assembled by someone like me who's read the studies about Dow's pesticide chlorpyrifos, tested the air for this chemical, and reviewed the basis of Dow's risk calculations, students are told to analyze and debate inane statements like this one: "Chemicals are toxic to the environment." Naturally, when they do so, they discover that *everything* is composed of chemicals. The take-home point they unconsciously grasp is that people concerned about toxic chemicals are emotional, uninformed, and foolish.[449]

These are just a few of countless cases of well-known polluters using funding to influence K to 12 education. Other corporations are also at it. McDonald's, Coca Cola, Scotch-Brite, and many more use donations to buy influence in our schools.

Presidential Promotion of Corporations in Schools. Wealthy corporations are finding it easier and easier to infiltrate and influence our school systems. One reason for this is that they are being aided by whichever party happens to be in the White House. The Obama Administration, like prior administrations, heavily promotes corporate-school "partnerships." Among other things, Obama started

"Change the Equation," a nonprofit that matches funds from corporations for STEM education. Articles praising this development report that "corporations like ExxonMobil, Dell Computers and Lockheed Martin, for example, have invested..." in schools. Five CEOs of major conglomerates helped launch the Change the Equation coalition, which has grown rapidly to include over 100 members.

In response to a question about why there is an emphasis on STEM, the Change the Equation CEO noted that, "We know that a functioning democracy needs citizens who can reason numerically and scientifically. People have to look at the global warming debate with some lens of scientific understanding; they have to see the health care debate with some grasp of the statistics of the dollars involved. Our democracy demands that all students achieve this form of literacy. A literate nation not only reads, but calculates, analyzes, and innovates."[450]

All of these statements are true. The real question is this, however: In a democracy, why would we place the vital functioning of schools in the hands of corporations that have a vested interest in ensuring that children adopt a perspective that will not threaten their corporate profits? It is precisely because we need to truly understand what is going on with global warming, health care, and other important issues that we need to be so concerned about corporate infiltration of our schools.

White House support for corporate access to schools goes well beyond launching and supporting programs like Change the Equation. There are myriad ways in which government officials regularly help corporations insert themselves into our schools. For example, in an article announcing a Syngenta grant focusing on recruiting, retaining, and honoring agricultural science teachers, a spokesman for the U.S. Department of Education opined, "The key to success with improving the future for agricultural education is partnerships between the public and private sectors." He expressed his hope that "this agriculture education program, sponsored by Syngenta, will be a model for how such partnerships can work."[451] Bayer's corporate materials mention the company's strong relationship with the U.S. Department of Education.[452]

Desperate Times for Schools. Another reason for growing corporate infiltration in schools is the sorry state of public school funding. Traditionally, private donations—from foundation grants to bake sale revenues—amounted to just 1% of K through 12 funding in the U.S.[453] That money went to extras like new computers or playground remodels. But now, reductions in public funding have left schools in the lurch, forcing them to rely on private donations to fund core functions.

Faced with inadequate budgets, school administrators and teachers must make unacceptable choices. Referring to the idea of asking Nike and other corporations to provide $30,000 to $50,000, a California school district staffer said, "[t]hat $30,000 could buy a part-time music teacher, a resource teacher, or books for the library." Presumably, students will go without music education and other important things unless the schools fall in line with the concept of "partnerships" with corporations.

A 2010 Wall Street Journal article illuminated the degree of desperation felt by more and more schools.[454] It provided some startling examples of schools taking private contributions to get by:

* A Lakeland, Florida, elementary school is "adopted" by a local church when the budget for pencils, paper, and other essential supplies is cut by a third. "We have inroads into public schools that we had not had before," Pastor Dave McClamma, is quoted as saying. "By befriending the students, we have the opportunity to visit homes to talk to parents about Jesus Christ."

* Another Florida elementary school asks local businesses to sponsor classrooms in return for promotion on the school marquee. Among those stepping up is Rogers & Walker Gun Shop.

* At another elementary school, the principal hands out flyers urging parents to go to "McTeacher's Night" at the local McDonald's, where teachers flip burgers with a portion of the proceeds going to the schools.

There is another option: insisting that ample public funding is provided for schools so they don't need to rely on private funding. But school boards act as if this is impossible. They stoically roll up their sleeves to make painful cuts or they scurry around seeking more private funding. Thus with each passing year, the super rich have more and more of a say in how children are educated. This increases the stranglehold the wealthy few have on the rest of us.

Controlling the News Media

Almost all media outlets that reach a large audience in the United States today are owned by for-profit corporations. This creates a dynamic that further empowers the super rich. Instead of providing unbiased information to guide our political and personal actions, the media has increasingly become a powerful conduit for the PR messages of large corporations.

Corporate mergers and acquisitions have consolidated control over media into the hands of remarkably few people. In 1983, 50 men and women, chiefs of their corporations, controlled more than half the information that reached 220 million Americans. By October 2011 the number had dropped from 50 to 20. A handful of corporations within those 20 controlled the lion's share of the information and ideas reaching people.[455]

Lists of major media outlets and who owns them are quite shocking. As I wrote this General Electric co-owned NBC and media giant Viacom was a major owner of CBS, for instance. Moreover, individuals who serve on the boards of major corporations dealing in oil, financial investments, pharmaceuticals, and other interests also serve on the boards of the major media corporations.[456]

Media ownership is in a state of constant flux. In 2013, for example, Amazon.com's CEO Jeff Bezos bought the *Washington Post* for $250 million. Printed in the nation's capital, the *Post* offers Bezos a unique means of promoting his company's profits and political agenda.[457]

"What you have is a plaything for these billionaires that they can then use aggressively to promote their own politics," explains Robert McChesney, author and co-founder of FreePress. "[I]t's not like Jeff Bezos has to march into a newsroom and say 'Cover this. Don't cover that.' It rarely works that way," McChesney noted. "You basically set an organizational culture, and smart journalists who want to survive internalize the values, and those that don't internalize the values get out of the way."[458]

In 2013 the Koch Brothers, of Koch Industries, famous for funding attacks on climate science, were in the news as potential buyers of the Tribune Company newspapers. These included the *Chicago Tribune*, *Baltimore Sun*, *Los Angeles Times*, *Orlando Sentinel*, and *Hartford Courant*. The sale would have been among the largest sales of newspapers by circulation in the U.S. Nonetheless, with an annual revenue of about $115 billion, Koch Industries would hardly have noticed paying the estimated price of $623 million for the newspapers.

Ultimately, the Koch Brothers decided not to buy the Tribune Company papers. A spokesman for Koch Industries noted, however, that "Koch continues to have an interest in the media business and we're exploring a broad range of opportunities where we think we can add value."[459]

A Koch acquisition of major media resources would be in keeping with an agenda laid out at a meeting the Kochs sponsored several years ago. The ultra-wealthy brothers proposed a three-pronged strategy for shifting the country toward their perspective: educating grass-roots activists, influencing politics, and influencing the media. Guests at that meeting included Philip F. Anschutz, a Republican oil mogul who owns the companies that publish the *Washington Examiner*, the *Oklahoman*, and the *Weekly Standard*.[460]

"It's a frightening scenario when a free press is actually a bought and paid-for press and it can happen on both sides," said Ellen Miller, executive director of the Sunlight Foundation. Seton Motley, president of Less Government, said, "[a] running joke among conservatives as we watched the G.O.P. establishment spend $500 million on ineffectual TV ads is 'Why don't you just buy NBC?'" As Motley sees it, "[i]t's good the Kochs are talking about fighting fire with a little fire."[461]

Media outlets have become more and more dependent on advertisements for income. Most aren't selling content to audiences; they're selling audiences to advertisers.

All of these developments dramatically undermine the role that media outlets should be playing in a democracy[462]:

- Wealthy private owners and sponsors have disproportionate influence over what we see, hear, and read. They avoid content or voices that make them or their products look bad.
- They also avoid content or voices that support policies and candidates they dislike.
- Censorship happens not only as the result of owners selecting news stories, reporters, hosts, programs, movies, and music that advance their own private interests and those of advertisers. Reporters also self-censor to stay in favor and keep their jobs.
- Advertisers steer programming and coverage toward the audiences they most want to reach, which tend to be young, white, and affluent.
- The push to maximize profits for media corporations leads to more sensational news, designed to grab readers' and viewers' attention.
- The profit motive leads media outlets to reduce costs by cutting the numbers of reporters they employ. This has left remaining reporters with very little time to engage in investigative journalism.

As the number of journalists has declined, the number of paid employees at PR firms has skyrocketed. Not counting in-house PR staff at major corporations, nonprofits, and government agencies—numbers that are likely quite high—there were over 50,000 PR employees in the U.S. in 2007, a

30% increase compared to 10 years earlier. In contrast, numbers of newspaper reporters and editors in the U.S. declined from almost 57,000 in 1990 to 41,600 in 2011, with much of the decline coming since 2007. It is estimated that network news employment today is half what it was in the 1980s.[463]

Here's another way to look at the numbers. In 1980, there were about 0.45 PR workers for every 100,000 people, but only 0.36 journalists for those people. By 2008, there were 0.90 PR employees and only 0.25 journalists per 100,000 people. The PR industry had increased its edge over journalists to a ratio of more than three to one, and the PR workers had a lot more money to play with than the journalists.[464] The ratio is likely even more disturbing today.

Environmental issues are more important than ever. Nonetheless, the number of reporters covering environmental issues has dropped precipitously in recent years. The *New York Times* closed its environment desk early in 2013, assigning its seven reporters and two editors to other departments and eliminating the positions of environment editor and deputy environment editor, for example.[465]

Fewer reporters means less investigative journalism. Covering broader topic areas, reporters are less able to focus, gain expertise on a particular issue, and ferret out details for stories.

PR staffers are more than willing to make things easy for stretched reporters. They constantly provide news releases and even ready-made video clips.

As a result, the number of original stories featured by news outlets is declining. A study in the Baltimore area published in 2010 found that only 14% of the news stories on the topics it tracked started with reporters. Sixty-three percent were generated by the government, and 23% came from interest groups or public relations staffers.[466]

Many media outlets run materials provided to them verbatim, with minimal investigation, if any, of the claims those materials make. Other media outlets then pick up and widely disseminate these "news" stories, creating a huge ripple effect. Thus, stories written by

PR experts designed to promote private interests are constantly in wide circulation in our world today. Widespread dissemination of a PR message increases the chances that people will accept it as true, never knowing its source.[467]

A recent analysis by the Union of Concerned Scientists documented how what's happening to the news media is undercutting environmental reporting. UCS found that news outlets failed to note the fossil-fuel funding of climate-denying organizations in two-thirds of the stories in which they were cited during a two-year study period.[468] The two newspapers with the biggest circulations in the U.S. did the worst job: *USA Today* reported funding sources in only 18% of the 28 stories and op-eds it ran, and the *Wall Street Journal* did so in only 11% of 46 stories and op-eds it ran. Too often, the news media have "provided a platform for fossil-fuel industry-funded groups to make misleading claims about global warming and renewables and allowed them to pass themselves off as independent disinterested parties," the UCS report concluded.[469]

Some corporations and their PR firms bypass traditional news outlets altogether, broadcasting their "news" stories far and wide directly and via "third parties" who seem independent but are not.

Public stations are not immune to corporate influence. PBS regularly reads tag lines from corporate sponsors that are ads in all but name. Worse, stations like PBS provide airspace for much bigger corporate PR. Dow Chemical, for example, sponsored a four-part series on PBS entitled Food Machine. Each episode dealt with topics that affect Dow's profits. Genetic modification was presented as a positive game changer, even as Dow sought EPA approval of its genetically modified products.[470]

Media corporations regularly make large donations to both Democrats and Republicans. They make these donations while concurrently accepting millions of dollars in payment for political ads they are running.[471]

Presidents as Products

Driving home just how pervasive and influential PR is in our world, Advertising Age awarded its Marketer of the Year Award in 2008 to Barack Obama.[472] Candidates for public office have become products to be packaged and sold to the American people via huge public relations campaigns. In winning the marketing award, Obama received the votes of hundreds of marketers, agency heads, and marketing-service vendors attending the Association of National Advertisers' annual conference. He edged out Apple, Zappos.com, Nike, Coors, and his Republican rival John McCain.

Appreciative PR experts gushed over how effective Obama's marketing had been. "I think he did a great job of going from a relative unknown to a household name to being a candidate for president," said Linda Clarizio, president of AOL's Platform A. "I honestly look at [Obama's] campaign and I look at it as something that we can all learn from as marketers," said Angus Macaulay, Vice-President of Rodale Marketing Solutions.

Central to Obama's success as a marketer was his "brand." He was marketed as the "Yes, We Can" candidate, the candidate of youthful exuberance, and the candidate of change. An iconic poster of Obama appeared everywhere, as did his logo. The logo is so well known that many Obama supporters simply used it together with the number 2012 to signal their support for Obama being reelected. In short, the PR experts who worked with Obama knew what they were doing.

Many have noticed the remarkable similarity between the logo used to symbolize and sell Obama and that used by Pepsi.[473] The themes of the two campaigns—Obama's and Pepsi's—are also remarkably similar. Pepsi, like the Obama campaign, strives to exude youthful energy, reaching out to the "Pepsi generation."

Public Relations: A Recap

One way corporations and wealthy individuals use their wealth to exert control is by implementing public relations strategies. They create self-serving messages and distribute these widely, using front groups and other means. They malign and discredit those who interfere with corporate profits. They buy influence in education. And, they own and control the major news media outlets.

The impact of all of these PR activities on public discourse and action cannot be overstated. At times it appears that very little of the information with which we come in contact has *not* been shaped by invisible private interests seeking to maximize their profits. Even presidential candidates can be sold like products with the right corporate backing and a slick PR machine.

CHAPTER 15

Other Things Money Buys

• • •

THERE REALLY IS NO END to what those who accumulate mountains of wealth can do to advance their interests. Here are glimpses of a few other things money can buy.

LAWSUITS

The rich can retain huge numbers of lawyers to bring lawsuits on their behalf. Each year, big corporations challenge environmental laws and regulations that interfere with their profits.[474]

They also attack activists with what are known as SLAPP suits. SLAPP stands for Strategic Litigation Against Public Participation. Corporations accuse someone who criticizes them of slander or libel, forcing them to spend time and money defending themselves. Professor Penelope Canan, an expert on SLAPP suits explains, "We don't think that they are intended to win on their legal merits, and it turns out way more than 95% get thrown out of court, eventually. It's just the 'eventually' and the ordeal of the time that essentially is such a chilling effect on citizens."[475]

Giant agribusiness corporations regularly sue farmers over issues related to genetically modified (GMO) crops. As of December 2012, Monsanto had filed 142 seed patent infringement lawsuits, involving 410 farmers and 56 small farm businesses in 27 states. This prompted one judge to label the company "incredibly litigious." In 72 record judgments, Monsanto has been awarded $23,675,820. As early as 2003, Monsanto had a department of 75 employees with a budget of $10 million solely for pursuing farmers for patent infringement. DuPont, the world's second largest seed company, hired at least 45 farm investigators in 2012 to look at Canadian farmers' planting and purchasing records and to perform genetic analyses on their fields. In the U.S. DuPont was expanding this work in 2013, hiring approximately 35 investigators, many of them former police officers.[476]

Monsanto's website defends the corporation's suits against "farmers who save seeds," claiming that patents are essential and ultimately benefit farmers and consumers. Monsanto emphasizes that most of its confrontations with farmers over patent violations result in settlements, as if threatening lawsuits and taking money from farmers is a benign activity. Monsanto uses the term "relatively rare" to describe the numbers of suits it brings, but most people would consider an acknowledged average of 11 suits per year over 13 years far from rare. The company boasts that it has won every case that has not been settled, driving home just how powerful it is compared to farmers.[477]

SPIES AND INFILTRATORS

In recent years, government agencies like the Central Intelligence Agency (CIA), the National Security Agency (NSA), and others have outsourced core tasks to private intelligence firms. As a result, spying has become a domestic market worth nearly $50 billion a year.[478] There is an immense pool of private investigators available for corporations to hire.[479]

Many large corporations also now have their own internal "intelligence" capabilities. These often employ former CIA, NSA, Secret Service, and other agency staffers, as well as people who have worked for local police, law enforcement agencies, or the military. "The private sector has virtually all the same techniques as the government," says Jack Devine, who worked for the CIA for 32 years.[480]

While we can only catch glimpses of what goes on in the murky world of espionage, big corporations are clearly making use of the spying resources at their disposal. In a 2010 article, for example, journalist Mary Cuddehe describes being approached by one of the world's largest private investigation firms, which does espionage work for Fortune 500 companies. The firm flew her to Colombia where she stayed in a very nice hotel and was offered $20,000 to go to the Ecuadorian Amazon to gather information for an oil corporation that had been sued by activists over its pollution there. "If I went to Lago Agrio as myself and pretended to write a story, no one would suspect that the starry-eyed young American poking around was actually shilling for Chevron," Cuddehe wrote.[481] She refused the offer, but how many other seemingly independent people are actually spying for major corporations?

For multiple examples of investigative firms going through nonprofit organizations' recycling bins, infiltrating groups, potentially breaking into offices and more, see the report, *Spooky Business: Corporate Espionage Against Nonprofit Organizations*, published in November of 2013.[482]

Ultra-rich corporations can work hand in glove with government spies. The same huge corporations whose names show up repeatedly in this book are formal "partners" within the U.S. government's vast surveillance network. Bank of America, Citigroup, ConocoPhilips, Walmart, and scores of other corporations partner with the FBI and the Department of Homeland Security via the "Domestic Security Alliance Council," for example. Many of these corporations have also participated in the Department of Homeland Security's Private Sector Information-Sharing Working Group, alongside other banks and corporations. That working group consists of 79 representatives from 51 Fortune 500 corporations. It was instrumental in drafting a plan that called, unsurprisingly, for increasing resources to public-private intelligence-sharing partnerships.[483]

Surveillance and other intelligence work for these public-private partnerships were originally rooted in concepts of preventing terrorism and protecting "critical infrastructure/key resources" from terrorism-related threats. The agenda quickly widened, however. Surveillance and other actions are now undertaken to address "all hazards/all crimes," rather than just terrorism-related ones. "Critical infrastructure" and "key resources" encompass privately controlled resources as well as those that are publicly controlled. Virtually anything that may be deemed a "hazard" to the public or to certain private sector interests is fair game for spying and related activities.[484]

The Center for Media and Democracy and DBA Press used freedom of information laws to obtain thousands of pages of emails and other documents produced in 2010 and 2011 by federal and state intelligence, enforcement, and Homeland Security agencies. Together, these paint an astonishing picture of the vast U.S. surveillance network and how governmental agencies join with major corporations to investigate people protesting actions of those very corporations. Instead of protecting people from terrorist attacks, surveillance is undermining our most basic freedoms.[485]

Documents made public by NSA whistleblower Edward Snowden have exposed the jaw-dropping breadth of U.S. government spying on everyday Americans and on people and leaders in other countries. The programs and mindset of government surveillance officials are in and of themselves a huge concern for Americans because they undermine our most fundamental liberties. Knowing that corporations are considered "partners" by surveillance agencies and that information obtained by governments can end up in corporate hands is cause for even greater concern.

One of the most shocking things revealed by the Snowden documents is that the NSA and equivalent agencies in other countries work together on "Joint Threat Research Intelligence."[486] They explicitly

* Put false material on the internet in order to destroy the reputations of targets.
* Use various techniques to manipulate online discourse and activism, leading to outcomes the governments desire.

There is little to prevent the use of these tactics to discredit social justice activists and steer political discourse away from topics that threaten corporate profits. We've already seen that U.S. ambassadors act as agents for big corporations in other countries, undercutting local laws and community movements that interfere with corporate profits (see chapter 12). Why would anyone doubt that government officials would help corporations use espionage against activists to advance corporate interests?

We also have documentation of prior government undercover activities targeting and disrupting political movements. The FBI went after social justice organizations and political leaders via its COINTELPRO program, for example.[487] The Mississippi Sovereignty Commission hired spies to infiltrate the civil rights movement, fight desegregation, and undermine voter-registration efforts, as another example.[488]

VIOLENCE

Large corporations have had notoriously close relationships with oppressive regimes that have engaged in violence and other human rights abuses against their citizens. The documentary *Drilling and Killing* provides disturbing insights into the relationship between corporations extracting oil in Nigeria and the military dictatorship there, for example. In the film, Chevron's general manager of public affairs acknowledges that Chevron flew in the soldiers who injured and killed young people protesting its offshore drilling practices. Earlier, Shell's parent company had drawn international criticism for failing to use its close relationship with the Nigerian government to halt the execution of environmental activists convicted in sham trials.

Around the world, activists, reporters, and others who have exposed environmental problems and injustice have been murdered. Did corporations who profited from the silencing of their critics play a role in those murders? In most cases we will never know, but it is important to recognize that those controlling unfathomable amounts of money have the capacity to promote violence without leaving a trail.

The ultimate violence is war, and there is a clear correlation between wars and the financial interests of wealthy corporations. Weapons manufacturers thrive whenever there is war, regardless of which side wins.[489] Oil and gas corporations profit when wars give them access to previously inaccessible fossil fuels. A recent study found that foreign governments are 100 times more likely to intervene in civil wars if the country involved is oil-rich.[490]

Author Greg Muttitt's tenacious investigations have produced valuable materials on this topic.[491] These include minutes and summaries of meetings between UK government officials and British oil giants BP and Shell prior to the U.S.-led invasion of Iraq. These documents show that Shell and BP were extremely interested in access to Iraqi oil, and top British officials were committed to helping them gain it.[492] The oil corporations and British governmental officials strategized on how to get "a fair slice of the action for UK companies in a post-Saddam Iraq."[493] Remember these discussions occurred *before* the invasion.

The British companies expressed concern that the U.S. might be cutting deals with the Russians and French over access to Iraqi oil. The UK Minister of Trade noted that "it would be difficult to justify British companies losing out in Iraq...if the UK had itself been a conspicuous supporter of the U.S. government throughout the crisis."[494]

In one meeting, BP reported on its recent visit to meet with U.S. officials and explained why the U.S. favored having U.S. oil companies follow *after* other oil companies. The BP representative's take was that "perhaps this was to avoid any political fall-out in the U.S. from allegations that the issue with Iraq was all about oil in the first place."[495]

Since the invasion, British and U.S. officials have continued to work closely with oil corporations to maximize their access to Iraqi oil. For example, they have lobbied for contracts and conditions most favorable to the oil corporations.[496] They have also facilitated military protection of corporate interests. A *USA Today* article reported that the U.S. is selling unarmed drones to Iraq's navy to help protect oil exports. "They understand the importance of the mission to protect its oil platforms," explained Army Lt. Gen. Robert Calen.[497]

Most people don't want war, but war is what we keep getting. It destroys lives and lands. It also diverts money and resources from the things we need like better schools, housing for all, decent health care, and food security. Those with massive wealth have the power to promote war, and there is every reason to believe that their use of that power is key to why we find ourselves endlessly at war and endlessly facing cuts to social services to fund those wars.

CHAPTER 16

Controlling Resources, Controlling Lives

• • •

WE'VE EXAMINED NUMEROUS WAYS IN which the few who hold most of the world's wealth use it to exert control. Big Money buys elections, laws, rules, trade agreements, scientific research, public relations strategies, media outlets, spies, lawsuits, and more.

But we've not yet explored more direct ways in which inequity disempowers us. When the wealth that workers produce is owned by someone else, we don't have access to it for meeting public needs. Moreover, when an elite few own major industries and natural resources, they get to decide what goods and services will be produced with these and how products will be distributed. We may try to influence them, but when it comes right down to it, we're not in charge regarding important decisions that affect our environment, hunger, and other public matters. We also find ourselves beholden to a limited number of job providers, instead of shaping employment ourselves.

The Wealth Grab. Chapter 8 laid out the details with respect to how much money the 1% has hoarded and how much that leaves for the rest of us. The gap between rich and poor is huge and growing larger by the day.

There's lots of money in the world, but most of it now lies beyond our reach. It isn't in our pockets and our governmental treasuries for us to use for public needs. Instead it is owned and controlled by a wealthy few. We are told that we must *cut* public programs, not expand them.

The Farmland Grab. Corporations and the super rich are relentlessly expanding their ownership of land. Farmland, for example, is now considered a great investment opportunity for those with money to spare.

"Hot money turns from stocks to farmland. Investors of every stripe flock to the nation's breadbasket," the *StarTribune*, a Minnesota newspaper, proclaims. About a quarter of farmland buyers in Kansas and elsewhere are now "investors or non-operator buyers of some sort," the paper reports. A young man who checks out land for investors notes that his firm "has clients lined up waiting for farms. Most of them are sophisticated investors with a net worth of more than $1 million."[498]

"If you want to get rich, you should be investing in farmland," a legendary Wall Street trader is quoted as saying in a financial advice column, which features a section entitled, "Milking Profits From Farmland." In a particularly sobering paragraph, the article notes that the average U.S. farmer is 58 years old, and the U.S. Department of Agriculture estimates that over one-third of all farmland owners have less than 15 years left to live. "That aging population represents a window of opportunity for investing in farmland."

Many different websites now cater to investors interested in farmland purchases. The Global AgInvesting site, for example, steers would-be investors to its conferences, which it proudly describes as very well attended. You can only read part of the site's materials, however, unless you wish to pay the annual membership fee of $1995.

Occasionally ag investment websites include lofty references to farms feeding the hungry world, but the obvious driving factor for investors is profit. Land purchases are clearly not propelled by a commitment to growing the foods we need, using sustainable practices, and helping those who want to farm do so.

When they buy up farmland, investors can then rent it to farmers who can be made to pay not only rent but also royalties. Farmland has been described as "gold with yield" because it can produce stable income streams.[499]

The increased focus on agriculture-related investment by the private sector is leading to a spike in U.S. farmland prices, which prevents many would-be young farmers from starting or continuing small-scale farming operations.[500]

Different aspects of increasing financial insecurity combine to facilitate investor-takeover of farmlands. Many older farmers need to sell their land at as high a price as possible because they do not have adequate funds for retirement. Meanwhile, young people don't have the financial resources to take on the kind of debt that buying land and farming now requires.[501] According to recent census data, farmers now own only 60% of the land they farm.[502] That number will likely drop further as investors make offers that financially strapped farmers can't refuse.

Wealthy interests have advocated policies that increase their control over farmland. As part of signing onto NAFTA, for example, Mexico was required to amend its constitution, privatizing formerly communal lands, or *ejidos*, cultivated by the rural poor. Privatization dislocated rural populations and facilitated corporate exploitation of those lands.[503] Displaced farmers who migrated to other nations have often ended up working as underpaid farm workers on someone else's land, denied the rights of citizens.

The farmland investment frenzy overlaps with ongoing loss of farmland to development. Given how difficult it is to make a living farming, many family farmers succumb to offers from developers to buy their land. According to American Farmland Trust, the U.S. has been losing more than an acre of farmland per minute for many years. Between 2002 and 2007, more than 4 million acres of farmland—an area nearly the size of Massachusetts—were developed for non-agricultural purposes.[504]

Contrary to popular belief, globally, small farms are more productive than big ones. They remain the major food producers for the planet. But the amount of land dedicated to them is swiftly declining. Small farms now comprise less than a quarter of the world's farmland.[505]

Land statistics in other countries are often hard to come by. In general, however, it appears that a few wealthy interests own a lot of land, while vast numbers of people are landless. In Brazil, less than 2% of the population owns more than half of the nation's land. A large movement of landless rural workers has been struggling for decades to claim land to farm for themselves.[506] Meanwhile, news articles and U.S. Embassy cables made public by Wikileaks reveal steady efforts by foreigners to buy up Brazilian agricultural land.[507]

The implications of investors' grabbing up farmland go well beyond depriving individuals of a livelihood. "When non-operators own farms, they tend to source out the oversight to management companies, leading in part to horrific conditions around labor and how we treat the land," says Anuradha Mittal of the watchdog group Oakland Institute.[508] Moreover, investors are driven by a desire to maximize profits rather than a commitment to ensuring that land is used for what people need most. Thus, land that could grow food crops to feed people may be used instead for biofuels, luxury items like coffee and beef, or other foods favored by the wealthy that make inefficient use of the land.

Other Land Grabs. Land and the rights to what's under it are also being bought to gain control over access to oil and gas. Chesapeake Energy is reportedly now the largest leaseholder in the United States, owning the drilling rights to about 15 million acres—an area more than twice the size of Maryland. According to an in-depth report published in *Rolling Stone*, the company's primary profit comes not from fracking and selling gas itself, but from buying and flipping land that contains gas. The report quotes the head of Chesapeake as saying, "I can assure you that buying leases for x and selling them for 5x or 10x is a lot more profitable than trying to produce gas at $5 or $6 per million cubic feet."[509]

Fossil-fuel corporations that hold leases to oil and gas under public lands use their wealth to lobby for low royalty payments. "Our past work has shown that [the U.S. Department of the] Interior does not have reasonable assurance that it is collecting the public's fair share of revenue from oil and gas produced on federal lands," the U.S. General Accounting Office (GAO) has noted.[510]

CNN Money's 2012 list of the 500 wealthiest corporations in the world ranked by revenues includes Royal Dutch Shell, Exxon Mobil, BP, Chevron, and ConocoPhillips.[511] Meanwhile, countries and states that lease land to these and other oil and gas giants tell citizens that there are not enough funds for basic public programs.

Here's one last example of the land grabs underway all around us. Over time, fewer and fewer people own their homes and the land those homes sit on. In fact, banks now own more of the housing in the U.S. than people do. Stagnant wages, rising debts, foreclosures, and other factors have all contributed to this new reality.[512]

The Water Grab. One of the most precious natural resources of all is water. Now formally labeled a "commodity" in trade agreements (adopted with heavy corporate involvement), water, like land, has become an investor's dream. Citi (formerly Citigroup), the same folks who wrote the "plutonomy" memo urging more investment in products and services for the ultra rich, produced an equally appalling memo in July of 2011. It described why investing in water is a wise financial move.

The 2011 memo features an essay by Citi economist Willem Buiter, which opens with the Oscar Wilde quote: "A cynic is a man who knows the price of everything and the value of nothing." Buiter quips that he never understood this aphorism, so he became an economist. His failure to understand the quote is indeed evident throughout the essay. Buiter explains that water is a "regular commodity," a "private good" that "can be allocated effectively and efficiently by markets, and provided by private profit-motivated producers." Water is "excludable" which means someone who owns water "can easily…prevent unauthorized use of the good or service by others." By being able to exclude people, owners can charge for consumption, which is a great thing in Buiter's mind.

With financial giants like Citi zeroing in on water, you can rest assured that the grab for water is well underway. Land purchases may often be undertaken as a way to control the water that flows through or next to a parcel of land. Diversions, dams, privatization of public water works, and foreign-owned, investor-serving agricultural projects receiving water rights are all part of major shifts occurring in the ownership and control of water.[513]

Early in 2013, Goldman Sachs co-sponsored an event entitled "Water: Emerging Risks and Opportunities" with GE and World Resources Institute. Despite inclement weather, nearly 300 water infrastructure and energy sector executives and asset managers attended to learn about opportunities for investing in water. Among other things, they learned about the "unconventional energy" sector's growing demands for water. Extreme fossil-fuel extraction techniques like fracking require a lot of water.[514]

In March of 2011 on World Water Day, UN Secretary General Ban Ki-moon warned, "[a] shortage of water resources could spell increased conflicts in the future. Population growth will make the problem worse. So will climate change. As the global economy grows, so will its thirst. Many more conflicts lie just over the horizon."[515]

Corporate Ownership of Other Things

The list of public resources being transferred to private hands does not end with wealth, land, oil and gas, water, and other natural resources. Anything that can possibly be commoditized is being fenced off and sold for a profit.

With the advent of genetically modified organism (GMOs), for example, large agricultural corporations now own seeds, a symbol of life itself. When farmers use GMO seeds, they must sign a contract ensuring that they will not save seeds to plant in the future. They are forced to go to Monsanto, Dow, or other seed-selling corporations year after year.

Some farmers get on the GM seed treadmill against their will because they can't find conventional seeds anymore. An Iowa farmer in this situation explains, "You know, I held out for years on buying them GE [genetically engineered] seeds, but now I can't get conventional seeds anymore. They just don't carry 'em."[516] Genetically modified plants exude pesticides, or they resist them, enabling growers to broadcast pesticides without harming crops. Genetic modification has increased pesticide use and the harms that accompany it.[517]

Private control over seeds has already been consolidated within a very few corporations which gives them enormous power. Monsanto, DuPont, and Syngenta now control 53% of the global commercial seed market. The top ten seed firms account for 73% of that market.[518]

In the past, we might also have thought of our *food supply* as a public resource. But consolidation of land in investors' hands, loss of farmland to development, patenting of seeds and other factors have been eroding public control over our food supply. Some claim that we retain control as consumers, but "food deserts"—large areas where it is hard to find nutritious food—are rampant in urban and rural areas. Even if nutritious sustainably grown foods are available, high prices may make them unaffordable for vast numbers of people as poverty deepens in the U.S. and around the world. Thus, our supposed influence over food as consumers is an ineffective substitute for actual control.

As one last example, the public resource of knowledge—once a freely shared product of universities and schools—is now increasingly locked away behind patents and copyrights. Only those who pay can access the information, life-saving medicines, and other benefits of research.

The Upshot: Beggars Not Choosers

If we do not own the profits our work produces and we lack control over land, natural resources, and key industries, we are disempowered. We cannot do the things we want to do.

We are told that we can't hire more teachers because there's not enough money, even as vast financial resources we have produced sit in corporate accounts. We long for sustainable agriculture, producing the nutritious food people need, but watch helplessly as huge tracts of farmland produce non-nutritious profit-maximizing crops instead. Even as the ability to rely on alternative energy sources lies within grasp, we watch as corporations proceed to take every last bit of fossil fuel out of the ground, dooming us all to more pollution and global warming.

By handing control over wealth and resources to a few individuals and corporations, we have lost our ability to establish the policies and programs we need. We have also given private interests the power of extortion over us. Those with limited resources have no choice but to do whatever those hoarding resources demand. As the saying goes, "Beggars can't be choosers."

Instead of the majority calling the shots and creating the society we want to see, we find that we are:

- Lessees and renters, forced to pay someone else for the use of land and buildings and limited in what we can do with these.
- Grantees and individuals beholden to donors. We are forced to ask wealthy individuals, foundations, and corporations to pay for education, the arts, food banks, and more. Everything we do is shaped by what our funders want. Instead of using our own resources to implement measures we have decided upon democratically, we are reduced to begging, and we can only do what donors allow.
- Employees with very little say over our jobs and workplaces and beholden to employers for our ability to pay our bills and survive.
- Consumers with little real ability to control the products and services available to us. We consume what others decide to provide, based on their analysis of what will maximize their profits.

Jobs as Extortion. One of the most important tools wealthy individuals and corporations have for controlling our world is their ability to offer and withhold jobs. Having appropriated the profits produced by workers, bought up land and other resources, and used political power to divert public funds to wars and other ventures benefiting private corporations, wealthy interests wield power over jobs. With limited resources and even less political will, governments bend over backward to create "business-friendly" environments, in order to persuade corporations to create or maintain jobs. Individuals and even unions and other organizations we form to represent us increasingly succumb to job extortion, accepting ever worse employment and workplace conditions.

In 2012, for example, Boeing let it be known that it was deciding where to make its new 777X airplane, noting that peak production by 2024 would involve 8500 direct jobs. Boeing said it preferred a location that "will share in the cost of capital expenditures including acquiring site, constructing facility, building infrastructure and procuring equipment/tooling." Among the "desired incentives" sought by Boeing were items like

* "Site at no cost, or very low cost, to project,"
* "Facilities at no cost, or significantly reduced cost,"
* A low tax structure with corporate income tax and other relevant taxes significantly reduced,
* Accelerated permitting, and
* Low overall cost of doing business, including local wages, utility rates, and other expenses.[519]

States from California to Alabama scrambled to persuade Boeing to choose them. Democratic Governor Jay Inslee of Washington State called a special legislative session in which $8.7 billion in tax breaks over 16 years were swiftly approved for Boeing.

Boeing approached its Seattle area workers when they still had three years left to go in their contract which forbade strikes. The company used the threat of making the 777X elsewhere to pressure for major concessions. It asked workers to accept major reductions in pensions and wages for new workers.

Despite pressure from the governor and legislators, the Machinists Union voted two to one in November of 2013 to reject Boeing's proposal. Another election was held in early January of 2014 on a day when many workers were on vacation, however. Fearing the loss of jobs and under pressure to vote yes, in that second election the Boeing workers voted by a narrow margin (51 to 49%) to accept the new contract.[520]

This is just one of countless examples of the extortion that now rules our lives. Ohio residents long for the jobs fracking may provide despite huge environmental and health risks.[521] Townspeople in the "Chemical Valley" of Virginia wish chemical corporation employers would return despite having endured deadly explosions, toxic exposures, and widespread local contamination with dioxin.[522] The CEO of a timeshare resort firm sends a memo to 7000 employees warning that if the presidential candidate he opposes is elected he will "have no choice but to reduce the size of this company."[523]

One of the barriers to criminal prosecutions against polluters is that it's tough to find people willing to testify against their bosses. One EPA investigator who had previously been an investigator with the Drug Enforcement Agency told researchers, "[i]t's at least as hard to flip somebody in a corporation as it is in a Colombian drug cartel, maybe harder." The reason? "It's hard to get somebody to flip against a paycheck."[524]

Despite all the things communities do to entice them to stay, corporations regularly leave. Jobs are offshored from the U.S. and other developed countries to places with lower wages, fewer worker protections, and weaker environmental standards.[525]

In the U.S., manufacturing jobs have been particularly depleted by corporate decisions to move production elsewhere. In June of 1979, 19.5 million people had manufacturing jobs. By December of 2009 that number had shrunk to 11.5 million. Between August 2000 and February 2004, manufacturing jobs were lost for 43 months straight. The number of manufacturing plants has declined sharply along with the number of jobs.[526]

As manufacturing has begun to rebound slightly, the jobs created are non-union. Non-union workers in manufacturing earn salaries that are about 7% lower than union-represented workers in similar jobs.[527]

In general in the U.S., low-wage jobs have replaced middle-income work. Three notoriously low-paying industries—food services, retail, and employment services—account for 43% of all jobs created during the economic recovery, while better-paying jobs have failed to recover. The median retail worker gets $11 per hour, and the median food service worker gets $10 per hour.

Cuts in government jobs are also part of the picture. Lay-offs of teachers and others have lowered the overall average earnings of workers.[528]

In short, corporations hold a lot of power as employers. Lacking control over our workplaces and the wealth our labor produces, we are beholden to corporations who pay our wages or dangle the prospect of future jobs in front of us. The power employers hold over working people is growing as our financial insecurity deepens.

Investment as Extortion. The wealthy play the extortion game at the international level with assistance from ambassadors and other diplomats. Corporations offer countries not only jobs but also the investment and infrastructure that come with them. These are conditioned on accepting concessions like low wages and weaker labor and environmental laws. The U.S. Embassy cables made public by Wikileaks provide documentation of this extortion in country after country.[529]

CHAPTER 17

The Giant Who Calls the Shots

• • •

WE ARE UP AGAINST AN absolute giant. Call it "the 1%", "Big Money," the "super rich" or whatever you like. Whatever name we choose, the giant we face has sucked up most of our wealth. It uses that wealth to manipulate the world around us, leading to policies and programs that serve elite private interests rather than the public good.

The problem is much larger than the ultra wealthy influencing elections and pouring money into lobbying. Big Money manipulates perceptions, shapes what scientific evidence exists, and severely limits public access to vital information. It fosters an extremely narrow script that keeps the real issues and the real solutions off the table and out of the conversation. The bizarre discourse we experienced on farm worker issues in Washington State, in which topics like transitioning farms to organic pest control methods were off-limits, exemplifies what is happening everywhere on environmental issues. Much of the control exerted by the ultra wealthy happens out of sight.

When an elite few control most of the world's productive capacity, financial assets, and natural resources, that leaves the rest of us in a bind. How can we invest in jobs for all, clean energy, sustainable food production, schools, health, cultural programs, and other social needs without controlling the wealth we produce and the resources and information that should belong to all? Attempts to do these things are stymied by the set-up all around us, and victories are small and temporary.

Trying to create the world we want as things stand now is rather like playing the children's board game Chutes and Ladders, with a board that includes lots of chutes and no ladders whatsoever. We do our best, trying to move forward bit by bit, despite the shackles imposed by the unjust system around us. Invariably, just as we think we've made some progress, we land on a chute, and find ourselves swiftly funneled backwards to a lower seat. We may finally pass a law, only to find that it is not implemented, for example. Or it is reversed as the result of a corporate challenge under international trade agreements.

While we may creep forward over and over again, we will never reach the top of the class.

The giant we face is getting bigger and more powerful every day. It is gorging on the wealth we produce, and grabbing more and more of the world's resources. We are losing. Indeed we are moving faster and faster in the wrong direction.

But we don't need to continue on this path. We have the power to defeat the giant and put in place policies and programs that lead to justice and survival. To do that we need to take a look at how we've been fighting back so far. That's what we'll do in Part IV.

PART IV

Not Fighting Back Effectively

• • •

Most people deeply concerned about the environment put their faith in environmental organizations to lead the way forward. There are tens of thousands of these organizations in the U.S. alone and tens of thousands more beyond our borders.[530] As concern for the environment has increased, so have the number of nonprofits with environmental missions. Revenues for nonprofits working on "environment and animals" increased by 76% between 1999 and 2009. Assets increased by 98%.[531]

We give environmental organizations our money and participate in their campaigns. Some of us work as staff and board members. We assume that they are an effective vehicle for winning the environmental policies and programs we so desperately need.

On the whole, however, environmental organizations are not delivering. In fact, many of the strategies and behaviors in which they engage undermine our chances of turning things around. In this section of the book we examine this dynamic.

Chapter 18 looks at how foundations and other funders shape and influence the world of environmental organizations. Chapters 19 through 24 look at common environmental organization behaviors that undermine our struggle for a just and sustainable world. Chapter 25 uses the healthcare debate to demonstrate that the same dynamics at play on environmental issues are at play on other social justice issues as well. Finally, Chapter 26 reviews the big picture of environmental activism as it exists today. It discusses the broader implications of continuing to fight for justice and survival the way we have been fighting so far.

CHAPTER 18

The Influence of Funders

• • •

A REVIEW OF THE WORLD of non-governmental organizations must begin with a look at its funding. Funders greatly influence which groups get to exist and the rules by which they must play. Previously we examined how the ultra rich create front groups whose actual, albeit hidden, mission is advancing private profits. Here we examine an additional way in which Big Money subverts public discourse: influencing the real environmental groups, i.e., organizations truly founded for the purpose of protecting the environment.

FOUNDATION FUNDERS

As individuals and corporations have amassed wealth, they have created foundations in order to store some of that wealth, enjoy tax advantages, and influence society. In 2010 there were over 120,000 private foundations in the U.S. with combined assets of more than $582.5 billion. The total revenue for those foundations that year was over $43.8 billion.[532]

Foundation grants are a major source of funding for many organizations addressing environmental issues. In 2009, by one estimate, U.S. foundations distributed approximately $2.7 billion in environmental funding, representing just over 7% of the total giving by U.S. foundations that year.[533]

WHO DOESN'T GET MONEY

Foundations influence the world of environmental organizations not only by what they fund, but also by what they *don't* fund. Overall foundations systematically exclude certain communities, perspectives, and issues.

Excluding Environmental Justice Communities. When I worked for the Farm Worker Pesticide Project, I was one of only a handful of paid staffers in the U.S. working with farm workers in their struggle against pesticide exposures. I may well have been the only one with the luxury of working *solely* on pesticide issues.

By any measure, farm worker families deserve much more support. Millions of people, including children, are regularly exposed to extremely toxic chemicals. These exposures trigger acute poisonings, and there is strong evidence linking chronic exposures to other serious health problems. Nonetheless, funding is just not there for farm worker environmental organizations.

The farm worker pesticide situation is not an anomaly. It reflects the sorry state of funding for "environmental justice" (EJ) communities in general. "Environmental justice" is the term used to highlight the *injustice* of low-income populations and communities of color bearing disproportionate environmental burdens[534] compared to others.[535] Foundations have acknowledged this reality for decades and much lip service has been paid to the need to direct more funds to those who face the most extreme environmental conditions.

Despite the rhetoric, the statistics on funding remain appalling. According to Northeastern University Sociology Professor Daniel Faber, the environmental justice movement receives only 4% of all foundation grants dedicated to the environment.[536] The numbers may be worse now than they were in 2010 when Faber made his comments. At the end of 2012, for example, the Funding Exchange Board voted to cease all programmatic operations. Funding Exchange was one of the few foundations that put its money where its mouth was by supporting environmental justice groups.[537]

Excluding EJ groups from funding perpetuates the injustice borne by communities forced to breathe factory air, cope with drifting pesticides, drink from contaminated wells, and deal with homes devalued by local contamination. This is wrong in and of itself.

Failing to fund EJ communities also reduces the effectiveness of environmental organizations overall. The conditions endured on the frontlines of environmental issues are the most egregious. They make the most compelling case for reform. EJ groups are also less likely to accept cosmetic changes that don't address the roots of an environmental problem. Living and working where they do, EJ activists see immediately and directly that Band-Aids aren't enough.

Excluding Boat-Rockers. Foundations exclude not only environmental justice groups, but also other groups that might rock the boat. Over 85% of foundation funding to environmental organizations goes to politically moderate groups.[538] According to Professor Faber, most liberal foundations engage in "the philanthropic exclusion and/or marginalization of popular social movements on the Left."[539] When nonprofit advisers urge grant-writers to keep "controversial ideas" out of their proposals, they know what they're talking about.[540]

In general, foundations prefer groups led by professionals over those led by community members without professional degrees. They favor lobbying and litigation over direct-action and grass-roots organizing, single issue approaches over multi-issue ones, and political compromise over principled stances. And as a whole, foundations are not interested in groups seeking to expose and take on the links between environmental degradation, inequality, corporate power, and lack of democracy.

According to Professor Faber, "[t]he impact of this funding pattern is to 'channel' the environmental movement into more moderate discourses and conventional forms of action. This approach also serves to systematically limit the range of progressive viewpoints represented in the public arena, and restrict participation of citizens in their own governments. It is this ideological and class-based affinity on behalf of mainline foundations for single-issue forms of environmental regulatory reform that remains the greatest obstacle to building a Left ecology movement."[541]

Excluding Whole Issues, Elevating Others. As one would expect, foundations only give money for the things they care about. As one grant-writing advice book puts it, "[t]he grantmaker may not—no, almost certainly does not—care what you have in mind, unless it happens to mesh exactly with the terms of the RFP or guidelines" they are issuing.[542]

Some environmental groups actually choose to work on a particular issue because it fits with foundations' priorities, as long as it doesn't conflict with their general mission. Advisors to nonprofits certainly encourage that kind of mindset. "[C]reative fundraising is looking at what's hot and what's not…You should be asking yourselves, 'How can I fit into change without changing my mission?'" offers one funder quoted in an advice book for nonprofit organizations.[543]

Other groups may alter the approach and emphasis for an issue they're already working on to suit a foundation's priorities. An alliance of pesticide groups I was part of invited a guest speaker to one of our strategy sessions to explain how we could frame our efforts as climate action work, for example. Lots of foundations wanted to fund climate action campaigns, and we wanted to get those grants.

Regardless of what groups seeking funds do and don't do, foundations fund the issues they care about, period. Thus, if the foundation world decides that a particular issue is the cat's meow, that issue will get a lot of attention from environmental groups. Other issues will fall by the wayside, no matter how important they may be.

Other Foundation Influences

Foundations also affect the world of environmental organizations in other important ways:

* **Even When They Claim To Support Grassroots Organizing and Movement-Building, Foundations Generally Undercut**

These. Increasingly, for example, foundations give "project support" rather than "general support." This means grantees get money for a specific project and a detailed action plan. Deviating from the plan in response to community desires jeopardizes grant renewals. General support, in contrast, goes to an organization as a whole for whatever it needs. General support lets an organization be nimble and flexible, going with community needs as issues develop.

Groups most committed to grassroots organizing are the least likely to get general support. Two-thirds of 26 grassroots organizations reviewed in a study by the National Committee for Responsive Philanthropy said they did not receive general operating support from foundations. The ten wealthiest conservative advocacy organizations received 90% of their foundation funding as general operating support, while left-leaning organizations received only 16% of their foundation funding as that kind of support.[544]

Foundations are also giving fewer multi-year grants now than they used to. Single-year grants are inconsistent with the idea of slow, patient community organizing efforts. It's hard to show grantors concrete results for such small periods of time, even though the groundwork laid is essential for ultimately achieving real change.

Single-year grants also tighten foundation control over organizations by keeping the threat of non-renewal imminent and constant. Activists are keenly aware that grantors could pull funding in a matter of months if they are not pleased with an organization's activities.

* **Foundations Impose Significant Administrative Burdens on Environmental Organizations, Diverting Time and Energy From Working on the Actual Issues.** Single-year funding exacerbates this problem by making grant proposals and reports due every year instead of every two or three.

Activists regularly find themselves working on a proposal for grant renewal when the grant year has barely begun. This is particularly true for the many foundations that insist upon pre-applications or letters of inquiry well in advance of proposal due dates, which themselves occur long before the foundations make their decisions. For groups unable to pull in large grants from big foundations, just keeping track of multiple small grants with their various project timelines, report deadlines, and renewal requirements is a time-consuming stress-filled nightmare. Because each proposal has been crafted to mesh with a particular foundation's priorities, things become even more difficult to manage. The heavy workload associated with grants diverts energy from the actual work at hand.

* **Foundations Push Environmental Organizations to Act Like Businesses.** Environmental organizations are supposed to champion the public interest, motivated solely by a desire to protect health and the environment. Unlike businesses, they are not supposed to be influenced by or focused upon making money. But as a book on grant-writing emphasizes, "[t]rustees of foundations tend to be businesspeople...."[545] And increasingly, foundations are demanding that environmental organizations think and act like businesses. Experiences like the one the Farm Worker Pesticide Project had with the Kresge Foundation, described in chapter 2, are becoming more and more common.

Many foundations now want to see a potential grantee's "business plan" before deciding whether to "invest" in it. They want to be assured that the organization will put plenty of resources into fundraising and organizational development, preferably hiring professional staff in these areas. This creates pressure on groups to adhere to a fundraising/ development/ business model. One grantmaker had this advice for nonprofits: "Build a development staff and align programs of the organization in an orderly way to secure additional diverse funding."[546]

The emphasis on fundraising and organizational development demanded by foundations is supposed to ensure that organizations live to fight another day. But fundraising and organizational development can become ends in themselves, fundamentally altering organizations and how they behave. This is particularly true as organizations hire more and more staff to focus on funding and development instead of issues and affected communities. Over the course of my career I witnessed an increasing obsession with raising money and an increasing tendency for work on the issues to take a back seat to that.

*   **Foundations Pressure Environmental Organizations to Add Inappropriate Individuals to Their Boards.** By law, the board of directors of an organization is in charge. It hires and fires lead staff, adopts budgets, establishes goals and plans, adopts positions and strategies, and so forth. The board literally determines what an organization does and does not do. It is also privy to confidential discussions and documents.

Given this power, boards should be composed primarily of individuals from the community an organization purports to represent. They should include only those who are committed to the organization's mission and have no financial conflicts of interest.

Even if people representing other interests and views are in the minority on a board, they can significantly undercut an organization. They can block consensus, steer conversations, tell outsiders about organizational plans, and more. Their influence may be particularly large if they are major donors who have the power to suspend donations if decisions don't go their way.

Most foundations do not understand this. They successfully pressure environmental organizations to dilute their power by recruiting inappropriate board members. The Farm Worker Pesticide Project maintained a board composed solely of farm worker community members and true allies. Certain foundation staffers who urged us to invite others to the board were not pleased. Our principled position and ability to resist that pressure was unusual.

Foundations Pressure Environmental Organizations to Collaborate With Polluting Corporations. Many foundations pressure grantees to sit down and negotiate with corporations. They may even set up meetings with polluters and ask grantees to attend. "At Tides Canada we are working to bridge these two polarized camps," said Ross McMillan CEO of Tides Canada Foundation, referring to environmentalists and oil companies.

"Leverage resources—building public-private partnerships," suggested one grant-maker quoted in a grant-writing advice book for nonprofits.[547]

All of these are examples of the ways foundations influence environmental organizations. But the biggest influence of all, of course, is the knowledge that continued funding depends on doing things grantors want and avoiding behaviors and positions they dislike. Fundamentally, by holding the purse strings, foundations exert tremendous control over the campaigns and strategies of the organizations we are depending on for environmental salvation.

Foundations as Government Helpers and Mediators

But there's more. Increasingly, foundations are acting as gatekeepers and moderators between the government and environmentalists. The Bullitt Foundation played this role when EPA asked it to help organize its "public" meeting in Seattle in 1999 shortly before the WTO's arrival, as explained in chapter 2. As another example the Cummings Foundation has from time to time invited activists of its choice to participate in online briefings with Obama Administration officials.[548]

When foundations are used by governments as go-betweens with environmental activists, the resulting pressure on activists is twofold.

If we boycott the process, we may hurt our chances of future funding with the foundation. And if we participate, foundation staff will be watching us, and we will be hesitant to contradict the approach and positions they espouse.

Those who are unknown to funders or disliked by them will not have a seat at the table. The disturbing assumption is that foundations, by virtue of having accumulated wealth, have the right to act as gate-keepers for government access.

GIANT FOUNDATIONS, GIANT INFLUENCE

Some foundations are gigantic. Their influence is gigantic as well.

A prime example is the Bill & Melinda Gates Foundation. As of this writing, it has distributed some $23 billion in grants since 1994. Grants have been made to organizations in all 50 states, the District of Columbia, and more than 100 countries.[549]

In 2011 alone, the Gates Foundation gave away more than $3.2 billion in grants. Its total assets were worth $34.6 billion.[550] The value of its furniture and fixtures was nearly $8 million.[551]

In that year the foundation gave $371,135,000 to agriculture development programs.[552] Clearly, that kind of money has the power to dramatically shape the discussions that occur and the policies and programs that are implemented.

In fact, in December of 2010, 100 organizations and individuals working on agricultural issues sent a letter to the Gates Foundation objecting to the impact the Foundation is having. The letter complained that Gates funding is "heavily distorted in favor of supporting inappropriate high-tech agricultural activities." The Foundation "is mistakenly funding an antiquated thrust to industrialize agriculture in Africa—including chemical fertilizers, pesticides, monocropping of 'improved' and genetically engineered (GE) crop varieties, further deregulation of trade, and regulatory frameworks that will privatize seed—which science and historical precedent indicate will come at the expense of the hungry, small farmers, consumer health, and the environment," the letter said.[553]

The Gates Foundation influences agricultural policies not only by funding nonprofit organizations, but also via a revolving door between the foundation and the corporations and grantees it supports. The 2011 Gates Foundation annual report proudly announced, for example, that their new president of Global Health had previously been the global head of development for Novartis Pharma AG.[554] The financial conflict of interest inherent in his past (and potentially future) connections with a corporation whose profits are affected by international health policies is not even mentioned in the annual report. Agriculture activists have raised concerns about Gates staff members who have connections to corporations and firms promoting genetically modified products.[555]

The Gates Foundation funds not only nonprofits but also key governmental bodies. It is one of the main funders of the World Health Organization (WHO), a United Nations agency focusing on international health, for example. The Foundation's 2010 tax return includes three full pages listing grants provided to WHO and its programs.[556] Many other UN programs besides WHO receive major financial support from the Gates Foundation.

By virtue of wealth alone, Bill Gates receives a bully pulpit from which to put forth his views about the world, complete with huge media coverage whenever he speaks. In his 2012 annual letter on the Foundation's website, Gates jokes about having been invited by French President Sarkozy to write a report for the G20 summit and present it in person. "The organizers weren't even sure what country to put on my badge since I wasn't coming as part of the U.S. official delegation," Gates notes. "They decided to put 'Invitee' on my badge, making me briefly the head of government of Invitee!"[557] While Gates treated this as amusing, there's nothing funny about individuals superseding national governments simply because they are rich. It is not a laughing matter that the ultra rich heavily shape our destiny without any democratic accountability whatsoever.

Wealth as extreme as that controlled by Bill and Melinda Gates creates a bizarre and disturbing dynamic. They can orchestrate entire public debates, pulling the strings for all the main characters. The voices of community groups and organizations with very different perspectives are drowned out by huge, extremely well-funded nonprofits funded by the Gates Foundation. These nonprofits present information and offer their perspective (i.e., the Gates perspective) to governmental bodies, which are themselves recipients of grants from the Foundation. On top of all this, Bill Gates himself—a man who presumably has never experienced real hunger, has no experience as a farmer, and has limited understanding at best of toxic exposure and GMO issues—is the keynote speaker at huge events.

Other wealthy donors are trying to help get the ball across the line on issues they care about, said one panelist at an event examining Gates's philanthropy. Gates, on the other hand, is "creating the ball, building the team, hiring the referees" and "funding the instant replay." Another panelist noted that one day a person might read an article about a Gates-supported health project, printed in a newspaper owned by Gates, reported by a journalist trained by Gates, and citing research by scientists funded by Gates.[558]

While the Gates Foundation is exceptionally powerful, it is by no means the only foundation exerting extreme influence on an issue.[559]

CORPORATE FUNDERS

Corporate giving to environmental organizations generally occurs through foundations that the corporations set up. Those grants are encompassed in the statistics shared in the prior section on foundation funding. But corporate donations to environmental organizations deserve a discussion of their own.

Corporations Make Lots of Donations. Corporate philanthropy is a key component of what is known as "Corporate Social Responsibility" (CSR). As one business analyst put it, "[i]n this day and age, it's no longer necessary to persuade corporations to undertake CSR—it's simply a matter of identifying the most appropriate opportunities."[560]

In fact, in 2011, 82% of companies reported having a corporate foundation. The most common structure was the "pass-through" model, where the company annually funds a foundation that typically distributes 100% of those funds within the year.[561]

A survey in 2011 of 214 corporations, including 62 listed in the top 100 companies on the Fortune 500 list, provides a glimpse of overall corporate donations. In total, survey responders reported giving away more than $100 billion that year.[562] While money donated to non-environmental causes dwarfed amounts given on environmental issues, these other donations are still relevant to environmental activism. Giving money to a school program can affect students' perceptions of environmental issues and discourage criticism of a corporation's environmental record, for instance.

There are other ways to catch a glimpse of corporate donations, such as funding lists sometimes available from specific corporations. According to an ExxonMobil document available online, the corporation and its affiliates gave $7,791,410 worldwide toward "public information and policy research" in 2011, for example. The bulk of that ($7,396,950) went to entities within the United States.[563] ExxonMobil gave $100,000 to the Aspen Institute for a Global Energy Forum in Washington, D.C. as well as $200,000 for other activities. It gave $86,500 to the American Legislative Exchange Council (ALEC), the organization that provides model legislation to undercut environmental protections, discussed in an earlier chapter.[564]

Funding Environmental Groups. Corporations regularly fund front groups that strive to undercut environmental policies and programs in order to maximize corporate profits. But plenty of organizations generally considered "real environmental organizations" take corporate funding as well. Big environmental groups like The Nature Conservancy, World Wildlife Fund, and Conservation International do. Many corporations on "The Toxic 100" list—a list of the worse corporate air polluters compiled annually by the Political Economy Research Institute at the University of Massachusetts—are major contributors to environmental groups. These include ExxonMobil, Dow, General Electric, and others.[565]

All sorts of social justice groups are feeling pressure to seek and accept corporate funding as competition for other funding increases, due to increased numbers of nonprofits and other factors. According to a report on Washington State nonprofits, the percent of organizations in the state obtaining funding from corporations rose from 13% in 2009 to 34% in 2010. Fifty-two percent of the responding nonprofits collaborated with businesses.[566]

Corporate donations to environmental organizations come in different forms. The Sierra Club reportedly accepted a deal with Clorox in 2008, in which the Club received a percentage of sales revenue in exchange for endorsing Clorox's new "green" household cleaners.[567] Outgoing Sierra Club chair Carl Pope, who brokered the Clorox deal, said that it brought the Sierra Club $1.3 million over the four-year term of the contract.[568] The arrangement spurred major objections within the Club and was not renewed.

The anger over Sierra Club's Clorox funding was nothing compared to that triggered by another corporate funding source for the Club. While supporting natural gas drilling as a "bridge" from coal to better energy alternatives between 2007 and 2010, the Sierra Club accepted over $25 million in donations from Aubrey McClendon, CEO of Chesapeake Energy. Chesapeake is one of the biggest gas drilling companies in the U.S. It is heavily involved in fracking. McClendon's donation was listed as "anonymous." Club members were kept in the dark about it until a 2012 article spilled the beans.[569]

The fracking industry has targeted other environmental groups as well. In Pennsylvania, the industry considered providing $30 million for a research project that would be staffed by conservation groups.[570]

Here's another example of corporate funding of an environmental organization. In February of 2001, the National Wildlife Federation (NWF) and BP/Amoco formed a "partnership" involving the sale of stuffed-toy endangered animals, like timber wolves and panda bears, at BP/Amoco gas stations.[571] Brightly colored posters proclaimed "Endangered wildlife friends are here!" and urged people to "Collect All 5—Only $2.99." The logos of both Amoco and NWF appeared on the poster, and the sales helped raise funds for NWF. As part of a special promotion, customers who bought at least eight gallons of BP/Amoco gas would receive one of the stuffed toys, tagged with the NWF logo and bearing the message that fossil-fuel consumption contributes to global climate change.

Interviewed about the partnership, NWF's President of Communications noted that "BP is one of a huge number of partners that we've dealt with….This is a small one compared with others we've done." BP/Amoco got to brand themselves as environmentally sensitive and somehow supportive of endangered animals. NWF got cash and name recognition, too.

The Nature Conservancy regularly accepts huge donations from some of the most polluting corporations in the world, such as Shell Oil[572] and Dow Chemical.[573]

These are innumerable other examples of environmental groups accepting funding from polluting corporations.

Why Do Corporations Give Donations to Environmental Organizations and Others? Advice from PR consultants over the years provides insights.

A leaked document from the 1990s exposed the advice PR consultants were giving corporations on how to neutralize environmental organizations at that time. "Help them raise money….Offer to sit on their board of directors," an expert from the Hill & Knowlton PR firm says. Also consider hiring staff from environmental groups, he adds, noting that they are available "at very reasonable rates."[574]

Today, readily accessible PR firm articles continue to advise corporations to give away money as a strategy for increasing profits. While these articles occasionally include a statement about the nobility of giving, the self-serving thrust of corporate philanthropy is crystal clear. An article entitled "Why Corporate Social Responsibility is so important in 2013" explained that "[p]ublic relations is a potent tool for shaping consumer perception and building a company's image.... Getting the word out about corporate donations, employee volunteer programs, or other CSR initiatives is a powerful branding tool that can build publicity for you in both online and print media...." The article elaborated that "[c]orporations that place an emphasis on corporate social responsibility typically have an easier experience when dealing with politicians and government regulators....The more positive the public perception is that a corporation takes social responsibility seriously, the less likely it is that activist groups will launch public campaigns and demand government inquiries against it."[575]

By making donations to environmental groups, corporations gain lots of benefits:

* <u>They can directly influence an organization's agenda, positions, strategies, and tactics.</u> A Sierra Club leader claimed that the millions of dollars donated by a fracking corporation CEO had come with no strings attached and didn't impact the Club's positions on natural gas.[576] The Club's own report on oil and gas industry campaign contributions and other expenditures influencing government noted that "savvy givers don't give money for nothing," however.[577]

* <u>They receive lots of publicity, getting the corporate name out there in general.</u>

* <u>The publicity gives them an image of benign, selfless generosity.</u> Instead of being seen as profit-seeking private entities, they are seen as organizations motivated by the public interest.

    This positive trust-inspiring image arises not only from corporations making donations but also from environmental organizations accepting them. By taking the money, those organizations put the imprimatur of public interest on private corporations. They also create confusion about environmental issues, further advancing corporate interests. It is difficult to think of anything that could create more confusion than environmental groups and oil companies distributing cute stuffed animals together at gas stations.

In gratitude for funding, environmental groups sometimes go even further than simply linking their green karma to polluting corporations. The Nature Conservancy gave Shell "a conservation leadership award" only a few years after the Nigerian government executed Ken Saro-Wiwa and other environmental activists. Shell had a close relationship with that government. Many felt the corporation could have prevented the executions. Despite its destructive products, poor environmental record, and close ties to violent dictators, Shell received an award that cast it as an environmental hero.

* Those accepting corporate funding are reluctant to criticize their funders. This is the case whether or not the fund recipient works for the environment or on other social justice causes. Indeed, grants to groups focusing on hunger, domestic violence, and other issues help divide social justice activists from one another. Those taking money from corporations look away from those corporations' records. They may even speak proactively in support of their corporate donors.

* The noble, generous image fostered by corporate philanthropy buys assistance and cooperation from elected officials.

OTHER FUNDING SOURCES

Environmental organizations can also receive grants from government agencies. These generally come with major strings attached. Often recipients can't sue the government, they can't use funds for involvement in government rulemakings, and they must establish partnerships with the very corporations they're fighting.

Other sources of funding include memberships, events, individual donors giving small amounts of money, and product sales. Chasing big grant and donation checks remains extremely important for most organizations, however.

Statistics regarding money given to nonprofits by individuals are quite interesting. Traditionally, middle-class and lower-income people have contributed far more to nonprofits than wealthy individuals. While the growing gap between rich and poor has shifted things a bit, the majority of individual donation income in the nonprofit world still comes from middle- and lower-income folks.[578] This is one of the reasons for hope that we'll discuss later in the book.

The World of Environmental Organizations—Shaped by Big Money

There is an irony underlying the phenomenon of wealthy individuals and entities giving large donations and grants. "Big Philanthropy" is only *possible* because money has accumulated in the hands of a very limited number of individuals and corporations. It is also only *necessary* for the same reason. If the wealth hoarded by a few belonged to society as a whole instead, working people could have what we need without begging others for help.

Understanding this is a crucial part of figuring out our path forward to a sustainable and just world.

Some day people will look back at our current era and marvel at the bizarre situation we accept as normal. Wealth produced by working people goes not to those who produce it but to a dwindling number of individuals and corporations. Those ultra-wealthy entities use the money they've amassed to establish policies and programs that further increase their holdings and power. At the same time, they serve as primary funders for the groups we count on to fight for the public interest. What a strange and dysfunctional arrangement.

CHAPTER 19

Self-Defeating Behaviors: An Overview

• • •

WITH SO MANY ENVIRONMENTAL ORGANIZATIONS in the world, why are we still losing? The answer lies in the self-defeating behaviors that permeate those organizations. The next several chapters describe these behaviors.

We've already discussed one of the reasons self-defeating behaviors are so dominant. Wealthy interests determine which groups are raised up and influence what those groups do.

But other factors are in play as well. Advice from nonprofit consultants reinforces the self-limiting mindsets fostered by funders. PR strategies implemented on behalf of wealthy corporations flood society with messages that promote those mindsets as well, influencing environmental activists whether we realize it or not.

Meanwhile, activists hooking up with environmental groups tend to assume that how things are done is, well, how things are done. Moreover, they soon become so swamped that it's hard to come up for air, let alone meaningfully evaluate whether we're on the right course or not.

I know from my decades working with environmental groups that they are populated by some of the most brilliant, compassionate, and committed people on the planet. Nevertheless, overall, those groups are holding us back despite the hard work and best intentions of staff, volunteers, and other supporters. I offer these observations about what we're doing wrong with love, and in the hope that this much-needed assessment will help us find the way forward in time.

CHAPTER 20

The First Three Behaviors

• • •

PROBLEMATIC BEHAVIOR NUMBER 1
NOT TAKING ON THE GIANT

WE'VE SEEN THAT THE GAME is rigged. No matter how hard we try, we can't make real headway.

Ignoring the giant that stands between us and the world we long to create dooms us to failure. Yet that is precisely what most environmental groups do. We just keep plodding along, playing with a deck that is stacked against us. We don't talk about the fact that we can't win. We don't adopt positions and launch campaigns to change that reality.

A few groups do acknowledge that Big Money influences elections and legislation. They spotlight campaign donations and lobbying expenditures, hoping to trigger public outrage that will outweigh the power of moneyed interests. One problem with this strategy is that both the Democratic and the Republican parties are awash with donations from the wealthy few, and most people know this already. Most are also aware of the mega bucks spent on lobbying by rich corporations and individuals each year. Spotlighting additional examples just adds to the sense of powerlessness many feel. *So and so accepted oil and gas money just like most elected officials did? Ho hum. What else is new? And what difference will it make to get riled up about this latest example of the legalized bribery that envelops our entire system?*

Some groups have endorsed Move to Amend, a national effort to amend the U.S. Constitution "to firmly establish that money is not speech, and that human beings, not corporations, are persons entitled to constitutional rights." The Sierra Club did so in January of 2012, for instance.[579] Most environmental organizations have not taken even this step, however. Moreover, as we will see later, the proposed constitutional amendment fails to truly take on the forces that disempower us, and it may even provide those forces with additional tools to use against us.

For the most part, environmental organizations just keep on keeping on. While some individuals bemoan our disempowerment, serious focused organizational discussions about what to do about it are not happening. Some of the other problematic behaviors listed below flow from this fundamental failure.

PROBLEMATIC BEHAVIOR NUMBER 2
WORKING IN SILOS

As we plod along with our particular environmental campaigns, not mentioning the giant we're up against and not discussing how to overcome it, we are also largely oblivious to other activists struggling all around us. We wear blinders, believing that focusing solely on our narrow task is a virtue, when it is actually a huge mistake.

In particular, we are almost entirely disconnected from those taking on non-environmental issues. We fail to recognize the connections between those issues and our own.

Let's look at one non-environmental issue and see how this dramatically affects our ability to win environmental reforms: national economic policies.

- As we examined in Part III of this book, economic policies that enrich the few have given them the power to call the shots. They can buy elections and much more.
- At the same time policies that impoverish people leave them little time for participating in environmental campaigns. Nor are people trying to make ends meet likely to prioritize those

campaigns. And those counting pennies are generally unable to participate in consumer pressure campaigns because they can't afford more expensive sustainable products and services.

*   Policies that leave corporations in charge of employment give them the power to extort. Some people vocally support environmentally degrading industries in exchange for the promise of jobs. Others simply remain silent about environmental problems created by local employers.

Despite these major connections, environmental organizations as a whole ignore the growing poverty all around us, the growing gap between rich and poor, and the economic policies associated with these realities. We act as if these things are irrelevant to environmental efforts, but they're not.

Immigration issues provide another example of how "non-environmental" struggles dramatically affect campaigns for environmental reform. How can we win strong environmental policies when a significant portion of the population, including people who bear the brunt of toxic chemical exposures in their workplaces and communities, face reprisals for speaking up and cannot even vote? Yet, most environmental organizations never discuss immigration policies, the underclass of non-citizens they create, and how these impact our work.

What about war and the bloated military budget? Is that on environmental organizations' radar screens? No, these issues are generally ignored as well, even as we are told that there is no money for vital environmental programs.

By failing to link with people working on other issues we ignore factors that directly undercut our chances of success on environmental campaigns. But just as importantly, we fail to see the opportunity for addressing the roots of our overall disempowerment. Those who focus on promoting peace, human rights, equitable wages, health care for all, and other social justice reforms are losing to the same giant that blocks us on environmental issues. Together we can defeat that giant.

Unfortunately, as we toil in our environmental silos, we not only fail to make use of shared interests with other justice movements. We also often aggressively undermine those other movements. Environmental awards given to corporations with horrendous labor practices and human rights records are just one example. They hurt other important causes and create divisions when we need to be uniting.

Our lack of communication with other justice activists also means that *their* actions can directly undercut *our* campaigns. Poverty groups accepting funding from major polluters and issuing statements praising those corporations as good neighbors is a case in point.

By focusing solely on our narrow campaigns, environmental organizations end up in a competitive posture vis-à-vis other organizations. We compete with them for members, donations, grants, media attention, governmental funds, legislative attention, public participation in our campaigns, and more. This makes no sense given the fact that the multiple injustices and threats addressed by social justice groups are all interconnected. And each is critically important. Only by leaving our silos and working together can we build the world we want.

Problematic Behavior Number 3
Focusing Unduly on Money and Acting like Businesses

Earlier we examined the pressure funders and consultants exert on environmental groups to focus on fundraising and behave like businesses. The Alliance for Nonprofits Washington says that the business model is "at the heart of successful management" for nonprofits, for example. Revenue streams and assets are key factors in that model, according to the Alliance.[580]

Unfortunately, many environmental groups are succumbing to this pressure. They focus excessively on money and they act like businesses, thereby greatly undercutting us all.

Diverting Time and Energy from Organizing. In general environmental groups spend far too much time preparing grant proposals, funder updates, business plans, and the like.[581] These burdens are exacerbated by the fact that there is now more competition for fewer funds. Foundations have lost money, the number of organizations seeking funds has grown, and nonprofits now provide basic services formerly provided by governments.[582] Some experts say that groups are doing well if they receive one grant for every ten applications they submit. Most foundations and government grantors reject 80 to 90% of the applications they receive.[583]

Fundraising is supposed to enable organizations to do their work, but it can end up undercutting that work in important ways. Yes, development staffers bring in money but they also spend a lot of it and sometimes the net gain for actual issues work is questionable. Moreover, fundraisers regularly pull other staff away from the work they should be doing to help on fundraising efforts. They also pressure organizations to moderate their positions, messages and tactics in order to please funders.

Disconnected Professional Staff and the Revolving Door. In the past, environmental organizations generally employed individuals deeply moved by an environmental problem. Now, increasingly, as the business model has taken hold, they employ professionals without personal connections to the issues addressed. Development staffers may be trained in raising money for anyone and anything. They may work for an environmental organization for a while and then move on to a better position.

Increasingly, executive directors at environmental groups receive substantial compensation, including six-digit salaries and, in some cases, extraordinary benefits packages. There is a huge and growing gap between what top employees at environmental groups earn and what others on staff earn. This mirrors and contributes to the very inequity that subverts democracy and fosters environmental degradation in our world.

A Revolving Door stands between environmental groups on the one hand and for-profit corporations and their consulting firms on the other. The former executive director of the Washington Conservation Voters, for example, showed up as a public relations firm spokesperson promoting a new coal terminal in Longview, Washington, as I worked on this book.[584] Similarly, Mark Tercek, President and CEO of The Nature Conservancy (TNC), was an investment banker for two decades. His banking career included a stint heading up Goldman Sach's environmental strategy. At TNC, Tercek has emphasized market strategies consistent with his background.[585]

Benefiting from high salaries, viewing their positions as career stepping stones, and being aware of future opportunities in corporations and government can lead top environmental staffers to steer their organizations away from actions they should be taking. Issues are handled as abstract matters to be addressed using models that can be applied to any business. As outsiders not grounded in issues and communities, environmental group executives often just "don't get it." They aren't moved by the impacts their compromises have on environmental issues and the communities affected by them.

Focusing on Rich People. People working for environmental organizations spend a lot of time seeking and hanging out with those who have money to give away. They take to heart advice like that offered by the book *Fundraising for Dummies*, which encourages sleuthing to identify potential donors and hanging out at locales frequented by rich people. "Certain places in your community are equated with a certain status," the book notes.[586] Special attention should be paid to nurturing big donors because they are "primary stakeholders." The "Holy Grail" of fundraising is the major gift.[587]

"Meeting your donors' expectations" gets its own section in this book, which suggests "peer-to-peer contact" for approaching major givers. "If Joe is the president of a local bank, prepare and send your board president, a company CEO, or a board member who is similar in professional and social standing."[588]

Environmental organizations are bombarded with offers of assistance in reaching wealthy donors. One consulting group offered to help the Farm Worker Pesticide Project build deeper relationships with donors for $55 per month.[589] Another group offered us information on "Wealth Screened Decision Makers." With a 60% discount, it would cost $3500 to receive a list of 60,000 wealth-screened individuals, who were owners, directors, and CEOs at large and medium U.S. organizations.[590,]

These services exist because there is a market for them. Nonprofits are working hard to find and court rich people. This takes time away from hanging out with the communities we are supposed to be serving. Instead of focusing on how to make the victims of environmental injustice heard, activists hobnob with those who already dominate public discourse by virtue of their wealth.

Putting Rich People and Corporate Representatives on Boards. Vast numbers of environmental groups appoint people to their boards who should not be there.[591] All sorts of corporate representatives, foundation staffers and investors serve on environmental groups' boards. It is difficult to find individuals who are among the 48% of Americans considered low income or living below the poverty line.

This behavior hands authority over our positions and strategies to those who have a vested interest in maintaining the economic status quo.

Seeking Corporate Funding and Collaborating with Corporations. Environmental groups also regularly accept funding from corporations that hurt our environment, as already examined in a prior chapter. This gives those corporations undeserved green credibility, creates confusion about what's happening in the world, and otherwise undercuts the environmental movement.

Nonprofit advisers join funders in urging environmental groups to get chummy with the very corporations we're fighting. In fact, business donors are suggested as a good place for small organizations to *start* when seeking funding. "If you can show how a grant to your organization will bring broad recognition or publicity to the [business] donor" that will please them,[592] suggests *Fundraising for Dummies*. Concepts like financial conflicts of interest and not wanting to help polluters "greenwash" their images are not mentioned.

The book points out that by courting corporate funders, you may not only get funding from the corporation itself. You'll also connect with wealthy company executives.[593] With enough effort, any organization can find "the perfect company" to take money from, readers are assured. "Remember that with a corporation (as with every donor, but even more so with a corporation), giving is an exchange—something for something," the authors note, apparently oblivious to the disturbing implications of this statement. "Corporations want to get something out of the relationship, so consider what you have to offer and who may want to 'buy' what you have," the book continues.[594] As "logical" corporate connections, it lists a pharmaceutical company funding a community clinic, and "the large smelting plant that used to have issues with polluting the air" giving money "to fund an environmental study."[595]

Funders and nonprofit advisers also urge nonprofit organizations to engage in broader "collaborations" with corporations. *The Only Grant-Writing Book You'll Ever Need*, like many other advice books, strongly recommends forming collaboratives that include for-profit corporations. True collaboration means "leaving a lot of baggage at the door," the book notes. One must come to the table committed to finding the best possible solution to the problem, even if that solution doesn't necessarily benefit everyone.[596]

Why exactly must we limit what we seek to only those things that private corporations with financial conflicts of interest will agree to? The book doesn't explore that topic. It simply asserts that we should voluntarily limit our goals and expectations and spend our time in "collaborative" meetings, as opposed to exerting the authority we should have in a democracy. We've already seen how the nice-sounding word "collaboration" masks dynamics that disempower us, and we will return to this topic later in the book again.

Large numbers of environmental groups accept corporate money and enter into collaborations with polluting corporations. "Almost all the major environmental groups are now engaged in some way with corporations," says a spokesperson for Environmental Defense Fund, an organization known for collaborating with industry. "That just wasn't the case fifteen years ago."[597]

Seeking Government Funding. In chapter 18 we identified some of the major limitations placed on organizations with respect to using funds received from governments. Environmental organizations regularly go after government funds despite this censorship.

Accepting Tax Status Limits on Organizational Activities. To be eligible for most grants and to provide donors the incentive of a tax deduction, many organizations apply for tax-exempt status under section 501(c)(3) of the Internal Revenue Code. This greatly limits what they can do. Lobbying cannot be a substantial part of their efforts. Nor can 501(c)(3) organizations endorse candidates or otherwise participate in political campaigns. Receiving 501(c)(3) tax status engenders timidity in environmental organizations as staffers worry about exceeding lobbying limits or being seen as having taken a political position, even when the circumstances demand that people speak up.

Adjusting Organizational Messages and Activities in Order to Build a "Brand." A key business model concept that permeates environmental organizations is that of building an organizational "brand". A large section of the book *Fundraising for Dummies* is dedicated to "Telling Your Story and Building Your Brand." The Alliance for Nonprofits Washington remarks that "some of the strongest and best-recognized brands" in the nonprofit world are built on sturdy nonprofit business models.[598]

In a nutshell, a "brand" is how an organization is perceived. Nonprofit advisers suggest a five-step brand development process: 1) Analyze strengths, weaknesses, opportunities and threats for the organization, 2) Review these to identify brand messaging opportunities, 3) Determine what your audience wants or needs to hear by surveying a representative subsection of it or conducting a focus group, 4) Create a "messaging package," and 5) Go back to the focus group to see how they react to that package.[599]

The messaging package is composed of things like a tagline, a positioning statement, supporting statements, and a logo. Its purpose is to help people in an organization "stay on message" whenever they communicate information to others.

Requiring everyone to stick to a focus-group-generated message is one of the ways that behaving like a business conflicts with grassroots organizing. Public-interest group reps start acting like politicians, deftly turning everything into a chance to repeat well-practiced talking points. Even if the facts on the ground cry out for honest reactions that go "off message", they stick to the script. Branding discourages conversations that are organic and real.

By playing the messaging and branding game, environmental organizations lose their authenticity. They tend toward vagueness so as to not risk accidentally going outside allowed boundaries. They lose their principles. Moreover, since only things that generate positive reactions in audiences will generally be worked into brands and messages, branding makes it difficult for environmental organizations to tell the truth about disturbing facts. It contributes to keeping supporters and the general public in the dark about what's really going on and what we really need to do in response.

Building Organizations, Undercutting Movements. Nonprofit advisors warn that there are not enough funds to go around. They claim to be able to give select groups an edge that assures them a bigger piece of the funding pie. An outfit called Guidestar invited the Farm Worker Pesticide Project to participate in an online development training that "helps organizations thrive, while others struggle to survive," for example.

Messages like these promote a competitive mindset. *Don't worry about other groups and the work they do that may fall by the wayside. Don't ask why there is such a need for non-governmental organizations to address societal problems. Don't think about how your work is entwined with that of all justice activists and how you all need to defeat the same giant. Go for the money for your own group and don't look back! Focus on yourself and on rising above the fray.* The business model divides people when we need to be united.

Having a "brand" is all about standing out so "consumers" will flock to our particular product or service instead of someone else's. But the idea of having something to sell makes no sense for groups promoting fundamental change. What we're fighting for is not ours to sell. It belongs to everyone and will only be achieved when we work together. Carving up the vision we all share so individual organizations can hawk pieces as their own is fundamentally at odds with what we need to be doing.

In fact, striving to stand out in order to grab more funds at the expense of others imposes upon the environmental movement the very mindset that made the movement necessary in the first place.

Environmental groups came into existence to counter environmental degradation. Originally there was no assumption of organizational permanency. Now many organizations treat ensuring their own perpetual existence as a top priority.

It is true that most environmental problems are entrenched and solving them may take time. The paradox, however, is that a mindset of organizational permanence leads to a focus on how to build and sustain organizations. This alters what they are willing to do because everything is run through a screen related to how it affects longevity. The bold actions we need have trouble getting through that screen.

Moreover, by embracing an approach of incremental change slowly unfolding over time, organizations discourage the appropriate urgency people should feel looking at the environmental problems we face. They funnel justified public outrage into timid ineffective strategies that perpetuate individual organizations but endanger our species. With time running out on various crucial fronts, focusing on organizational longevity doesn't make sense. We need to secure major changes *now* to have any chance of turning things around.

Many have remarked that it is getting harder and harder to tell the nonprofit world from the for-profit world, as if this were a good thing.

"[T]he lines that divide the business, government, and charitable sectors are blurring," exults a July 2007 prologue to the book *Forces For Good*.[600] Referring to a nonprofit that licenses its logo for use on bottles of California wine, the book approvingly quotes the nonprofit's founder as saying, "It's no different than Disney licensing *Lion King* merchandise to Burger King."[601]

But the transformation of environmental organizations into entities that act like businesses is not something to celebrate. It has everything to do with why we are moving ever faster toward an abyss instead of building the movement we need to turn things around.

CHAPTER 21

Problematic Behavior Number 4
Tactical Errors

• • •

OVERALL, ENVIRONMENTAL GROUPS AREN'T MAKING wise decisions about which tactics to use and how to use them. This chapter explores available tactics, their limitations and potentials, and whether and how they should be used. It provides examples of the tactical errors that are common at environmental groups.

If a tactic reinforces the undemocratic system that disempowers us, using it is generally a bad idea, even if short-term gains are possible. Yet, many groups rely on these sorts of tactics, as will be examined below. They are not securing meaningful and lasting victories. Worse, they are sowing confusion and reinforcing the system that keeps us down.

Other tactics *are* consistent with democracy, even though they won't get us far in the current rigged game we're in. Relying on them can be okay if we're honest about their limitations and use them to build the movement for systemic change. Unfortunately, most environmental groups fail to tell the truth about what can and cannot be achieved. They urge people to join in, pretending that significant policy reforms will result. This fosters confusion precisely when we need clarity.

LOBBYING

Environmental organizations spend a lot of time and money trying to get good laws and regulations adopted. They meet with government officials, submit written comments, testify at hearings, mobilize people to contact their legislators, and engage in all sorts of other activities.

In the face of Big Money forces detailed earlier in the book, however, lobbying ultimately can't get us much. We almost always come out of lobbying campaigns with watered-down bills and rules or with nothing at all. Often the price of one step forward is two steps backward. Moreover, the benefits we think we've won may never even be realized, given the power the wealthy few have over implementation and enforcement.

Given the huge resources needed to advance even a weak bill or rule, environmental groups can take on only a few lobbying battles at a time. Thus, even if individual lobbying campaigns produce good policies that are actually implemented, we still lose on a huge array of other important issues.

In a world beyond inequality, we will have the power to adopt laws and rules that promote the public good rather than private profits. Right now, however, lobbying uses vast resources with little chance of delivering meaningful policy victories.

Environmental groups generally don't acknowledge the limits on what lobbying can achieve. By repeatedly mobilizing people to lobby, without articulating the broader picture, they create the misimpression that lobbying works. This diverts energy from more effective strategies and from building a movement for real change.

STAKEHOLDER CONSENSUS GROUPS

There is no end to the opportunities environmental organizations have to serve on stakeholder committees convened to seek consensus on this or that environmental matter. The Washington State Department of Agriculture workgroup on pesticide issues described in chapter 2 is one of countless examples.

"Stakeholders" are those organizations and individuals that a government agency or other administrative authority believes represent the key parties affected by a particular issue. The corporations that are causing an environmental problem are always considered stakeholders. Therein lies a key reason that participating in these consensus-based meetings is a bad idea.

Even if public-interest representatives were to dominate a stakeholder group, a single corporate participant could block consensus regarding environmental protections. Of course, in reality, public-interest dominance on these committees is extremely rare. Usually, one or two environmental advocates struggle to be heard amidst a room full of people representing corporate interests. Even the topics up for discussion are narrowly limited by group participants whose profits are at stake.

Government agencies sometimes sponsor stakeholder groups without stipulating that they will only act on things for which consensus can be reached. But even without such a clear stipulation, the mindset is often one of encouraging consensus and selecting discussion topics based on the narrow parameters that parties they're supposed to be regulating will tolerate.

Environmental groups regularly send people to participate in stakeholder groups. This wastes a lot of time and money. It also validates the notion that those with financial conflicts of interests can and should steer public policies. It implies that the best we can do is try to reason with them and hope they'll do what we want. Reliance on this tactic is not only ineffective but also self-defeating with respect to our efforts to gain the power that should be ours.

NEGOTIATING WITH INDIVIDUAL CORPORATIONS

Some organizations choose to work with a particular corporation collaboratively, hoping to persuade it to change its behaviors.

Environmental Defense Fund (EDF) and Walmart have had a collaborative relationship for many years, for example. "We're working with the world's largest retailer to measurably reduce the environmental impacts of its operations and products," EDF's website declares.[602]

Walmart's annual Global Responsibility Report paints a picture of a caring organization doing more and more for the environment each year. EDF solidifies this image by regularly praising the corporation's supposed green leadership.[603]

Does Walmart deserve the green image it has cultivated? Absolutely not. Take the issue of garbage. Walmart makes much of the fact that its stores produce less trash than they used to, but Walmart still remains a major force increasing the generation of garbage in our world. "Walmart's price pressure on manufacturers is undermining the durability and quality of products, which has contributed to a sharp increase in how much Americans buy and how much we discard," explains Stacy Mitchell, of the Institute for Local Self-Reliance. "The majority of what the company does is designed to accelerate consumption."[604]

Peeling back the hype about Walmart's environmental leadership on other fronts, we find similar disappointing realities. After Walmart made a big splash about selling organic foods, the watchdog group Cornucopia Institute investigated its stores around the country and discovered "widespread problems with signage misrepresenting nonorganic food as organic,"[605] for example.

EDF is quick to defend Walmart when supposed gains are questioned. In response to people pointing out Walmart's role as a global garbage creator, an EDF spokesperson said that "a retail model in this country, starting back in the '50s, was planned obsolescence and increased consumption, so I don't think you can lay the burden on Walmart."[606] In other words, *all* the big corporations follow this unsustainable planet-destroying strategy, so you can't criticize Walmart for it.

A conversation about the enormous power and devastating impacts of huge corporations is precisely the conversation we need to be having. Steeped in the mindset of collaboration, EDF is discouraging this essential conversation. It is pretending that the way things are currently set up is an immutable reality that cannot be changed. All we can do is chip away at a superficial level, helping big corporations make cosmetic changes while their entire thrust is destroying the world around us.

Walmart has a terrible record on other social justice issues too. It is known for its low wages, finding ways to avoid paying benefits, and fostering extremely bad working conditions in factories where its products are made. Walmart has obstructed efforts to make factories safer, even in the wake of the horrific collapse of a Bangladeshi clothes factory in 2013 that killed over 1100 workers. "Walmart is the king of discount retail," said Scott Nova, Executive Director of the Worker Rights Consortium. "They also enjoy royal status when it comes to empty promises about the rights and safety of workers in their supplier chain."[607]

Despite its horrendous record, Walmart's strategy of adopting new "sustainability" initiatives blessed by groups like EDF has paid off for the corporation. About a quarter of Americans now have a favorable impression of Walmart, which is about double what the percentage was in 2007. This has made it easier to build new stores.

EDF emphasizes that it does not accept contributions from Walmart, but that statement is misleading. EDF has received over $66 million from the Walton Family Foundation. The Waltons are the children and grandchildren of Walmart founder Sam Walton. They control Walmart. As of late 2013, they owned over half of Walmart's stock and had several seats on its board, including the chair.[608]

The limitations of collaborating with corporations in an attempt to reduce the harm they do are apparent from the EDF-Walmart example. Collaboration generally yields superficial changes at best, despite the substantial resources and time groups put into it.

Author Paul Hawken warns that claims of social responsibility create illusions that keep society from recognizing and coming to grips with the dangers we face. "If every company on the planet were to adopt the best environmental practices of the 'leading' companies—say, Ben & Jerry's, Patagonia, or 3M—the world would still be moving toward sure degradation and collapse," he notes. With corporations like Monsanto proclaiming their credentials as members of Business for Social Responsibility (BSR), the designation has become meaningless.[609]

By praising corporations for tiny environmental advances, we also undercut those fighting for justice on other fronts. To applaud Walmart, even as it blocks efforts to make factories in Bangladesh safer, is to undercut the connections environmentalists should be making with other social justice groups.

Even the tiny steps forward we believe we've won through collaborating with a corporation may not be real. For example, when a corporation saves money through energy efficiency—the "win-win" everyone is looking for—this actually backfires on us. The savings are channeled into increased production, and therefore increased energy use and pollution. "This backfiring is known as the Jevons Paradox—a concept forged in the mid-nineteenth century by the economist William Stanley Jevons—whereby greater efficiencies lead to greater resource use rather than less," explains author Heather Rogers. She quotes Wes Jackson, a plant geneticist and president of the Land Institute: "When the Walmarts of the world say they're going to put in different lightbulbs and get their trucks to get by on half the fuel, what are they going to do with the savings? They're going to open up another box store somewhere. It's nuts."[610]

The larger problem with collaborating with individual industries to encourage them to protect the environment is this: it implies that our proper role is that of a supplicant, asking a corporation to please hurt our environment less. It embraces an arrangement wherein we hope that those in power will do what we want, when we should instead hold the power and make the decisions ourselves.

Numerous prominent environmental groups use the ineffective and harmful tactic of collaborating with corporations and praising them for supposed environmental advances. This is undercutting us in multiple ways. It sends a message that is confusing and disempowering.

POLLUTION OFFSET AND TRADING SCHEMES

Some environmental organizations advocate programs that enable certain polluting activities to continue in exchange for promised pollution reductions elsewhere. The theory behind these programs is that they will reduce pollution overall while giving corporations flexibility and cost savings.

In reality, offset and trading schemes can create the impression that overall emissions are going down when they're not:

- A California program let major stationary sources get around limits on sulfur dioxide (SO2) and nitrogen oxide (NOx) emissions by paying owners of old, polluting cars to take them off the road. Unfortunately many of the vehicle owners scrapped their cars but transferred the dirty engines into other vehicles.[611]

- The British rock band Coldplay paid nearly $50,000 through an offsetting firm for 10,000 mango trees to be planted in India. The carbon dioxide stored in these trees was supposed to offset carbon emissions associated with producing one of Coldplay's albums. An investigation revealed, however, that the forest project was poorly implemented and fell dramatically short of its clean air objectives.[612]

- The Reducing Emissions from Deforestation and Forest Degradation (REDD) program is supposed to reduce overall carbon emissions by letting polluters fund projects that protect forests from logging. There have been significant problems with the program, however.

    Working with The Nature Conservancy, for example, British Petroleum, PacifiCorp, and American Electric Power made arrangements to protect 3.9 million acres of tropical forests in Bolivia from logging, which was supposed to keep 55 million tons of CO2 out of the atmosphere. This was used to justify an extra 55 million tons of emissions from the corporations' coal and oil operations. Some logging companies simply moved to another rainforest to keep cutting. In the end, the project kept only 5.8 million tons or less of CO2 out of the atmosphere—a tenth of what had been projected.[613]

Offsetting proponents say they're working to prevent such outcomes in the future, but accurate tracking is a daunting task. Even if loggers don't shift operations to another forest, how can we possibly guarantee that protected trees will stand for centuries and beyond? That's how long the extra carbon spewed into the atmosphere as a result of the offset deal will heat the planet.

● Nineteen manufacturers of coolant gas have profited handsomely from selling credits they receive for destroying waste gas under a United Nations carbon-trading program. To ensure a steady income stream, however, the plants have *boosted* their production of waste gases in order to destroy them and cash in on the credits. "I was a climate negotiator, and no one had this in mind," said David Doniger of NRDC.

Supposed reductions from waste gas destruction were not real given the boosted production of those gases. The 19 plants also invested profits they made through emissions trading to keep the price of coolant gas low. This discouraged air-conditioning companies from switching to less-damaging alternatives.[614]

Credits for destroying waste gas have reportedly been the most common type of credit in the UN system. Since the UN program began, 46% of all credits have been awarded to the 19 coolant factories.[615]

Even in the absence of fake offsets, pollution trading may be less effective than other pollution reduction programs. Yes, U.S. SO2 emissions reportedly dropped by 31% between 1990 and 2001 under an emissions trading program. But over the same period, Germany used traditional regulations to reduce its SO2 emissions by 87%. Italy dropped its emissions by 62% and Western Europe as a whole dropped its emissions by 57% using traditional regulation. Western Europe and individual countries within it had far better results than the U.S. in both absolute and per capita terms.[616]

Pollution trading can exacerbate the disproportionate burdens of environmental degradation already borne by low-income communities. The California trading program based on scrapping old cars reportedly led to toxic hot spots in low-income areas near facilities that bought permission to pollute at higher levels, for instance.[617]

Pollution trading sets up yet another playing field for the same financiers and Wall Street traders whose actions have triggered global financial crises. As of 2008, emissions trading programs were driving a booming $5 billion-a-year global carbon trading business.[618] Remember how Wall Street financiers didn't hesitate to create and sell "toxic" financial products? The same sort of shenanigans can occur with the *literally* toxic products involved in pollution trading programs. A *New York Times* article in August of 2012 described a convoluted drama playing out with the credits owned by the 19 companies that created gas in order to profit by destroying it. Those companies apparently stand to earn huge sums of money from the credits they hold, even though the "credits" have nothing to do with reducing pollution.[619]

The worst thing about pollution trading and offset schemes is that they contradict the mindset we need to truly protect our environment and our lives. We should minimize pollution *everywhere* as a matter of course. We should both plant trees *and* halt carbon emissions. Instead, pollution trading and offset schemes create a "right to pollute"—a right that can be bought and sold.

Unfortunately, some well-funded environmental groups are promoting pollution trading and offset schemes, even though these are ineffective, create confusion, exacerbate environmental injustice, and enshrine the right to pollute. This tactic is a prime example of one that has no place in our strategies.

Urging Individuals to Change Personal Behaviors

Many groups put resources into encouraging people to take the bus, buy organic food, buy non-toxic products for home and garden, install solar panels, and otherwise tread lightly on the Earth.[620]

Many factors limit the impact that campaigns of this type can have. Here are a few:

A lot of people don't have enough time and money to make green choices. Organic food and green household products are often out of people's price range. Public transit systems are so bad in most places that people have to drive to get where they need to go. And forget about a substantial proportion of the population putting solar panels on the roof. Even if people actually own their home—something that is not the case for many—the expenditure is simply out of the question.

If alternatives are not available, people can't choose them. The selection of sustainably produced products is generally quite limited for most people.

Often it is extremely difficult to determine which item is environmentally preferable to the others. Information may be completely missing regarding product ingredients, and even if you know the ingredients, you still have to figure out what each one means. That's where groups like the Washington Toxics Coalition play a role, but there are only so many products they can evaluate among the tens of thousands out there and new products springing up all the time.

Labeling doesn't make environmentally sound choices clear to consumers. At one point, many of us hoped that certification by independent groups would make clear which products were best for the planet. Now there are so many competing certification programs that it is hard to know what to trust. Private industries have created certification programs that compete with those created by public-interest groups. Meanwhile, public-interest-based certifications, like those for organic food, are under constant attack, forcing us to fight hard to keep them from being weakened.

Even beyond competing certifications, there's the matter of other wording on product labels. Terms like "natural" and "environmentally friendly" are now so prevalent that it is impossible for people to figure out where the truth lies. Two-thirds of foods sold in Whole Foods Market or Trader Joe's are not organic, but rather 'natural.'[621]

The $30 billion spent each year on organic products is overshadowed by the $50 billion spent on "natural" products. Polls indicate that many consumers wanting to buy "green" are confused about what the difference is between "natural" and "organic." Many believe that "natural" means "almost organic" or that it is even better than organic. In reality "natural products" may well include genetically modified organisms, pesticide residues, and other toxic chemicals. They likely come from farms and factories that fail to adhere to organic principles.

By one count, there are more than 400 "eco-labels" in the marketplace today, creating confusion and information overload for consumers.[622] Massive, well-funded PR campaigns help corporations target consumers who want to buy green products.[623] With mega PR bucks spent to convince people that particular products are environmentally sound whether or not they are, nonprofit campaigns that provide accurate information don't stand a chance. If you are also concerned about whether the people who produced a product labored under decent working conditions, the task of product vetting becomes even more confusing.

The most important thing to know about consumer pressure as an overall strategy for bringing about environmental change is that it's not working. Toby Webb of *Ethical Consumer* magazine put it this way: "The numbers do not lie: 'ethical consumers'...no matter where you look, are simply not revolutionizing markets and company product and service line-ups at any kind of scale."[624] Green consumer expert Joel Makower had this to say in 2010: "One thing hasn't changed all that much: green consumers. That is, there don't seem to be that many more today than in 1990, in terms of people making significant changes to their shopping and consuming habits in ways that move markets toward green products and services, never mind actually 'saving the world.'"[625]

There are benefits to encouraging people to make green lifestyle choices. Doing so disseminates important information about how we each need to live to sustain our environment. It helps people see through corporate lies. People who have grown their own organic garden are more likely to question assertions that there is no way to farm without highly toxic pesticides, for example. Finally, while exploring environmentally sustainable lifestyles, we develop relationships with each other that can help build the movement we need for political change.

The problem is that the world is set up in a way that prevents most people from having money, time, information, and opportunity to live in an environmentally sustainable manner. Many groups are urging people to change their behaviors without acknowledging this important fact. They foster guilt rather than empowerment. They promote false faith in our ability to save the world by how we shop and how we live our daily lives. This creates confusion as to what we're up against and what we need to do to turn things around.

In short, helping people choose sustainable lifestyles must be carefully framed when used as a tactic. We must ensure that it empowers people and shines a light forward instead of sowing confusion, guilt, and disempowerment.

TARGETING PARTICULAR CORPORATIONS

Some environmental organizations target a specific corporation and rally public pressure to persuade it to change some undesirable behavior. They hope that convincing one corporation to change will spur others to follow suit.

At any given time there are all sorts of environmental public pressure campaigns under way, targeting all sorts of corporations.[626] Here's a sampling of things I was asked to do as I was writing this book:

* Contact Avon and ask them to take hazardous chemicals out of their beauty products.

* Engage in a social media day of action urging Campbell's and Progresso to stop lining their soup cans with dangerous materials.

* Join in a mini-day of action at Disney stores across the U.S. and help make an image go viral to pressure Disney to get toxic chemicals out of school supplies and other products it sells.

* Sign a petition to Graco about toxic chemicals in its strollers and other products.

* Join a "Twitter party" to pressure Proctor & Gamble to take particular toxic chemicals out of Tide® Free & Gentle.[627]

* Take various actions vis-á-vis Pepsi. Some groups wanted me to complain to Pepsi about the money it had given to defeat a California referendum that would have required labeling of products containing genetically modified organisms. The Sierra Club wanted me to urge Pepsi to use fuel-efficient vehicles in its "fleet," and to use non-tar-sands fuel. The Club also wanted me to contact Coca Cola and Dr. Pepper-Snapple to encourage them "to compete to meet" certain climate goals.[628]

Public pressure campaigns sometimes succeed in meeting their specific goals. After one such campaign, for example, Johnson & Johnson announced that it would remove potential carcinogens and other dangerous chemicals from most of its adult toiletry and cosmetic products. Pressure that preceded this victory included sign-on letters, a report co-released by environmental groups, and more. Similarly, Proctor &

Gamble agreed to remove particular chemicals from Tide® Free & Gentle after public pressure and a lawsuit targeted the corporation.[629]

Despite these victories the tactic of public pressure on individual corporations has serious limitations. First of all, it's hard to enlist people in such efforts because it's hard to get their attention. We are all bombarded by a multitude of messages each day, including but not limited to appeals to pressure various corporations.

Secondly, persuading corporations one-by-one to change practices is inherently resource-intensive, providing little bang for the buck. A particular product ingredient may be removed or a specific practice may be ended, but these developments are dwarfed by the tens of thousands of other damaging products and practices that continue unabated. In fact, environmental organizations tend to keep requests narrow in order to have "winnable" campaigns.

Moreover, since victories result from voluntary corporate action, they can be undone at any time. A corporation may change its mind, or it may be taken over by another corporation that doesn't adhere to promised practices.

A bigger problem with campaigns targeting specific corporations is the confusion they create and the divisions they foster among people working for a better world. Take campaigns targeting Pepsi as one example. As the two requests mentioned above for me to contact Pepsi sat in my inbox, news outlets reported that another Pepsi-targeted campaign had achieved its goal. Pepsi had agreed to remove brominated vegetable oil—an ingredient linked to neurological disorders and other health problems—from Gatorade in response to an online petition.[630]

Just think of the confusion created by these three Pepsi-focused pressure campaigns alone, even without other campaigns likely targeting this corporation. When one campaign succeeds, its leaders urge people to thank Pepsi. The corporation enjoys good publicity about listening to people's concerns, and the message is that it's now fine to drink Pepsi. All of this undermines the *other* campaigns targeting Pepsi.

An even bigger problem with targeted public pressure campaigns is that they implicitly accept whole product lines and industries as legitimate when it is those very product lines and industries we should be challenging. Many campaigns are really quite bizarre when you stop to consider them. Do we really want to spend a lot of time persuading the manufacturer of an air freshener to alter its ingredients when the whole concept of spraying chemicals in the air to address odors is misguided?

Do we really want to make a fuss to get Pepsi to repent its ballot donations, change its fuel, or alter an ingredient in its soft drinks? Isn't the real problem that Pepsi sells products that undermine nutrition and promote obesity? Should environmentalists thank Pepsi for supposed environmental advances when its products are such bad news for health? Won't doing so undercut nutrition advocates who should be our allies?

But the biggest problem with the tactic of mobilizing public pressure on individual corporations is that it embraces a model of government in which the only thing we can do to stop the destruction of our environment is ask corporations to please do things differently. This tactic reinforces a system in which power has been stolen from us.

In summary, many different environmental groups are engaging in public pressure campaigns targeting particular corporations, a tactic which uses lots of resources, can't win us very much, and divides us from those who should be allies. This tactic reinforces the system that is disempowering us by implying that change comes from powerful corporations voluntarily deciding to make superficial changes to please consumers. If corporate pressure campaigns are to be useful adjuncts to efforts that move us forward, they need to be designed and explained as such, and much more strategically implemented. Uniting with other social justice movements rather than engaging in conflicting struggles vis-á-vis particular corporations will also be essential.

Procurement Campaigns

Another tactic regularly used by environmental groups is persuading major purchasers to procure environmentally preferable materials, thereby creating a market for those materials. Major purchasers can include government bodies, big institutions like hospitals, large corporations, and anyone who buys a lot of a particular product and can make an impact via their procurement choices. Examples of procurement campaigns include urging health care facilities to demand products made without certain toxic chemicals, urging school districts to serve organic food, and urging state and federal agencies to buy recycled paper that has not been bleached with chlorine.

Moneyed interests sometimes influence procurement criteria, enabling themselves to win contracts despite the fact that they don't offer a true environmental advantage. Vague criteria, such as a requirement that suppliers have sustainability plans, leave the door open for most suppliers to win contracts. In addition, procurement policies can be quickly reversed, such as when there are budget cuts or a change in administration.

In many cases, the overall impact of procurement policies is negligible. When San Francisco announced that it would no longer buy Apple desktop and laptop computers because Apple had removed a green electronics certification (known as EPEAT) from its products, for instance, the impact turned out to be largely symbolic. "Given the relatively small percentage [of organizations] that require 100% EPEAT compliance, it's not going to make a whole lot of difference to Apple," said analyst Michael Gartenberg.[631]

In summary, procurement programs are not at all in conflict with the world we need to build. Environmental organizations sometimes overstate their potential impact, however. And they fail to use procurement campaigns to build towards a larger well-articulated goal of systemic change that unites and empowers people.

Shareholder Resolutions

Some organizations attempt to pressure corporations by enabling shareholders to file resolutions calling for better practices. The premise is that people and organizations holding shares in a corporation can combine their votes at annual shareholder meetings to require the corporation to make changes. If they assemble more than 50% of the votes, the corporation will need to do as told. Even if they can't secure that many votes, shareholder resolutions may persuade corporate executives to sit down and talk and to make some improvements.

Shareholder resolutions have become a major tactic for public-interest organizations. As of mid-February 2013, 365 resolutions on various issues had been filed with corporations for consideration in 2013. Resolutions concerning environmental issues and sustainability accounted for 36% of that total.[632]

It is difficult, however, to force fundamental change via shareholder resolutions. At most corporations, a core group of people who have profited immensely from the corporation's activities own the majority of its shares. This core group is unlikely to agree to substantial changes.

This is particularly true where the very purpose of the corporation is itself a problem, such as at corporations formed to extract, refine, and sell fossil fuels. We need to eliminate these corporations altogether, but core shareholders will not agree to dissolve them or to fundamentally alter their purpose. Even shareholders outside of the core group will be loathe to take such action because they don't want to jeopardize the money they've invested. Thus, when the corporation's primary product or service is the problem, shareholder resolutions at best nip around the edges of that problem without ever truly addressing it.

Shareholder resolutions targeting fossil-fuel corporations like Chevron, ExxonMobil, and Chesapeake Energy in 2012 illustrate this reality well. The resolutions asked for things like "increased transparency" and a reduction of risks associated with fracking. They didn't call for an end to fracking and other fossil-fuel extraction, which is what we really need. "This year's effort builds on the remarkable success achieved by investors last year, when similar proposals received an average 40 percent vote," exulted Richard Liroff of the Investor Environmental Health Network. "These high votes send strong messages to companies that significant portions of their shareholders required increased disclosure on this issue," he said. "In order to maintain their social license to operate, companies must fully disclose the steps they are taking to minimize risks," said Laura Berry of the Interfaith Center on Corporate Responsibility.[633]

Why are people talking about maintaining the social license of these corporations to operate instead of about *repealing* that license?[634]

Even when a corporation's purpose is not inherently environmentally destructive, shareholder resolutions tend to be weakly worded in order to garner maximum support. The few resolutions that take a stronger stand lose by very large margins. Targeted corporations are urged to do things like disclose the chemicals they use, track emissions, and prepare reports about environmental damage and alternatives. If these resolutions are adopted or if the corporations agree to do something in exchange for their withdrawal, corporations get good PR without really having to change how they do business.

In 2009, for example, environmental and shareholder activists celebrated a "historic" shareholder agreement reached with McDonald's on pesticide use reduction. McDonald's promised to survey its potato suppliers, compile a list of best practices in pesticide reductions, and communicate findings to shareholders in an annual corporate social responsibility report. Newground Social Investment CEO Bruce Herbert referred to McDonald's commanding presence in the marketplace, noting that its new commitment offered "the promise of significant reductions of pesticide use…"[635]

Unfortunately, the actual impact of this 2009 victory appears to be minimal. McDonald's website is extremely vague about what has and hasn't changed regarding pesticide use among its potato suppliers. I contacted the Investor Environmental Health Network, which helped broker the 2009 deal, but they had no data. USDA data regarding one of the most common highly toxic potato pesticides used in 2009 indicate that its use remains as high as ever.[636]

I also emailed McDonald's sustainability staff asking if they could provide data on pesticides used by farmers supplying McDonald's potatoes. What percentage of suppliers was organic? What volumes of the pesticide metam sodium were applied on what percentage of McDonald's potato acres, and did they have any information on other specific pesticides? Here's how they replied:

> …the information you are specifically requesting is considered proprietary business information or is otherwise unavailable at this time. I'm sorry I cannot answer your specific questions… thank you for contacting McDonald's. We hope to have the opportunity of serving you again soon under the Golden Arches.

In short, no one seems to be tracking the impact of McDonald's pledge and available data don't bode well for there having been any real reductions in pesticide use as a result of it.

The bigger problem with the shareholder tactic, however, is that it promotes an undemocratic model of government. Instead of having direct majority control over things that affect us like whether or not our environment will be polluted, we try to control our destiny through resolutions at corporate meetings we don't control. Furthermore, to submit and vote on resolutions someone needs to buy shares. Pay to play is the antithesis of how democracy is supposed to work.

Shareholder activism creates the impression that our power lies in trying to nudge corporations to take small steps forward from within their annual meetings. This is the wrong message to be spreading at this pivotal time in human history.

In summary, a lot of money is being spent on shareholder resolutions that have little potential for achieving real change. This tactic creates confusion about what we need to do to save our environment.

DIVESTMENT

Closely related to the tactic of shareholder resolutions is that of divestment. This tactic involves persuading those who own shares to "divest," i.e., sell them. There is a growing movement in the U.S. to persuade colleges, cities, unions, and other major institutions to divest from the fossil-fuel industry.[637] Student leaders in that movement have labeled divestment "a form of economic non-cooperation." By divesting, colleges and others send a message of not wanting to be complicit with the fossil-fuel industry's destructive practices. They are also free to invest their money in alternatives.[638]

Some divestment leaders have described divestment as a moral and political strategy, rather than just an economic one. "This is an Abolitionist Cause," they say. "If slavery is wrong, is it wrong to make a profit from it? If it is wrong to wreck the planet, then it is wrong to profit from it."[639]

Unfortunately, the economic impact of divestment on targeted companies may not be as great as some hope. To divest means to sell one's shares to someone else or to let the corporation buy them back. Exactly who owns stocks makes little difference to a corporation and its bottom line. Buying back shares can even improve a corporation's finances by reducing the money it needs to pay out. It could actually use those savings to escalate its environmental destructive actions.

In addition, many corporations are not publicly owned. Koch Industries is a good example of an environmental destructive corporation that is not vulnerable to divestment campaigns since the public can't own shares in the company.

A small number of corporations hold most of the world's assets, and many corporations are tied to others financially and through interlocking directorates. (Directors for one corporation also serve on the boards of other corporations.) Thus, any harm from a divestment campaign felt by a targeted corporation or its shareholders is likely mitigated by income at interconnected corporations that have not been targeted.

This brings us to another major limitation of divestment—the likelihood that divested money will be redirected to some other environmentally damaging company. Sure, it's nice seeing institutions and individuals divest from fossil-fuel corporations. But we're not really winning overall if those investments are transferred to Monsanto, Coca Cola, Citigroup, and the like.

Divestment campaigns often elevate a particular environmental problem as "the most important" or "the most urgent." But we face multiple important crises that need to be addressed simultaneously. If investments in corporations fuel their destructive behaviors, shifting funds from one corporation to another may be like shooting ourselves in one foot to avoid shooting ourselves in the other. This will be the case until we address the system itself.

In summary, failing to acknowledge the limitations of divestment can promote confusion about what it can achieve. Divestment campaigns can divide people working on different issues by shifting funds from one industrial sector to another.

On the other hand, divestment campaigns can raise awareness about our economic system and how it leads to environmental degradation and injustice. If its limitations are acknowledged, divestment can be used to build the movement for fundamental change that we need. Many student divestment leaders understand this.[640]

Lawsuits

Environmental organizations bring lawsuits to try to force environmental protections. Lawsuits can lead to good outcomes and they can provide other benefits such as access to documents obtained through discovery—the ability of each party to obtain relevant documents from the other.

Lawsuits are limited in what they can accomplish, however. Many suits brought under environmental laws only challenge agencies for failing to adhere to some *procedural* requirement. An agency may have failed to do an environmental impact statement or to consider certain factors in making a decision. It may have missed a statutory deadline for taking action. Thus, after investing lots of time and money in lawsuits, we may still end up with a bad outcome. The agency will finally issue a rule for which a deadline had passed but the rule is inadequate. Or it will go back and change *how* a decision was made, but the new decision will still be a bad one.

When laws do allow challenges on substance rather than just procedure, outcomes will likely still be disappointing. The courts are extremely deferential to governmental agencies with respect to the substance of their decisions.

Here's an example of a procedural win that the Sierra Club declared a "landmark victory" in April of 2013. A federal judge ruled that federal authorities broke the law when they failed to consider the environmental impacts of fracking before leasing 2700 acres of public land in Monterey and Fresno counties in California to oil and gas drillers.[641] This court decision may buy time, but federal authorizes will likely end up leasing the land anyway after a cursory examination of environmental impacts.

It can take years for litigation to lead to a court decision or a settlement. During that time, resources are diverted from other strategies. In addition, agency personnel may refuse to talk about the issue because it is "in litigation." Environmental group staffers may also be hamstrung regarding what they can say and do. And even when a lawsuit results in a victory, Congress or a state legislature may turn around and change the law on which the decision was based, rendering the decision moot.

Lawyers can also bring suits on behalf of toxic exposure victims under "tort" law, charging a polluter with negligence or using other common law theories. I know from working as an organizer with communities injured by toxic pollution, however, that few want to go through what is entailed in filing such a suit. Moreover, getting a lawyer to take these cases on contingency is very difficult.

Most law firms can't afford to represent people hurt by pollution or other environmental problems. They can't afford to hire the needed experts or to properly investigate a case. They can't compete against the huge resources invested by corporations to defend themselves.

Organizing for a lawsuit can divert communities from other important organizing work. In addition, if a case is settled, there may be a "gag order" forbidding the toxic exposure victims from talking about what happened and from sharing valuable information they gained about the polluter.

In short, lawsuits should not be a primary tactic in our fight for justice and survival. They are too resource-intensive, generally produce victories of limited value, and can undercut community organizing. Our resources and time are better spent on tactics that build our movement for fundamental change.

Lawsuits can be beneficial at times, however. In some instances, they can produce outcomes that are useful. They can also buy us time for organizing and garner media attention for our issues. When we file lawsuits, we must carefully integrate them into our broader efforts. We must make sure that they invigorate rather than deflate the movement we are building.

PROTESTS

Environmental organizations can also organize protests. These include things like marches, rallies, and street theater. They also include acts of civil disobedience like blocking traffic, locking oneself to a gate, and stopping trains that carry oil. In their most advanced form, protests include strikes—people refusing to work unless and until demands are met.

In light of how broken our democracy is and the major limitations of other tactics, protests are the most important tool available to environmentalists for saving our environment. They can be used to expose problems that have previously been swept under the rug, demonstrate popular anger about these, and articulate solutions. They take place out in the open rather than in smoke-filled backrooms, and they demand *public* discussion of the issues. This can radically change the terms of the debate.

Protests can also help activists find each other, thereby fueling the next stages of organizing. Groups of people united by Occupy Wall Street are still working together towards the next big leap forward, for example.

Most important, when enough people join together in protest under a strong agenda for change, nothing can stop us. Our power arises from the fact that working people do the work of society. When we withhold our labor we can bring the economy to a halt until the changes we want are made.

External forces create challenges when we use protest as a tactic. Corporate-owned news media outlets may fail to report on protests or they may misrepresent them. This makes it harder to reach people with our message and increase the numbers of people taking to the streets.

As momentum builds and protests grow, we may also face police crackdowns. Those opposed to change may even send infiltrators to protests who do things that government officials use to justify no-protest zones, curfews, and violence against protesters.

There are also forces within our own ranks that work against protests. Environmental and other social justice groups may fail to put resources into them, for example, preferring instead to focus on lobbying, lawsuits, negotiating with corporations, and other tactics. Over the last several decades, resources spent to organize protests have been dwarfed by those expended on futilely working within the system for reforms that never come.

Another threat from within revolves around what protests look like. Organizers can frame them in a manner that limits their effectiveness.

Consider two protests organized early in 2013 by 350.org, the Sierra Club, and others on global warming issues. One involved fifty or so environmental activists and celebrities who were arrested outside the White House. The other involved an estimated 40,000 people convening on the Mall in Washington, D.C.[642]

Organizers and speakers for these events—at least those quoted in organizers' materials, activist blogs, and news coverage—made sure to not criticize the Obama Administration. In fact, they praised Obama for his vague rhetoric about global warming in the State of the Union address. They said things like "We want him to know that when he takes these bold actions to stabilize the climate, the American people will support him every step of the way."[643] The organizers and speakers made a point of not expressing anger and dismay at the leadership Obama had shown in the *wrong* direction on global warming. Organizers even went so far as to use the Obama logo on signs and other materials. The logo for the protest was itself a modified Obama logo. In an upcoming chapter we'll review why this praise for Obama is completely inappropriate given his actual fossil-fuel promoting record and agenda.

This posture of praising those in power and not detailing and criticizing their abysmal records severely undercuts the effectiveness of protests. It reinforces for elected officials that there will be no price to pay no matter how much damage they do to the environment. More importantly it creates a confusing message for those who participate in protests and those who read about them. Refusal to criticize Democrats is one of the most common self-defeating behaviors of environmental organizations and will be discussed in more detail in an upcoming chapter.

The two global warming protests also did not disrupt society in any way. Even the civil disobedience actions were purely symbolic. Traffic was not blocked. Government officials promoting fossil-fuel extraction were not kept from their offices. Those seeking to be arrested politely refused to disperse and chatted amiably with forewarned police officers who politely arrested them and led them away. Most, if not all, were asked to pay minor fines and released within a couple of hours of their arrests. Media attention focused on celebrities like Daryl Hannah and paid almost no attention to the global warming issues protesters sought to address.

The ultra-courteous, orchestrated, non-disruptive nature of the protests prompted some observers to coin terms like "designer protests" and "celebrity catch-and-release."[644]

In short, these two protests raised awareness about global warming, and they spotlighted the deep concern people are feeling. But they also created some confusion, and they channeled people's concern into highly choreographed non-disruptive activities that didn't interfere with fossil-fuel production and the system that promotes it.

It will take time to build a movement that is broad and cohesive enough to use the full power of the working class. In the meantime, less sweeping protests play an important role in moving us forward. Even symbolic non-disruptive civil disobedience and marches that don't have clear strong messages can be important tools for building momentum for change.

If we are not careful, however, protests can lose their power over time. They can become everyday events that are part of the status quo rather than a challenge to it—happenings that one hardly notices, like wallpaper. Protests can become parades that feature elected officials who are feverishly undermining the environment behind the scenes on behalf of private corporations. They can become a forum in which people let off steam without changing anything.

If protests don't tell the truth about who and what we are up against, and if they don't ultimately disrupt the system that is hurting us, they become meaningless. We need to be discussing how to prevent that outcome, ensuring instead that our protests become steadily more powerful over time.

How do we deal with the external and internal threats to the power we can have through protest? Our best weapon is talking honestly about what we're up against as much as we can, fostering ever-broadening discussions about what we need to do about it. The more widely we cultivate a clear understanding of the need for systemic reform and a detailed vision of what that looks like, the harder it will be for those who prefer the 1%-enriching status quo to derail our efforts. The more we speak up within our own movement about the message we need to deliver and the stances we should take, the more we block the self-crippling messages and stances many current leaders espouse. We must also nurture communication networks that circumvent Big Money-controlled media outlets. These sorts of steps will be explored later in the book.

Protests have a long history of ushering in major social reforms. Marches, rallies, civil disobedience, boycotts, sit-ins, and other protests were crucial tactics that ultimately forced the repeal of racist Jim Crow laws and passage of the 1965 Civil Rights Act, for example. Teach-ins and other environmental protests in the 1960s and 1970s led to important environmental laws. Historically, some of the least progressive leaders have been forced to advance progressive measures as the result of public pressure exerted though marches and other mass protests.

The spirit of Occupy, the WTO Battle of Seattle, and other past protests is alive and spreading. Harsh "austerity" measures have prompted huge marches in various countries. People are now turning out for rallies against global warming in the hundreds of thousands, and large numbers are engaging in civil disobedience on this issue. Increasingly, civil disobedience is actively disrupting things such as by blocking oil trains and drilling rigs.

What happens now with respect to protests and what they look like depends on us. If we are to survive as a species, building upon the protest movements of the past is essential. Being aware of how protests can be co-opted and derailed and keeping that from happening will be critical.

Tactical Choices

Environmental organizations often rely on self-defeating or ineffective tactics that need to be left behind. Sitting down with corporations one by one to ask them to please take this or that step, supporting corporate-backed schemes like pollution trading that create a right to pollute, and buying shares hoping to pass weak resolutions from within corporations all embrace the inequitable set-up that disempowers us. The message they deliver is not one of claiming our power but rather of ceding it to the wealthy few. Unfortunately, some of the best-funded groups rely heavily on these self-defeating tactics, undermining our movement immeasurably.

Environmental groups also commonly rely on other tactics that are ineffective but not inconsistent with the new world we need to build. If we lived in a functioning democracy, they would work. Lobbying would lead to the passage of strong public-interest laws, for example.

Unfortunately, however, environmental groups fail to frame their use of these other tactics appropriately. They imply that the tactics will lead to policy reforms even though that is not possible with the deck stacked against us. This causes confusion when we desperately need clarity. Instead of building awareness about the need for systemic change and nurturing a movement that will fight for that change, reliance on these tactics is reinforcing the misperception that dead ends are the way out.

In a world in which everything is set up to advance the interests of the wealthy few, protest stands out as the tactic with the greatest potential to get us where we need to go. It acknowledges that the game is rigged against us and that we must go outside the system to claim the power that should be ours. That is the message we need to be emphasizing.

Protest can be used to build a mass movement for democracy, justice, and survival. When that movement is strong enough, protests can evolve into an exercise of the power that has always been ours. Together we will refuse to make the wheels of an unjust system turn anymore, and we will establish a just system in its place.

Environmental groups are beginning to use protests more aggressively and more effectively. Overall, however, they still don't understand this tactic, what it can accomplish, and how to use it effectively.

CHAPTER 22

Problematic Behavior Number 5
Aiming Too Low and Compromising Too Readily

• • •

OVERALL, ENVIRONMENTAL GROUPS AIM TOO low and compromise too readily, thereby contributing significantly to the sorry state of the environment today. This behavior may be prompted by a desire to get a win, even a small one, in order to keep people's spirits up. It may also result from needing to have something to show to funders so they'll renew their support. In general it is tied to unjustified faith that tiny incremental gains eventually add up to big changes.

Several historical compromises stand out as ones that have most damaged our basic rights and our ability to prevent environmental catastrophe:

> **Selling Out on NAFTA.** While the vast majority of environmental activists opposed the North American Free Trade Agreement (NAFTA),[645] some environmental groups supported it. The Audubon Society, Natural Resources Defense Council (NRDC), Environmental Defense Fund, National Wildlife Federation, and others formed "the Environmental Coalition for NAFTA." As NRDC leader John Adams put it: "We broke the back of the environmental opposition to NAFTA. After we established our position, Clinton only had labor to fight. We did him a big favor."[646]

In exchange for their support, the compromising environmental groups got access. "I can't tell you how wonderful it is to walk down the hall in the White House or a government agency and be greeted by your first name," Brock Evans, the Audubon Society's chief lobbyist exulted.

They also got toothless "side agreements" to NAFTA. As a legal services attorney, I prepared materials for a hearing under such an agreement on labor. While we were able to raise concerns in an international forum about the treatment of farm workers, the side agreement gave us no real power to change that treatment.

NAFTA set the stage for the WTO and other so-called trade agreements to follow. The devastating impacts of these agreements on environmental protection, financial regulation, and social justice in general cannot be overstated.

Selling Out on the Precautionary Principle. John Adams of NRDC told EPA Administrator Carol Browner at a meeting in 1993: "You are our general. We are your troops. We await your orders."[647] Apparently he really meant it because NRDC and other big environmental groups lined up in support of Browner's plan to exclude pesticides from the "Delaney clause." That clause in the Food, Drug, and Cosmetic Act prohibited the adding of known cancer-causing chemicals—including pesticides—to processed foods. It should have been expanded to raw foods but instead President Clinton helped his agribusiness friends by exempting pesticides from its coverage. Thus, with the support of environmental organizations, Clinton eliminated a clear precaution-based law that said "zero" cancer-causing chemicals could be added to certain foods we eat. In its place, he established a "Risk Assessment" approach, allowing cancer-causing chemicals to be added as long as the risks they posed were supposedly "negligible."

This capitulation by big environmental organizations was part of a broader ushering in of the age of "Risk Assessment." With their assistance, the precautionary principle gave way to a policy of gambling with health and the environment. The travesty of ongoing farm worker family exposures to deadly pesticides described in Part I of this book is just one of countless terrible consequences of the Risk Assessment model.

Selling Out on Fossil Fuels. Aiming low and compromising has impeded fossil-fuel activism for a long time. The Sierra Club and other organizations long embraced fracked natural gas as a "bridge" to renewable energy, for example. They facilitated expansion of this dangerous extraction method and gave natural gas a good name it does not deserve. While fewer organizations now overtly support fracking, many still focus on "fixing" it. This directly undercuts campaigns to ban fracking and keep natural gas and oil in the ground where they belong.[648] Groups like NRDC also endorsed Obama's pick for Secretary of Energy in 2013: Ernest Moniz, a strong supporter of fracking.[649]

Numerous major environmental groups have been avid proponents of carbon pollution trading schemes,[650] an approach to global warming that doesn't work, as discussed earlier. In April of 2011, EDF's President Fred Krupp lambasted those not joining him in pushing cap and trade when a bill embodying this approach failed to pass. Appearing at a *Fortune* magazine conference with Duke Energy Corporation—which also supported the bill—Krupp used terms like "arrogant" to denounce those opposing the bill and his market-based policies. "There has to be shrillness taken out" of environmentalists' language, he said. "The idea of humility means we need to be open to any solution," Krupp said. By "any solution" he meant any of the dead-end, self-serving policies fossil-fuel industry representatives will agree to.[651]

EDF, NRDC, and World Resources Institute were founding members in 2007 of the "U.S. Climate Action Partnership" (USCAP.) Other founding members included BP America, Duke Energy, DuPont, and other corporations. Soon, other major environmental organizations and corporations joined, including Shell, ConocoPhillips, Chrysler, Ford Motor Company, PepsiCo, Dow Chemical, the National Wildlife Federation, and The Nature Conservancy, among others. Many of the members of USCAP had been involved with the Global Climate Coalition, which has been described as "one of the most outspoken and confrontational industry groups in the United States battling reductions in greenhouse gas emissions."[652]

The submissive posture of key environmental groups and the confusion this engenders have played a major role in preventing meaningful action on global warming.

THE DYNAMIC OF BIG GROUPS' COMPROMISES

These historic examples spotlight a dynamic that has plagued the environmental movement for decades. Large, well-funded organizations sign on to policies that environmental justice and other more principled groups oppose. Corporations, and the elected officials who serve them, point to the support of the compromising environmental organizations to add legitimacy to their cause. Groups that hold firm for policies in the public interest are ignored.

While recalling these examples and the ongoing dynamic they represent, it is useful to keep in mind a speech given by public relations consultant, Ronald A. Duchin in 1991. Duchin's talk was entitled "Take An Activist Apart And What Do You Have?" It described how to defeat those who work in the public interest. Duchin suggested that corporations classify activists as radicals (i.e., people who want to change the system), opportunists, idealists, or realists. He then explained how to win over certain categories and thereby marginalize others. As Duchin put it, "[w]ithout support of the realists and the idealists, the positions of radicals and opportunists are seen to be shallow and self-serving."[653] Foundations and corporations ensure that "realist" organizations are well funded. These organizations aim low and compromise readily, undermining the work that needs to be done.

Low Goals and Compromises Continue All Around Us

The propensity to aim low and readily compromise is getting more pronounced with each passing year. Weak goals, weak positions, and weak outcomes now dominate environmental organizations' campaigns.

For example, environmental activists concerned about toxic chemicals in products have been working hard for years to win amendments to the federal Toxic Substance Control (TSCA). What's the solution they propose? Making TSCA more like the federal pesticide law, "FIFRA." Pesticide activists have pointed out that FIFRA is failing abysmally to protect us from pesticides, but our warnings have gone unheeded.

And now, as I write this book, the usual scenario is playing out. The TSCA reform bill garnering support in Congress is one that most environmental activists oppose. It won't accomplish our goals, and, indeed, will make things worse. It prohibits state action on toxic chemicals, thereby undercutting the primary tool that activists have used on toxics issues for years. The American Chemistry Council helped draft the bill and supports it.[654]

Predictably a large well-funded group, Environmental Defense Fund (EDF), is supporting this atrocious bill.[655] EDF maintains that any bill must be sure to sustain the economic health of the chemical industry, and it lauds protection of companies' proprietary interests in the chemicals they develop. An argument used in support of the bill is the fact that it could actually be enacted into law. (In other words, according to EDF, we must base what we support on what corporate-controlled legislative bodies are willing to pass rather than on what is actually needed to protect the environment.)[656] Even though most health and environmental groups vehemently oppose the proposed toxics law, elected officials can point to EDF and claim that they have environmentalists' support.

And so, we are in a familiar situation. A harmful bill is moving forward with the support of a well-funded "green" group, despite the opposition of most other groups. The bill these other groups prefer is itself absolutely insufficient. But that's the debate we have: a god-awful bill that will set us back dramatically versus a weak, ineffective bill that won't do us much good. And it's the former that will probably pass.

On issue after issue, groups object to the state of things, but take as a given that really addressing problems isn't an option. One group chronicles how the Obama Administration is attacking regulations through its Office of Information and Regulatory Affairs (OIRA), but states that they "have little hope that the Obama Administration will contemplate the fundamental overhaul of OIRA's role that is genuinely needed." Solely "for the record" they briefly list the reforms that are really needed, like getting rid of OIRA review altogether, before focusing on the more pragmatic reforms, like increasing "transparency."[657]

Fighting for more "transparency"—i.e., more disclosure of information—has become the go-to, winnable reform that is all the rage these days. Shareholders file resolutions asking fracking corporations to disclose the chemicals they use. Activists demand disclosure of the contract between the University of Michigan and Dow Chemical regarding the latter's massive gift to the university, while saying little about the inappropriateness of the gift altogether. The Union of Concerned Scientists details how fossil-fuel corporations undermine science and block science-based climate reforms, but then offers weak recommendations that emphasize increasing transparency.[658]

Environmental groups are broadcasting the message over and over again that we can't win real victories, so why go for them? Incremental advances that don't really get us anywhere are the best we can hope for, they say. This mindset is a major barrier to our survival as a species.

Mired in a defeatist mindset, environmental groups regularly accept false frames put forth by wealthy interests. When it is asserted that ours is a time of austerity with tough choices about what to fund, they don't challenge this false framework. When Risk Assessments are praised as sound unbiased analyses, they don't point out the absurdity of that praise.

By accepting false frames and classifying what really needs to be done as impossible, we lose before we even begin to fight. By aiming low and compromising readily, we let ourselves be pushed ever backward despite the power we have to instead create the world we want.

CHAPTER 23

Problematic Behavior Number 6
Overstating Accomplishments

• • •

CLOSELY RELATED TO AIMING TOO low and compromising too readily is the tendency of environmental organizations to overstate their accomplishments. At times organizations even celebrate losses as if they were victories. And when a small advance is later rescinded or put on hold, often those who celebrated it don't tell people that the victory has evaporated.

There is no end to the chorus of celebratory messages surrounding us from environmental organizations. Action alerts, updates to supporters, quotes in news articles, and other communications all convey the impression that these organizations are making progress. There may be references to set-backs and the battle being uphill. These statements often precede requests for donations to fund the ongoing work. But overall, communications are designed to give the impression that strategies are working. Progress may be slow, but environmental organizations' efforts will gradually get us where we need to be, we are told.

❧ "We've got the chemical industry on the run," the Washington Toxics Coalition declares in an email to supporters. Unfortunately this statement couldn't be further from the truth. Later, when the chemical industry has derailed the latest toxics bill desired by the Coalition, the follow-up message to supporters puts a happy face on this failure. Lobbying for the failed bill raised awareness about the issue.

The Coalition also finds something to cheer about with respect to a different bill that did become law after the chemical industry gutted it. The new law was supposed to force manufacturers to let consumers know when certain highly toxic chemicals are present in specific products. As passed, it only requires that they list chemicals used within *categories* of products. This gives consumers no information about whether specific products contain dangerous chemicals. Nonetheless, the Coalition claims a partial victory, literally because we are no longer *completely* in the dark.

* An Oregon group says that "[t]his is a great time to be engaged in protecting the environment. WE'RE WINNING!" The only evidence of this grand statement is passage in one of two state legislative houses of a bill related to integrated pest management. Bills have to pass both houses and be signed by the governor to become law.

* Various environmental organizations praise Washington State's governor as a visionary leader when she signs an executive order calling on state government to "reduce greenhouse gases and battle climate change." We're told that "it's immensely exciting" to see her "demonstrate her tenacity and continued leadership on climate change." The only problem is that the order doesn't actually impose limits on emissions. It's a toothless document directing state agencies to work toward setting limits and to talk with industry about cutting emissions.

* Culminating months of intense work, the Environmental Priorities Coalition (EPC) of Washington State sends out a legislative update. It celebrates "victories," but what are they? One bill that actually passed is a "climate action" bill that yet again doesn't really mandate any action. It requires the gathering of information and that state officials map out a clean energy

strategy. Despite the decidedly unimpressive nature of the new law, and the déjà vu sensation anyone working on climate issues should have looking at it, environmental organizations dutifully praise it: "The Governor's climate action bill keeps our state in the game," says Joan Crooks of the Washington Environmental Council.[659] This is standard spin for casting little or no progress in a positive light. Environmental organizations are continually "laying the groundwork" for future action and "setting the stage" for change.

The other EPC victories are even less concrete. The EPC groups celebrate having "fought off" over 70 bad bills, sent over 8000 emails to legislators, called over 19,000 voters, and engaged over 600 activists on lobby day.[660] Unfortunately, using resources to call for change is not the same thing as achieving it. Blocking bad laws isn't the same as moving forward.

* One sees similar missives from groups that address a range of issues rather than just the environment. A December 2012 email sent by the Washington State progressive group Fuse to its members makes vague claims about past victories ("We stayed true to our values and we won!" How exactly? What exactly?) The tangible items listed in the email are more about motion than action. Accomplishments include: 275,000 voters reading the groups' voter guide, organization members knocking on lots of doors, and the like. Based on these enthusiastic assertions about victories, Fuse asks me to chip in some cash so they can build on their "incredible record of success."[661]

* Here's a victory that was years in the making: in September 2012, participants at the 3rd International Conference on Chemicals Management reached consensus that endocrine-disrupting chemicals are officially a global emerging policy issue. This new status was highly celebrated by activists, and it does represent a step forward. But being considered an emerging issue doesn't mean that anything will

actually be done to address it. Look at how well the world is doing with long-established global issues like crashing fish populations and climate change.

* A Sierra Club Insider report to supporters labels 2012 a "banner year for environmental accomplishment." According to the Club, "making our grassroots movement an unstoppable force" had yielded "truly inspiring" results. When you click on the link to learn what those results are exactly, you're treated to a slick music video pulsing with youthful energy that is very short on actual victories. Coal plant closures (facilitated by low natural gas prices due to fracking) and weak, long-delayed Obama fuel efficiency standards are mentioned. So is the Administration's narrow carbon rule for some new power plants. (We'll discuss these more in the next chapter.)

But most of the Sierra Club video is vague fluff showing people protesting various things, as if campaigning for change is the same as winning it. Parts of the video are downright misleading. An uninformed viewer would get the distinct impression that offshore drilling and Arctic drilling have been halted, for example, even though these are moving forward with Obama Administration encouragement. Sierra Club members are shown fighting for fair trade in a way that implies we are winning on trade, when the opposite is in fact the case.

The video culminates in all-out worship of Obama. He is identified as a "green champion" that Sierra Club helped elect. Ignoring Obama's record on oil, gas, climate change, and other issues, the video features photos of the president on election night, interspersed with images of fireworks, as the music crescendos. The video's presidential adulation is an example of another problematic behavior that will be discussed in the next section—that of praising and endorsing Democratic candidates despite their records and agendas.[662]

What's Wrong With All This? Placing chemicals on lists, getting bills introduced, and other things organizations celebrate do represent accomplishments of some kind. The problem is that these accomplishments are almost always minuscule or illusory. We get a toothless policy that calls for more studies and discussions about an issue when we've had plenty of those already. We get a law so gutted by industry lobbyists that its original purpose has been destroyed. We get a pollutant placed on a list where it will likely sit for years without real action. We see defeats recast as having laid groundwork for future success yet again.

Moreover, the things we do win are often tied to other things that drag us down. Big environmental organizations celebrated those toothless side agreements to NAFTA even while NAFTA handed corporations powerful tools to dismantle environmental laws, for example.

When action is taken on an issue it is used as an excuse for blocking further discussion for years to come. *We've already dealt with that, and it's time to move on to other things,* we are told. This makes celebrating minute and questionable gains doubly problematic.

By reflexively putting out celebratory messages no matter what, environmental organizations are flooding the world with messages of success and well-being. The problem with this is that we are actually losing on specific campaigns. And we are losing on saving our environment overall, as was laid out in painful detail in Part II of this book. Time is running out. We've got to stop, acknowledge the truth, and change our strategies.

A steady flow of messages claiming that we've won lulls people into a false belief that continuing to do what we've been doing will work. It prevents the discussions we should be having about changing our approach so we can turn truly succeed.

Why Do Environmental Organizations Over-Celebrate? Environmental organizations are under a lot of pressure to report victories. If you want funding and membership support, you need to look like you're getting things done.

Those who advise environmental groups emphasize this. "When you talk up your recent successes, no matter how small they might be, you inspire the people listening to think positively about your organization," notes *Fundraising for Dummies*, for example, in a section of the book entitled "Talking Up Your Successes and Building Relationships."[663]

The tendency to always declare victories arises from more than a desire to sustain organizational funding and membership, however. Individuals working for environmental organizations sincerely believe that it's important to keep people's hopes up. If we admit that we're losing, they say, people will become discouraged and apathetic.

It is indeed important to give people hope. The way to do that is to identify the *real* problem we face, develop strategies to take it on, and unite with others to use our collective power.

Ironically, the current obsession with manufacturing things to celebrate and implying that we're doing fine when we're not, ends up creating despair rather than hope. Despite the inundation of positive messages from thousands of environmental organizations, the truth keeps seeping through. People catch sobering news headlines. They observe the increase in extreme weather conditions associated with global warming. They notice that various victories sound a lot like ones we're supposed to have already won, and that problems yet to be addressed seem to be the same ones we've already celebrated solving.

Faith-Based Incrementalism. The tendency to over-celebrate also arises from a mindset that permeates the world of environmental organizations that I call "faith-based incrementalism."

Incrementalism is a method of achieving change that relies on incremental steps. Small victories are stepping stones to other small victories, which are stepping stones to others, and so on, ultimately leading to big changes.

Incremental struggles and victories can indeed lead to big changes, but only if they challenge the underlying system that creates problems. If that underlying system is not challenged, small victories never get us where we need to go. Unaddressed, underlying forces ultimately assert themselves and undo our victories.

I use the adjective "faith-based" to describe the incrementalism dominating environmental organizations today because people are trusting that incrementalism is working without actually examining the facts. They are taking on faith that all boats rise when one group makes progress, and that step by tiny step we're moving forward and will achieve our goals in time. But the fact is that we're moving backwards rather than forwards. What we've been doing is not working. If all boats are rising these days, it's due to global warming and rising sea levels, not environmental victories.

It's time to take off our rose-colored glasses and figure out what we need to do differently. Having faith that things will somehow work out when the evidence points in the opposite direction is suicidal.

<u>Criticizing Those Who Tell the Truth.</u> The problem goes beyond environmental groups asserting (without factual support) that we're moving forward step by step. Some groups also attack anyone who challenges faith-based incrementalism.

When the Copenhagen climate summit ended without producing meaningful agreements, for example, NRDC's policy director David Doniger directed his anger not at fossil-fuel corporations and the governments they control, but at the people who protested this outcome. In an opinion piece entitled "The Copenhagen Accord: A Big Step Forward," Doniger denigrated the "howls of protest in European media, and rather tepid reviews in many U.S. news stories." Doniger said that people were "holding the accord to standards and expectations that no outcome achievable at Copenhagen could reasonably have met—or even should have met."[664]

Doniger's essay exuded disdain for the idea of people holding firm for the policies that we actually need. He readily agreed that the worlds' leaders had failed to ensure the carbon reductions needed to forestall disastrous temperature increases, but said that's just how things are. We're powerless to do more, so get over it. World leaders, including Barack

Obama, would not have attended the summit if participating countries had not shifted their expectations away from securing a legally binding agreement, he explained.

This analysis is shocking, given the urgent need for swift action. As columnist Johann Hari put it: "Doniger believes it is 'reasonable' to act within the constraints of the U.S. and global political systems, and unreasonable to act within the constraints of the climate science."[665]

Doniger's praise for summit outcomes (that actually warranted strong criticism) and his disdain for those who told the truth about what is needed to really address climate change illustrate one of the most problematic behaviors within environmental organizations. The facts about where we are going as a species laid out in this book make it clear that we are losing. We urgently need to talk about this reality and figure out what to do differently. Unfortunately, on the whole, environmental organizations are preventing that discussion by pretending we are winning and marginalizing those who refuse to go along with that pretense.

CHAPTER 24

Problematic Behavior Number 7
Demophilia

• • •

SOME OF THE SELF-DEFEATING BEHAVIORS discussed above such as aiming low, compromising, and over-celebrating are often linked to another common behavior that renders environmental organizations ineffective: "Demophilia."[666] This is the tendency widely prevalent among environmental organizations and those who work with them to support the Democratic Party.

IS SUPPORT FOR THE DEMOCRATIC PARTY WARRANTED?

Before discussing examples and consequences of this behavior, we need to take on the underlying question. Is the support environmental organizations give to the Democratic Party warranted? The Party enjoys an aura of environmental leadership, but is it deserved?

Looking at the facts, the answer is a resounding No. The Democratic Party has not delivered what is needed to protect the environment. Nor will it. In fact the Party embraces and advances policies that directly undercut environmental protection. It is important to take some time to examine this as background to document why Demophilia is so destructive.

Overall Environmental Record. We've already discussed some of the egregious environmentally destructive actions led by Democrats during the Clinton Presidency, such as the push for NAFTA and WTO trade agreements and the promotion of Risk Assessment over precaution-based policies. Some assume that times have changed and that now we can count on Democrats for environmental leadership. They are wrong. Let's look at the actual record of the leader of the Democratic Party as of this writing: President Barack Obama.

As was detailed earlier, Obama and his party have accepted huge sums of money from polluting corporations and their executives for campaigns throughout his political career. Oil, gas, nuclear, agribusiness, and other environmentally destructive industries bankrolled Obama's ascension to the highest elected office in the United States.

As was also shown earlier, President Obama has not taken urgently needed action on important issues. In fact, in significant ways he has led us in the wrong direction on these issues. He has:

* Sided with chemical corporations over and over again, ignoring the pleas of those injured by pesticides and other toxic chemicals.
* Made numerous horrible appointments to key governmental positions. Examples include Islam Siddiqui, a senior executive at the pesticide group CropLife America,[667] appointed as the lead U.S. trade negotiator on agricultural issues; Ernest Moniz, an individual with close ties to fossil-fuel and nuclear corporations, appointed as head of the U.S. Department of Energy;[668] Tom Vilsack, the Biotechnology Industry Organization's Governor of the Year, appointed to head the U.S. Department of Agriculture;[669] Colorado Senator Ken Salazar, appointed to head the Department of Interior, a move that drew praise from oil and gas companies;[670] Michael Taylor, a former Monsanto executive, appointed to top positions at the Food & Drug Administration;[671] and Cass Sunstein, an avid proponent of cost-benefit analysis—who, among other things, supported discounting the value of senior citizens' lives—appointed as head of the White House Office of Information and Regulatory Affairs.[672]
* Used the Office of Information and Regulatory Affairs (OIRA) to do end-runs around EPA regulations at a rate that surpassed

that of his Republican predecessor. Obama also expanded OIRA's reach to encompass existing regulations as well as new ones.

* Directed his ambassadors and other State Department officials to use their positions to pressure other countries to promote U.S. private corporate interests, such as by approving genetically modified crops.

* Failed to renegotiate existing trade agreements, despite promises to do so, and aggressively pushed new environmentally destructive trade agreements. Obama has kept corporations in the driver's seat for these new agreements while excluding the public.

* Facilitated corporate infiltration of and control over public education. Obama treats large polluting corporations as "partners," and paves the way for them to increase their power over our public institutions and resources.

Obama and Global Warming. Obama's record on energy and global warming issues is particularly troubling. Scientists warn that we should be eliminating the extraction and burning of fossil fuels, but Obama is aggressively expanding these activities. He talks a good line to environmentally concerned crowds, but his actions exacerbate global warming and enrich the fossil-fuel corporations.

As detailed in a prior chapter, fossil-fuel corporate executives bundled major contributions to Obama's election campaigns. One reason for their support was Obama's "All-of-the-Above" energy policy, which is consistent with the Republican agenda and made them less afraid of being regulated by the Obama Administration. An Exxon attorney who gave $2000 to Obama for his 2012 campaign explained that Obama has "been fine. He's left us to compete in the free enterprise system."[673]

Obama's Unabashed Promotion of Fossil Fuels. Obama is very clear about his goal of helping fossil-fuel corporations get every last bit of fossil fuel out of the ground. He brags about America producing more oil during his tenure than at any time during the prior eight years. He boasts that his Administration has "added enough new oil and gas pipeline to encircle the Earth and then some." He is particularly proud of opening up *public* lands to fossil-fuel corporations. "We're drilling all over the place....And you have my word that we will keep drilling everywhere we can," Obama says. "As long as I'm President, we're going to keep on encouraging oil development and infrastructure."[674] This is not the language of a climate hero.

Obama supports even the most environmentally egregious fossil-fuel extraction methods and locations. Take offshore drilling. Obama is aggressively expanding it despite the BP disaster in 2010. [675] BP itself remained the leading leaseholder in the Gulf of Mexico with about 620 leases as of early 2014.[676] "Offshore, I've directed my administration to open up more than 75 percent of our potential oil resources," Obama proudly declared less than two years after the BP explosion and spill. "And that includes an area in the Gulf of Mexico that we opened up a few months ago that could produce more than 400 million barrels of oil—about 38 million acres in the gulf."[677]

BP and its employees gave more than $3.5 million to federal candidates over the 20 years preceding their 2010 Gulf disaster. The largest chunk of that money went to Obama.[678] BP earned $7 billion in profits in the first quarter of 2011 despite the death and destruction it had caused in 2010. This was a 17% increase over the first quarter of 2010 (prior to the disaster.)[679]

Obama has authorized seismic exploration for oil and gas in the Atlantic.[680] He has even encouraged and approved offshore explorations in the vulnerable Arctic.[681] Oil company executives say the Arctic could eventually yield a million barrels of crude oil a day.[682]

And what about the risky practice of fracking for oil and gas? Obama enthusiastically supports it. While issuing weak rules for some pollutants at fracking sites, EPA's air quality chief literally told reporters that the ultimate goal was to control pollutants "without slowing natural gas production."[683]

EPA's 2014 carbon emissions rule set a standard for natural gas plants they could already meet, thereby giving them a green light. Even if the climate footprint for natural gas is smaller than that for coal, it is still substantial. In a best-case scenario that replaces coal with natural gas, there will still be major global temperature increases.[684] There is also strong evidence that natural gas may have a *bigger* global warming footprint than coal when methane releases from extraction are taken into account. [685]

And what about coal? Obama's power plant rule does effectively block new coal-powered plants in the U.S., but plummeting natural gas prices and other factors had already shifted the coal industry's strategy. Few utilities planned to build new coal plants even before the EPA rule was issued. [686]

Yet with Obama's blessing, coal companies are as busy as ever taking coal out of the ground. They're just exporting more of it now than before. Over a billion tons of coal were mined in the U.S. in 2012—the same amount as was mined in 2005. [687]

Obama has leased huge coal deposits in the Powder River Basin of Montana and Wyoming to coal companies.[688] The burning of this coal will lead to nearly 4 billion tons of carbon pollution in the air—the equivalent of building 300 new coal-fired power plants.[689] In terms of global warming, it doesn't matter whether that burning happens in the U.S. or abroad. Burning abroad could actually make matters worse if fewer pollution controls result in more emissions compared to those from U.S. plants. As of July 2014, Obama's Bureau of Land Management had leased 2.2 billion tons of publicly owned coal.

Obama's White House has also given the coal industry a helping hand with respect to EPA rules drafted in response to a huge coal ash spill. A leaked document shows that the Office of Information and Regulatory Affairs (OIRA) redrafted the long-awaited rule, rendering it toothless after meeting 33 times with industry groups.[690]

Even on the matter of extracting oil from tar sands, Obama hasn't been an environmental leader. He approved the southern leg of the

Keystone XL (KXL) pipeline. It connects an existing KXL pipeline from Alberta to Nebraska with the Gulf Coast. After years of delay, during which he failed to denounce oil production in general and tars sands extraction in particular, Obama finally rejected a proposed second northern KXL pipeline. With other pipeline expansions and massive increases in rail transportation of tar sands oil, this action was certainly no death knell for Alberta tar sands mining.[691]

"This project, somewhat bizarrely, took on an almost mythical status as the ultimate political hot potato between Republicans and Democrats," energy analyst Pavel Mochanov said of the rejected northern KXL pipeline. "But in actuality, it is simply not that big a deal in the grand scheme of things—not for U.S. refiners, and not for oil sands producers. This may be the only pipeline that most Americans have heard of mentioned on TV, but the reality is that new pipeline projects are being approved, and built, on a regular basis."[692]

Newspaper stories about the KXL decision failed to mention that Obama had declared 800,000 acres of public lands in Utah available for shale and tar sands leasing. More oil could be recovered from these lands than has been used so far in all of human history.[693]

At the international level, Obama has undercut meaningful negotiations at global warming summits. At the same time, he has aggressively pushed trade agreements that will help fossil-fuel corporations export their global warming fuels. [694] Thus, as he carries out the fossil-fuel industry's agenda domestically, Obama also serves their interests internationally.

The "All-of-the-Above" Hoax. Obama engages in his all-out promotion of fossil fuels in the context of his "All-of- the-Above" energy policy. The patently absurd premise of All-of-the-Above is that we should promote and maximize use of *all* the different sources of energy available to us, including fossil fuels, rather than just solar, wind, and other renewables. This strategy posits that, somehow, full throttle promotion of domestic fossil fuel is a prudent course of action that complements and even supports renewables. Nothing could be further from the truth.

Scientists have noted that burning the oil trapped in the Alberta tar sands alone represents "Game Over" in our attempts to forestall complete climate disaster. [695] Game Over can also come from other massive fossil-fuel caches now opening up under Obama's All-of-the-Above travesty. These include Powder River Basin coal, Utah tar sands oil, vast reserves of frackable natural gas, and offshore oil reserves in the Gulf of Mexico, the Arctic, and other locations.

We need to end fossil-fuel drilling and mining as quickly as possible, doing everything in our power to immediately wean ourselves from these deadly energy sources. All-of-the-Above is directly at odds with the path we should be taking.

Obama's Support for Renewable Energy. It is in the context of All-of-the-Above that Obama's actions to promote renewables must be examined. Support for renewables is dwarfed and undercut by the all-out promotion of fossil fuels that is underway.

Be careful reading statistics on how much money has supposedly been invested in clean, safe, and renewable energy under the Obama Administration. Climate-warming, unsustainable, nonrenewable energy sources like "clean" coal and natural gas are often casually included in these statistics. So are biofuels, despite the deforestation, pesticide use, and loss of food-producing lands associated with them. Nuclear energy is also included as a "clean" technology, despite its devastating impacts on health and the environment.[696]

Obama's proposed budget for 2013 gives a glimpse of the reality behind the renewables rhetoric. The Energy Department budget proposal allocated some money to solar, wind, and geothermal energy, but most went to nuclear weapons upgrading. No more than 20% was proposed for actual energy activities. Within that category nuclear energy dominated research and development spending.[697]

Statistics can also be used to mask the fact that the amount of energy currently generated from renewable sources is pathetically small. According to some accounts, for example, wind energy production doubled in the U.S. between 2009 and 2011. Wow! That sounds wonderful until you realize that after the doubling, wind accounted for only about 3% of U.S. electricity production, climbing to only 4% in the first months of 2012.[698]

Obama has increased investments in renewable clean energy compared to prior presidents, but those investments remain token compared to advantages offered to fossil-fuel corporations. In addition to ongoing subsidies, the fossil-fuel industry is not held accountable for the impacts of its activities. Costs related to public health, climate and environmental degradation are externalized, to be borne by the rest of us while the corporations reap all the profits.

More important, Obama's huge promotion of fossil fuels directly undercuts renewable alternatives. Low natural gas prices resulting from pro-gas drilling policies have contributed significantly to declines in investor support for renewables.[699] In January of 2012, the wind energy producer NextEra Energy Inc. canceled plans for new wind projects, for example. According to news reports "[n]atural gas is now the cheapest option for power generation, which has led companies to shelve wind and nuclear power projects in the country."[700]

Faith Birol, the chief economist of the International Energy Agency (IEA) explains that "[i]f gas prices come down, that would put a lot of pressure on governments to review their existing renewable energy support policies....We may see many renewable energy projects put on the shelf." Birol notes that if the world fails to invest in renewable energy, a new generation of gas-fired power plants would have a lifetime of at least 25 years, effectively "locking in" billions of tons of carbon emissions per year. The IEA estimates that there are at least 250 years of recoverable natural gas resources at today's demand levels.[701]

Obama says "...as long as I'm President, we're going to keep on encouraging oil development and infrastructure..." He couples that statement with the claim that "we're going to do it in a way that protects the health and safety of the American people. We don't have to choose between one or the other, we can do both."[702] But that claim is nonsense. Of course we have to choose between promoting oil and building an environmentally sustainable, life-supporting world. The science is abundantly clear on the matter. Expanding oil infrastructure and facilitating the burning of as much oil as possible is the opposite of protecting the health and safety of the American people, and of people in other countries as well. It is also clear that renewables can meet all of our energy needs.[703]

A recent green investor report concluded that "[p]rogress in green investment continues to be outpaced by investment in fossil-fuel intensive, inefficient infrastructure."[704] "We're still not seeing clean energy deployment at the scale we need to put a dent in climate change," said Mindy Lubber, President of Ceres Investments.

Another signal that renewables are not moving forward as they should comes from the 2012 annual State of Green Business report. A chapter entitled "Carbon Intensity. We're Moving the Needle… Backwards," notes that the economy is growing, but not as quickly as carbon emissions. "Carbon intensity"—the green business world's measure of energy-related CO2 emissions per dollar of gross domestic product—increased 2.2% from 2009 to 2010. Globally, in 2010 carbon emissions rose 5.8% while the economy grew 5.1%. In the United States, energy-related CO2 emissions rose 4% after declining for several years. The authors refer to several factors contributing to the global rise in carbon intensity in 2010, including the fall in the price of coal relative to gas and a drop in renewable energy deployment.[705]

With a policy of "Drill Baby Drill" ruling the land, renewables don't stand a chance, even when investments in them are larger than they have been in the past. You cannot simultaneously promote fossil fuels and prepare the world for their elimination.

CAFE Standards. In July of 2011, flanked by Ford, GM, Chrysler, Honda, and other corporations, Obama proposed a new "CAFE" standard. "CAFE" stands for Corporate Average Fuel Economy. The final rule was issued in August of 2012.

The new standard is an average of 54.5 miles per gallon to be achieved by 2025, up from 28.6 at the end of 2011. But credits and flexibilities bring the estimated mileage down to about 47 miles per gallon. Cars commercially available today already meet and exceed that standard.

In the long run, improved gas mileage under the new standard will not offset total emissions from increasing numbers of cars driving more miles. The standard also has loopholes for SUVs and heavier pickup trucks during the early years of the rule's implementation, allowing them to get by with less improvement. Those loopholes encourage production of the vehicles that should be most discouraged.

The Administration considered and rejected more effective standards that would have reduced total vehicle greenhouse gas emissions despite increasing numbers of cars on the road driving more miles. Moreover, the flexibilities and credits mentioned above mean that the actual outcomes from the standard in 2025 are not as climate-protective as the standards proposed for 2020 in the European Union, Japan, and China. "Setting fuel economy standards for 2025 that are lower than what we can achieve right now is not the kind of progress we urgently need," said Vera Pardee of the Center for Biological Diversity.[706]

To put the CAFE standards in perspective consider this: two coal lease purchase opportunities for the Powder River Basin offered by the Obama Administration in the fall of 2013 together allow the extraction of almost 316 million tons of coal from the ground. Burning this coal will release 523,524,951 tons of carbon dioxide into the air. That is equivalent to the emissions from nearly 109 million passenger vehicles each year. Overall, there are about 253 million vehicles in the U.S. [707] In 2011 and 2012, Obama's Bureau of Land Management leased over 2.1 billion tons of coal in the Powder River Basin, an amount that will add 3.5 billion tons of carbon dioxide to the atmosphere when burned.[708]

Nuclear Power. As part of All-of-the-Above, Obama is aggressively promoting nuclear power. His administration approved $6.5 billion in loan guarantees to enable construction of the first new nuclear power plant in the U.S. in over 30 years.

What makes this promotion of nuclear power particularly astounding is that it continues despite the Fukushima nuclear disaster. That disaster began with a triple meltdown triggered by an earthquake and tsunami in March of 2011, and it is ongoing. Even as the extremely difficult cleanup continues and scientists document health impacts near Fukushima and as far away as the United States,[709] Obama has not missed a beat in promoting nuclear power.

Without Obama's assistance, it is unlikely that nuclear power could be revived. Wall Street and the insurance industry are unwilling to invest in this expensive and very risky energy source.[710] The contributions made by nuclear corporations to Obama since his time as an Illinois state legislator have paid off for them big-time.

The Grand Climate Plan of 2014.[711] In June of 2014, the Obama Administration proposed its long-awaited Clean Power Plan. It is deplorable.

Key international bodies have issued multiple urgent calls for major reductions in global warming emissions to prevent climate catastrophe. Specifically, we need 15 to 40% reductions below 1990 emission levels by 2020, and up to 70% reductions before 2050, with groundwork for that being laid in the next 15 years.[712] Scientists at Stanford and other institutions have laid out a mix of existing renewable technologies that can be used to achieve these reductions.[713]

The Obama plan ignores all of this. It deals only with carbon, omitting methane and other greenhouse gases. For carbon, it fails to establish a standard that must be met at existing plants nationwide. Instead it establishes a "carbon intensity" goal for each state. This is a ratio of how much carbon is produced for each unit of power produced. It is not a limit on carbon.

The goal for each state takes into account what EPA thinks that state can do, resulting in very different goals across the nation. The plan calls on coal-dependent Kentucky to cut its carbon emissions rate by 19%, whereas hydro-power-using Washington State is asked to cut its emissions rate by 84%, for example. Each state is to submit a plan to EPA choosing whatever way it wants to reach its own special EPA-provided goal.

EPA *hopes* that the states' actions will result in actual carbon reductions of 30% compared to 2005 emission levels. It makes it clear that there isn't a baseline against which actual reductions will be assessed, and it is the *rate* of emissions per volume of power produced that will be examined.

The plan is deeply troubling on numerous fronts:

* Obama's targets leave U.S. emissions above 1990 levels in 2030 in direct contradiction to what international agencies say is needed to prevent climate disaster.

* Even the weak targets set by the plan may not be met. If overall power production increases, emissions may not decline as quickly as hoped or *at all* even if *rates* of emissions decline.

* The plan gives maximum deference to the states. They can claim to meet targets by establishing or expanding pollution credit trading, for example, a scheme that doesn't work, as discussed previously.

* By leaving things up to the states, Obama's plan creates a nightmarish hodgepodge instead of a cohesive plan to address a grave threat facing humanity. The plan will be difficult for EPA to oversee.

* By setting weaker standards for states with the worst carbon pollution records and by letting power plants emit at higher rates if they buy pollution credits, Obama condemns communities living near power plants to disproportionate toxic exposures. This is a classic form of environmental injustice.

* The plan encourages states to subsidize nuclear power plants that are "at risk for retirement" and will apparently allow such subsidies to count towards states meeting their carbon reduction goals. The nuclear plants "at risk for retirement" are the most antiquated and most dangerous plants of all, in other words, the ones we most urgently need to close.[714] Policies that "discourage premature retirement of nuclear capacity could be useful elements of CO2 reduction strategies...." EPA says.

* The plan promotes natural gas as a panacea, which it is not.

The science is clear. We need aggressive, enforceable policies that rapidly end the extraction and burning of fossil fuels, and that transition us to renewable energy. Obama could have proposed such a plan. It could have included moratoriums on permits to fossil-fuel corporations, phase-out timelines for fossil-fuel plants, funding and other support for renewable technologies, a plan to transition displaced fossil-fuel workers to other jobs, programs to ensure sustainable farming methods that sequester carbon and minimize fossil-fuel use, and more. These are the measures that can get us where we need to be.

Obama did not propose such a plan despite ample authority under federal environmental statutes. Instead he chose to serve the interests of the fossil-fuel and nuclear energy industries.

Is Environmental Support for Democrats Warranted by the Party's Record? Obama's environmental record is composed of weak measures that don't adequately advance renewables, combined with full-throttle advancement of polluting corporations' agendas. He is not an anomaly within the Democratic Party. Indeed, he is the leader of the Party, held up as the pinnacle of its values.

As you proceed downward from the top office of the land, you find the same sounds-good rhetoric accompanied by polluter-serving actions within the Democratic Party. On occasion, a Democratic governor will do something positive for the environment, but these actions are dwarfed by ongoing subservience to corporate interests. True leadership for a sustainable, pollution-free future is sorely lacking.[715]

Obama, other Democrats, and the Party as a whole regularly receive huge sums of money for their campaigns from Big Oil, chemical corporations, and other polluters. True to the priorities of their funders, these politicians fail to champion the strong environmental policies and programs we need.

Do the Democratic Party and its candidates deserve the trust and support of environmental organizations? Absolutely not.

EXAMPLES OF DEMOPHILIA

Even though the Democrats don't deserve trust and support, they are lavished with these. Demophilia permeates the decisions, statements, strategies, and campaigns of many environmental organizations.

FORMALLY ENDORSING AND CAMPAIGNING FOR DEMOCRATS

Some environmental organizations have a tax status that allows them to endorse political candidates. These organizations almost always endorse Democratic candidates. They also funnel money and volunteers into Democratic Party campaigns. In doing so, they lend those candidates and their party an undeserved aura of environmental leadership.

To support their endorsement decisions, organizations grossly overstate candidates' environmental accomplishments. They downplay or fail to mention major anti-environmental actions and positions.

The endorsement of Barack Obama for president by the Sierra Club, Environment America, League of Conservation Voters, and Clean Water Action in April of 2012 is an example. This was the earliest endorsement ever given by the Sierra Club in a presidential contest.[716]

Each of the groups' statements lavished praise on Obama. He had, in three years, "accomplished more for the environment and our families' health" than what had been accomplished since landmark environmental laws were passed 40 years before. Obama was "an environmental champion." Four years earlier "we had hope, now we have evidence that Barack Obama is the right choice for the environment," they said.[717]

What earned Obama this over-the-top praise? The groups provided a sparse list of accomplishments, such as Obama's carbon emissions rule for new power plants. As you'll recall, this rule ratified what was already occurring: the coal industry's increased emphasis on exports instead of new plant construction, and the expansion of the natural gas industry despite its global warming impacts.

Obama's new fuel efficiency standards were cited repeatedly. The Sierra Club called them "the Obama administration's biggest climate accomplishment"[718] claiming they were "dealing a big blow to Big Oil."[719] The Blue-Green Alliance commended Obama for "outstanding leadership on this critical issue."[720] Nothing was said about the loopholes and exceptions, other countries having stronger standards, and the ineffectiveness of the standards in light of more cars driving more miles in coming decades.

The most crucial thing the environmental groups did to justify their endorsement of Obama was ignore his huge anti-environmental record. While spinning an image of Obama "dealing a big blow to Big Oil," the groups didn't mention that he had, in his own words, added "enough new oil and gas pipeline to encircle the Earth and then some," "quadrupled the number of operating rigs to a record high," opened up vast offshore areas to drilling, and otherwise honored his openly stated commitment to aggressively promote oil and gas production. They failed to mention Obama's expansion of coal mining in the Powder River Basin and other actions promoting coal. Obama was portrayed as a climate hero even as he led the way backwards on climate issues and scuttled global climate change forums.

Nor did the endorsing groups make mention of any of the other anti-environmental activities Obama was spearheading. Pollution-promoting trade agreements drafted by corporations, environmental regulations derailed and gutted by the White House, industry-friendly appointments to key environmental positions, support for nuclear power, and promotion of genetically modified crops were all simply ignored. Also missing from the groups' statements was any mention of the major funding Obama and his party got from Big Oil, the nuclear industry, chemical corporations, and other polluting industries.[721]

The Sierra Club warned that "[i]f the president is defeated, big polluters will get free rein to turn back the clock and begin polluting our air and water without fear of repercussions." Polluters will get free rein? They'll *begin* polluting? Hello! The reins were already firmly in polluters' hands under Obama and massive pollution was ongoing. Polluters were drilling, building pipelines, constructing new chemical plants, providing the language for self-serving trade deals, using the White House to derail much-needed environmental regulations, and engaging in other environmentally-destructive actions. What was BP's Deepwater Horizon explosion and its 87-day spew of oil into the Gulf of Mexico, followed by new offshore permits and huge profits, if not "polluting our air and water without fear of repercussions"?

The Sierra Club Voter's Guide stated that "[i]n contrast to Obama, Romney has embraced the agenda of oil, gas, and coal companies. Romney's energy plan was admittedly crafted with the assistance of oil and gas executives, and proposes significantly weakening Clean Air and Clean Water Act protections as well as throwing open public lands to drilling and mining..." Reading statements like these one would have no idea that Obama was working hand in glove with fossil-fuel corporations and actively opening public lands to drilling and mining.

The Club had to do some fancy footwork after the presidential debates to continue to cast their candidate as an environmental hero. The debates were noteworthy for the absence of statements about climate change and other environmental issues. Nonetheless, the Sierra Club declared, "The debates are over, and the differences between the two candidates could not be clearer."

The obvious truth was that they could have been much clearer. They would have been clearer if one of the candidates had actually talked about climate change and laid out an agenda for addressing it, for example. Yes, Romney had said at one point: "I will fight for oil, coal, and natural gas." But Obama had been openly fighting for them as President. He had declared: "as long as I'm President, we're going to keep on encouraging oil development and infrastructure."

"[V]oting today could be the most important thing you do for the environment all year," the Club claimed,[722] even though the actual debate and Obama's record contradicted this declaration.

When the election was over, the false presentation of Obama as an environmental leader reached a new crescendo. We had *defeated* "Big Oil and Coal all across the country," we were told. The country had triumphed over the billions spent by dirty fossil-fuel interests. After fighting the fossil-fuel industry for decades, the momentum was on our side.[723] These pronouncements falsely implied that Obama and the Democrats were not funded by fossil-fuel interests and that they were leading the charge against those interests.

The news media magnified the misleading spin about Obama being an environmental hero. "Environmentalists joined President Obama this morning in taking a victory lap" exclaimed one news article. Since green groups were "significantly outspent by oil and other energy interests," the results showed that clean energy and environmental issues resonate with voters, it claimed.[724] No mention was made of the huge donations from dirty energy corporations and other polluters to Obama and the Democrats in the 2012 election and before. Obama's silence about climate change and other major environmental issues during the presidential campaign was also glossed over. Despite the lack of discussion on these issues on the campaign trail and in the debates, strangely the election was declared a referendum on them.

In January the Sierra Club sent out a Happy New Year message featuring a video about accomplishments in 2012 which culminated in all-out Obama worship, complete with fireworks and swelling music as footage of Obama on election night was shown. The intended message could not have been clearer: electing Obama was an environmental accomplishment. His actual record, positions, statements, and funding sources were ignored.

Demophilia Beyond Endorsements

Many environmental groups are organized under sections of the U.S tax code that prohibit them from endorsing candidates or political parties. That doesn't mean they don't play favorites, however. Whether or not they openly take positions on candidates and parties, environmental organizations generally put their faith in Democrats and engage in behaviors that lend them support.

They Limit Criticisms of Weak and Even Overtly Bad Environmental Policies Advanced by Democrats. Demophilia-prone environmentalists praise dubious Democratic Party accomplishments, often effusively. Even when Democratic leaders engage in activities that are clearly harmful to our cause, Demophiliacs offer muted criticisms at best. More often, they simply don't mention those harmful activities at all. The silence has been deafening.

Obama was lauded for simply talking about climate change in his Inauguration speech in 2013. The National Wildlife Federation celebrated a renewed sense of hope because of those few empty words.[725] The Environmental Defense Fund urged its members to thank the President for talking about climate action. "Tell President Obama you stand with him," they urged, even though we clearly need to stand *against* Obama's climate-destroying policies.

The pathetic climate plan Obama proposed in 2014 elicited the same undeserved praise. "Time is running out, but today the president is reminding us that we have the solutions," said Frances Beinecke, president of the Natural Resources Defense Council.[726] How strange that a politician who has whole-heartedly promoted global warming activities and bragged about it, was supposedly *reminding* us about solutions. And why was NRDC not expressing outrage about the plan's details?

MoveOn.org sent out giddy emails describing the President's plan as "the biggest action ever taken by an American president to limit global warming," a compliment which actually doesn't mean much when you think about it.[727]

Many groups did criticize the President's plan, but their criticism was muted. They made sure to preface objections with deferential statements about the plan being a huge step forward, which it isn't.

Here's an interesting sentence offered by one blogger: "The EPA's emission-reduction targets fall a little bit short of what environmentalists hoped for, and well short of what is technologically feasible and what will ultimately be needed to actually avert climate catastrophe."[728] We should ask: why are environmentalists only hoping for something that will still doom us to climate catastrophe? Why are environmentalists' goals less than what we actually need? Moreover, why doesn't the fact that Obama's proposal is even more out of line with what's needed (or what environmentalists hoped for) prompt them to express outrage and demand a much stronger proposal? We *are* trying to prevent climate catastrophe, right?

The upshot of all this is that Obama and his Party come off as environmental leaders, saving the day despite all odds, and are supported by grateful environmentalists.[729] With this as the starting point, the already inadequate plan will surely be watered down even further. Meanwhile, the temperature rises, fossil-fuel production and infrastructure expand, and we move closer to the point of no return.

As Democrats receive praise for each limited pro-environment step they take and even for steps that are ineffective or harmful, the myth of their environmental leadership grows. As a result when people do have something negative to say about some Democratic Party action or proposal, they feel compelled to first assert that, of course, as everyone knows, overall Democrats have done all sorts of great things for the environment.

Reporters and others outside of environmental groups further build the myth of Democratic environmental leadership by paying homage to it in their articles. A *Mother Jones* article in 2011 about how the Obama White House undercut environmental rules began by first asserting that Obama's environmental record had at times been "great." Few readers probably took the time to follow the link provided with the word "great." It led to an article about Obama's November 2011 announcement that he was temporarily rejecting the Keystone XL Pipeline's northern leg.[730] This was hardly evidence of greatness, given his approval of the pipeline's southern leg, his openness to approving the northern leg with a different route, and his all-out promotion of other pipelines and oil production. Yet, readers of the *Mother Jones* article were given the impression that the White House's outrageous attack on environmental regulations was balanced by greatness on other issues.

Muting or omitting criticism creates bizarre disconnects in environmental groups' materials. Funding appeals and other letters talk about attacks on the environment without mentioning the fact that the attacks are being led by Democrats. They use the passive voice—*our environment is under attack*—or they name corporations as the perpetrators without noting that Democrats gave those corporations the green light.

A Sierra Club Insider article in April of 2013, for example, warned that "Big Oil wants to double down on more dangerous drilling in the Arctic and off our coasts..." despite recent disasters like the BP Gulf spill, Shell's rig running ashore in Alaska, and a major ExxonMobil pipeline spill in Arkansas. The article urged us to "[t]ell President Obama we need to protect our communities, coasts, and public lands from dangerous oil and gas drilling and spills." What makes this letter so bizarre is that they imply that Big Oil has done all these bad things on their own, and that we need to ask superhero Obama to do something about it. In reality Obama has been Big Oil's champion.[731]

It's as if we're being asked to rely on a wolf dressed up in our grandmother's clothes as an ally. At some point, shouldn't we notice how big grandmother's teeth are? Obama and the Democratic Party have been serving the oil and gas industry's interests, not ours.

This kid glove approach toward Democrats carries over to various pundits and columnists. Jim Hightower, for example, wrote in his newsletter that "Barack Obama went to Washington promising change. What greeted him was a swarm of Wall Street bankers, the war machine, 13,000 corporate lobbyists...weak-kneed Democrats... and other powerful forces of business-as-usual politics." One would think from reading this that Barack Obama had not himself had countless fundraisers with Wall Street executives and that he hadn't accepted mountains of funding from war-supporting corporations, lobbyists and other powerful supporters of business-as-usual.[732]

The kid glove approach for Democrats contrasts sharply with how environmentalists respond to anti-environmental activities carried out by Republicans. Bemoaning environmentalists' silence when Obama appointed the anti-environmental Cass Sunstein as his regulatory czar in January of 2009, the president of Clean Air Watch noted that "[p]rogressives would've screamed" about such an appointee put forth by Bush. [733]

Environmentalists make a point of pinning blame for environmental problems on Republicans while imposing no such accountability on Democrats for their wrongdoings. "If Shell and their allies in Congress get their way, pristine habitats like the Polar Bear Seas could be riddled with oil rigs someday soon," a typical Sierra Club missive reads. It will also be Obama getting *his* way since he is an avid proponent of offshore drilling, including in the Polar Bear Seas, but the Club doesn't mention that.[734]

Similarly, an Earthjustice funding appeal celebrated Obama's reference to global warming in his second inaugural address and blamed Congressional Republicans for any future problems in addressing climate change. "Yet the recent election left us saddled with one of the most environmentally hostile U.S. House of Representatives in history," Earthjustice lamented. "They'll be pushing the destructive agenda of their Dirty Energy backers and they'll be doing everything they can to sabotage President Obama's leadership." While the anti-environmental agenda of Republicans in Congress is crystal clear, so is Obama's, to anyone paying attention. Remember that Obama is heavily funded by Dirty Energy backers too.

Here's another example of the double standard employed by environmental organizations. In 2011, Health Care Without Harm (HCWH) and Natural Resources Defense Council (NRDC) joined forces to target members of Congress with ads and letters denouncing their efforts to undercut EPA.[735] "People feel EPA should be left alone to do its job, which is to protect public health," an NRDC spokesperson said. "Failure to allow EPA to safeguard our air supply exposes thousands of people with chronic illnesses, including our children, to increased health episodes," a HCWH staffer noted. The HCWH/NRDC strategy did include three Democrats as targets while mainly going after

Republicans, but the participation of those Democrats in attacks on EPA did not spur environmental groups to denounce the Democratic Party as a whole. The Party as a whole is immune from criticism for the actions of its members.

Moreover, it is grossly misleading to imply that but for Congressional attacks EPA would be free to do its job. As discussed earlier, Obama has used his Office of Information and Regulatory Affairs (OIRA) to aggressively undercut EPA, forcing the agency to rescind its smog rule, and weakening and derailing other rules. Yet these attacks on EPA do not prompt denouncements of the Democratic Party.[736]

Designing Strategies and Campaigns Based on Electoral Impacts. The drive to help Democrats win elections regularly affects the action plans developed by environmental organizations. Research and organizing tend to be focused in districts where they can help Democrats get elected.

Demophilia can also prompt environmental organizations to drop entire efforts because they might make Democrats look bad. As described in chapter 2, a staff member at another environmental organization in Washington State urged the Farm Worker Pesticide Project to stop giving reporters documents exposing the governor's subservience to the agrichemical industry because it was making her look so bad. Pulling back from getting more press coverage was the wrong thing to do, and we refused. But other groups hold their punches all the time to favor Democratic candidates by hiding things about them that contradict carefully concocted images of environmental leadership.

THE ULTIMATE DEMOPHILIA: TAKING INSTRUCTIONS DIRECTLY FROM DEMOCRATIC PARTY OFFICIALS

Environmental groups don't just shape their strategies and silence themselves to help Democrats as the result of internal planning processes.

They sometimes literally take directions from Democratic Party leaders about what to say and do.

Here's one disturbing example. In 2009 Obama's green team invited various environmental groups to the White House to talk about climate change. At the meeting aides handed around a one-page memo providing polling data and talking points. Climate change, it was explained, was not a winning message. Therefore, even with Democrats controlling both Houses of Congress and the White House, Obama would not talk about climate change, the threat it poses, and the changes needed to address it. He wanted environmental groups to silence themselves as well. The assembled groups were asked to talk about clean energy as an economic opportunity, rather than climate change as an urgent environmental problem. "My most vivid memory of that meeting is this idea that you can't talk about climate change," said Jessy Tolkan, who was a leader of the climate youth group, Power Shift, at the time.[737]

The Guardian newspaper learned of the secret meeting in 2012 and investigated. According to *The Guardian*, "most of the environmental groups were inclined to go along" with Obama's request. Indeed, in the months and years following the meeting, the Obama Administration and lead environmental groups failed to say much about climate change. Media coverage of climate change, its devastating impacts, and campaigns to address it head-on dwindled. Public relations firms and front groups funded by the fossil-fuel industry, however, got lots of climate denial "news" published.

Maggie Fox, chief executive of the Climate Reality Project, acknowledged that the strategy of censoring talk about climate change "in the end... proved to be unwise." An Environmental Defense Fund spokesperson on the other hand insisted, "I don't think it was a mistake."[738]

Ultimately, Hurricane Sandy forced climate change back into the national dialogue a few days before the presidential election in November of 2012. Ironically, the man who'd fostered silence on the issue for years was showered with praise by environmental organizations for merely mentioning climate change in his inaugural address in January of 2013.

The Reuters news service noted that climate change had been "a mostly dormant issue during last year's presidential campaign, and environmentalists hoped that Obama would put the topic squarely on his agenda in a second term."[739] Knowing what we now know about the willing self-censorship carried out by environmental organizations at Obama's request, the Reuters statement takes on new meaning.

EDF's President Fred Krupp praised an Obama pledge to take on climate change in June of 2013, declaring, "Thanks to the President, the days of silence and inaction on climate are over."[740] How ironic to praise Obama for ending a silence he himself had fostered.

The Demophilial Fight Against the KXL Pipeline

The fight against the northern leg of the KXL pipeline was one of the most visible global warming campaigns waged by environmentalists. Opponents gathered more than 2 million voices together to urge Obama to reject the pipeline.[741] Over 86,000 activists signed a "Pledge of Resistance" indicating that they would commit civil disobedience if Secretary of State Kerry recommended pipeline approval. The organization 350.org coordinated 15,000 rallies in 189 countries, a bus tour to campuses across the United States, and various protests including one in which 350.org leader Bill McKibben and others were arrested after chaining themselves to the White House fence.[742] On March 3, 2014, nearly 400 young people were arrested at the White House protesting the pipeline.[743]

With the pipeline slated to carry over 800,000 barrels of especially dirty oil every day from Alberta, Canada, to the U.S. Gulf Coast, it made sense to organize around it. Demophilial framing and other behaviors dominated the KXL campaign, however, causing confusion and undermining our long-term ability to stop global warming and address other global crises.

McKibben explicitly stated, "We won't attack the President. We will only hold him to the standard he set in 2008."[744] Obama's campaign

logo was used on anti-XL campaign materials and protest signs, implying faith in Obama and glossing over his horrendous record on global warming. Photos show McKibben and others wearing prominent
Obama buttons at protests.

This blatant display of Demophilia was accompanied by a more
subtle but equally important type of Demophilial behavior: framing
KXL issues in a way that was highly favorable to Democrats. Anti-
KXL organizations repeatedly declared that Obama's KXL decision
would "determine his legacy."[745] It would be his "defining moment
in the history of the world." [746] These statements indicated that
the damage he had done and continued to do on other fronts didn't
matter. Pushing fossil-fuel production, scuttling global summits,
promoting nuclear power, pushing through bad trade agreements,
gutting EPA regulations, serving the chemical industry, launching
illegal wars and more—these things would all be forgiven if Obama
nixed the northern leg of KXL. This was a sweet deal for Obama
and the Democrats. They could enjoy savior status bestowed by environmental organizations. Meanwhile oil industry backers wouldn't
be unduly impacted because they were already transporting Alberta's
oil through other avenues that were expanding.

The anti-KXL campaign groups insisted that Obama wants to
lead us forward on global warming issues, despite voluminous evidence to the contrary. According to the messaging that permeated
the campaign, Obama had our backs, and we just needed to let him
know that we had his as he took on the big bad fossil-fuel industry. The absurdity of this imagery is obvious to anyone who follows
Obama's actions.

McKibben has lately been a bit clearer about Obama's actual record,
such as in a December 2013 article he wrote for *Rolling Stone*.[747] But he
still stops short of the obvious implications regarding the Democratic
Party: Obama has never had our backs. He and his party are a force we
need to fight, not praise.

The Consequences of Demophilia

Democratic and Republican Administrations alike have advanced the agendas and the fortunes of the 1%, exacerbating environmental problems. We need to acknowledge this and figure out what to do about it. There is no time to waste. By failing to tell the truth about the Democratic Party, environmental organizations are blocking the conversations we need to be having. By striving to help Democrats get elected and stay in office, they are diverting resources away from effective strategies including building our own political party.

The Democratic Party is not our friend. And it's not just a matter of Republicans blocking Democrats. Even when Democrats control both houses of Congress and the White House, they serve polluting corporations. Obama and other Democratic Party leaders have an aggressive, proactive agenda that harms our environment and our ability to protect it.

Nonetheless, stoked by environmental organizations, a sideshow dominates everyone's attention: the never-ending battle of Democrats versus Republicans. Since campaigning for the next election begins not long after votes are counted, electoral conflict creates a constant distraction from gaining the power that should be ours. We never get to the real battle—wresting control from the 1% and establishing a system that empowers us to put in place the policies we need.

Given the Demophilial behaviors that dominate environmental organizations, Democrats know that they will not be held accountable for their actions. They need only use simple tricks to keep environmental groups in line. If they make statements now and then about global warming being a real problem, that's enough to satisfy many environmentalists.

Demophilia obfuscates. It obscures the downward spiral we are in, constantly fueling the false impression that by supporting Democrats we are taking on the problems that plague us. It diverts resources from the battles we should be waging and replaces the powerful concept of holding firm to principles with one of analyzing our actions in terms of impacts on Democrats' electoral success. Demophilia dramatically undercuts our struggle for justice and survival.

Lesser Evilism—the Perfect Mindset for Perpetuating Our Downward Spiral

Many argue that support for Democrats is warranted because things will be worse if Republicans are elected. Lesser-evilism—the practice of supporting candidates we don't like to avoid a greater evil—is a toxic strategy, however.

We need to change direction on a slew of urgent environmental issues. Democrats and Republicans alike are taking us in the wrong direction. Sure it's nicer to head more slowly towards the abyss, but continuing on our suicidal path is not okay, no matter the pace. We really need to turn the ship around now, and electing Democrats is not making that happen. The question to ask is not who is better, the Democrats or the Republicans, but rather how do we get real environmental action—something that is not offered by either party.

A strong argument can be made that Democrats are actually the greater evil, not the lesser one. Black Agenda Report (which provides "news, information and analysis from the black left") uses the phrase "the more effective evil" to describe Barack Obama. While their analysis has focused on non-environmental issues, it holds true for Obama's environmental record as well. Obama appears to be much more effective at advancing anti-environmental policies and programs than Republicans would be. One of the main reasons for this is Demophilia.

If Mitt Romney had expanded offshore and onshore oil drilling, promoted nuclear power and fracking, attacked EPA rules, and pushed through trade agreements written by private corporations there would have been huge protests. Yet Obama does all these things with impunity while environmental organizations barely object. Demophilia enables the Democratic Party to get away with it, virtually unchallenged.

Regardless of who is the real lesser evil, however, it is quite clear that basing our actions and votes on "lesser evilism" has not served us well. Both the Democratic and Republican parties have become more and more entrenched in serving the interests of the 1%. Over the years, the downward march into greater disparity between rich and poor, increased poverty, rising global temperatures, depleted fish stocks and other crises has been unrelenting. The pace of decline has increased over time, not decreased. It's time to break free, tell the truth and demand real change.

The Democratic Party Can't Be Fixed From Within

"But," some insist, "we can fix the Democratic Party from within." This strategy is clearly not working. With each passing year, the Democratic Party moves farther away from serving the public interest, rather than closer to it. We now have a Democratic President who openly espouses a "Drill Baby Drill" approach to fossil fuels, pushes nuclear power, advances trade agreements drafted by corporations, promotes the GMO interests of Monsanto and other agrichemical giants, and more.

The Democratic Party, like the Republican Party, is a wholly owned subsidiary of Wall Street, Big Oil, the chemical industry, Big Pharma, and war profiteers—in short, of the 1%. Hoping to change it into an organization that puts human needs before profits makes as much sense as believing you can turn a wolf into a sheep.

Regardless of their intentions, environmentally oriented Democrats end up propping up the Democratic Party rather than transforming it. By endlessly identifying as Democrats they give the impression that the Party takes strong stances on environmental issues, even as it does the opposite. In other words, they give the Party cover.

"Progressive" Democratic officials hold their tongues or deliver only muted criticisms when it is Democrats who act against the environment. Under Republican Administrations, Democrats strongly criticized plans to open up the Arctic to drilling, for example, loudly denouncing the Republican Party and its leaders as a whole for their disregard for the environment. Now that Barack Obama is giving oil companies the go-ahead in the Arctic, there has been some criticism from within Democratic Party ranks but it has been very restrained. It is certainly not used to denounce Obama and the Party as a whole.

By remaining Democrats as they criticize Democratic Party actions, "progressives" send a clear message that overall the Party must be doing a good job. Seeing someone who seems to care about the environment stick with the Party persuades members of the public that its environmental record must be good in general, even though it isn't.

Democratic politicians usually vote with Party leadership no matter how bad bills or appointments may be. Only five Democrats opposed the appointment of Cass Sunstein as Obama's regulatory czar despite the fact that his positions are every bit as bad as those of Bush nominee John Graham. By contrast, 37 Democrats opposed Graham's confirmation.[748]

"Progressive" Democrats do sometimes cast votes at odds with Party leaders, but these votes rarely make a difference in the anticipated outcome. That outcome has been determined by Party leadership and a few protest votes are tolerated because they don't alter it.

When their votes actually could make a difference, Democrats are pressured to ignore their consciences and they cave. Denis Kucinich's plan to cast a principled vote on health care, for example, led to a personal visit from the President. Kucinich then cast a vote that directly contradicted principles he had stood for his entire career.

Environmentally concerned Democrats serving as heads of government agencies are allowed by Party leaders to go only so far in protecting the environment. When Obama forced EPA Administrator Lisa Jackson to rescind her smog rule and reinstate a legally indefensible Bush-era rule, she did so without criticizing him or resigning.

In making appointments to key agency positions, the Democratic Party selects loyalists who will remain quiet in the face of anti-environmental actions. For elected offices, it promotes those who will toe the line for wealthy interests. The few mavericks allowed through provide the illusion of change within the Party, persuading voters to not break away, diverting us from the work we need to be doing.

DEMOPHILIA—A RECAP

Given its record on environmental issues, the Democratic Party does not deserve the support of environmental organizations. Favoring the Party based on lesser-evilism or a belief that it can be fixed from within is not a winning strategy. In fact, the Democratic Party is much further away from environmental leadership now than it was in the past. We're losing on every front and the Democratic Party is part of the problem. Widespread Demophilia at environmental organizations is undercutting our ability to win the changes we need.

CHAPTER 25

Beyond Environmental Issues

• • •

THIS BOOK FOCUSES ON ENVIRONMENTAL issues. But the same dynamics explored here apply to the other major issues of our day. At best we are running in place. More often we are losing ground at an alarming pace.

Just as with environmental issues, solutions for other problems are obvious, but we can't seem to achieve them. One reason is that ultra-rich individuals and huge corporations control resources and wealth, blocking our way forward. Another reason is that the organizations we look to for leadership engage in self-defeating behaviors.

Wealthy individuals and foundations have a lot to say about which advocacy organizations exist and are heard on issues well beyond environmental ones. Taken together, national policy groups "tilt strongly in the direction of the haves," Professor Kay Schlozman of the University of Chicago concludes, based on comprehensive analysis of the world of non-governmental organizations (NGOs).[749] "Organizations representing those with ample political resources and deep pockets vastly outnumber advocates for the economic interests of the middle class and the poor," she says. Organizations representing the wealthy, she points out, also tend to have far bigger budgets than other groups.

Schlozman found that of the billions of dollars devoted annually to lobbying in Washington, 72% is spent by organizations representing business interests. Only 2% is spent by public-interest groups—a category that includes both liberal and conservative advocates. One percent is spent by unions, and less than 1% is spent by organizations advocating on behalf of social welfare programs or the poor.

Health Care

Let's take a look at access to health care as an example of how the same dynamics at play on environmental issues are at play on other issues as well.

<u>The Health Care System We Deserve.</u> A strong majority of people in the U.S. support a "single-payer" health care system.[750] People understand that healthcare is a basic right, and that it makes much more sense to have a "single payer"—the federal government—cover everyone's medical expenses than to continue the crazy hodgepodge of multiple payers we have now that is dominated by greedy, for-profit insurance companies.

The U.S. could save $400 billion per year by switching to single payer.[751] Money would no longer be wasted on insurance corporation's profits, their CEO's exorbitant salaries, and unnecessary paperwork and procedures. As a single payer, the government would also have leverage to lower costs of medicines and care.

Because of these savings, we could provide health care, including dental and vision, to absolutely everyone. Nobody would be left out.

And our health would improve. Under our multiple-payer largely for-profit system, the U.S. has far worse health outcomes than other developed countries despite paying so much more into our health care system. U.S. health care is ranked 37th in the world by the World Health Organization.[752]

It would be easy to put a single-payer system in place in the U.S., bringing us in line with most developed nations of the world. All we have to do is remove the words "65 and older" from the Medicare statute and expand funding for that wildly popular program. Activists have been working for "Improved Medicare for All" for a long time.

What We Got Instead. In 2010, President Obama signed the "Affordable Care Act," better known as ObamaCare. The law entrenches and enriches insurance corporations. Americans who don't qualify for Medicaid or Medicare are now required to buy health insurance or face a fine. Moreover, to supposedly make insurance affordable, ObamaCare provides subsidies for some people to help cover monthly premiums. In other words, insurance corporations get millions of new customers and taxpayer money is funneled to for-profit corporations.

The details of the law we got are appalling:

*   ObamaCare leaves tens of millions without any health care coverage. The Congressional Budget Office had projected 27 million left out in the cold as of 2021. With 26 states not expanding Medicaid[753] despite the law's encouragement that they do so, the projection rose to 30 million.[754]

*   For vast numbers of Americans supposedly helped by ObamaCare, "affordable care" provides neither affordability nor care. Subsidies are based on pre-tax income and fail to take into account the financial realities of our lives.[755] Even with subsidies, people are still paying large amounts of money each month for insurance and/or they are selecting low-quality plans. Those plans have high deductibles (amounts we must pay before insurers help on medical bills);[756] high co-insurance rates (the percentage of medical costs we pay even after deductibles are met—40% is typical of plans offered on ObamaCare exchanges); and high annual maximums for out-of-pocket payments.[757] Lots of people who have insurance can't go to the doctor because of cost.[758]

    Moreover, because ObamaCare leaves insurance companies in charge, people will continue to regularly find that medical costs are not covered under this or that exclusion or excuse. Insurance corporations want to maximize their profits and are very good at finding ways to do so. And they helped write ObamaCare.

A policy update sent recently to someone I know states that the insurer will only cover various important medical treatments if they are "medically necessary," for example. His doctors are required to notify the insurer in advance so it can "assure that proposed treatment is effective based on the latest scientific evidence." Why do we still have a system in which profit-seeking insurance companies get to tell our doctors what treatments to prescribe?

Similarly, in the fall of 2012, Change.org circulated a petition that began with the words: "My 13-year-old brother Seth is sweet and extremely sick....But according to our insurance company Cigna he's 'not sick enough' for the health insurance company to cover the medication his doctor says he desperately needs."[759]

Even ObamaCare's much-touted ban on insurers refusing to cover people with pre-existing conditions is not iron-clad. Insurers can accuse people of "fraud or intentional misrepresentation" to get around the ban. Will they do this? Probably. A 2010 investigation found that in pre-ObamaCare days, the insurance company Wellpoint used a computer algorithm to automatically target policyholders recently diagnosed with breast cancer, thereby triggering immediate fraud investigations of them. A news article shared stories of women who had their insurance canceled right after finding out they had cancer.[760] While this story dealt with pre-ObamaCare actions, the law leaves the fraud and intentional misrepresentation loophole intact.

Here's another trick insurers are using to leave people in the lurch: narrow networks. If people use "in-network" health care providers, insurers help pay bills, after deductibles, and minus co-pays and co-insurance. There are caps on what insured people will have to spend over all. If people use "out-of-network" doctors on the other hand, there's less or no coverage, and there are no caps. Unsurprisingly, narrow networks abound under ObamaCare.

Only one insurer offering plans through the Washington State online exchange includes Seattle Cancer Care Alliance in Seattle, and only three include Seattle's Children's Hospital, for example. "In our view it is unacceptable for an insurer to have no qualified pediatric surgeons in network," Mark Del Beccaro of Children's said.[761]

Similarly, a *New York Times* article chronicled the ordeal of a family whose nine-month-old needed emergency heart surgery. Although they chose an "in-network" hospital, their medical team included doctors who worked *in* the hospital but not *for* it, and were therefore "out-of-network." This is a common arrangement. Instead of focusing solely on their daughter's health, the parents had to spend time fighting massive medical bills.[762]

There really is no end to the schemes insurance corporations use to get out of paying our medical bills. Having these superfluous profit-seeking middlemen act as gatekeepers between us and the care we need is insane. With insurance companies in charge, people will pay lots of money for health care and/ or go without that care. Medical bankruptcies will remain a problem.[763]

Other Problems. Much more could be said about the negative impacts of ObamaCare. It undermines workplace health care coverage in various ways, for example. [764] It adds to the stress we each feel as we navigate a morass of ever-changing policies and options, dealing with insurance company agents and government officials who specialize in obfuscation.[765]

The Democrats Deliver ObamaCare. As a state senator running for the U.S. Senate in Illinois, Obama declared himself "a proponent of a single-payer universal health care program." He said that to get single payer "first we have to take back the White House, we have to take back the Senate, and we have to take back the House."[766]

In 2009, Democrats did indeed control both houses of Congress and the White House. But President Obama did not champion single payer. Instead, he took it "off the table" before the health care debate even got underway. Obama refused to admit single-payer advocates to White House summits.[767] When a Senate committee held a public roundtable discussion on health care issues, no single-payer supporters were included. One by one, eight single-payer advocates stood up in the audience to object to their exclusion. They were arrested, hand-cuffed, and charged with "disruption of Congress."[768]

While single-payer supporters were given the cold shoulder, insurance and pharmaceutical corporations were welcomed with open arms. Obama met repeatedly with their CEOs.[769]

Well-placed past and future industry employees played key roles within Congress. The point person on health care for Senate Finance Committee Chair Baucus, for example, had previously worked for a large insurance company. After helping draft, pass, and implement ObamaCare from within government, she went to work for a giant pharmaceutical corporation.[770]

Despite Democratic control of both houses of Congress, Obama claimed he had to compromise early and big to get bipartisan support. This self-crippling approach was illogical.[771] Did blocking discussion of single payer, caving on the public option, and other huge compromises create bipartisan support? No. Even though Obama jumped out the window to avoid being pushed, ObamaCare was ultimately adopted without a single Republican vote.

Big Money: Paving the Way for ObamaCare. The health care industry has long loved the idea of forcing people to buy private insurance. After the ultra-right-wing Heritage Foundation called for such a program in 1989, Republicans introduced ObamaCare type bills in the U.S. Congress.[772] In 2008 Republican Governor Mitt Romney put the model into effect in Massachusetts[773], where it has not worked.[774,]

The industry gave over $20 million to Obama during the 2008 election cycle and over $7.7 million to his opponent John McCain.[775] Blue Cross/Blue Shield alone invested $207,750 in Obama and $97,730 in McCain.[776]

Healthcare industry money was spread across Congressional races as well. Blue Cross/Blue Shield gave a total of $539,223 to 141 Democrats and a total of $537,716 to 130 Republicans in the House of Representatives. Meanwhile, in Senate races 37 Democrats received a total of $514,002 and 35 Republicans received a total of $462,935 from this corporation.[777] Pharmaceutical giant Pfizer money flowed not only to Obama ($119,275) and other Presidential candidates but also to 99 Democrats in the House, 122 Republicans in the House, 21 Democrats in the Senate, and 29 Republicans in the Senate.[778]

Electoral contributions were supplemented by massive lobbying expenditures. In 2009, the health insurance industry had six lobbyists for every member of Congress.[779] Over 350 former government staff members and retired members of Congress were among the ranks of those lobbyists. More than 50 former employees of the pivotal Finance Committee or its members lobbied on behalf of the health-care industry.[780]

The pharmaceutical/health products industry reported 1797 lobbyists in 2009. Of these, 61.8% were "revolvers," i.e., they went through the revolving door between government and industry. In 2010, the figure was 1633 lobbyists, and 62.5% were revolvers.[781]

In 2009 alone, the pharmaceutical/health products industry spent over $272 million on federal lobbying, while the insurance industry spent over $163 million. In 2010, the figures were over $246 million and $157 million respectively.[782]

What Did Social Justice Groups Do? Various organizations have worked tirelessly to promote single payer for a long time. Physicians for a National Health Plan (PNHP) and its chapters throughout the U.S. have been active since 1987, for example. The Health Care Now coalition has been campaigning since 2004.

The world of non-governmental organizations (NGOs) fighting for health care reform changed in 2008, however. The Robert Wood Johnson foundation gave large grants to state groups to promote "public-private partnership health reform"—in other words, ObamaCare-type programs. In July, a new coalition was formed to champion this kind of reform. It was called Health Care for America Now (HCAN), a name that was confusingly similar to Health Care Now, the single-payer coalition. [783] HCAN had more than 1000 organizational participants, including a number of large unions, which were a big funding source. It received some huge grants, including a $5 million grant from billionaire George Soros.

Flush with funds, HCAN carried out a $50 million campaign, replete with staff throughout the U.S., meetings with government officials, T.V. ads, and thousands of organizing actions. HCAN worked in concert with the Obama campaign and Democratic leaders in Congress to build consensus for ObamaCare. It verbally attacked the big bad insurance companies—a message that resonated with most Americans—even as it championed a system that empowers and enriches those companies.[784] [785]

Single-payer advocates were appalled by HCAN's stance. Rose Ann DeMoro of the California Nurses Association objected that HCAN had "surrendered in advance on the only overhaul that will actually cure the disease, a single payer, expanded and improved Medicare-for-all reform."[786] Other single-payer advocates wrote that HCAN was "sucking up all the air in the room" and waving "the white flag of surrender before the first shot is fired."[787] Reacting to HCAN's campaign director declaring single payer off limits for discussion, Dr. David Himmelstein of PNHP said, "When he says there's a debate that single payer can't be part of it's because organizations like his—the big money organizations with $25 million to spend—decide in advance that they're not going to actually do anything that is going to take on the insurance industry. If we had that sort of resources to actually mount a campaign for single payer, we could actually win."[788]

Despite being excluded, single-payer advocates kept pushing hard. At a breakfast meeting with reporters in April of 2009, House Speaker Nancy Pelosi (D-CA) noted with exasperation, "Over and over again, we hear single payer, single payer, single payer. Well, it's not going to be a single payer."[789]

It wasn't single payer because Big Money wanted ObamaCare and well-funded NGOs gave the Democrats cover to support that law. HCAN, MoveOn, and others supported ObamaCare and put their resources into fighting tooth and nail for "the public option." This was a government insurance plan made available in health exchanges alongside private plans.

Many people hoped the public option would set the stage for single payer. But single payer works because there is a *single* payer. By definition it can't be embedded within a multiple insurer system. Moreover, Obama himself made it very clear that the public option was in no way a Trojan horse for single payer.[790,791]

Whatever the public option would have accomplished really didn't matter though. Even as NGOs fought for it, Obama had already secretly bargained it away.[792] Later when Obama declared the public option dead, these NGOs moved seamlessly from insisting that the public option was an absolute bottom line to acting like it didn't matter. MoveOn had sent many emails urging people to punish elected representatives who supported any bill without the public option. Suddenly, they flip-flopped, and we were urged to punish our elected representatives if they *failed to* support ObamaCare, which contained no public option.

When ObamaCare passed, HCAN's website declared "We Did It!" MoveOn declared ObamaCare "a huge step towards universal health care." Then both groups became insurance sales agents. MoveOn ran ads in college newspapers and on Facebook.[793] "Republicans think you're stupid. Prove them wrong—get coverage today," a typical ad said.

New "nonprofit" organizations were also formed to help insurers sell policies including Enroll America, for instance, which had raised about $6 million by December of 2012. Its financial backers included health care corporations like Aetna and Blue Cross Blue Shield.[794]

Enroll America held focus groups around the country and commissioned a nationwide survey to help hone its message. Their survey found that even with federal subsidies, many uninsured people might balk at the cost of coverage. Only about one-third of respondents leaned toward thinking monthly premiums of $210 for a single person earning $30,000 a year were affordable. The survey company recommended that Enroll America not cite specific dollar amounts when talking to uninsured people about new coverage options.[795]

Insurance Companies Rake in the Dough. Insurance companies are doing extremely well under ObamaCare. They posted better-than-expected profits in 2013 with rosy predictions for 2014. Nine of eleven insurance companies had their stocks close, during the first week of June in 2014, at near 52-week highs. Humana's share price had increased more than 53% over the prior year. Aetna's share price was up 31%, Cigna's 32%, United's 28%, and WellPoint's 39%.[796]

Insurance industry CEOs have been rewarded with huge compensation packages. Mark Bertolini, CEO of Aetna, for example, got $30.7 million in 2013, which was 131% more than what he got in 2012. Centene's CEO Michael Neidorff's compensation increased 71% from $8.5 million to $14.5 million. Molina Healthcare's Mario Molina got a 140% raise from $4.95 million in 2012 to $11.9 million in 2013. The compensation packages in 2013 for the 11 largest for-profit insurance companies totaled more than $125 million.[797]

In raising Wellpoint's earnings estimates in October of 2013, CEO Joseph Swedish noted the long-term membership growth opportunity created by the ObamaCare exchanges. UnitedHealth Group CEO Stephen J. Hemsley similarly celebrated that "[t]he emergence of public exchanges, private exchanges, Medicaid expansions…have the potential to create new opportunities for us to grow and serve in new ways."[798]

Health Care: A Recap. What happened on health care parallels what has been happening on environmental issues. Ultra-wealthy corporations have used their massive wealth to influence elections, legislation, perceptions and more. Democratic Party leaders co-opted the language of single-payer groups, criticizing big bad insurance corporations even as they did the bidding of those corporations. Big Money NGOs gave Obama cover as he declared single payer off-limits and championed a law originally advanced by Republicans. Those NGOs didn't balk at the idea of tying tiny gains to huge backsliding. Nor did they question why Obama forbade even consideration of single payer when both houses of Congress were under his party's control.

And so we find ourselves mired in ObamaCare even though Improved Medicare for All has majority support in our country and is the obvious solution to our health care problems.

OTHER ISSUES

The story is the same on each of the important issues of our day. Huge corporations and ultra-rich individuals make giant contributions to electoral campaigns, fund massive lobbying efforts, pay for public relations strategies, file lawsuits, and otherwise use their enormous resources to steer things their way. Public-interest groups do not fight back effectively.

On economic issues, Democrats and Republicans alike have been abject servants of Wall Street for decades. The Clinton Administration gutted welfare, pushed through Wall Street-serving trade deals, and repealed the Glass-Steagall Act, thereby deregulating financial institutions, for example.[799]

Obama and the Democratic Party took piles of campaign contributions from Wall Street in 2008 and 2012, as discussed earlier in this book.[800] Once in office, Obama filled economic positions in his Administration with the best friends Wall Street could want: former executives from Citigroup, Goldman Sachs, and other financial firms, and individuals who had pushed for financial deregulation under prior Administrations.[801]

Despite populist rhetoric, Obama has led the charge for policies that enrich and empower Wall Street. Huge bailouts have been delivered without giving the public any real control over those bailed out.[802] Ineffective reform legislation has been advanced which does not truly rein in the perpetrators.[803] Obama has failed to amend existing trade agreements that require deregulation of financial institutions and he has pushed through new agreements that are even better deals for his Wall Street friends.

Obama and his party have focused public discussion on things like the "Bush tax cuts" and whether they would be allowed to expire. These matters are a side show of little real importance.[804] Meanwhile the huge loopholes the wealthy use to minimize taxes have remained intact. The tax rate for the richest Americans is only 35% now, as compared to 91% in the 1950s and 1960s, and 70% in the 1970s.[805] There are very low tax rates on dividends and capital gains income.[806] Scores of major corporations pay no net federal income taxes.[807]

Worldwide, between $29 trillion and $32 trillion dollars has been squirreled away in over 120,000 dummy offshore companies to avoid taxes. At least a quarter of that total, and probably more like half of it, comes from the U.S.[808] The entire U.S. federal budget for 2012 was only $3.7 trillion. A recent Philadelphia school system budget shortfall of $304 million was about one ten-millionth of a percent of the amount of money hidden by the ultra rich in offshore accounts each year.[809]

Mega banks and other financial institutions that engaged in abusive and irresponsible behaviors have emerged richer and more powerful than before.[810] Meanwhile, supposed benefits to the rest of us from bailouts, settlements, and legislation have been illusory.[811] For us there has only been more and more pressure to accept austerity and belt-tightening as the new normal. As our money has been funneled upward into the coffers of the ultra rich, we have coped with cuts to basic public services, privatization of public programs, and a stagnant minimum wage. Even Social Security is on the chopping block. While Obama sometimes makes statements implying he doesn't want cuts to Social Security, he appointed individuals who support cuts to positions that will shape what happens next.[812]

And what have non-governmental organizations that work on financial policies done through all this? They've pretended that the Democrats have been fighting for the little guy and against Wall Street. They've focused on the side shows while ignoring the mammoth ongoing backward slide perpetrated by Democrats and Republicans alike. In short, they've aimed low, compromised readily, engaged in Demophilia, and displayed all the other self-defeating behaviors we saw among environmental organizations.

What we see on economic issues, health care, and environmental issues, we see on all the other big issues of our day. People don't want war, but that's what we have—endless spreading war that makes money for weapons manufacturers but is horrendous for everyone else.[813] We want immigration reform, but instead we've seen the largest numbers of deportations ever under Deporter-in-Chief Obama and increased militarization of the U.S.-Mexico border. Even when Democrats controlled both houses of Congress as well as the White House, legislation creating a pathway to citizenship did not move forward. As of this writing, we're being asked to celebrate Obama's latest token gesture—a vague promise to let some people get temporary work permits without any pathway to citizenship or assurance that this status will last.

The list goes on and on. Instead of increasing funding and support for public education, our elected officials are handing our schools over to private corporations.[814] Instead of revoking "trade" agreements that undermine our sovereignty, environmental protection, and social justice, both parties are pushing through more international agreements drafted by corporations.

On each issue, the ultra rich are using their unfathomable wealth to call the shots. NGOs are not fighting effectively, and we are losing ground.

What is happening on other issues is highly relevant to environmentalists. People can't join our campaigns when they've got more imminent problems to deal with or when their employment depends on them keeping quiet. And more money flowing into the coffers of the 1% means those elite few have even more resources to use in blocking environmental reforms.

Financial policies that serve the wealthy few, our inability to secure a decent health care system, downward spiraling environmental trends, and other crises are all symptoms of the same underlying problem. Social justice activists, regardless of our areas of focus, are all blocked by the same giant—one that is created by ceding our resources and wealth to a few corporations and individuals. We must unite to defeat that giant.

CHAPTER 26

Is This What Democracy Looks Like?

• • •

Tens of thousands—perhaps even hundreds of thousands of organizations—are carrying out countless campaigns to right wrongs in our world. Groups focusing on the environment, health care, workers' rights, immigration, poverty, racial equality, civil liberties, peace, education, and all sorts of other important issues are all out there fighting for justice. For the most part, these campaigns are carried out separately from one another.

The result is pure chaos. Organizations churn out their messages, competing for our attention, media coverage, legislative action, funding and more. We are bombarded by a dizzying array of requests for assistance: Sign this petition. Call that Congressperson. Show up at this hearing. Pressure that corporation. Any given month, we hear scores of disconnected and often conflicting declarations about what the important issues are, how good or bad particular corporations are, and so forth.

We are told repeatedly that it's necessary to invest huge resources in an issue in order to win and maintain victories on it. Seeking money to defend Social Security, MoveOn declares, "[W]e'll need at least $200,000 to get noticed."[815] Bill McKibben of 350.org muses that, "You know, environmentalists never win permanent victories. That's the thing. I guess we've got to keep this fight, as with many others, going strong."[816]

We are even told that if we don't implement big campaigns on particular issues we deserve to lose on them. In his speech at a climate change rally, attorney-activist Van Jones said, for example, "if you don't fight for what you want, you deserve what you get."[817]

But all of this is insanity. Think about it.

Even if hard work does produce real victories on selected issues, which is rarely the case, we can't possibly wage enough campaigns to address all the crucial threats we face. We don't have enough time and resources for that.

In other words, by accepting as normal a model in which people must mount resource-intensive campaigns to get anything done, we also accept as normal the concept of consciously ignoring important issues. We pretend that the multiple problems that plague us are disconnected and best addressed sequentially when that is simply not the case. We learn to look at the menu of campaigns that groups are mounting, plug into the "most important" ones, and not dilute our energy by fighting on other issues.

This approach makes no sense. It doesn't work to choose between stopping global warming, saving pollinators, demanding nuclear disarmament, pulling millions out of abject poverty, preventing toxic contamination of our water supply, and countless other critical matters. They are *all* extremely important. Failing to address any of them may lead to irreversible catastrophic impacts. These impacts may even undo advances on issues we do choose to address. It is a Pyrrhic victory, for example, to preserve wildlife habitat only to see wildlife populations crash because of widespread exposures to reproductive toxicants.

Moreover, most of the major issues we face are intertwined with one another. They *can't* be dealt with sequentially, but rather must be dealt with together. They stem from common roots and will only be solved when we address those roots. Social justice groups that promote narrow campaigns as if other issues are unimportant and unrelated do us a disservice. They divide us when we need to unite.

The most troubling thing about the mindset we have embraced is that it doesn't mesh with how things are supposed to be in a democracy. If the majority of us want a policy implemented, we should be able to easily put it in place without having to fight an uphill, multi-year, resource-intensive battle. How have we come to accept as normal a situation in which we pick a few issues, invest huge amounts of time and energy on these, and ignore the fact that we're careening towards disaster on other fronts?

It is incredibly dangerous to accept this model of social activism. It keeps us hurtling in the wrong direction and threatens our very survival.

There is overwhelming support for environmental protections and for other life-sustaining policies that create a just and sustainable world. There is overwhelming opposition to policies that further enrich and empower the moneyed few. But we, the people, can't seem to translate our will into the policies we want. As Professor Martin Gilens notes, based on research documenting our disempowerment: "[a] democracy that ignores most of the public most of the time has a tenuous claim to legitimacy."[818]

In many ways, as a whole, the complex of social justice groups on which we are relying fosters a mindset of "No We Can't"—a deadly self-fulfilling prophecy that stands between us and the changes we need. No, we can't frame our issue campaigns broadly. No, we can't take principled positions seeking what we truly want. No, we can't hold firm for those positions. No, we can't vote for someone we agree with and refuse to support candidates whose positions contradict our own. No, we can't have actual democracy.

I am *not* saying that we should drop the narrow causes on which we're working. Campaigns being waged on specific problems are the way people will ultimately find one another and articulate a larger vision. I *am* saying that we have to find each other and articulate that vision as soon as possible, because time is running out. We have to reject the notion that we *deserve* atrocious policies on issues if we don't mount a huge campaign to address them. We need to stand up and shout for all to hear that the current set-up is not normal. It's not right. It's not democracy, and we must unite to change how things work.

The time has come to claim "Yes, We Can" as our own. Given the threats our world faces as the direct result of "No We Can't" activism, we have no choice but to do so.

The compassion and caring that spurs so many to plug into social justice groups' campaigns reflects the enormous power available to us. When we identify the giant we're up against and refuse to be splintered any longer, and when we refuse to accept an undemocratic set-up, we will swiftly transform our lives and our world.

PART V

How to Defeat the Giant

• • •

THIS BOOK HAS TAKEN READERS on a harrowing journey. We've confirmed that the human race is rapidly losing ground on do-or-die issues, and there is no time to waste in turning things around. We've seen that a Big Money giant stands between us and the policies we urgently need. A small number of corporations and well-heeled individuals control much of the world's wealth and resources, leaving the vast majority of us without control over our individual lives and our collective destiny.

We've also learned that Big Money shapes the groups we've been depending on to lead us to safety, and those groups engage in self-defeating behaviors that keep us running in circles.

All of this is daunting.

But things don't have to stay the way they are.

CHAPTER 27

Beyond Capitalism

• • •

THE OVERWHELMING MAJORITY OF PEOPLE on Earth want sane and compassionate policies that protect our environment. We want justice and equity. We don't want to crash and burn.

But we can't achieve these goals, no matter how hard we fight. Not with the game rigged against us like it is.

Why do we lack the resources and power we need to do what we want? Because our economic system ensures that. Why does a Big Money giant call the shots in our world—a giant that grows bigger and bigger by the moment? Because our economic system creates and feeds that giant.

The problem is capitalism. We must move beyond it.

Capitalism 101. Capitalism is an economic system in which major industries and natural resources are privately owned. A limited number of individuals own the land, machinery, infrastructure, and materials involved in producing important goods and services. They decide what will be produced, how and where production will take place, and who will do the work. They own the goods and services that are produced and the profits that accrue from selling them.

In contrast to these wealthy owners, most people within capitalist economies work as wage laborers. They rent their muscles and brains to business owners by the hour or the month. These workers have little or no control over workplace conditions, over what is produced, or even over where production will take place. If corporate owners decide to move production to another country, workers find themselves laid off. Workers do not own the profits their labor produces or control how these are spent.

Under capitalism, businesses compete against each other as they strive to maximize profits. This arrangement creates incentives for them to minimize pollution control expenditures and drive down wages in order to lower production costs. It also creates incentives for them to advocate policies that foster unemployment. Wages can be kept low when lots of people don't have jobs.[819]

It is primarily "the market" that determines how resources are allocated and how goods and services are distributed in a capitalist economy. In other words, industrial titans set important public policy based on their desire to maximize profits. Moneyed interests influence the market through advertising and through their influence on government intervention.

Do we need to expand production of toxic chemicals? No, we need to reduce it. But the price of natural gas is low, so chemical corporations are gleefully building new facilities to cash in on new chemical sales. [820] A major environmental decision that hurts us all is being made by a limited number of corporate owners.

In a capitalist society we may try to plan, but we are limited by our lack of ownership over key resources. Instead of deciding what needs to happen and just doing it, we must instead devise incentives to try to entice private owners to implement our wishes.

For example, there are obvious solutions to the climate crisis we face. Various experts have produced blueprints for every state and country, identifying a mix of existing renewable technologies that could be swiftly deployed to end reliance on fossil fuel. Can we decide together to put these in place and get on with it? No. We don't control energy corporations. Instead, we come up with tax credits and other indirect measures to try to get corporations to change. It's like trying to do brain surgery while wearing boxing gloves. And it's not working.

Owners are allowed to accumulate as much wealth as they want under capitalism. Indeed, accumulation of capital is encouraged. Prior chapters document the massive success the top 1% of the world's population has had in accumulating wealth.

Capitalism is based on the concept of a few individuals and corporations controlling vital resources and accumulating the wealth produced by the majority. The existence of an empowered upper class and a disempowered lower class isn't an unexpected consequence; it's the very basis of the capitalist economic system.

<u>An Alternative to Capitalism.</u> We are so trapped by the stress of capitalism that many people are skeptical that we can ever get beyond it. What's the alternative, they ask.

Earlier chapters examined the powerful ways in which those who accumulate wealth under capitalism have limited the conversation on environmental issues and other topics like health care. The biggest censorship of all, however, results from the taboo that permeates society when it comes to the topic of socialism.

We still feel the impacts of the Joe McCarthy era in the 1950s. Some 10,000 to 12,000 workers lost their jobs during the decade's "Red Scare" based on alleged connections to anti-capitalist thinking. Hollywood power brokers maintained a list of actors and others who were ostracized due to their "subversive" views. Hundreds of people went to jail for their anti-capitalist political beliefs.[821] In 1958, as a condition of employment, an estimated one-fifth of the U.S. workforce was subjected to "loyalty oaths," many of which entailed swearing to have no affiliations with the Communist Party.[822]

The message of McCarthyism was clear. Don't question capitalism, and don't talk to people who *do* question it.

Despite this repression and its legacy, people still questioned capitalism. So, in the 1970s, business interests got organized to defend it. A memo written by corporate lawyer Lewis F. Powell, Jr. to the chairman of the U.S. Chamber of Commerce's Education Committee in August of 1971 sheds light on their game plan. [823] (Powell was appointed to the

U.S. Supreme Court shortly after he sent this memo. There he could directly implement his pro-capitalist agenda.)

Powell bemoaned evidence of discontent with capitalism, such as college campus polls in which almost half of the students "favored socialization of basic U.S. industries."[824] He called on businesses to mount a full-court press to defend "free enterprise." Powell urged the Chamber to become a major voice for capitalism dedicating substantial financial resources to that work. He recommended that businesses invest heavily in public relations campaigns to defend capitalism, including allocating 10% of annual advertising budgets for that purpose. Powell called for the creation of cadres of media-savvy pro-capitalist thinkers, writers, and speakers; getting pro-capitalism courses and materials into colleges and high schools; and major increases in political spending.

"[T]he time has come—indeed it is long overdue—for the wisdom, ingenuity and resources of American business to be marshaled against those who would destroy it," Powell said. "There should be no hesitation to attack the [Ralph] Naders, the Marcuses [a Marxist professor] and others who openly seek destruction of the system. There should be not the slightest hesitation to press vigorously in all political arenas for support of the enterprise system. Nor should there be reluctance to penalize politically those who oppose it."

The Chamber responded to the memo by forming a task force composed of 40 business executives (from GE, GM, U.S. Steel, Phillips Petroleum, CBS, and other companies) to come up with specific proposals based on it. They adopted those proposals in November of 1973.[825] Not long after the Powell memo was written, numerous family and corporate foundations created new groups to promote capitalism, such as the Heritage Foundation, the American Legislative Exchange Council, the Cato Institute, and other powerful think tanks.

The Chamber has indeed become an extremely powerful entity with millions of dollars at its disposal, much of which comes from major corporations. Together with dozens of think tanks and legal foundations, it has helped shape a powerful "business civil liberties" movement to block challenges to capitalism and restrictions on businesses.

Much more could be said about the systematic well-funded campaign to keep capitalism in place and prevent socialism from even being discussed. U.S. involvement in deposing democratically elected leaders in other countries has limited the examples of socialism we can examine and point to, for example.[826]

The upshot of all this is that it has been taboo for decades to even raise the topic of socialism. Hence, while suffering the consequences of our current economic system, many have little understanding of the alternatives.

I personally assimilated pro-capitalism messages early on, even though I questioned so many other things. I remember thinking that people handing out socialist pamphlets were "out there," without making any effort to hear what they had to say. I did not want my credibility brought into question by associating with them. This powerful message had been drummed into my psyche.

Yes, "socialism" has been demonized, and those who dare to support it have been marginalized. There has been an extraordinary absence of discussion about it. But socialism is precisely what we need to be talking about if we want to establish democracy and steer the human species away from disaster. Why? Because we need a name for the post-capitalist democracy we hope to build. What else are we to call an economic system that moves beyond the limits and hazards inherent in capitalism, ensuring that decisions are made for public good rather than private gain?

Socialism 101. Socialism is an economic system in which major industries and resources are publicly owned. Working people control what these industries produce and the profits associated with them, which we can invest as we see fit.

Note that it is only "major" industries that are publicly owned. Mom-and-pop stores, restaurants, and other small businesses can still be privately owned. We can also still own our homes and personal property.

Note also that working people being in control is part of the definition of socialism. Vibrant democratic grassroots structures are an essential element of this economic system.

In a socialist society, workers will participate in workplace decision-making councils that coordinate with community councils and feed into regional and national decision-making bodies. Those elected to serve at higher levels of government will earn no more than the people they represent and they will be subject to instant recall.

Currently, most people experience democracy as voting every two or four years, and a large percentage of Americans don't even vote. In contrast, democratic participation will be a meaningful daily activity for everyone in a socialist economy. Issues and what to do about them, as opposed to candidates and their personalities, will become the focus of attention.

In all workplaces, workers will make important decisions about working conditions and other factors affecting their lives and the products and services they produce. In some cases, workers will be direct owners of their businesses, and will have discretion regarding what happens to the products and services they produce and how the surplus will be invested.

In other cases where national planning is needed, workers will own their businesses collectively with others in society. Some industries and the jobs they provide will need to be phased out in order to protect our environment and otherwise serve the public interest. When this happens, displaced workers will not lose income. They will be paid well and retrained for other jobs. As we phase out fossil-fuel extraction and processing, for example, we must provide fully paid transitions for fossil-fuel workers.

Under socialism, we will be able to make and implement plans to solve environmental problems and arrange for rational distribution of things like food. Decisions will be driven by cooperation and meeting public needs rather than by competition and promoting private financial gain. As the owners of major industries and the wealth they produce, we will be able to take direct action. On energy issues, for instance, we will be able to identify the mix of renewable energy sources needed in each region and put these in place.

There are no incentives for keeping wages down and fostering unemployment under socialism. In fact, in a socialist economy it will be easy to guarantee a job with a livable wage to everyone. There's plenty of work to go around, including building renewable energy grids and equipment, creating comprehensive mass transit systems, improving education with reduced class sizes, building housing, growing food, improving health care, repairing the environment, and creating art and so much more. We'll be able to collectively make plans to employ people accomplishing this work and to directly implement those plans. We will no longer be limited to pleading with the 1% to do what we want, or hoping to stimulate their good will through profit incentives.

We will even be able to reduce the numbers of hours people work each week without reducing pay. Worker productivity has steadily increased for decades,[827] yet capitalist owners have depressed workers' wages and pocketed the gains for themselves. In a socialist economy we will jointly decide what to do with the extra money that results from increased productivity. One likely decision will be to reduce work hours, giving each of us more time for civic involvement, our friends and families, art and music, learning new things, and simply relaxing.

A guaranteed job won't be the only basic economic right enjoyed by every person in a socialist economy. We will also be able to guarantee good incomes for those who can't work, free health care, and free education from preschool through college. Worrying about whether we or our loved ones will miss out on a decent education, go without medical treatment, or end up living on the street will become a thing of the past.

All of this will be paid for by harnessing the collective wealth produced by working people—wealth that is now funneled into a few hands as profit. Resources currently squandered on the military, spying, police repression, risk assessments for unneeded pesticides, and other wasteful endeavors linked to securing and enhancing corporate profits will also be redirected to social good.

There are many details to figure out regarding what a socialist world will look like, and there are many variations on how to set things up. But our survival depends on having this discussion and moving forward to socialism.

Arguments Used to Prevent Discussion of Socialism. All sorts of myths are circulated to discourage public discussion of socialism. Each swiftly falls apart upon examination.

Myth: Socialism means Stalinism. Many proponents of capitalism falsely equate socialism with Stalinism, even though they are completely at odds with one another. Stalinism represented the *derailment* of socialism in Russia.[828] State ownership of key industries without true democratic control over decision-making (established from the ground up in workplaces and communities) was not the goal of socialist revolutionaries. Nor are China and other countries with state-owned industries, in which working people lack democratic control over their lives, examples of the socialist system we need to establish.

Many factors led to the degeneration of the Russian Revolution.[829] Invasions by armies from four capitalist countries (including the U.S.) and the backward, impoverished state that the country was in at the time of the revolution were both key. We can and should study what happened in the Soviet Union to learn from experiences there, as we transition to democracy-infused socialism.

Myth: People won't work without profit as an inducement. Others say socialism isn't viable because people won't work unless driven to do so by the profit motive. Anyone who has ever been involved with a nonprofit organization or a charitable cause knows that this claim and the assumptions on which it is based are ridiculous. People volunteer all over the place, motivated by love, the joy of being creative, and the pleasure of being useful.

Repairing trails in a park? Building a local playground? Lots of people turn out to help on things like these. When a tornado devastates a neighborhood, people show up in droves to help their neighbors.

In 2010, 26% of U.S. adults volunteered through a nonprofit organization. Volunteers contributed 15 billion hours worth $283.84 billion in average wages.[830] These statistics do not encompass those who did volunteer work separate from a nonprofit and others whose efforts were not tracked.

Ironically, some of the most ardent proponents of capitalism point to people's generous hard-working spirits when it suits them. President George H. W. Bush coined the phrase "a thousand points of light" referring to people's willingness to help others without pay. In his 1989 inaugural address, Bush said that "[t]he old ideas are new again because they are not old, they are timeless: duty, sacrifice, commitment, and a patriotism that finds its expression in taking part and pitching in."

Obama has also made volunteerism a theme of his presidency. In 2009, he signed legislation to more than triple the size of the AmeriCorps program from 75,000 volunteers to 250,000 by 2017. Praising Bush for his thousand points of light initiatives, Obama said that "volunteerism has gone from something that some people do some of the time to something that lots of people do as a regular part of their lives."[831]

The argument that, without the capitalist profit motive no work would get done, rings hollow.

Myth: People will trash collectively held property. In his book, *Saving Capitalism*, Robert Reich argues that private property has "obvious advantages over common ownership." He cites Garrett Harden's tale of cattle owners letting their cows overgraze on the town commons in *The Tragedy of the Commons*. Reich then points out that, to his knowledge, "no customer has ever washed a rental car."[832]

Here's the thing about the cattle example. The herdsmen are operating within a capitalist system. As Hardin explains, each is seeking to maximize their individual gain. Each receives all the proceeds of selling an extra cow while being allowed to externalize the effects of overgrazing by sharing those with other herdsmen. Moreover, the capitalist model measures the success of each herdsman by his or her individual profit alone. Under this model, it would be self-defeating for herdsmen to sacrifice their own income for the good of the commons. The capitalist economic model harshly punishes that kind of altruism.

This tale would play out quite differently in a socialist economy. In such an economy we are all owners of major industries and their aggregate proceeds. Moreover, each of us is assured of a good job, health care, pay when we can't work, and other benefits. We are not forced to compete with others, and we don't need to worry that by cooperating to protect the environment we might not have enough money to pay for food.

As to rental cars, I certainly have never washed one. On the other hand, I've pulled ivy from my children's school grounds. Many other people engaged in this blatant protect-our-commons activity alongside me. I could provide countless other examples of people joining together to protect and maintain the commons. Just think how much more we would do, if we had more leisure time and less stress because our jobs, incomes, health care, and educations were guaranteed.

A key principle affecting the commons under capitalism is "alienation." In an economy where everything is privately owned, individuals learn that it pays to care most for those things that belong to *you*. We become "alienated" from most commodities, having no say and no direct stake in their disposition. Washing a rental car provides no benefit to the renter. Under socialism, however, the commons includes all essential industries and resources, and all are managed cooperatively and democratically. In such a system, it is far more likely that an individual will take an interest in maintaining a shared resource, even if they don't *personally* own it.

<u>Myth: People won't innovate without profit as a motivator.</u> Proponents of capitalism also argue that innovation will be stymied if people don't earn patents and other protections for their inventions and discoveries. But the same non-monetary motives that spur people to engage in volunteer work are also at play with respect to research and invention.

In fact, devices like patents and other means of tying creativity to profit can actually undercut innovation. Take agricultural research, for example. For decades land-grant universities produced countless valuable innovations for growing food efficiently and shared this information freely with farmers and other researchers. But after laws adopted in the 1980s prompted these universities to "partner" with private corporations, all that changed. Now research is steered heavily towards the interests of for-profit corporations rather than the interests of farmers and the general public. Corporations are granted patents, and they use these to prevent research beyond the narrow scope that will further their financial interests. Scientists eager to study patented seeds are barred from that research by the patent-holder. Far from encouraging discovery and the expansion of knowledge, the profit motive is squelching both.[833]

Recall also how Myriad Genetics, Inc. claimed patents for certain naturally occurring human DNA segments, thereby holding a monopoly on BRCA (breast cancer) gene testing for 15 years. This stifled genetic research by others. Ultimately the Supreme Court ruled that "a naturally occurring DNA segment is a product of nature and not patent-eligible merely because it has been isolated," thereby ending Myriad's monopoly. But the case leaves intact other patents, including ones related to human genetics. In addition, Myriad still retains control over the results of research it did during the 15 years of its monopoly. In a socialist world, that "proprietary" data would be available to all, spurring research by others that could help save lives.[834]

In a socialist society, people will be less stressed, work shorter hours, and have more time to be creative. For the first time, our ability to innovate will be truly freed.

<u>Myth: Socialism will deny people the high incomes they deserve.</u> Yet another argument made by proponents of capitalism is that that those at the top deserve the huge wages they earn because they work hard or because they create jobs and products of value to society as a whole. This ignores well-documented damage done by major corporations

to our environment, public health, and workers' financial fortunes. It also assumes that there is no way to create jobs other than the capitalist model, an assumption readily contradicted by alternatives like the worker-owned Mondragon Corporation in Spain. Composed of many cooperative enterprises in industry, finance, retail, and knowledge, this corporation operates democratically. It employs over 100,000 people.[835]

Moreover, every invention or innovation you can name has a multitude of people that contributed to its creation. Teachers help educate and inspire future inventors. Doctors and healthcare workers protect the well-being of budding innovators. Research and technology from publicly funded universities makes new breakthroughs possible. And each new discovery stands on the shoulders of countless others that came before, without which the latest leap forward would not have been possible.

An original, socially useful idea is worth something, but surely not thousands or tens of thousands of times the amount paid to those whose labor brings the idea to fruition. Likewise, some jobs may be harder than others. But the huge differences in today's world between what the lowest and highest-paid workers earn are clearly inappropriate.

Most people recoil at the assertion that the executive of a major corporation deserves to earn huge sums each year, while people growing our food, teaching our children, and engaging in other vital work deserve so much less. Something is very wrong in a society where so many people's work does not produce income that covers their needs, while a lucky few are awash in wealth.

Finally, let's not forget that many wealthy individuals receive giant incomes not because of hard work but because interest and dividends roll in without their lifting a finger. Many inherit huge sums of money and other assets.

<u>Myth: People won't be able to own property.</u> Often capitalism is defended as protecting a fundamental right to own private property. This is ironic, because even a cursory glance at property ownership under capitalism reveals that it isn't all it's made out to be.

Chapter 8 laid out the disturbing details. Sure, a small number of people do own lots and lots of private property. But most people own very little. Take our homes, for example. Vast numbers rent apartments or houses, living there at the whim of landlords. Even home "owners" aren't necessarily real owners. In the U.S., banks have owned more of the housing stock than people do, for a while now.

In fact, lots of people have "negative" ownership—in other words, "debt."

When we go to work, most of us produce goods and services but have no claim to them. A key characteristic of capitalism is that we're renting our bodies and our brains to someone else who owns the things we produce and the profits associated with them.

In short, most people in capitalist societies don't own as much private property as capitalism's proponents imply. And we certainly don't control our individual lives and our joint destiny the way we should.

We can still own homes and personal items under socialism. In fact, we'll be much more likely to truly own them as opposed to possessing them while someone else is the actual owner, as is so often the case in our world today. More importantly, we'll own our political system. We'll own our lives and what we do with them. We'll have much more control over the future we bequeath to our children.

<u>Myth: We won't be free. We won't have democracy.</u> Capitalism is regularly held up as synonymous with democracy. Terms like "free enterprise" are often used to emphasize the "freedom" we have to own things or to become entrepreneurs.

But capitalism is antithetical to democracy.

As individuals, we spend most of our waking hours at workplaces over which we have little or no control. We have to fight for every dollar we are paid and every "fringe benefit" we receive. Many of us are trapped in jobs that don't cover our expenses, unable to voice concerns because we can't risk being fired. This situation is a recipe for oppression.

At the societal level, we don't have control over the resources we need to build a just and sustainable world. Instead of democratically discussing how to allocate the ample wealth produced by our collective labor, we find ourselves discussing how to impose an insane austerity agenda. Trillions of dollars exist that could be used for all the things we need—including food and shelter for all, free universal health care, grids and infrastructure for 100% renewable energy, excellent mass transit, reduced classroom sizes, and much more. But the trillions generated by our collective labor sit in private bank accounts, leaving us powerless to implement rational, life-affirming policies.

The wealthy few largely determine the direction our society will take through the decisions they make about what products and services to produce next. We may try to plan for a different direction but we lack real power to implement our plans.

At the same time, those who hoard wealth use it to buy things that distort public discourse and policymaking. As detailed in this book, buying elections and legislation are only a small part of that picture.

Capitalism divides people into the "haves" and the "have-nots." Accumulated wealth and control over vital resources lead to enormous power in the hands of the few, and severe disempowerment of the many—the direct opposite of democracy. Under capitalism, working people lead splintered lives, unable to choose work we like, unable to enjoy financial security and the leisure that comes with it, and unable to establish the policies and programs we want.

When we don't control our workplaces and the jobs that are available to us, and when the fruits of our labor are appropriated by those few at the top who *do* own and control so much, we lose our most basic freedoms. We watch helplessly as the climate grows more volatile, fisheries and bee colonies collapse, toxic contamination spreads, wars escalate, poverty deepens, and hunger holds hundreds of millions in its grip. The fundamental rules of our economic system disenfranchise the majority and favor policies that benefit an elite few. That's not democracy.

We Can't Fix Capitalism. Many people these days agree that things are not going well under capitalism. But they claim we can and should save it. Robert Reich's latest book is even called *"Saving Capitalism."* In the first Democratic Party presidential debate in the fall of 2015, Hillary Clinton declared that we need to "save capitalism from itself."

Even Naomi Klein, author of the book, *This Changes Everything: Capitalism vs. the Climate*, generally refers to our problem as "deregulated capitalism," rather than just capitalism. This implies that capitalism can be fixed by better regulation.

We need to be very clear. We can't fix capitalism. Its basic structure is the problem. The reforms we win under this undemocratic system will be limited and subject to reversal.

As long as major industries remain in private hands, we will lack real control over our lives and our destiny:

1. We will not decide which products and services are produced. A few private owners will do that, even though their decisions dramatically affect our world.
2. We will lack the wealth required for the things society needs, even though wealth abounds and is created solely by working people.
3. Members of the owning class will accumulate money and use it to buy scientific research, front groups, media outlets, academic institutions, public relations strategies, spies, and so forth. These expenditures will massively distort public discourse, undermining the public interest.
4. Workers will continue to have little or no control over our workplaces, even though many of us spend the majority of our waking hours there.
5. Workers and communities will continue to depend on corporate owners for jobs, an arrangement that subjects us to extortion.

These fundamental features of capitalism will stymie us, no matter how hard we try to create the world we want.

We can attempt to mandate specific environmental decisions at corporations by fighting for policies that limit bad behaviors or require good ones. But Big Money's influence over science, elections, education, the news, jobs and more will continue to derail us time and again. Under capitalism, putting even one much-needed policy in place requires massive resources and single-minded focus, and then we can count on corporate shenanigans undercutting implementation and enforcement. We can also count on steady pressure to repeal our victory and on new problems replacing the ones we've "solved." Different toxic products will replace the ones we've finally banned, and so on and so forth.

And what about all the environmental problems for which we can't mount campaigns to win specific regulatory mandates—the problems that fall by the wayside as we engage in triage? They will continue unabated.

We can also try to influence specific corporate decisions through market mechanisms. But the 1% uses its wealth and position to undermine these efforts as well. Moreover, it is inherently difficult to achieve the outcomes we want in a complex world with multiple players and countless corporate decisions each day. In fact, attempts to steer corporate behaviors on one issue can undercut attempts to influence them on others, as examined in previous chapters.

Some maintain that we can save capitalism by taking a broader approach. We can redefine the ground rules for corporations, insisting that they make profits secondary to serving the public interest. But corporations will easily circumvent such directives. They will do what they've already planned on doing and simply declare it benign. Minor investments in spin doctors and scientists who vouch for their environmental stewardship will provide cover. Corporations are adept at wrapping a mantle of public service around the most despicable affronts to humanity.

Some proponents of capitalism argue that we can make things better via economic reforms that shift wealth from the 1% to the 99%. We can increase taxes on the rich, enforce antitrust laws, increase the minimum wage, keep banks from taking risks with people's savings, and more. But we've been there and done all that before. The New Deal adopted reforms of this type while leaving capitalism itself in place. With time, the super rich reversed much of it. The same can be expected if we again implement limited economic reforms while leaving capitalist production and property relations intact. If anything, capitalist owners are more adept now at blocking and undoing public advances than they've ever been.

In short, as long as we leave private owners in charge of major industries, we will limit ourselves to nipping around the edges of the problems we face. We won't be able to end economic inequity, address social injustice, or save our environment.

As another example of what happens when we don't challenge the underlying economic set-up, consider ObamaCare. It left the basic capitalist structure of our dysfunctional health care system intact. It even reinforced that structure by requiring Americans to buy insurance. ObamaCare limited some of the tactics insurance companies have used to deny medical coverage, but kept those companies firmly in charge of our health care. They have had no trouble finding ways to continue to foist medical costs onto us: High premiums. High deductibles. Narrow networks. Refusing to cover treatments they deem inappropriate. You name it.

Under capitalism, fighting for the public interest is like playing Whack-a-Mole at an amusement arcade. No matter how many times we whack problems down, others pop up to take their place. Capitalist owners always find a way to get what they want. And we find ourselves perpetually disempowered.

The truth was stated succinctly by Seattle City Councilmember Kshama Sawant at a global warming event in New York City in 2014. "It's really straightforward. You cannot control what you do not own."[836]

Under capitalism, our victories are few, small, and temporary. Because vital industries and the products and wealth they produce are privately owned, a small number of ultra-rich individuals call the shots in our world. Working people do not, even if we pretend otherwise. This undemocratic arrangement is at the heart of capitalism. Saving capitalism means denying ourselves control over our individual lives and our joint destiny.

Capitalism can't be fixed. And we won't be able to protect our environment and create a just world until it is replaced.

This is not to say that we shouldn't push for interim reforms. Raising taxes on the rich, ending police brutality, increasing the minimum wage, adopting specific environmental regulations, and implementing other reforms should indeed be part of our agenda. But we need to be clear that these are but steps on the way to replacing capitalism with a more democratic, more rational economic system. They are measures that lay the foundation for socialism. We must use advocacy for reforms to educate about the need for *systemic* change and to build a movement for that change.

What About Campaign Finance Reform and Amending the Constitution? In recent years a new coalition called "Move to Amend" has gathered momentum in response to the U.S. Supreme Court's decision in the Citizens United case.[837] The coalition is justly concerned about the undue influence of money in elections. To address these concerns, its members are working to amend the U.S. Constitution.

If Move to Amend succeeds, monetary expenditures will no longer be considered a form of speech protected by the First Amendment. In addition, constitutional rights will apply only to people and "not to government-created artificial legal entities such as corporations and limited liability companies."[838] Proponents hope that when the daunting task of amending the Constitution is complete, we will be able to persuade Congress and other legislative bodies to pass new laws limiting electoral expenditures and other activities of ultra-wealthy individuals and corporations, thereby giving the rest of us more control over our lives.

Unfortunately, the proposed amendments will not succeed in ending Big Money's influence in elections, nor will they address other barriers to democracy.

Ultra-wealthy individuals and corporations have found a way around every prior campaign finance reform.[839] They would almost certainly find a way around future laws adopted after a Constitutional amendment as well.

Several pathways are already obvious. Bundling will likely continue. The rich will still groom future candidates who serve their interests, quietly pulling the strings behind the scenes to assure their ascension when the time is right. Private corporations will ensure that "public" debates still exclude candidates who don't serve their interests. Major corporations and wealthy individuals will buy up even more media outlets, where they will present slanted news and editorialize about candidates right up to election day.

More importantly, all of the other ways in which capitalism subverts democracy will continue unabated. We will still have no control over our natural resources and our productive capacity. We will still face massive expenditures by private interests on public relations campaigns, front groups, scientific research, schools and more.

Money in politics is a *symptom*. The accumulation of vast sums of wealth in the hands of a few and our lack of control over resources and the productive process is the real problem. In fact, money influencing elections is a rather small part of how democracy is undercut in the larger scheme of things. As long as capitalism remains in place, we will be disempowered, even if Move to Amend were to achieve its stated goals.

But Move to Amend's proposed constitutional amendments would not only be ineffective at curtailing the power of the 1%. They would also curtail our own constitutional rights, something we would likely regret. Except for the misguided 18th amendment, which prohibited alcohol and was later rescinded, we have never before amended the Constitution in a way that curtails rather than expands our rights. Do we really want to go there? It is the bloated corporations and their ultra-rich CEOs that will most aggressively use an amended Constitution to their advantage, not us.

If governments can pass laws restricting expenditures of money related to disseminating views, what's to keep lawmakers from restricting *us* as well as those with whom we disagree? Our freedom of speech can be severely undercut by limits on spending money to produce and disseminate films, print brochures and reports, place open letters in local papers, put up yard signs, or rent halls for political events.

Moreover, if "artificial entities" no longer have constitutional rights, that means groups working in the public interest will also not have those rights. Unions, environmental groups, and others will become fair game for censorship, warrantless searches, and other abuses. If organizations needed to challenge any of the following governmental actions, for example, they would have a much harder time winning if due process and the freedoms of assembly, religion, and speech no longer applied to them:

- A city prohibits environmental groups and unions from holding a rally to protest pollution at a local factory.
- An ordinance or administrative policy denies business licenses to companies that won't post the Ten Commandments.
- The Internal Revenue Service selectively audits organizations that support bans on genetically modified foods. Meanwhile the FBI conducts warrantless searches of their offices, seizing materials without probable cause.
- An agricultural state prohibits organizations from criticizing state crops and the methods by which they are grown.[840]

Historically, all sorts of "artificial entities" have relied on the Bill of Rights for protection against unjust governmental actions. The National Association for the Advancement of Colored People (NAACP) won a case against the State of Alabama in 1958 because the Bill of Rights was intact, for example. Trying to force the NAACP out of the state, Alabama had subpoenaed documents, including membership lists, but the Supreme Court affirmed the NAACP's constitutional right to resist turning over those lists. Constitutional amendments limiting free speech and stripping "artificial entities" of constitutional rights will call this and other prior decisions into question.

There is a reason that the American Civil Liberties Union (ACLU) opposes Move to Amend's suggested changes to the Constitution. Limiting free speech and other constitutional rights is dangerous territory. The ACLU itself has been the subject of attacks that were only rebuffed because the First Amendment was intact. [841] Challenges to its right to criticize President Nixon for opposing school bussing in 1972 were held unconstitutional, for example.

Proponents of amending the Constitution argue that amendments and laws can be written in a way that exempts groups working in the public interest. Leaving aside the matter of whether such exemptions would be adopted in a form that actually protects true public-interest groups, this approach is problematic. For-profit corporations have mastered the art of creating nonprofit front groups to accomplish their goals. They can and will readily get around any Constitutional changes intended to apply only to them.

It is good that people are acknowledging that we have a democracy problem and that we need to think outside the box to change things. But we need to fully examine and understand the real roots of our disempowerment if we are to succeed in claiming our power. Move to Amend is proposing palliative solutions that would be ineffective and would likely lead to more harm than good. To gain control of our lives and destiny we need to get beyond capitalism.

Insisting That the Conversation Occur. The interesting thing about most of the arguments against socialism is that they are generally used as conversation-stoppers rather than conversation-starters. If someone brings up the topic of socialism, there is often a response like, "Ah, but that doesn't work; just look at the former Soviet Union and how socialism led to Stalinism." It's true, the Russian Revolution, which started out with such promise, did degenerate into a Stalinist dictatorship. But what's needed is a discussion of *why* and how to prevent that outcome in the future. Instead, the conversation generally dies at this point. People drop it like a hot potato and move on to other subjects. Part of what's going on may be that many have internalized that the topic is a dangerous one.

Whatever the cause of the instant stymieing of public discussion about socialism, it is time to get beyond that. We must insist on examining how to replace capitalism.

Capitalism destroys democracy. It creates inequities, pollution, and despair. Socialism offers a different path, one we must explore if we are to survive and create a just world.

We have been mired in capitalism for so long that we accept as normal countless things that are truly insane, including:

- People amassing huge debts to get a college education.
- People working full-time or multiple jobs but still living in poverty.
- People working longer and earning less despite big increases in productivity.
- The insurance company enrichment scheme that masquerades as health care in the U.S.
- Elderly people working years after they reach retirement age in order to pay the bills.
- Chemical and fossil-fuel production expanding as our environment teeters on the edge of collapse.
- Huge numbers of people longing for jobs while all sorts of vital work remains undone.
- Ultra-wealthy individuals earning thousands of dollars per hour while workers who grow our food barely get by and face harassment and deportation.
- Billions going hungry while food lays unused in warehouses. Farms producing luxury crops and biofuels instead of food. Land that could be farmed being developed instead.
- Empty houses as homeless people set up boxes to live in under the highway.

* Each of us spending inordinate amounts of time researching and buying products related to health care, dental care,
  financial planning, phone services, wifi, and more. Each of
  these could be handled more cost effectively at a societal level. But instead we each navigate a confusing melee of shifting
  options, knowing that in many cases (e.g., financial planning,
  health insurance) a misstep could spell disaster for our loved
  ones.

But it doesn't have to be this way!

As we make a point of noticing and questioning the injustices and
irrationalities of everyday life linked to capitalism, we need to also envision and articulate what the world *could* look like instead. A partial
glimpse might include the following:

* Jobs for everyone, each of which pays well, is useful, and doesn't
  harm the world.
* Reduced work hours at no reduction in pay, giving us all more
  leisure time.
* Free, comprehensive health care for all, including dental, vision,
  and prescription drugs.
* Free education for all from preschool through college.
* An agricultural system based on sustainable practices, providing
  nutritious food for all. No more hunger.
* A free and vibrant not-for-profit news media.
* Thriving arts and music.
* Open sharing of ideas, inventions, music and more.
* People in much better shape physically because we have the time
  for exercise, we can get health care whenever we need it, and we
  are no longer as stressed.
* All of our energy needs met by 100% clean, renewable energy
  after a swift transition period.
* Zero garbage produced.

- An end to global warming and reversal of other adverse environmental trends.
- Quality, affordable housing for all. No more homelessness.
- An end to poverty, injustice, racism, and all forms of discrimination as the financial incentive for these disappears with the ending of capitalism.
- An end to wars and violence.
- Being in charge of our lives, workplaces, communities, and the world.

Sound like pie in the sky? Why is that? As the next chapter attests, we have the capacity to accomplish all of these things. In a true democracy, people can establish programs that equitably allocate resources, solve environmental problems, and create the types of communities we want. It is time to fight for that democracy and make the vision laid out above a reality. Indeed, we have no choice but to do so, given the threat to our survival if we maintain our present course. False friends and dead-ends must be left behind.

We can't keep nipping around the edges of environmental crises, pretending that ineffective strategies will somehow save the day. We can't keep supporting organizations and political parties that prop up an economic system that cedes control over our destiny to a wealthy few.

Instead we must articulate a democracy-infused socialist alternative to capitalism, and devise our strategies based on moving to that alternative. There is no time to waste.

CHAPTER 28

Hope

• • •

THERE IS MUCH MORE TO discuss regarding a world beyond capitalism and how to get there. We'll get to those topics shortly.

First, let's consider a question that plagues anyone who understands the forces we're up against: *Is there any hope?*

Fortunately, the answer is yes. There is ample reason for hope.

Solutions abound. We have the power to create the world we want. And we're ready to use it.

1) We have the resources, technologies, and wealth we need to solve the world's problems.

Food and Agriculture. The world produces enough food to feed everyone. In 2002 it produced 17% more calories per person than 30 years before, despite a 70% population increase. That was enough to give each person 2720 kilocalories per day.[842] In fact we already produce enough calories on Earth to feed 9 billion people.[843] According to the United Nations, about $30 billion is needed per year to eradicate hunger. Several wealthy individuals have more than this amount in their personal coffers.[844] Hunger is a problem of distribution, not food shortages.

What's more, food can be grown sustainably. There are farmers everywhere who grow crops without poisoning the land, the workers, or the food itself.[845] In fact, the promise of increased food production lies with these sustainable techniques on small farms rather than with dependence on dangerous pesticides, genetic modification, and giant corporate-owned farms.[846] Organic farming can outcompete non-organic yields for almost all food crops studied, including corn, wheat, rice, soybeans, and sunflowers.[847]

Renewable Energy. Numerous energy experts have laid out in detail how the world's energy needs can be met within decades using current renewable technologies, with zero reliance on fossil fuels or nuclear power. Drs. Mark Jacobson (Stanford) and Mark Delucchi (University of California at Davis), for example, have produced a global plan that would provide all new energy from wind, sun, and water power by 2030, and phase out all remaining fossil-fuel-based energy by 2050. [848] According to Jacobson and Delucchi, "[b]arriers to the plan are primarily social and political, not technological or economic."[849]

Dr. Jacobson has also developed a 50-state roadmap for making the U.S. fossil-fuel-free by 2050. Go to http://thesolutionsproject.org/infographic/ and hover over each state with the cursor to see the mix of renewable energy sources that state could use.[850]

Enough sunlight hits the Earth's surface in one hour to power humanity for one year.[851] We have the know-how to capture enough of this and related renewable energy for our needs.

When public policies provide meaningful support, renewable technologies thrive. Germany already gets 10% of its power from renewables. One day in 2012 it reached a new record with 50% of the country's midday energy needs coming from solar energy. Texas leads the U.S. in installed wind capacity and on some days in 2012, wind generated a quarter of the state's power. Wind energy generated 20% of Iowa's energy from January through April 2011.[852] These milestones were all reached without renewables being given anything close to the support they deserve, and despite the huge promotion and proliferation of natural gas.

Drs. Jacobson and Delucchi note that "[c]hanging the 'dominant paradigm' may require concerted social and political efforts beyond the traditional sorts of economic incentives." They refer to the U.S. transforming motor vehicle production to aircraft production during World War II and the Apollo Program putting a person on the moon in just 10 years. These examples "suggest that the large scale of a complete transformation of the energy system is not, in itself, an insurmountable barrier."

"With sensible broad-based policies and social changes, it may be possible to convert 25% of the current energy system to WWS [wind, water, and sunlight] in 10-15 years and 85% in 20-30 years, and 100% by 2050," Jacobson and Delucchi say. "Absent that clear direction, the conversion will take longer."

On top of all this, organic agricultural practices can take carbon from the atmosphere and sequester it in the soil, thereby countering global warming. A report published by the Center for Food Safety in April of 2015 concluded that "Unlike geoengineering, rebuilding soil carbon is a zero-risk, low-cost proposition. It has universal application, and we already know how to do it. All that stands in our way is a greater awareness of the opportunity and the political will to make it happen."[853] According to a 2014 Rodale Institute study, data from trials around the world show that "we could sequester more than 100% of current annual CO2 emissions with a switch to widely available and inexpensive organic management practices."[854]

Financial Resources. We are regularly told that there's not enough money for the things we want to do. That's nonsense. There's plenty of money in the world. It's just unjustly distributed.

U.S. corporations held up to $5 trillion in liquid assets globally as of mid-2012.[855] Eighty individuals own as much wealth as the bottom half of the global population. Chapter 8 is full of statistics like these. When the wealth produced by workers is funneled into the coffers of private owners, this is the lopsided situation that results.

To make matters worse, the ultra rich further deplete our financial resources by regularly raiding public treasuries. Taxpayer money ends up being spent on corporate bailouts, contracts that enrich weapons manufacturers,[856] and other things that advance private fortunes. The military-industrial complex has succeeded in regularly diverting a huge percentage of public funds into military and defense programs. A whopping $643 billion were spent on these in 2013.[857]

Public funds are used not only to *directly* subsidize big corporations but also to *indirectly* subsidize them. Taxpayers provide $243 billion in assistance like food stamps and Medicaid each year to *working* families because employers pay them so little. In other words, we are covering basics that corporations should cover via decent wages. Fast-food workers average nearly $7 billion per year in public assistance. Even working 40 hours a week, 52% of front-line[858] fast-food workers must obtain this assistance for their families.[859]

Walmart earned $17 billion in profits in 2012, or $1.9 million per hour, but it pays an average sales associate an hourly wage of only $8.81.[860] Medicaid payouts for employees at a single Walmart Supercenter in Wisconsin cost taxpayers an estimated $904,542 to $1,744,590 per year!

Walmart has 100 stores including 75 Supercenters in Wisconsin alone. It employs about 1.4 million people in the U.S. and 2 million worldwide.[861] The amount of extra money we would have in public treasuries if Walmart paid decent wages is staggering.

Phenomenal amounts of our money are also wasted each year on unnecessary bureaucracies implementing programs that serve private corporations. Vast numbers of risk assessors and other environmental agency staffers work full-time on risk assessment calculations for chemicals that can and should be replaced by non-chemical alternatives, for example. It would be interesting to know how many millions of taxpayer dollars have been spent just on EPA's massive, never-ending risk calculations for chlorpyrifos, one of the neurotoxic pesticides we targeted at the Farm Worker Pesticide Project.

Similarly, the annual cost of operating the ObamaCare exchanges is between $15 million and several hundred million dollars per state. This money goes to sorting people by their incomes when we could have quality health *care* (as opposed to *insurance*) for everyone under single payer without any of this waste. Part of the federal ObamaCare spending goes to "navigators" and "assisters" who help people buy insurance, a completely unnecessary occupation that does not exist in any sane health care system. The Obama Administration announced in 2013 that it would direct $200 million to states, private groups, and local health centers to hire navigators.[862]

In short, there are ample financial resources in the world to pay for mass transit, renewable energy, transition programs for fossil-fuel workers, assistance to farmers as they adopt sustainable agriculture methods, housing and health care for all, free higher education, and all the other things we need. Money is not scarce. It is simply diverted to private interests, a situation we do not need to accept.

2) Members of the 99% are generous with their money and time.

Even though the 1% appropriates most of the wealth that should be ours, members of the 99% are remarkably generous with the money they do have. As a result, ample resources could be available for a people's campaign that takes on the roots of our disempowerment.

Seventy percent of adults in the U.S. donate money. The majority of givers are low- and middle-income people, who together account for 50 to 80% of money donated. The vast majority of donations come from families earning less than $90,000 per year. About 20% of people on welfare give away money, with an average gift being $74. Most people who give to nonprofits give to at least 5 and as many as 15 groups.[863]

A lot of money is flowing from the 99% to non-governmental organizations that we believe are making the world a better place. An estimated 20 to 30 million people are members of environmental organizations in the U.S. alone.[864] Vast numbers also pay membership dues and donate to other groups working on other issues. Bringing even a small portion of these supporters together behind joint efforts to address the roots of the problems we face as a species would enable us to make swift progress.

Groups that successfully tap into Americans' innate generosity now raise lots of money from small donations in a short period of time using internet solicitations and payment options. MoveOn, for example, is constantly putting out requests for cash and pulling it in. An email I received from them in September of 2012, for instance, told me that 15,743 MoveOn members had already donated $504,829 for the cause MoveOn was championing that day.[865] In this case it was getting out the vote for

Obama, despite his unprogressive record. They were trying to reach $600,000 and probably ended up making it.

Of course, it isn't just monetary donations that people can bring to a united joint campaign to address the roots of our environmental and other problems. More important, people can bring themselves, including their time and energy. In 2010, 26% of U.S. adults volunteered through an organization. Volunteers contributed 15 billion hours worth $283.84 billion in average wages.[866] These figures don't reflect volunteer hours that are not tracked.

Labor unions have substantial financial resources and the ability to put lots of volunteers on the ground in support of causes they like. They have generally invested heavily in the Democratic Party despite the harm it does to workers and its failure to deliver strong policies.

OpenSecrets.org's listing of 140 "Top All-Time Donors" for 1989 to 2010 includes over 25 unions. The combined giving of these unions exceeded $553 million.[867] These figures represent only a portion of the funds available to unions to use in organizing for policies, programs, and political parties that benefit working Americans.

In short, people are very generous with money even when they don't have a lot of it. A lot of the money flowing through nongovernmental organizations and our political system comes from regular people wanting to make the world better. People are also very generous with their time, volunteering extensively for things they believe in. A united front for real change has large financial and people-power resources potentially available to it.

3) People support policies that protect our environment and create a just and sustainable world.

Polling of U.S. voters in 2010 found that a large majority (73%) believe that exposure to toxic chemicals in everyday life presents a serious threat. An overwhelming super-majority of those polled favored stricter regulation of chemicals, with a majority *strongly* favoring stricter regulations. The research found that 57% of respondents looked at environmental groups favorably, with only 32% seeing them unfavorably. Meanwhile, 45% of respondents viewed chemical companies and 60% viewed oil companies unfavorably as compared to favorable ratings for these companies of 32 and 28% respectively.[868]

A whopping 83% of American adults say that protecting the world's ecosystems is important.[869] Nationally, 70% of Americans disapproved of Obama's decision to block the ozone pollution standard, with only 30% approving his decision. Nearly four out of five Americans (78%) want EPA to hold corporate polluters accountable for what they release into our communities.[870] And a 2011 poll jointly conducted by Democratic and Republican polling firms showed 75% support for EPA setting new emissions rules.[871]

A solid majority of people—58%—prefer organic food. Those who supposedly favor non-organic food, according to NPR-Thomson Reuters pollsters, give high prices and lack of availability of organic as their rationale. In other words if our economic system didn't discourage and overprice sustainably grown food, more Americans would likely choose it.

A full 83% of Americans approve of renewable energy, including 63% of Republicans and 84% of Independents.[872] Recent polls show that 70% of the American public believes that climate change is a real phenomenon that requires action.[873] This is the case despite limited media coverage on this issue from 2009 to 2011 as the result of President Obama's policy of not discussing it and his success in persuading environmental organizations to join him in this silence as discussed earlier. It is also the case despite public relations campaigns funded by fossil-fuel corporations spreading misinformation about climate change.

Solid public support for policies that protect and improve the lives of the 99% goes well beyond environmental issues. For example, in a September 2010 NBC/*Wall Street Journal* poll, 86% agreed that U.S. companies outsourcing work to foreign countries is one of the reasons for unemployment and economic struggles in the U.S. Sixty-eight percent *strongly* felt this way.[874]

Multiple polls have long shown that over half of all Americans support single-payer health care, also known as "Improved Medicare for All." Many polls found support in the mid- to high-60% range. Interestingly, when the questions gave a clearer picture of what single payer is by referring to it as a program like Medicare run by the government and financed by taxpayers, support was higher (65%) than for the less clear version of the question (54%). Even though public discussion of single payer has been extremely limited, polls found majority support for it even in the absence of clarification as to what it is.[875]

4) People recognize that the system is broken and are ready for fundamental change.

People are not only continuing to support rational environmental and social policies despite PR campaigns designed to confuse the issues. They are also noticing and objecting to the fact that the system is rigged against the public interest. Consider the following:

* For at least two decades, at least 80% of Americans have felt that "big companies" "have too much power and influence" in Washington D.C. In 2012, the figure was 86%. That year 81% felt that banks and financial institutions also had too much power and influence there. "Public opinion," on the other hand, had too little power and influence according to 78% of those polled.[876]

* These perceptions were shared by Republicans, Democrats, and Independents alike. Over four in five people in each of these groups felt big companies have too much power.[877]

* By 2011, while it remained a "negative" term for 60% of respondents overall, "socialism" was viewed more favorably than capitalism among three important categories: young people, African Americans, and those earning $30,000 or less. See Table 1. [878]

Table 1: Reactions to Capitalism and Socialism

	Capitalism Positive	Capitalism Negative	Socialism Positive	Socialism Negative
Blacks	41	51	55	36
Ages 18-29	46	47	49	43
Family Income Below $30,000	39	47	43	46

- By mid 2015 (when a self-proclaimed socialist entered the presidential race running as a Democrat), nearly half (47%) of all Americans said they would vote for a socialist for president, according to a Gallup poll. Nearly 7 in 10 (69%) Americans ages 18 to 29 said they would vote for a socialist. The figure for people ages 30 to 49 was 50%.[879]

- A global poll by Pew Research found that in 11 of 21 nations surveyed, only 50% or less of the population now believe that people are better off in a free market economy than in some other system. The ongoing global financial crisis has significantly eroded faith in capitalism.[880]

- Polls in the fall of 2011 showed 44% of Americans supporting the Occupy Wall Street movement, compared to 35% opposing. Forty-eight percent agreed with concerns the protesters raised, as compared to 30% who disagreed. A 61% majority of Americans said that the economic system in the U.S. unfairly favors the wealthy, as compared to only 36% who said it is generally fair to most Americans. A whopping 77% said that a few rich people and corporations have too much power. About half of Americans (51%) felt that Wall Street hurts the American economy more than it helps it, as compared to only 36% who felt Wall Street helps more than it hurts.[881]

All of these statistics indicate that the time is ripe for change. People are dissatisfied with how things are working. Most of us see that we have no power and that big business is calling the shots. People are aware of the gap between rich and poor, and do not like it.

5) Support for the Democratic and Republican Parties is at an all-time low.

Another indication that the time is ripe for change is the notable increase in people identifying themselves as "Independent" rather than "Democrat" or "Republican." A Pew Research Center poll in the summer of 2012 found that 38% of the public self-identify as Independent—a

75-year high—as compared to only 32% and 24% self-identifying as Democrats and Republicans respectively.[882]

The face of the Independent voter has also changed. More young voters—traditionally a key Democratic Party voting bloc—now consider themselves Independent. Nearly half of Americans born since 1981 say they are Independent. Similarly, the percent of Hispanics considering themselves Independent rose from 31 in 2006 to 46 in 2012.

Even with limited public discussion about the giant we're up against and how to defeat it, there are signs of change in elections around the U.S. that show the way forward.

For example, in November of 2010, a progressive 3rd party slate of candidates won the position of mayor and two city council positions in Richmond, California, despite refusing to accept corporate donations and spending a tiny amount of money compared to that spent by corporate party candidates. Chevron Corporation put at least $1.08 million into the race to support incumbent council members and a different mayoral candidate. The Democratic Party endorsed Democratic candidates, and numerous unions joined them in doing so. This election illustrates the potential for third-party candidates to win elections despite vastly fewer resources than those going to Democrats and Republicans.[883]

In Seattle, Washington, socialist candidate Kshama Sawant took 28% of the vote in her challenge against Democrat Frank Chopp, Speaker of the State House of Representatives in November of 2012. Although Sawant lost, the large number who voted for her was notable given her shoe-string budget. It illustrated the fact that clear statements demanding policies that serve the 99% resonate with people, and could go far if we, the people, invest our money and time in our own candidates rather than 1%-serving candidates of the two corporate parties.

Sawant didn't stop there. Again running as a socialist, she challenged a long-time Democratic Party Seattle City councilman and won. Sawant's campaign became a rallying point for people who were sick of politics as usual. Sawant did not accept corporate contributions and articulated a strong platform, calling for a $15 per hour minimum wage, rent control, and taxes on the rich to fund social services. Many labor and other progressive groups failed to endorse Sawant, although her positions aligned with theirs. They behaved in typical Demophilial fashion, endorsing her Democratic opponent despite his weaker record and positions and his acceptance of corporate cash. At a victory rally, leaders of some of these organizations gave Johnny-come-lately speeches celebrating Sawant's victory. Despite their loyalty to the Democratic Party, voters had put a socialist with a strong pro-worker, pro-environment, pro-democracy platform into office.

A socialist candidate for city council in Minneapolis ran a race similar to Sawant's and lost by only 229 votes. Socialist and other groups are running more candidates nationwide to build on what has happened so far.

6) Young people are particularly ready for change and equipped to bring it about.

As noted earlier, young adults react favorably to the word socialism and negatively to the word capitalism, and they are more likely than other age groups to be political Independents.

PR analysts advising companies on how to market their products to young people have interesting things to say about them. "Millennials"—those born between 1980 and 2002—apparently describe themselves as open-minded, intelligent, responsible, thoughtful, and independent. They "believe that, as civic-minded and active participants in today's world, it is up to them to assume the responsibility of making a lasting, positive impact on the future." Millennials are computer- and internet-savvy and have been exposed "to an entire Global Community." They have increased awareness of news and world events. Moreover, "as a group, the Millennial Generation embodies a spirit of optimism and cooperation."[884]

While marketing consultants compile these facts in order to devise strategies to persuade Millennials to buy something, their findings illuminate opportunity for global movement building. Millennials are relatively free from the strictures on thinking that have limited prior generations. They also think globally, are aware of others on the planet, and are able to connect with them in ways that were impossible 30 years ago. Yes, the powers against us are huge, but we have much going for us, including potentially the energy, connections, and social media prowess of the young.

In his 2013 "Riskmap Report," consultant Richard Fenning warned his corporate audience about unstable conditions in the world.[885] "The last two years have shown how susceptible a highly interconnected world is to rapid political change (the Arab spring)..." he noted. "[T]he world has long suffered from political, economic and natural upheaval—but the taut connectivity of supply chains and communication networks means that the velocity with which local problems become global issues has increased substantially." Let's hope he's right about the potential for demands for democracy and justice spreading like wildfire via our modern connections to one another.

7) People are creating sustainable, cooperative, public interest-serving enterprises.

While capitalist structures and systems continue to dominate, many people are quietly building alternatives. These provide models of how we can live and work together. They help build momentum for real change.

The large and successful worker-owned Mondragon Corporation in Spain and other democratically managed Worker Self-Directed Enterprises (WSDEs) are inspiring people to form WSDEs around the world. Some WSDEs come into existence when private owners sell companies to the employees. Others are created by groups of workers from scratch. Groups like *Democracy At Work* and *Toolbox for Education and Social Action (TESA)* provide educational materials and other assistance to the burgeoning WSDE movement.[886]

At the same time, many people are turning to credit unions for their banking needs. Credit unions are nonprofit, member-owned financial cooperatives, democratically controlled by their members. Many credit unions emphasize support for local community development.

In 2011, more than 1.3 million Americans opened new credit-union accounts, bringing the number of credit-union members to a record 91.8 million. This change has been attributed to Occupy Wall Street's focus on the problems with banking institutions, combined with new fees for debit cards initiated by certain banks. The $96 billion in credit union accounts is much smaller than the over $12 trillion in the U.S. banking system,[887] but it is an indicator of people's willingness to switch to alternatives when they know about them.

In the agricultural realm, despite agribusiness dominance and other pressures, small farmers are still out there farming sustainably. Organizations that help people access land and learn to farm report a surge in interest among young people spurred by environmental concerns. Community Supported Agriculture and farmers' markets are directly connecting local farmers with the people who eat their food.

A growing movement of *urban* farmers is transforming plots of land in cities into food-producing oases. In Seattle, Marra Farm engages people in sustainable agriculture while producing healthy food for low income communities, for example.

Consumer food cooperatives like the Seattle-based Puget Consumer Coop are thriving. These member-controlled entities sell sustainably produced products. They provide markets for local organic growers, give grants to them, and support other socially beneficial programs.

Around the world people are engaged in all sorts of endeavors that emphasize cooperation, sustainability, and the public interest, rather than private profit. They are installing renewable energy technologies in their neighborhoods, living in co-housing communities that share common areas and chores, forming independent journalism outlets, and engaging in other such endeavors.

8) People are steadily organizing and building the mass movement we need.

The developments of the last several years have been nothing short of amazing. The Arab Spring, activists taking over the Wisconsin State Capital Building, Occupy Wall Street, huge protests against austerity in Europe, massive demonstrations against global warming, and very well-attended international Social Forums have unfolded before our eyes. All over the world, people are rising up to demand real change.

Proponents of the status quo try to label these outpourings of discontent a "flash in the pan." "Occupy is dead, it failed," they say, a message which probably disheartens many.

Don't be disheartened! Occupy and the fire it carried forward from prior uprisings is very much alive. Terms like "the 99%" and "the 1%" have become part of our language. They are shaping the discussions we're having, focusing attention on the root of our problems at last. People inspired by Occupy and other rebellions have been moving forward with new projects, building new networks. Slowly but surely the taboo on talking about alternatives to the undemocratic system in which we live is receding.

Fast food workers and other low-wage workers have been fighting hard for $15 an hour and the right to form a union, for example. They've organized numerous strikes and other protests across the United States and around the world.[888] Occupy themes permeate these actions. Echoed by "the people's mic"[889] for example, at a protest outside a McDonald's across from the Empire State Building, protester Letitia James pointed out the inequity of wages at the bottom compared to those at the top at McDonalds. "Fast-food workers, on average, only make between $10,000 and $18,000, less than what it costs to live in New York City," she said. "But yet, the CEO of McDonald's makes—are you ready?—$9,200 an hour."[890]

In a major victory, low-wage workers in Seatac, Washington, fought for a $15 per hour minimum wage and won.

The election of socialist Kshama Sawant to the Seattle City Council is a direct outgrowth of Occupy Seattle and the victory in nearby Seatac. And what has been accomplished through the grassroots movement that put her into office has been extraordinary. In less than a year, this movement forced the city of Seattle to adopt a $15 minimum wage.[891] Three years earlier this seemed impossible.

Democrats on the Seattle City Council brought big business to the table and supported provisions that weakened the minimum wage ordinance. Some activists collaborated with those Democrats instead of standing firm. As a result, corporations succeeded in imposing some delays and loopholes, but overall, the big increase in wages for workers in Seattle is a huge step forward. It spotlights how swiftly we can make gains when we unapologetically demand what we want and build a movement to support it.

Sawant and her Socialist Alternative Party used the electoral campaign to build a grassroots movement. That movement created the pressure that led rapidly to victory. Sawant uses the media attention associated with her position to spotlight issues and further empower the grassroots movement from which change comes.

People are organizing 15 Now efforts across the United States. Campaigns for a $15 minimum wage are underway in multiple cities and states.

There are other broad organizing efforts underway which arise from people's frustration with the control that wealthy interests have over our political system. The "Move to Amend" campaign—although of questionable efficacy, as discussed earlier—is mobilizing substantial numbers of people eager for systemic change. Campaign finance reform efforts, "backbone" projects attempting to force elected officials to stand up to private interests, and other endeavors all show how ready people are to work for societal transformation.

Around the world, people are continuing to fight back against corporations seeking to frack, drill, transport fossil fuels, dump toxic wastes, and otherwise threaten the environment. They are lying down in front of bulldozers and on train tracks. They are marching in the streets. The numbers are swelling, particularly with respect to opposing activities linked to global warming. Nearly 400,000 took part in a climate action march in New York City on September 21, 2014, for example, with other protests happening the same day in 150 countries around the world.

Some of these events have received very little coverage in the mainstream news media. A tiny Tea Party protest may garner multiple news stories while thousands of people at a global social justice forum will get no news coverage whatsoever.

Whether reported or not, however, organizing for fundamental change is happening. The groundwork for creating the world we want to see is being laid. There are quiet heroes all around us patiently building alliances and paving the way forward. Their resilience and dedication is an important reason for hope.

None of us can stay out of the fray. We are approaching the point of no return on critical environmental issues and we must all stand up to demand real change in order to save our species and create a just world. But we could be a lot closer to the tipping point for achieving major change than we think.[892]

9) We are the 99%. The other big reason for hope lies in the role working people play in society. Without working people, things literally don't get done. Trains don't move, factory machines sit idle, buildings are not built, students aren't taught, food isn't grown and so forth. If and when we unite around an economic democracy agenda, nothing can stop us. We are the many, and we can bring the economy to a standstill. This gives us true power.

Some Final Thoughts About Hope.

They say it's darkest just before the dawn. We need to keep this in mind as we watch environmental and social crises deepen. We actually do have enormous power, and there are indications all around us that we may at last be learning how to wield it. The following chapters discuss what it will take to use the power that is ours to create the world we want.

Recently, I was chatting with the author of a book on how to live sustainably at the local level. I told him that I thought those efforts were important, but that it was essential that we all work for economic political change as well. Local sustainable living is limited by barriers created by the market system and by the fact that wealth and resources are controlled by so few. I really hadn't said more than a few sentences to that effect when a bystander jumped in to disagree with me. Young people today need hope, she said. They need to hear about positive things like local urban farms, not about depressing, negative things like the power corporations wield.

Her statements grew from concern about the emotional state of young people today—individuals who, like her daughters, are inheriting a troubled world from us. I had run into the same sort of admonition before, such as when parents my age noted that they agreed with my analysis of the Democratic Party presidential candidate, but felt that their teenagers and young adult children needed hope, so they were going to support him and not criticize him.

I share the same deep concern for the emotional well-being of my own young adult children, and for all young people and others longing for hope in a world full of frightening news.

But ignorance is temporary bliss at best. Pretending that things are different than they are—that incremental steps forward are saving us when they're not, that candidates dedicated to increasing the power of the 1% are champions of the 99%, and the like—these things do not help young people or anyone else. Encouraging blinders to protect people from uncomfortable realities only ensures that things will keep getting worse. It sets in stone ineffective strategies that condemn humankind to an uncertain and increasingly unpleasant future.

We must talk openly and honestly about where we are now and where we are headed as a species. We must expose false hope for what it is to ensure that our efforts are no longer wasted on dead-ends.

When we do these things and when we illuminate the enormous power we have to create the world we want, we offer real hope. This is the best gift we can give to our children and to all the people of the world.

CHAPTER 29

An Economic Democracy Agenda

• • •

It is critical that we articulate a clear vision of what our economic and political system needs to look like and the fundamental changes required to get us there.

Ultra-rich individuals and corporations who benefit from the status quo spend billions each year to persuade us that everything's fine, and if that fails, to steer us toward phony solutions. Meanwhile, authors and activists who have identified capitalism as a problem dance around what that means. They falsely imply that capitalism is fixable or they fail to state clearly what it means to get beyond it.

Let's be clear about where we need to go.

Public Ownership of Major Industries and Resources. To save humanity, we need to establish economic democracy. That means first and foremost that we must nationalize key industries and associated natural resources under the democratic control of those working in and affected by those industries. Energy production; mineral extraction; chemical manufacturing; agribusiness; banking transportation; and large-scale manufacturing of things like steel, cars, and airplanes all need to be nationalized and managed democratically for the public good. Only then will we be able to solve the environmental and other social problems we face.

Notice that we need to demand both public ownership *and* democratic structures that give working people—the 99%—real control over decision-making. A broad network of workplace and community councils must be developed to foster vibrant public discussion and self-governance. Those elected to represent us in higher levels of government must earn the same wages as the people they represent and be subject to instant recall.

By nationalizing major industries and resources and building true democratic control over these, we will empower people individually and at the societal level. Individuals will finally have a real say over the conditions of their everyday lives, including their workplaces. Matters like how goods and services are produced and worker safety will no longer be governed by decisions handed down from on high. At the societal level, we will be able to craft and implement policies for the public good, using the collective resources and wealth that belong to us all. Decisions about pollution, our energy future, what jobs exist and more will no longer be determined by a few individuals and corporations seeking to maximize their private profits.

Economic Rights. As part of establishing economic democracy, we must also declare and enforce basic economic rights. We must insist that every person has:

- The right to a job with union wages, reasonable hours, and good working conditions.
- The right to a livable income when they cannot work.
- The right to free government-funded health care covering all health needs including dental, vision, and prescription drugs.
- The right to affordable housing and food.
- The right to free education from preschool through college.
- The right to form a union and organize for workers' rights.
- The right to help set economic and political policy.

Recognition and enforcement of these rights will transform our world. Freed from the threat of unemployment and poverty, we will no longer be subject to extortion. Corporations will no longer be able to threaten us with unemployment or loss of income if we don't accept pollution and bad working conditions. We'll also have more time and energy for self-governance because we'll not be wasting these on things like researching health insurance plans. Stress levels will plummet, further fostering our ability to participate fully in decision-making for our society.

Public Planning. Our call for economic democracy must expressly state that we have a right and a responsibility to adopt plans for energy production and for all other basic societal needs. We must make it clear that these plans will mandate actions that are needed, rather than merely establish them as goals we hope to accomplish through indirect means. The plans we produce and implement will also create jobs and provide training linked to our societal needs. They will ensure transition assistance for those working in industries we decide to eliminate, including full wages while shifting to other jobs.

In the context of the economic rights we have articulated and embraced, we will frame planning discussions the way they ought to be framed. *What do we want our lives, communities, and world to look like? What are the things that need to happen to make those visions a reality? What jobs are needed to make those things happen?* With resources and wealth under our control, we can swiftly do what needs to be done instead of futilely relying on private profit-seeking interests to save the day.

Other Actions. These measures—public ownership and democratic control of major industries, recognition and enforcement of the economic rights listed above, and public planning—are all essential elements of the agenda we must advance.

Of course, there will be additional elements in that agenda, but an all-inclusive list of these is beyond the scope of this book.[893] To help transfer wealth from the 1% to the 99% that produces it, we need to support major tax increases on the wealthy, for example. A comprehensive agenda will also include multiple measures that address racism and discrimination. It will demand immigration reforms that end the disenfranchisement of millions.

Whatever we ultimately include in our complete agenda, the systemic changes outlined in this chapter must be retained up front as clear indispensable priorities. Only through these changes will we establish economic democracy, enabling us to create the world we want.

The Time for Clarity Is Now. Most of us consider it self-evident that each person is endowed with inalienable rights, including life, liberty, and the pursuit of happiness. Yet, these rights are denied for the majority of people on Earth. Despite abundant resources, massive inequity relegates huge numbers to poverty and creates conditions that curtail liberty and the pursuit of happiness. Inequity is so severe that many lose their lives due to avoidable problems like hunger and preventable disease. Moreover, we now face the threat of *all* life being extinguished, because those who hoard public resources are blocking urgently needed environmental and social reforms.

Capitalism is inherently undemocratic and unjust, and it is leading us towards extinction. There is no time to waste in jointly advancing an agenda for economic change. That agenda must explicitly identify the essential elements of the new economic system we need to put in place.

CHAPTER 30

What We Need to Do

• • •

WE KNOW WHERE WE NEED to go: beyond capitalism to economic democracy, justice, and survival. How do we get there? This chapter offers a roadmap.

PRINCIPLES FOR TURNING THINGS AROUND

As we move forward in our do-or-die struggle, we must adhere to several fundamental principles. Failure to adhere to these principles has kept us running in circles for far too long.

Principle Number 1: Truth, Not Lies

It's time to tell the truth. We don't have the chemical industry on the run. Incremental gains aren't saving the day. We are not winning, nor can we win under our current economic set-up. We won't win unless and until we get beyond capitalism.

It's a bad idea to keep people's hopes up via misrepresentations. Let's give people real reasons for hope, not fraudulent ones. We can and should spotlight solutions to the world's environmental crises, the unstoppable power working people have when we unite, and multiple indications that the time for change is nigh.

Principle Number 2: Explicit, Not Vague

We need to be clear about the changes we want. If we are vague about what economic democracy looks like, we risk being swept away by more false friends into more dead-ends. Many who use labels like "social democracy" or "democratic socialism" do not actually espouse public ownership of major industries, true grassroots democracy, or other essential elements of socialism. Others mention socialist-sounding goals in their materials, but then advocate superficial reforms as if those are the ultimate objective.

As the thirst for system change grows and people's interest in socialism skyrockets, all sorts of pretenders are co-opting the language of change to serve the status quo. Hillary Clinton and others who want to "save capitalism from itself" are suddenly denouncing the symptoms of capitalism—including symptoms they personally exacerbated with their prior actions. These false friends are tapping into people's justified anger about the consequences of capitalism, while proposing fixes that leave its undemocratic life-destroying structures intact.

If we want to mobilize behind real change—if we want to save the Earth rather than capitalism—we need to be very clear about what socialism entails. We need to articulate and advance an economic agenda based on public ownership of major industries, democratic control over workplaces and communities, empowered public planning, and a full and enforced economic bill of rights. (See chapter 29 for details.)

Principle Number 3: Unity, Not Competition

Social justice activists must reject the competitive mindset encouraged by funders and others. Instead of fighting from separate silos, we need to unite for economic democracy. Instead of focusing on perfecting individual brands that give us an edge over others, we need to focus on building alliances.

Bringing diverse social justice movements together must be a priority for each of us. Ignoring and undercutting other groups and their campaigns is not an option if we want to create a just and sustainable world.

Poverty, racism, police violence, exploitation, hunger, endless imperial wars, and the threat of nuclear holocaust. Toxic contamination, plummeting biodiversity, crashing fish stocks, bee colony collapse, and climate change. Each of these issues and countless others are of utmost importance. And they are all intertwined with one another.

Environmentalists won't get far when so many people live paycheck to paycheck. Education advocates can't win when public funds go to weapons manufacturers for never-ending wars instead of schools. Those fighting racism will be stymied as long as we live in a system that fosters poverty and makes racism profitable.

We're all butting up against the same brick wall. Only by joining forces will we be able to knock it down.

Principle Number 4: Every Choice Consistent With Building a Movement for Economic Democracy

We need to evaluate strategies, tactics, and messages in the context of our larger struggle for economic democracy. Can a contemplated action be used to expose the inadequacies of capitalism? Can it help people understand that there is an alternative we can fight for? Can it bring people into a broad movement for real change?

Everything we do must be undertaken in a way that serves our long-term system-change goals. Approaches that reinforce our current subservience must be left behind. (See Chapter 21 for an examination of specific tactics available to activists.)

In general, we need to aim much higher and compromise far less readily than we have in the past. To claim our power, we need to stop giving it away. Investing huge resources in lengthy "winnable" campaigns for increased corporate transparency, for example, doesn't really move us forward. On the other hand, hard-hitting campaigns demanding bans on environmentally destructive practices can be used to build momentum for economic democracy. They document our lack of control over important decisions under capitalism.

Principle Number 5: True Friends, Not False Ones

If a commitment to the principles laid out above is to mean anything, we must demand adherence to them by the social justice organizations, political parties, and candidates for office that we support.

STEPS TO TAKE TO DEFEAT THE GIANT

Guided by these principles, what specific steps should we take to advance economic democracy and solve the world's crises? The rest of this chapter provides examples.

1. SPEAK UP.

Each of us has endless chances to tell it like it is, giving hope and inspiration to others. Chats with friends, discussions at school or work, social media exchanges, public meetings, letters-to-the-editor, and other forums all provide opportunities to change the debate. We need to use these opportunities.

People-to-people persuasion is central to how things work in a real democracy. As we strive to create that system of governance, we need to start behaving accordingly.

Here are some of the scenarios in which we need to speak up, with suggestions in italics regarding the sorts of things we might say.

Countering the Myth of Austerity

We are inundated with claims that this or that essential social program must be cut or cannot be fully implemented because resources are too limited. We are presented with a tiny slice of the pie that is supposedly all there is left for the public services we need. We must refuse to accept this false framework:

- *No, we will not participate in a discussion about which schools to close. There's plenty of money to open more schools, reduce class sizes, and increase teachers' salaries. We need to get beyond an economic system that diverts public resources to an elite few.*

- *Existing renewable technologies can replace all fossil fuels, and we absolutely have enough money to make that happen. Leaving profit-driven corporations in charge of our energy future is the problem. It's time to get beyond capitalism so we can implement obvious solutions to urgent environmental problems.*

- *No, we won't let you raise the retirement age or otherwise cut Social Security benefits. Ample money exists for Social Security and other public programs. The real question is why we tolerate a system that gives the money workers produce to a few ultra-rich corporations and individuals.*

Many officials and activists dutifully accept the austerity framework and focus on coming up with ways to make cuts and divide supposedly inadequate resources "equitably." They see this behavior as "leadership" and are praised for it. We need to counter that message directly and clearly.

Leadership means stepping outside the box others place you in on these issues. Ample financial resources exist in our society for all our needs. The challenge of our day is creating a system that justly allocates those resources. We must refuse to go along with the austerity hoax.

Putting "Victories" in Context

Social justice groups go to great lengths to proclaim victories, even when we haven't really won anything. This confuses people and creates the dangerous misimpression that we are winning, even as we move steadily backwards overall.

When a victory is an actual but small step forward, we must insist that the context be understood: *Yes, this step forward is something to celebrate, but we need to recognize how small and vulnerable it is. Our most important work is changing the system that keeps us from winning real reforms.*

If something is actually a defeat or a step backward, we need to object to celebratory language. *No, I'm sorry, the gain we got with the new law is tiny and it is outweighed by the backward provisions attached to it.*

Similarly, when people point to windmills on the hill or solar panels on a neighbor's house as proof that we're winning the battle against fossil fuels, we need to challenge that perception. *It's nice to see windmills and solar panels, and we really can provide all the energy we need with clean renewables. But progress on renewables has been sporadic and minimal, and it has been totally overwhelmed by full-throttle expansion of fossil-fuel extraction. The amount of greenhouse gases in the atmosphere is increasing, as is the average global temperature. Despite some new renewable energy projects, overall we're losing badly. We will continue to lose unless and until we challenge the system that lets the fossil-fuel industry call the shots.*

Telling the Truth about Democrats Earlier chapters documented in detail why faith in the Democratic Party is misplaced. We must challenge Demophilia when we witness it and urge people to break with the Democratic Party.

When individuals and organizations criticize the Republicans for their ties to Big Money, we need to point out that Democrats are funded by Big Money as well. When they imply that Democrats are environmental heroes or champions of the 99%, we need to set the record straight. When someone talks about "having Obama's back" in the fight against the oil and gas industry, we should respond like this:

I'm confused. Why do you use that phrase? It implies that Obama wants to curtail fossil-fuel extraction and burning and just needs our help to fulfill his intentions. In fact, he's aggressively promoted oil and gas extraction, even bragging about approving pipelines, leasing public lands, and opening up offshore waters for drilling. The Republicans are not our friends. But neither are Obama and the Democrats. It is time for a party of, by, and for the 99%.

When others ask us to donate, endorse, or vote for Democrats, we need to respond that we cannot do so because we want a just and sustainable world. We need to be ready to explain that Lesser Evilism is a dead-end that has resulted in Democrats drifting farther away from the public interest over the years, not closer to it.

Calling Extortion What It Is

Earlier sections of this book described how wealthy corporations use their control over resources and jobs to impose unacceptable conditions on workers and communities. The problem is so widespread that it is now accepted as the norm. We need to call these corporate demands what they are: extortion. *No, we won't agree to the wage cuts, air pollution exemptions, and public subsidies demanded by the company. We refuse to give in to extortion.*

If a company insists that it will leave town if its demands aren't met, we need to stand up even taller. There are now many examples of workers finding ways to take over their workplaces and run them democratically as cooperatives. *If the company leaves town, that doesn't mean we need to close the factory. Let's find a way to keep the equipment and materials and create a worker-owned and worker-managed company.*[894]

It takes courage to speak up. Often those who tell the truth face harsh criticism. *You're uncooperative. You're negative,* we are told. And worse.

We need to let such criticisms roll off our backs as we continue to say what needs to be said. In fact, we need to claim for ourselves the adjectives that more accurately describe us. We are actually extraordinarily *positive* people with a rational vision of how society can be structured so all can thrive and we can survive as a species. We stand for fundamental values that most people share: government of, by, and for the people; equality under the law; and a democratic economy not rigged for some and full of landmines for others. While others say, "No, we can't put in place the policies we want," we are the ones who say, "Yes, we can, and indeed we must."

We are very *collaborative.* No, we don't go along with undemocratic procedures that misuse that term, such as those in which people with financial conflicts are given veto power over policy decisions. Instead we are collaborative in the truest and broadest sense of the word. We are uniting diverse people from around the world in a huge movement to establish and protect democracy.

2. BE CHOOSEY ABOUT THE SINGLE-ISSUE ORGANIZATIONS WE SUPPORT.

People who want to make a difference on particular issues generally plug into the world of non-governmental social justice groups. They get themselves hired, sign up as volunteers, make donations, and lend support to chosen organizations' campaigns.

Unfortunately, as this book documents, some social justice organizations are actually front groups for the very forces that have created the problems we're trying to fix. Others engage in behaviors that are ineffective and may even reinforce the capitalist system that disempowers us.

We have to rethink our relationships with environmental groups and other social justice organizations. We must insist that the ones we plug into adhere to the principles outlined above.

If the organizations we already belong to engage in ineffective or harmful behaviors and we are unable to change them, it's time to move on.

3. SUPPORT SOCIALIST ORGANIZATIONS.

We must support organizations that understand the need to get beyond capitalism and make fighting for socialism their primary focus. These groups will likely be active in some of the pivotal organizing fronts mentioned in the next section.[895]

Indeed, socialists have been active organizers from early on in some of the most powerful and successful mass movements in history. They were there in the Civil Rights movement, the fight to end the Vietnam War, workers' battles for basic rights like union organizing and the eight-hour day, and other important struggles.

Joining a socialist organization is important because we will only achieve our goals by working together with others. Moreover, there are countless decisions to be made about the details of the system we want to put in place and the best strategies for moving forward. Discussion and debate are central to the democracy we are trying to establish. Each of us has important insights and ideas to bring to the table and an important role to play in shaping what happens next. Socialist organizations foster the discussions we need to be having.

Be aware, however, that there are socialists and there are socialists. Neither groups that idolize Stalinist-type repression nor those that claim the next step toward socialism is to elect another Democrat are what we need. Seek out groups that are committed to workers' democracy, that tell the truth about history, and that believe that capitalism can and must be replaced *in our time* through the education and mobilization of masses of working people.

4. SUPPORT PIVOTAL PROTESTS AND CAMPAIGNS.

Periodically, people rise up in pivotal protests and campaigns that have the potential to trigger a quantum leap forward toward the fundamental changes we need. When that happens, we've got to be there. Our participation can help tip the balance.

Recent pivotal protests and campaigns include:

* Occupy Wall Street, which identified and objected to the most important dynamic in the world today: less than 1% of the world's population owning most of the world's wealth and calling the shots.

* The 15 Now Movement, which is demanding an increase in the U.S. minimum wage to $15 per hour. Those hardest hit by capitalism—the people we need to be the backbone of our economic democracy movement—are making swift progress on an issue that makes a big difference in their lives. They are radically affecting public perceptions about capitalism by spotlighting its egregious consequences. Organizers are asking why people working full-time still live in poverty. They're pointing out that in 2014, the CEO of JPMorgan Chase made more money in less than three hours than a minimum wage worker made all year.

* The Anti-Austerity Movement, which is also mobilizing those hardest hit by capitalism. Like 15 Now, this movement is exposing the true nature of capitalism. It is spotlighting the need to get beyond that economic system. Anti-austerity activists are pointing to the trillions of dollars workers produced that sit in the bank accounts of a few wealthy corporations and individuals. And they are refusing to accept proposed cuts to public services, pensions and more.

* Climate Change Protests. Growing numbers of people are rising up to protect the Earth, engaging in ever-larger mass marches and in smaller protests that some have dubbed "Blockadia." (Blockadia refers to protesters blocking coal trains and otherwise

trying to physically disrupt the extraction, transportation, and burning of fossil fuels.) Together, these protests have the potential to bring to the streets the numbers we need to tip the balance and begin to claim our real power. Moreover, they expose one of the most frightening impacts of capitalism: our seeming inability to halt the extraction and burning of fossil fuels even though these activities threaten the very survival of our species. Global warming protests have the potential to expose the fact that democratic control over our destiny is impossible in an economic system that gives private interests control over public wealth, resources and industries.

* The Black Lives Matter Movement, which was triggered by police killings of unarmed black men and women across the United States but has goals that are much broader than halting police brutality. Racism has its roots in class society. We live with the legacy of slavery, the epitome of putting the pursuit of profit above justice and human rights. Capitalism fosters racism by creating a dog-eat-dog society in which vast numbers compete with one another to get by. This is a breeding ground for manipulation that pits working people against working people, while those who hoard society's wealth profit from the results. Black Lives Matter is connecting the dots between economic oppression and racial discrimination.

These pivotal protests and campaigns deserve our support. We need to hit the streets with others, swelling the numbers demanding change. As we do so, we should talk with people we meet about the economic roots of the things we are protesting.

5: BUILD A POLITICAL PARTY OF OUR OWN.

We cannot get where we need to go by supporting the Democratic and Republican Parties and candidates who run under their auspices. Both of these parties are committed to perpetuating and expanding the very economic system that prevents democracy and advances private over public interests.

Obscene wealth in the hands of a few, privatization of public services, vast poverty, expansive wars, the inability of people to establish much-needed reforms, and other unacceptable situations all flow directly from policies advanced by both Democrats and Republicans. Both parties have promoted "trade" agreements that undercut financial regulation and environmental protection. Both are heavily funded by the 1%. The national candidates of both parties tend to be members of the 1% themselves.

We need a political party that is clearly and unabashedly of, by, and for the 99%. Our party needs to advance a platform that articulates the facts about our capitalist economic system and the need to move beyond that system. We must offer a stark contrast to the polluted two-party corporacracy that currently dominates elections.

Just any alternative to the Democrats and Republicans won't do, even if party organizers say lots of good things. Our party must have several important characteristics, including:

* A commitment to real economic democracy rather than merely cosmetic changes that leave unjust economic arrangements intact. The party must clearly understand and state that it only represents and advances the interests of the working class. It cannot claim to also represent the 1% and the institutions that enrich it. Representing the 1% is inherently inconsistent with representing working people and striving for an equitable economic system.

* Strong participation and leadership from labor unions and other worker organizations. It is the power of working people to bring our economy to a halt that will ultimately get us where we need to go. Thus, the organizations of the working class must play a central role in our party. Moreover, transferring the money

labor now invests in the Democratic Party to our own working people's party will give a vital boost to our efforts.

* A clear understanding that those elected as party candidates will actually support and advance the party's platform. "Blue Dog" candidates who don't agree with portions of it must not be put forth. While other parties package and sell personalities, ours will focus on the issues and the specifics of how to address them.

* A commitment to building workplace and community-based structures that will funnel decisions from the 99% upward in our society.

* A commitment within the party itself to grassroots-up democracy instead of top-down party governance.

* A commitment to truly seeking votes for the party's candidates even in elections where Democrats and Republicans are running neck in neck. A party that encourages supporters to vote Democratic in such elections doesn't understand the deadly dynamics of Lesser Evilism. It diverts us from the work we need to be doing.[896]

* A commitment to refusing corporate donations, limiting the size of contributions from individuals, and fully disclosing all donors. Where public financing is available, the party should use it.

* Candidate commitments to refuse or give away portions of the salaries they receive, if elected, that exceed average workers' wages.

Building our own political party entails many things. We must give our time and money to it and encourage friends and colleagues to do the same. We must encourage organizations that endorse candidates to endorse ours, and insist that they tell the truth about the inadequacies of Democrats and Republicans alike. Finally, building our own party means voting for the candidates it runs.

6. PUT PIECES OF A NEW WORLD IN PLACE, AS A SUPPLEMENT TO
POLITICAL ACTIVISM NOT A SUBSTITUTE FOR IT.

Previous chapters described some of the inspiring ways in which people
are breaking away from the insane, unjust, and unsustainable practices
promoted by our capitalist economy. These sorts of actions are part of
our path forward, too, but they must be supplements to political activism, not substitutes for it.

It is valuable to do things like:

* Move our money from big corporate banks to credit unions and
  community-owned banks.
* Install renewable energy equipment on our homes and in our
  communities.
* Support small, local, sustainable farming by becoming farmers
  ourselves, growing food in our gardens for our families, being
  part of a CSA (Community Supported Agriculture) program
  and frequenting farmers' markets and food co-ops.
* Be part of a cooperative business where workers democratically
  determine policies.

These steps are helpful because:

* They keep essential knowledge alive and expand that knowledge, including how to grow food and how to capture energy
  from the sun.
* They show people that there are alternatives. We don't need to
  spray toxic chemicals, injuring people and wildlife to grow food.
  We don't need to dig up and burn fossil fuels. Showing the
  world alternatives helps accomplish the radical task of getting
  people to question the "No We Can't Change Things" message
  promoted by those who profit from the status quo.
* They connect us with one another. When we choose to live
  in a cooperative life-sustaining manner we find others who are

questioning the set-up all around us. We find colleagues for the struggle for economic and political change.

* They give us hope. We learn that there really are adequate resources and technologies for our needs.

While these actions are useful, they are not enough. We must be very clear about that, and never imply otherwise. By themselves they will not save the day.

First of all, our economic system makes it difficult for most people to afford to buy organic, buy other "green" products, install solar panels on our homes, etc. Even if some have the ability to make those choices, most don't.

Secondly, our economic system promotes consumption and waste through massive public relations campaigns and a relentless need for "growth." Our best efforts as individuals are no match for this overwhelming promotion of planet-destroying products and behaviors. They're no match for the success major corporations have in intentionally blocking people's access to alternative products and services.

Thirdly, unless and until we wrest power from the 1%, we will be unable to engage in comprehensive planning. We will be unable to put in place the national and regional energy policies and grids that we need. We won't be able to establish good mass transit systems. We will lack the means to make meeting human needs a priority.

Fourth, even if we lead ideal lives, minimizing our own footprints on the planet, there really is no place to hide. Global warming, toxic pollution, radiation from nuclear disasters and other environmental problems affect people everywhere. As just one example, temperatures create droughts that can undo the hard work of even the most talented farmers, as just one example.

Moreover, as our insane economic system depletes resources and denies people access to basic necessities, the scourge of war expands daily. Violence over access to oil, water, and land will increase with time unless we turn things around. The threat of global holocaust from nuclear and chemical weapons remains very real, and none of us can hide from that no matter how lightly we tread on the Earth as individuals.

We have no choice but to work for political and economic justice, even as we also put alternative systems in place.

CHAPTER 31

The Path Forward

• • •

WE STAND AT THE MOST important crossroads in human history. Ever more rapidly, on multiple, crucial fronts, we are losing ground. With each passing day, the gap between rich and poor grows larger. The atmosphere gets warmer. Populations of pollinators, fish, and other species decline precipitously. Wars expand and with them the threat of nuclear holocaust. The fate of our children and grandchildren hangs in the balance as we engage in monumental struggles on these and other urgent issues.

We can keep fighting the way we've been fighting. Instead of making the key decisions that determine our future ourselves, we can still leave these to the owners of major industries. We can continue to nip around the edges of the world's crises.

Instead of challenging the funneling of wealth produced by workers into the coffers of an elite few, we can continue to accept this arrangement. We can keep battling selected consequences, while ignoring the countless other ways Big Money manipulates public policymaking.

We can maintain our faith in political parties bankrolled by the 1% and dedicated to its interests. Maybe this time the Band-Aids they offer will cover the gaping wounds engendered by their policies. Maybe this time the Band-Aids won't be torn off.

Yes, we can keep fighting the way we've been fighting.

But that's no way to save a planet. It's no way to create the just society we want and deserve.

The path we need to take is clear. We have to change how we fight and what we're demanding. It is time to move beyond capitalism and the class-based inequities in wealth and power it engenders. We must unite for economic democracy and the political democracy that comes with it.

Democracy—and the lack thereof—has been the issue all along. It was the issue when we took to the streets against the WTO and when I resisted EPA's insistence that the public be gagged at its meeting in 1999. It was the issue in every pesticide battle our farm worker organization undertook. It is the issue in each and every environmental and social justice struggle now underway.

Explicitly, unapologetically, and forcefully, we need to fight for real system change. We must leave false friends and dead-ends behind. It's time to straighten our backs and stand tall at last, because as Martin Luther King said so well: "…a man can't ride your back unless it is bent."[897]

Lessons from Occupy Wall Street

Powerful forces will try to derail us, of course. In earlier chapters, we glimpsed some of the tools they'll use to marginalize us and distort the issues.

Occupy Wall Street offers further insights on what to expect as we move forward. In the fall of 2011, as I started to write this book, thousands marched on New York City's financial district. They set up an encampment in Zuccotti Park. After videos of violent police behavior against protesters went viral, Occupy sprang up in other cities across the U.S. and around the world.

Occupy Wall Street did an extremely important thing. It pointed to the actual problem: wealth and power accumulating in a few hands leaving the rest of us unable to control our destiny. It gave us language to talk about this. "We are the 99%!" denounces the 1%'s power grab while simultaneously emphasizing that working people can turn things around because there are so many of us.

Occupy enjoyed instant widespread support across the U.S. An impressive 44% of Americans supported it, compared to only 35% opposed. Forty-eight percent agreed with concerns raised by protesters as compared with only 30% who disagreed. A whopping 77% of people polled said that a few rich people and corporations have too much power. People I knew who were politically conservative or not politically active at all were excited by Occupy.

Despite the way Occupy resonated with people, or perhaps because of it, external forces aligned against this movement from the get-go. At first the news media failed to cover Occupy at all, except for producing small local stories. Eventually, as the Occupy movement spread, coverage increased, but rarely did it give much information about the issues being raised.

Documents obtained by the Partnership for Civil Justice Fund through the Freedom of Information Act reveal that the FBI was actively spying on Occupy protesters as early as August 2011, a month prior to the first encampment. The documents also show that an incredibly large network of FBI, Department of Homeland Security, local police, and private security personnel coordinated with one another and treated Occupy protests as potential criminal and terrorist activity. There was ongoing coordination with and sharing of information about protesters' plans with big banks.[898]

It is likely that people serving corporate and government surveillance groups attended Occupy meetings without divulging who they were working for.[899] Infiltrators can play roles beyond gathering information for the corporate state. They can also steer discussions or prevent action. A Seattle activist complained to me that he was frustrated by Occupy meetings in which certain participants seemed to always block agreement on what to do next. He wondered if they were infiltrators.

A leaked PR firm memo sheds further light on the sorts of external threats Occupy faced. The firm Clark, Lytle, Geduldig & Crawford proposed a six-month $850,000 program to the American Bankers Association to discredit and derail Occupy.[900] The memo proposed in-depth research on Occupy leaders including their litigation history, bankruptcies, tax liens, and more. The firm would produce an analysis of Occupy Wall Street (OWS) backers, funders and "extremist" leaders, and figure out how to use this information in effective messages. They wanted to "construct fact-based negative narratives of the OWS for high impact media placement."

The memo noted that individual companies threatened by OWS "likely will not be the best spokespeople for their own cause...." It promised a report about allies and a coalition that would help get companies' messages out for them.

The American Banking Association says that it did not take the PR firm up on its proposal, and it is unclear whether the firm pitched the same proposal to others who said yes. Nonetheless, the memo gives a glimpse of the sorts of PR strategies that were likely in play. The focus on "extremist" people within Occupy, and the plan to make sure the media received news pitches about them meshes well with what we witnessed regarding media coverage of Occupy. Much attention was paid to small numbers of people who tried to damage property, i.e., the sort of people who would provoke negative reactions among readers and viewers of the news.

Occupy also faced the threat of co-optation. At one rally that seemed to spring from Occupy Seattle, for example, a Democratic Congressman was a featured speaker. He lashed out at specific major corporations and then incongruously concluded that what everyone needed to do was put all their energy into reelecting Obama. Obama had taken funding from those very corporations and had appointed people sympathetic to them and even employed by them. Obama's record showed his solid support for policies advancing the interests of the 1% at the expense of the 99%.

Similarly, in the spring of 2012, MoveOn.org grabbed the language and energy generated by Occupy. It launched a campaign called "the 99% Spring." Author Charles M. Young's account of a 99% Spring training reveals the sharp contrast between what MoveOn sought to do and what Occupy stood for.[901] After the trainings ended, the "99% Spring" campaign disappeared, never to be heard of again. Throughout the years, MoveOn has steadfastly portrayed Obama as a champion of the 99%, ignoring his actual record, positions, and plans.

Resisting Derailment

As the facts about Occupy reveal, there will be many challenges as we move forward on the path we must take. We can protect ourselves from being knocked off track, however.

To minimize the disruptive power of infiltrators, for example, we need to establish effective group decision-making procedures. Ample discussion and exchange of information is essential, but must not be used to permanently delay decisions. Consensus is a good goal, but lack of consensus must not prevent action. The democratic process of voting needs to be central.

Our greatest hope lies in as many of us as possible taking the steps laid out in this book, broadly sharing our vision and spotlighting the power we have to make it real. Despite the billions spent on creating the illusion of prosperity and democracy, people can see that we have neither. The more we talk honestly about what we're up against, and the more thoroughly we articulate the real changes we need, the less successful those who seek to derail us will be. The more of us who are committed to passing the information and the vision on to others, the more unstoppable we will become. As my favorite Occupy sign noted, "You cannot kill an idea whose time has come."

We need to take full advantage of the many ways we have to communicate with one another. For lots of people, corporate-owned news outlets are no longer a primary source of information. We must foster and use alternative ways of sharing information and keep moving forward, regardless of marginalization by the mainstream press.

Change Is Coming

The desire for justice, protection of our environment, and survival of our species is a bright flame that cannot be extinguished. We saw that flame burning brightly, creating hope for the future during the WTO protests described at the beginning of this book. Today we see it burning still as people take to the streets to protest low wages, austerity, global warming, trade agreements, racist police brutality, and more.

Meanwhile, less visibly but just as importantly, people who have found each other through Occupy and other movements are quietly working together, laying the groundwork for what to do next.[902] The movement we need is gestating. Hope is percolating beneath the surface.

While we go about the business of telling the truth, building alliances, forging new agendas and strategies, building our own political party, and otherwise setting the stage for what comes next, we need to all be in a state of readiness.

In early September 2011 most of us had no idea that the extraordinary leap forward known as Occupy Wall Street was about to happen. It seemed to come out of nowhere, but it really resulted from a convergence of all sorts of things. The next quantum leap forward could occur at any time.

Just before the New Deal, things looked pretty bleak. Few anticipated the major changes that were coming. While those changes helped individuals for a while, they didn't deal with the roots of the problems that had arisen. Instead they propped up capitalism. It was only a matter of time before those who hoard wealth and resources under capitalism began to chip away at New Deal advances, ultimately increasing their wealth and power astronomically. This has led to the obscene gap between rich and poor we now endure, and all that goes with it, including multiple serious threats to human survival.

The time for another major upheaval is nigh. This go-round, we must demand the fundamental changes to our economic system that are needed.

Polls have long shown that overwhelming majorities of Americans are frustrated with the control that ultra-wealthy corporations have in our country. There are more and more signs every day that we can harness that discontent and turn it towards the work of creating economic democracy.

Some people ridicule those who lay out a vision of the just world we want—one that ensures democracy, fair distribution of resources, food and shelter for all, guaranteed jobs, livable wages, secure retirements, and other rights. They criticize us for describing a "utopia" as if the concept of having such a fair and sustainable world is ridiculous.

But we really have no choice but to envision that better world. It truly has come down to choosing between what author and inventor Buckminster Fuller poetically described as "utopia or oblivion."

The path ahead is daunting but we really are the 99% and we are waking up. Together we have the power to create the world we need.

CHAPTER 32

Jobs in a World Controlled by the Wealthy Few

• • •

YEARS HAVE PASSED SINCE I sat down to write this book. Reviewing my experiences, researching political power and global trends, and contemplating what it all means have been quite helpful. I'm still very worried about what could be in store for us and our children, but I also have clarity about what we must do to turn things around. And I believe we can succeed.

This book is the distillation of what I've learned. I hope it will be one of many catalysts spurring the changes that are needed at this critical point in history.

But what about that other question I was grappling with when I started writing? I didn't just want to figure out what we need to do differently as a movement for social change. I also wanted to figure out my particular path. Should I continue to be an employee for environmental organizations, or do I need to chart a different course for myself? And what should I tell young people eager to make their livings as environmental activists?

GOODBYE PAID ACTIVISM

Lots of people fight for the Earth without being paid for their efforts. As a young woman, I assumed, however, that the best way for me to make a difference was to make a career out of my activism.

Law schools paint a rosy picture of the role lawyers play in our world. Supposedly, we represent all the various perspectives on important issues, ensuring that each is presented vigorously and effectively. There's an entire ethical canon about the legal profession's obligation to ensure that all have representation.

That happy image bears no connection to reality. Large corporations and wealthy individuals have all sorts of lawyers, not to mention public relations experts, scientists, and other professionals, at their beck and call. On the other hand, representation by lawyers and other professionals for middle- and low-income people is extremely sparse, particularly when it comes to influencing policy.

Agricultural pesticide issues are a typical example. Vast teams of highly paid professionals work around the clock with enormous resources at their disposal to ensure that policies favor agribusiness interests. Meanwhile, there are almost no such advocates for farm workers and others poisoned by farm pesticides. After funding ran out for my position at the Farm Worker Pesticide Project, I searched in vain for a similar position. I had very strong credentials, proven skills, and an intense desire to advocate policies that protect farm worker families and others, but relevant jobs weren't to be found.

Other public-interest environmental advocacy openings were also few and far between. Posted jobs were generally with groups that employ ineffective strategies and don't help the hardest hit communities. Most openings weren't even for advocates. They were for fundraisers and organizational development experts.

There were also frequent postings for what I call "generic activists." Public Outreach Fundraising (POF)[903], for example, was seeking people it could farm out as "fundraising representatives" to client organizations. POF claimed that its workers go home every day with the knowledge that they are "helping to make a difference in the lives of those most in need by informing the public about the issues that really matter and getting them involved." How does POF determine which issues really matter and which people are most in need? I'm betting they bestow that praise on whoever happens to have the money to hire POF.

Those seeking public-interest jobs are always limited to whatever positions happen to be funded, whether or not these positions effectively address issues truly worthy of attention. Rent-an-activist operations take things a step further, funneling people's skills and passion into shifting unnamed causes for whatever organizations happen to sign up next.

Month after month, I searched steadily for effective public-interest advocacy work to no avail. Meanwhile, Monsanto, the American Chemistry Council, and the U.S. Chamber of Commerce were all hiring people to influence policies on behalf of private corporations.

Many public-interest employees ultimately move into positions representing industry. Bruce Gryniewski, the former head of Washington Conservation Voters, was mentioned in a *Seattle Times* article in February of 2013 as a strategist for a coal company, for example. According to the article, state Representative Reuven Carlyle was disappointed to know that environmentalists were working for the coal companies. The Seattle Democrat noted, however, that he didn't take it personally. "It's just one of those realities when hundreds of millions of dollars are at stake," he said. "This is the gig, and the game we're in."[904]

I agree that this is the gig and the game we're in. But that's what we need to protest and change. And I'm not willing to play under these conditions.

Thus, I have decided to separate my activism from my income.

I am more committed than ever to working for environmental justice and survival. But I am officially giving up on finding a paid public-interest advocacy job.

I've reached this decision because I will almost certainly not find a job worthy of my skills, passion, and expertise. In fact, any opportunities that arise in the future would likely funnel these into ineffective or even harmful agendas and strategies. Moreover, employment at an environmental organization would limit what I do on my own time. An environmental employer would object to me publicly embracing tactics and positions it perceives as at odds with its own. It would not allow me to criticize a major funder.

Therefore, I now do other work to pay my bills. And I am an unpaid activist in my spare time, free of the tethers and censorship associated with doing that work for pay.

OUR JOBS, OUR WORLD

My employment dilemma is not unusual. This book provides glimpses of similar dilemmas faced by others. Would-be investigative journalists encounter dwindling numbers of jobs in their field and increasing control over media outlets by private interests. Scientists find that many positions are funded by those with a financial stake in research outcomes, and even those who remain independent are denied necessary materials and information because it is "proprietary." As public libraries reduce their hours, librarians get jobs at bookstores, selling books they used to loan to people without charge. And so on and so forth.

Meanwhile, the percent of jobs that pay low wages has been steadily increasing for years. Middle-wage occupations accounted for 60% of employment losses between 2007 and 2009, but represent just 20% of post-recession job growth.[905] Now, deep into the so-called recovery, job growth is still heavily concentrated in lower-wage industries.[906] When I searched for work, the overwhelming majority of positions posted were low-wage ones.

Many people can't find jobs at all, of course. Given the many unmet needs in our society, this is insane. How can we have unemployment when we should be installing alternative energy systems, building low-income housing, transforming empty lots into farms, adding teachers and special needs assistants to classrooms, building mass transit systems, and providing other necessary goods and services?

But wait! There is an industry that is expanding the number of jobs it provides, including "hundreds of thousands" at a level of pay claimed to be "significantly higher than the national average." It's the oil and gas industry! The American Petroleum Institute (API) launched a new recruiting website in June of 2014 to attract workers to keep up with its booming growth. API predicted that the industry will need 1.3 million new workers by 2030. Oil and gas job growth has been 40 times higher than job growth in the rest of the economy.[907]

An industry that should be eliminated if we are to have any chance of preventing climate disaster is growing by leaps and bounds. What clearer evidence could there be that we're heading in the wrong direction?

No, my job dilemma is not an anomaly. It is part of a larger societal crisis that plays out in the job choices faced by millions upon millions of people every day. My situation is far better than most people's.

The same forces that are pushing our planet towards environmental disaster also limit and control the jobs available to us as individuals. As each of us figures out what to do for pay, we need to remember that our personal employment experience is yet another symptom of a destructive economic system that has to go.

My Job Plan

To pay my bills I now work part-time at jobs that have nothing to do with environmental activism. They leave me time and energy to do activist work that is unpaid and unfettered.

For a while I toyed with doing legal work such as drawing up contracts and wills because I could earn more money in a few hours than I could in a lot of hours at other lower paid jobs. But it would have unduly drained me to come up to speed in those areas. Moreover, those legal jobs just didn't appeal to me at all, as compared to other things that were calling to me.

I'd been longing to spend more time with children, to have more music in my life, to teach, and to grow things.

And so my paid work includes providing child care and teaching family music classes. These feed my soul as well as give me money for the bills. Spending delightful hours with children recharges me for the work I do on their behalf as an activist.

I am also enjoying growing large quantities of food in our yard as part of the local organic urban food movement. I feel compelled to witness nature's abundance and how seeds planted today produce food tomorrow. While I'm not paid for this labor with cash, it does reduce our grocery bills. And it gives me hope.

Getting my new jobs going has been challenging, but gradually things have fallen into place. I am excited about this new phase of life and the freedom to advocate for change without the ball and chain of the nonprofit industrial complex attached to my leg.

I leave the door open for other sources of income that use my skills as an advocate, writer, organizer, and researcher. But the sort of job that uses those skills without undercutting the work I need to do is unlikely to come my way. I've made my peace with that, and feel quite liberated by my decision.

As for my unpaid activism, I am following the path this book has led me to, adhering to the principles and implementing steps laid out here. This book will be one of the tools I use in outreach to help build the movement we need. While working to persuade environmental activists and others to fight for economic change, I will also step up my involvement with Seattle-area campaigns to raise the minimum wage, control rent, and otherwise address major financial inequities. My involvement in third-party campaigns challenging the two-party corporacracy will also increase.

These activities are the best thing I can possibly do to address the environmental problems I fought so hard to address for so long. They are also the best thing I can do to address countless other critical issues that are inextricably intertwined with environmental issues.

So You Want to Save the World? Advice to Would-Be Career Activists

Regularly, while I was working for the Farm Worker Pesticide Project, people would approach me at meetings, quite enthused about the work we were doing. "How can I get a job like yours?" they would ask. Many were recent or future graduates of law schools or environmental programs at universities. They were deeply concerned about what is happening in the world and committed to using their talents to make things better.

Here's how I would answer their question now. Please do join with others in this struggle for justice and survival. There is an urgent need for your help. As you do your work, understand that you can't isolate environmental issues from other issues. Also understand that capitalism stands between us and the world we want. Our strategies must take it on. They must tell the truth and call for fundamental changes that foster equality and democracy.

Recognize, as well, that in many ways, social justice organizations have become part of the problem. If you are thinking about working for such an organization, be very careful. Keep in mind the principles that must guide our efforts and the actions we should be taking if we are to truly save our world. Take the time to assess whether you can fight the good fight through the organization you are considering. Will you be able to do its work in the context of the broader strategies and alliances we need to be building? Will you be censored or stymied in what you do? Will your work prop up systems that should be exposed as unacceptable and dismantled?

You may want to reassess your plans to engage in activism as a paid career. Finding a different way to make money may enable you to be a more effective agent for change. My dental hygienist cleans teeth to support her music, for instance, and the same concept can be used for activism. There are all sorts of other options to explore.

Whatever you do, good luck to you and thank you for adding your voice and talents to the most important struggle the human race has ever faced. I look forward to being with you in the huge movement we are building for a just and sustainable world.

ONWARD

And so the journey of writing this book has come to an end. I am excited about my new jobs for pay, and I'm eager to jump into the next phase of my activism, unencumbered by nonprofit employment and all that goes with it.

In parting, I'll share some of the words of a great Pete Seeger song I often turn to for inspiration when the going gets tough. Like so many others, I've been at this a long time. But loving my children, all children, and the miracle of life itself, it's time to give it one more try.

> One blue sky above us.
> One ocean lapping all our shores.
> One Earth so green and round.
> Who could ask for more?
> And because I love you, I'll give it one more try.
> I need to tell my rainbow race,
> It's too soon to die.
>
> ...Go tell, go tell all the children.
> Tell all the mothers and fathers, too.
> Now's our last chance to share
> What's been given to me and you.[908]

Acknowledgments

• • •

I AM INDEBTED TO COUNTLESS individuals for their help as I researched, wrote and published *What It Will Take*. Thank you to all who provided information and insights including especially Kate Davies, Jeannie Economos, Kathryn Gilje, Lin Nelson, Joanne Prado, Margaret Scott and the folks at the Center for Responsive Politics. Thank you to my wonderful editors A.T. Birmingham Young and Susie Hara for your gentle, thorough and excellent editing. Thank you to Bruce Lesnick for reading multiple drafts, making invaluable suggestions, and giving me the emotional sustenance I needed to complete this labor of love. Finally, thank you to everyone who is fighting for the Earth, including but not limited to the amazing individuals with whom I have been honored to join forces over the years. Your compassion, dedication and resilience give me hope.

Chapter 2

1   Earthjustice Legal Defense Fund, Chemical Industry Advisory Committee Lawsuit Backgrounder.

2   A Federal Register notice about the Advisory Committees stated that "For all committees, the Secretary [of Commerce] and USTR invite nomination of U.S. citizens who are executives and managers of U.S. manufacturing or service companies that trade internationally. The Secretary and USTR also invite nominations of executives representing trade associations whose members are U.S. companies that trade internationally. Companies must be at least 51 percent beneficially-owned by U.S. persons." In case any of us public interest types didn't grasp that we weren't welcome, the notice spelled out that "U.S.-based subsidiaries of foreign companies, non-government organizations, and academic institutions do not qualify for representation on a committee" (Federal Register Vol. 64, No. 42, Thursday, March 4, 1999, pp. 10448-10449.)

3   Thompson et al, "Identifying Constituents to Participate in a Project to Control Pesticide Exposure in Children of Farmworkers," *Environ Health Perspect* 109:443-448 (2001.)

4   Thompson et al, "Para Ninos Saludables: A Community Intervention Trial to Reduce Organophosphate Pesticide Exposure in Children of Farmworkers," *Environ Health Perspect*, May 2008.

5   Meanwhile detections and concentrations of phosmet increased by Year 4, indicating that many growers were apparently switching to this other organophosphate. EPA's ban only applied to Guthion.

6   Sources for this discussion include my notes and recollections and WSDA minutes for meetings that took place on July 22, October 19, and December 13, 2004.

7   Dan Wheat, "Ag Dept. Survey Results Misleading," *Wenatchee World*, Feb. 12, 2006. Wheat did a thorough review of the comment record after WSDA's director claimed that the count was closer to 50-to-50 than the accurate numbers FWPP had given reporters. (Pressed for details, WSDA had claimed that 41 people opposed the rule, 39 supported it, and 21 supported it if it were expanded.) Dan Wheat went through the comments and concluded that the accurate count was 270 for and 25 opposed. WSDA had also claimed that a phone survey of principals at 58 schools "did not produce any consensus about the value of the proposed rule." The Wenatchee World concluded that WSDA "misrepresented the results" of that survey. In fact, 82% (14 of 17) of the institutions that the rule was designed to benefit—those that bordered agricultural lands—supported the rule.

8   In 2008 Gregoire was endorsed by the Washington Conservation Voters, the Sierra Club, and other environmental and labor organizations. (See facts about Christine Gregoire, including key endorsements, *Seattle Times*, August 8, 2008.) She was proclaimed to be an environmental leader who had advanced public health and ecosystem protections. Gregoire was readily re-elected and continued to be portrayed within the state and nationally as an "eco-Governor." (See for example, Tracey D. Morsella, "Greenopia Ranks 50 State Governors for Environmental Responsibility," posted 2009, retrieved March 8, 2012.)

9   Valoria Loveland, WSDA, "Letter to Carol Dansereau, FWPP," March 4, 2005.

10   HalBernton, "A Pesticide Policeman's Fall," *Seattle Times*, August 31, 2004; Email from WSDA Assistant Director Bob Arrington to Gail Amos et al (WSDA staff), "Investigative Summary," Feb. 2, 2004, 10:26 a.m.; James Pitkin, "Ag Inspector Did His Job Right But He Still Won't Be Allowed to Return to It," *Wenatchee World*, Jan. 11, 2004; James Pitkin, "Agriculture Inspector Taken Off Pesticide Job. Move Appears to Be Retaliatory, Some Say," *Wenatchee World*, Nov. 20, 2003; Dan Wheat, "Numbers of Controversy. State Imposes Fewer Penalties for Area Growers After Removing Inspector Who Critics Say Was Too Strict," *Wenatchee World*, Feb. 10, 2008.

11   The state also tested the air for MITC near potato fields where the pesticide metam sodium was used, establishing that drift was a major problem for that pesticide as well. FWPP's efforts related to metam sodium are beyond the scope of this book. Our experiences related to that and other pesticides were similar to those recounted for chlorpyrifos here.

12   Source: WFFF website list of board of directors retrieved at that time.

13   http://www.pestfacts.org/rise/index.html, retrieved 5/9/08.

14   Sources include but are not limited to: Washington State Horticulture Association Hort Headlines, Jan. 19, 2007; Jim Hazen, WSDAH, Letter to Secretary of Health Mary Selecky, Feb. 12, 2007; Heather Hansen, WA Friends of Farms and Forests, Letter to Governor Gregoire, June 21, 2007.

15   RCW 70.104.090.

16   One email noted that "Jim [probably Jesernig] will check with PNNL management tomorrow, when he's there. He may suggest a quick call from the Gov... as management may have to loosen some of Timchalk's 'benchmark' requirements." Another message notes that "Jesernig is working PNNL to encourage Timchalk to say yes. Jim believes the lab managers may need to 'relax' some of his production requirements...and it may take a while to get that decision made/communicated. But he's working it...Given that, if Timchalk is leaning towards 'no'—maybe we hold off on accepting that answer, at least right away...."

17   Reference Exposure Levels go by many different names depending on whom you're talking to, which route of exposure you're dealing with, and other factors. Other terms include "reference doses," "reference concentrations," and "screening levels."

18   Richard Fenske et al, University of Washington, Organophosphorus Pesticide Air Monitoring, Project Final Report Submitted to Dr. Cynthia Lopez, Washington State Dept. of Health Pesticide Program, June 30, 2009 (Updated Sept. 15, 2009.)

19   The Stanford team reviewed 19 Dow studies bearing on the safety of chlorpyrifos, including nine studies they classified as "core" and 10 studies they classified as "secondary." From 78 to 100% of the core Dow studies contained errors of the most significant types. None of these studies were error free; 23% had more than 15 errors, and the average number of errors was 10.8. The report notes that "(b)y any standards that I am aware of in this field, these are extraordinarily high rates of errors."

Just as importantly, the analysis found that "no single error among these is a false positive (i.e., mistakenly presenting CPF [chlorpyrifos] as being more dangerous than it actually is), and the vast majority are false negatives (i.e. minimizing the danger of CPF). **In other words, this core literature of Dow papers concerning the safety of CPF is rife with errors that minimize its dangers"** (emphasis added.)

A similar analysis of the secondary studies found an error rate somewhat lower than in the core papers. Sapolsky noted, however, that "...there is once again by the standards that I am familiar with, an extraordinarily high rate of errors, with, at the extreme, 70% of papers having Category D errors (i.e. problems with interpretation of results.).... As with the core CPF papers, there is no instance in which an error exaggerated the dangers of CPF. Instead, they overwhelmingly lessened them."

Dr. Sapolsky and his team reviewed chlorpyrifos studies not done by Dow scientists for comparison. They found significantly fewer errors. These errors were not biased towards supporting the traditional stances of the scientists.

When FWPP submitted comments to EPA on a chlorpyrifos Risk Assessment in 2011 we included a new analysis by Dr. Sapolsky regarding a Dow study included in that assessment. (Comments of Robert Sapolsky, Professor of Biology, Neurology and Neurosurgery, Stanford University on MRID 44556901; October 19, 2011). Dr. Sapolsky said, "I have reviewed MRID 44556901. I find the same self-serving, scientifically indefensible analyses that run through all of Dow's CPF studies."

20 RichardFenske, Letter to Ann Wick, Washington State Department of Agriculture, Dec. 13, 2006.

21 DanWheat, "Pesticide Test Showing Danger to Children Disputed by Some," *The Wenatchee World*, Dec. 11, 2006.

22 The main federal pesticide law, which is supposed to protect workers and other people from exposures at work, through drift, and other direct avenues, is a cost-benefit statute. EPA also regulates pesticides in the context of their residues in food under the Food, Drug and Cosmetic Act (FDCA). That statute requires reasonable certainty of no harm from pesticide residues in food. At this writing, there is a chance that EPA will finally ban chlorpyrifos under the FDCA. The agency was forced by a lawsuit to meet statutory deadlines under it. Thus on October 30, 2015, it issued a proposed rule that would effectively ban chlorpyrifos, with a potential effective date of mid 2017, i.e., two more spray seasons away for Washington State farm worker families. EPA's analysis is narrow in scope, and does not consider occupational farm worker exposures and much of the data we presented to them. The agency has made it clear that it only acted because of the deadline and its current inability to establish certainty of no harm. It is emphasizing that it is very open to changing the proposal based on input from the pesticide industry. Might we finally see an end to chlorpyrifos in 2017? It's hard to tell. (U.S. EPA, *Prepublication Notice: Chlorpyrifos; Tolerance Revocation, Proposed Rule, Docket EPA-HQ-OPP-2015-0653;* October 30, 2015.)

23 Granatstein and Kirby, CSANR, Trends in Washington State Organic Agriculture—2008.

Chapter 4

24 The U.S. figure includes 877 million pounds used in agriculture. Referenced amounts only count the "active ingredients" in pesticide products. They don't count so-called inactive ingredients, which can themselves be harmful.

25 Agriculture accounted for two-thirds of those expenditures.

26 Research Institute of Organic Agriculture (FiBL) news release, "United States: Organic Market Surpasses 31 Billion US Dollars in 2011." April 5, 2012.

27 JasonMick, "Monsanto Defeats Small Farmers in Critical Bioethics Class Action Suit," *Dailytech.com*, March 1, 2012.

28 Research Institute of Organic Agriculture (FiBL) and the International Federation of Organic Agriculture Movements (IFOAM), *The World of Organic Agriculture. Statistics & Emerging Trends 2015* (2015.)

29   WSU Center for Sustaining Agriculture and Natural Resources, Current Status of Organic Agriculture in Washington State 2011, Data as of Nov. 2011; Feb. 21, 2012.

30   U.S. Geological Survey, "Pesticides in the Nation's Streams and Ground Water," News Release, March 3, 2006.

31   Schafer et al, Pesticide Action Network, *Chemical Trespass. Pesticides in Our Bodies and Corporate Accountability*, evaluating CDC data. May 2004, p. 7. TCP was present in the urine of 93% of the people sampled.

32   Mark Bittman, "Pesticides: Now More Than Ever," *New York Times*, Dec. 11, 2012.

33   Dashka Slater, "The Frog of War," *Mother Jones*, January/February 2012 Issue, p. 4.

34   Wu et al, NRDC, *Still Poisoning the Well. Atrazine Continues to Contaminate Surface Water and Drinking Water in the United States*, April 2010, pp. i-iv.

35   Pesticide Action Network, "Atrazine Fact Sheet," http://www.panna.org/resources/specific-pesticides/atrazine.

36   Jacob L. Kerby and Andrew Storfer, "Combined Effects of Atrazine and Chlorpyrifos on Susceptibility of the Tiger Salamander to Ambystoma tigrinum Virus," *EcoHealth* 6, 91-98, 2009.

Atrazine is just one of many pesticides in use that harm frogs and other aquatic species. *The Guardian* newspaper reported on a new study in 2013 in which researchers exposed frogs to the most widely used fungicides, herbicides, and insecticides. One product killed frogs within an hour at concentrations recommended by the label. Others were acutely toxic to frogs, even when applied at just 10% of the label rate. The insecticide dimethoate killed 40% of exposed animals within a week (Damian Carrington, "Common Pesticides 'Can Kill Frogs Within an Hour,'" *The Guardian*, Jan. 24, 2013).

37   Jacob L. Kerby and Andrew Storfer, "Combined Effects of Atrazine and Chlorpyrifos on Susceptibility of the Tiger Salamander to Ambystoma tigrinum Virus," *EcoHealth* 6, 91-98, 2009.

38   USDA-NIFA *Specialty Crop Research Initiative Project, Enhancing Biological Control in Western Orchards*, p. 10; Geraldine Warner, "Who's Making the Decisions? Scientists Want to Get Pest Information into the Hands of Growers," *Goodfruit*, May 15, 2011.

39   Tom Philpott, "Are Pesticides Behind Massive Bee Die-Offs?," *Mother Jones*, Jan. 10, 2012.

40   AP, "Pesticides: Popular Pesticide Harms Bees—Studies," *Greenwire*, March 30, 2012.

41 Tom Philpott, "New Studies Link Bee Declines to Bayer Pesticide," *Mother Jones*, March 29, 2012, 3

42 Beginning in October of 2006, some beekeepers have been reporting losses of 30 to 90% of their hives. A certain amount of loss is to be expected in the winter, but the magnitudes experienced have been very unusual. Wild pollinators, like bumblebees, are also experiencing major losses; USDA Agricultural Research Service, "Questions and Answers: Colony Collapse Disorder," http://www.ars. usda.gov/News/docs.htm?docid=15572&pf=1&cg_id=0, retrieved July 25, 2012.

43 Some sources indicate that the over-wintering average pollinator loss in the U.S. is 40%, with some experiencing losses closer to 70%; Paul Towers, "Beekeepers expect 'worst year for bees,'" *Pesticide Action Network*, Jan. 16, 2013.

44 Tom Philpott, "New Studies Link Bee Declines to Bayer Pesticide," *Mother Jones*, March 29, 2012, p. 3, citing *Environmental Science & Technology*, http://www.ncbi. nlm.nih.gov/pubmed/22292570; Krupke et al, "Multiple Routes of Pesticide Exposure for Honey Bees Living Near Agricultural Fields," *PLoS ONE* 7(1): e29268. doi:10.1371/journal.pone.0029268; Hopwood et al, The Xerces Society for Invertebrate Conservation, "Are Neonicotinoids Killing Bees?," 2012; Mullin et al, "High Levels of Miticides and Agrochemicals in North American Apiaries: Implications for Honey Bee Health," *PLoS ONE* 5(3): e9754. doi:10.1371/journal.pone, March 19, 2010; Tom Philpott, "Top USDA Bee Researcher Also Found Bayer Pesticide Harmful to Bees," *Grist*, http://grist.org/article/2011-01-21-top-usda-bee-rsearcher -also-found-bayer-pesticide-harmful; Starner et al, "Detections of the Neonicotinoid Insecticide Imidacloprid in Surface Waters of Three Agricultural Regions of California, USA, 2010-2011"; *Bulletin of Environmental Contamination and Toxicology*, Vol. 88, No. 3 (2012), pp. 316-321.

One study, for example, found that exposure to small doses of the neonic thiamethoxam significantly affects bees' ability to find their way back to their hives "at levels that could put a colony at risk of collapse." Tom Philpott, "New Studies Link Bee Declines to Bayer Pesticide," *Mother Jones*, March 29, 2012, p. 3, citing *Science Express* article, http://www.sciencemag.org/content/early/recent.

The researchers attached tiny radio transmitters to bees to track them, and those dosed with neonics were two to three times more likely to not come back than un-dosed bees were. AP, "Pesticides: Popular Pesticide Harms Bees— Studies," *Greenwire*, March 30, 2012; Henry et al, "A Common Pesticide Decreases Foraging Success and Survival in Honey Bees," *Science*, April 20, 2012, Vol. 336, No. 6079, pp. 348-350.

In another study, researchers exposed bumblebee colonies to "field-realistic levels" of imidacloprid and then allowed them to develop naturally under field conditions. The treated colonies had a significantly reduced growth rate and suffered an 85% reduction in production of new queens. The researchers concluded that, "[g] iven the scale of use of neonicitinoids, we suggest that they may be having a considerable negative impact on wild bumble bee populations across the developed world." Tom Philpott, "New Studies Link Bee Declines to Bayer Pesticide," *Mother Jones*, March 29, 2012, p. 3.

45 As cited in Avaaz.org alert: "Bee-ware of Pesticides," April 26, 2012.

46 USDA Agricultural Research Service, "Questions and Answers: Colony Collapse Disorder," http://www.ars.usda.gov/News/docs.htm?docid=15572, retrieved July 25, 2012.

47 Center for Food Safety & Save Our Seeds, *Seed Giants vs. U.S. Farmers*, 2013, p. 2

48 Center for Food Safety & Save Our Seeds, *Seed Giants vs. U.S. Farmers*, 2013, p. 5.

49 See for example, Carey Gillam, "Pesticide Use Ramping Up as GMO Crop Technology Backfires: Study," *Reuters*, Oct. 1, 2012. Also, note that genetic modification corporations sell "pesticide-ready" crop seeds, specifically intending that farmers will buy and use the pesticides for which the plants will be "ready."

50 See for example, Colin McConnell, "Monarch Butterfly Decline Due to Loss of Milkweed, New Study Shows," *The Star.com, Canada*, June 4, 2014.

The Obama Administration is steadily approving GMO products. In February of 2015, for example, USDA approved a non-browning GMO Arctic apple. (Lisa R. David & Food Democracy Now! Letter to Supporters, Feb. 14, 2015.) In the fall of 2014, as another example, EPA approved "Enlist Duo," a toxic herbicide that contains 2,4 D (a key ingredient in Agent Orange used in the Vietnam War) and glyphosate (a pesticide declared a probable human carcinogen by the International Agency for Research on Cancer). This herbicide will be used on Dow's new herbicide-resistant corn and soy seeds, which had already been approved by USDA. See Jon Queally, "Glyphosate, Favored Chemical of Monsanto & Dow, Declared 'Probably' Source of Cancer for Humans," *Common Dreams*, Mar. 25, 2015; David Murphy, Food Democracy Now!, Letter to Supporters: "BREAKING: EPA Approves New Agent Orange' GMO Weedkiller," Oct. 15, 2014; U.S. EPA News Release, "EPA Announces Final Decision to Register *Enlist Duo*, Herbicide Containing 2,4-D and Glyphosate," Oct. 15, 2014.

Chapter 5

51 Jennifer Sass and Daniel Rosenberg, NRDC, *The Delay Game. How the Chemical Industry Ducks Regulation of the Most Toxic Substances*, Oct. 2011.

52 Sandy Bauers, "Thousands of Chemicals Pose Risks to Health," *The Philadelphia Inquirer*, Jan. 20, 2013.

53   UN Environment Program, *Global Chemicals Outlook* (2013).

54   UN Environment Program, *Global Chemicals Outlook* (2013).

55   *Chemical and Engineering News,* Aug. 20, 2012.

56   UNEP, *GEO 5 Assessment,* Chapter 6, June 6, 2012.

57   UN Environment Program, *Global Chemicals Outlook,* 2013, p. 7.

58   Jared Hunt, "Official Predicts Chemical Sector Boost," *Charleston Daily Mail,* Mar. 22, 2013.

59   Washington Toxics Coalition, News Release, "Children's Product Makers Report Over 5000 Products Contain Toxic Chemicals of Concern to Kid's Health," May 1, 2013.

60   Frontier Group, News Release, "America's Waterways received 226 Million Pounds of Toxic Chemicals," Mar. 22, 2012.

61   Jeff Barnard, "Toxics from Everyday Life Reaching Columbia River," *The Seattle Times,* May 14, 2012.

62   *Democracy Now* Headlines, EPA: "Most U.S. Rivers, Streams Are in Poor Condition," *Democracy Now,* March 27, 2013.

63   UNEP, *GEO 5 Assessment,* June 6, 2012, Chapter 6, p. 177.

64   UNEP, *GEO 2012 News Release,* June 6, 2012, p. 6.

65   Center for Disease Control, *2009 Fourth National Report on Human Exposure to Environmental Chemicals, Executive Summary.*

66   Sandy Bauers, "Thousands of Chemicals Pose Risks to Health," *The Philadelphia Inquirer,* Jan. 20 2013.

67   Environmental Working Group, *A Benchmark Investigation of Industrial Chemicals, Pollutants and Pesticides in Umbilical Cord Blood,* July 14, 2005; President's Cancer Panel (U.S. Dept of Health and Human Services, National Institutes of Health, National Cancer Institute), *Annual Report of the President's Cancer Panel: Reducing Environmental Cancer Risk, What We Can Do Now, 2008-2009* (April 2010.)

68   Statement from the Work Session on Chemically-Induced Alterations in Sexual Development: The Wildlife/Human Connection, Wingspread Conference Center, Racine, Wisconsin, July 1991.

69   UN Environment Programme, World Health Organization, State *of the Science of Endocrine Disrupting Chemicals 2012 Summary for Decision-Makers* (2013, p. 10.)

70   Dr. Philip Landrigan, Mount Sinai Children's Environmental Health Center, News Release, April 25, 2012.

71   Dr. Brian Moench, "Utah Physicians for a Healthy Environment, Autism and Disappearing Bees: A Common Denominator?," *Common Dreams,* April 2, 2012.

72   National Academy of Science, *Scientific Frontiers in Developmental Toxicology and Risk Assessment,* 2000.   See also Granjean and Landrigen, "Neurobehavioural

Effects of Developmental Toxicity," *Lancet*, Vol. 13, March 2014. According to this analysis "Overall, genetic factors seem to account for no more than perhaps 30–40% of all cases of neurodevelopmental disorders. Thus, non-genetic, environmental exposures are involved in causation, in some cases probably by interacting with genetically inherited dispositions. Strong evidence exists that industrial chemicals widely disseminated in the environment are important contributors to what we have called the global, silent pandemic of neurodevelopmental toxicity."

73   President's Cancer Panel (U.S. Dept of Health and Human Services, National Institutes of Health, National Cancer Institute), Annual *Report of the President's Cancer Panel: Reducing Environmental Cancer Risk, What We Can Do Now, 2008-2009*, (April 2010).

74   Michael Hawthorne et al, "Flame retardants and Their Risks," *Chicago Tribune Watchdog*, May 10, 2012.

75   Washington Toxics Coalition website: "About Us. Our Work Is Making a Difference," retrieved Feb. 3, 2012.

76   Washington Toxics Coalition, "Nothing But a Game of Bait and Switch," letter to supporters, Oct. 3, 2011.

77   David Rosner & Gerald Markowitz, "You and Your Family Are Guinea Pigs for the Chemical Corporations," *TomDispatch.com*, April 29, 2013.

Chapter 6

78   UNEP, "World Remains on Unsustainable Track Despite Hundreds of Internationally Agreed Goals and Objectives," June 6, 2012 (emphasis added.) See also: UNEP, "All G8 Countries Back Action on Black Carbon, Methane and Short-Lived Climate Pollutants," *UNEP News Center*, May 22, 2012.

79   UNEP, "World Remains on Unsustainable Track Despite Hundreds of Internationally Agreed Goals and Objectives," June 6, 2012, and UNEP, *GEO5 Global Environment Outlook Report Summary for Policy Makers* (2012).

80   "Failed Pledges, Weak Draft Lower Hopes for Rio+20 U.N. Conference on Sustainable Development in Brazil," *Democracy Now*, June 20, 2012

81   UNEP, *GEO5 report Summary for Policy Makers* (2012), p. 6.

82   Barnosky et al, "Approaching a State Shift in Earth's Biosphere," *Nature* 486, p. 52-58, June 7, 2012.

83   UNEP, "World Remains on Unsustainable Track Despite Hundreds of Internationally Agreed Goals and Objectives," June 6, 2012; UNEP, *GEO5 Global Environment Outlook Report Summary for Policy Makers* (2012).

84   UNEP, *Keeping Track of Our Changing Environment: From Rio to Rio+20* (2011).

85   UNEP, "World Remains on Unsustainable Track Despite Hundreds of Internationally Agreed Goals and Objectives," June 6, 2012.

86   UNEP, "World Remains on Unsustainable Track Despite Hundreds of Internationally Agreed Goals and Objectives," June 6, 2012.

87   Charles Clover, *End of the Line*, Film directed by Rupert Murray, 2009.

88   UNEP, "World Remains on Unsustainable Track Despite Hundreds of Internationally Agreed Goals and Objectives," June 6, 2012.

89   UNEP, "World Remains on Unsustainable Track Despite Hundreds of Internationally Agreed Goals and Objectives," June 6, 2012.

90   UNEP, "Keeping Track of Our Changing Environment, From Rio to Rio+20 (1992-2012)."

91   UNEP, "Keeping Track of Our Changing Environment, From Rio to Rio+20 (1992-2012)."

92   UNEP, "Keeping Track of Our Changing Environment, from Rio to Rio+20 (1992-2012)."

93   UNEP, "Keeping Track of Our Changing Environment, From Rio to Rio+20 (1992-2012)."

94   A Friends of the Earth spokesperson who attended the summit had this to say: "Here what they've done is, firstly, by refusing to commit to the Kyoto Protocol, leading an exit strategy from the Kyoto Protocol. Others have followed behind, Canada and Japan among them." A Dartmouth professor who also attended the summit said "...we've seen...a startling lack of vision, a startling level of obstructionism, of defeatism...what we've seen the U.S. try to force the world to do here is to sort of throw out the baby that's called Kyoto, which is an agreement that's legally binding, and get the world to drink the dirty water, the bath water that's left behind." The U.S. State Department diplomacy "is about delay," he said "....pitching us out to five or 10 years to just begin a process..."; *Democracy Now*, Obama Admin Denounced for "Startling Level of Obstructionism and Defeatism" on U.N. Climate Deal, Dec. 9, 2011.

95   Interview with Severn Cullis-Suzuki, *Democracy Now*, June 21, 2012.

96   George Monbiot, "The Earth Cannot Be Saved by Hope and Billionaires. World Leaders at Earth Summits Seem More Interested in Protecting the Interests of Plutocratic Elites Than Our Environment," *Common Dreams.org*, June 19, 2012.

97   Talks in Doha in the country of Quatar in December of 2012 concluded with no new commitments from the United States to reduce carbon emissions or provide aid to countries most affected by climate change. Binding emissions cuts under the Kyoto Protocol were extended, but only a small percent of the world's greenhouse emissions are covered by that Protocol. Many countries such as Japan

and Canada have opted out of it, and the United States never ratified it at all. Describing the Doha summit, Alden Meyer of the Union of Concerned Scientists said, "The coal industry won here, the oil industry won here, the fossil fuel industry won here. You saw on display the power of these industries and their short-term profit motivation to dominate the governments of the world. This wasn't an environmental or science-driven discussion; this was a trade fair. This was a, who's going to share the spoils of the world as we drill in the Arctic and produce tar sands in Canada and mine coal in Indonesia for China." Climate activists labeled the U.S. "the most obdurate bully in the room" at the Doha session." *Democracy Now* headlines, Dec. 10, 2012.

98   "US on Brink of Strong Oil, Gas Growth, Senate Panel Told," *Oil & Gas Journal*, Feb. 1, 2012.

99   "All of the Above, President Obama's Approach to Energy Independence," http://l.barackobama.com/energy-info/, retrieved April 25, 2014.

100 In 2005 1.13 billon tons of coal were mined in the U.S. with 49.9 million tons of that exported. In 2012, the figures were 1.01 billion tons and 125.7 million tons, respectively. Source: National Mining Association, "Most Requested Statistics—U.S. Coal Industry," www.nma.org/pdf/c_most_requested.pdf.

101 Brian Rosenthal, 'Green' Strategists Hired by Coal Companies to Push Train Proposals," *Seattle Times*, Feb. 23, 2013; PR firms for the fossil fuel industry have hired former environmental activists, former aides to Democratic Governors, and others as spokespeople. "We're proud of our environmental commitment—the work we've done for a variety of sustainable enterprises, from clean technology to green buildings," said a former spokesman of Democratic Governor Gary Locke regarding his firm. "I don't see that being inconsistent with the work that we're doing here [promoting coal]."

102 Parametrix, *Coal Train Traffic Impact Study for City of Seattle*, Nov. 2012.

103 Barack Obama, Remarks by the President on March 22, 2012 in Maljamar, New Mexico, and Cushing, Oklahoma.

104 It is estimated that three oil trains already cross into the state of Washington each day carrying crude oil from North Dakota's Bakken Oilfields heading to refineries on our coast. The number and volume will likely increase eight-fold if 10 proposed oil terminals become operational. Martha Baskin, "Oil on the Tracks: Seattle Joins Spokane in Looking at Safety Issues," *Crosscut Public Media*, Feb. 20, 2014.

105 *Democracy Now* Headlines, "Train Carrying Crude Oil Derails, Spills in Virginia," *Democracy Now*, May 1, 2014.

106 Nick Snow, "ExxonMobil Sees Gas Displacing Coal as World's No. 2 Energy Source." *Oil & Gas Journal*, Dec. 11, 2012.

107 Abrahm Lustgarten, *Run to Failure. BP and the Making of the Deepwater Horizon Disaster*, 2012.

108 Sean Cockerham, "Feds Favor Use of Air-Gun Blasts to Track Oil, Gas in Atlantic," *The Seattle Times*, Feb. 27, 2014. In seismic explorations air guns blast compressed air underwater, sending intense sound waves to the bottom of the ocean. The blasts are repeated every 10 seconds or so for days or weeks. The deafening noise poses a threat to whales and dolphins by interfering with feeding, mating, and communication.

109 Sarah Lazare, "Cries of Betrayal, Calls to Organize as Obama Approves Arctic Drilling," *Common Dreams*, July 22, 2015.

110 Elizabeth Rosenthal, "Race Is on as Ice Melt Reveals Arctic Treasures," *New York Times*, Sept. 18, 2012.

111 Statement of Louis Allstadt, former Mobil Oil Vice President who is a vocal opponent of fracking; as cited in Lauren McCauley, "'Straight from the Horse's Mouth': Former Oil Exec Says Fracking Not Safe, Retired Mobil VP Confirms Technology Is Dangerous and Untested," *Common Dreams*, April 23, 2014.

112 Jonathan Wood, Control Risks, *The Global Anti-Fracking Movement, What It Wants, How It Operates, and What's Next* (Dec. 2012).

113 Potential Gas Committee, "News Release: Potential Gas Committee Reports Significant Increase in Magnitude of U.S. Natural Gas Resource Base," April 9, 2013.

114 Deborah Rogers, "Shale and Wall Street: Was the Decline in Natural Gas Prices Orchestrated?," *Energy Policy Forum*, Feb. 19, 2013.

115 R.W. Howarth et al, "Methane and Greenhouse-Gas Footprint of Natural Gas from Shale Formations, *Climatic Change*, Letter, DOI 10.1007/s10584-011-0061-5, (2011). A recent EPA report on greenhouse gas emissions included oil and gas production for the first time. Emissions from drilling including fracking, and leaks from transmission pipes totaled 225 million metric tons of carbon-dioxide equivalents during 2011, second only to power plants, which emitted 10 times that amount. The EPA report showed as benefits of fracking, reduction in coal use and increased use of gas as fuel by electricity generators.

116 Fiona Harvey, "Natural Gas Is No Climate Change 'Panacea,' Warns IEA," The *Guardian*, June 6, 2011.

117   University Corporation for Atmospheric Research, "Switching from Coal to Natural Gas Would Do Little for Global Climate, Study Indicates," *AtmosNews*, Sept. 8, 2011; Joe Romm, *ClimateProgress, A Bridge to Nowhere*, Sept. 9, 2011.

118   U.S. Climate Network, *The Trouble with Tar Sands*, www.usclimatenetwork.org, retrieved Oct. 31, 2014; Citizens ClimateLobby, "Are Tar Sands Dirtier Than Regular Oil?," citizensclimatelobby.org, retrieved Oct. 31, 2014.

119   James Hansen, "Game Over for the Climate," *New York Times*, May 9, 2012.

120   Danny Keating, "The Tar Sands—Capitalism's Threat to the Climate," *SocialistAlternative.org*, Apr 7, 2013.

121   Mat McDermott, "Canadian Tar Sands Look Like Tolkien's Mordor Says UN Water Advisor," *Treehugger*, Nov. 4, 2008.

122   Catherine Mann and Stacy Feldman, "Exclusive Map: The Tar Sands Pipeline Boom," *InsideClimate News*, April 30, 2012.

123   NOAA, *Technical Memorandum NOSOR&R44, Transporting Alberta Oil Sands Products: Defining the Issues and Assessing the Risks*, Sept. 2013.

124   "Fuel-Fix, Oil Industry Beats Buffett in Railroad Investments Surge," *Bloomberg*, Jan. 14, 2013. More than 200,000 train cars of oil were projected to be shipped in 2012, according to the American Association of Railroads' forecast. About 1 million barrels a day of rail-unloading capacity is being built in the U.S. according to an industry analyst. That's more than double the current level of shipments, which averaged about 456,000 barrels a day in the third quarter of 2012, according to the Railroad Association. Burlington Northern, which handles about 35% of U.S. oil shipments, itself plans to spend "a couple hundred million dollars" on capital improvements to help haul 40% more crude in 2013.

David Shaffer, "Canadian Crude Oil Finds a New Pathway Through Minnesota," *Star Tribune*, March 3, 2013; Tar sands oil producers aim to deliver their oil to not only the Gulf Coast but also the East Coast. On the East Coast, PBF Energy built a rail terminal at its Delaware refinery to accept heavy crude in 2012. The company ordered enough rail cars to carry 80,000 barrels of Canadian crude per day. "We are confident, very long term, on the movement of heavy Canadian crudes to the U.S. East Coast," said Tom O'Malley of PBF. "The people who are selling these crudes....seem to have that same view, since a number of them have made very, very large orders of rail cars." Canadian National, whose rail network extends from western Canada to the U.S. Gulf Coast, hauled 30,000 tank car loads of crude oil in 2012, a sixfold increase over 2011. It expected to double that in 2013. Crude oil shipments on Canadian Pacific also jumped in 2012.

125 "Utah's Carbon Bomb," State Plots Massive Tar Sands & Oil Shale Projects Despite Climate Concerns," *Democracy Now*, Mar. 14, 2014.

126 "Study: Global Temperatures Highest in 4,000 Years," *Democracy Now*, Mar. 8, 2013; "NOAA: U.S. Summer Was Third Hottest on Record," *Democracy Now*, Sept. 14, 2012; "NOAA: Last Month Was Globe's Fourth Warmest January Ever," *Democracy Now*, Feb. 21, 2014; "U.N.: 13 of 14 Warmest Years on Record Occurred Since 2000," *Democracy Now*, March 25, 2014.

127 AFP, "Extreme India Heatwave Kills 800 as Capital's Roads Melt," *The Telegraph*, May 26, 2015.

128 "Carbon Tsunami: World Bank Study Warns of Lethal Global Temperature Rise Even If Emissions Pledges Are Met," *Democracy Now*, Dec. 4, 2012.

129 "NOAA: U.S. Summer Was Third Hottest on Record," Sept. 14, 2012; *Democracy Now*, "U.S. Declares Natural Disaster Areas in Drought-Stricken Midwest," *Democracy Now*, Jan. 11, 2013.

130 "Tens of Thousands Remain Homeless 6 Months After Superstorm Sandy," *Democracy Now*, April 29, 2013.

131 "If Not Now, Then When?": Filipino Negotiator Pleads for Climate Deal After Typhoon Kills 500, *Democracy Now*, Dec. 7, 2012; "'Unimaginable' Devastation as Philippines Hit With One of Worst Storms in History," *Democracy Now*, Nov. 11, 2013; "After Typhoon Haiyan's Devastation, Filipino Calls for Climate Action Take on New Urgency," *Democracy Now*, Nov. 18, 2013; "Philippines President Lowers Death Toll as Haitian Survivors Seek Aid," *Democracy Now*, Nov. 13, 2013. The death toll was, at that time, listed as 2500. More than 670,000 people were thought to have been displaced by the storm.

132 See for example, "Weather Whiplash: As Polar Vortex Brings Deep Freeze, Is Extreme Weather Linked to Climate Change?" *Democracy Now*, Jan. 7, 2014; Robert Hunziker, "It's Climate Change! What's Driving the Polar Vortex?" *Counterpunch*, Jan. 10-12, 2014.

133 Craig Welch, "Sea Changes Harming Ocean Now Could Someday Undermine Marine Food Chain," *Seattle Times*, Nov. 25, 2012; A study published in the spring of 2013 found that average acidity of surface ocean waters around the planet has increased by about 30% over the past two centuries. Researcher Richard Bellerby said, "We have already passed critical thresholds. Even if we stop emissions now, acidification will last tens of thousands of years"; "Study: Acidification from CO2 Emissions Threatens Oceans," *Democracy Now*, May 7, 2013.

134 Justin Wm. Moyer, "Climate Change Alert: Global Carbon Dioxide Tops 400 ppm for First Time," *The Washington Post*, May 7, 2015.

135   Damian Carrington, "IPCC report: World Must Urgently Switch to Clean Sources of Energy," *The Guardian*, April 11, 2014; Ben Spencer, "The world must shift to solar and wind power rapidly to avoid catastrophic global warming, say UN scientists in major report," *Dailymail Online*, April 12, 2014.

Chapter 8

136   Sylvia A. Allegretto, Economic Policy Institute, *The State of Working America's Wealth, 2011. Through Volatility and Turmoil, the Gap Widens. EPA Briefing Paper #292* (March 23, 2011).

137   Allegretto, *The State of Working America's Wealth, 2011.*

138   Median households are those with net worths that are at the midpoint of the net worths of all households.

139   Sylvia A. Allegretto, Economic Policy Institute, *The State of Working America's Wealth, 2011. Through Volatility and Turmoil, the Gap Widens. EPA Briefing Paper #292* (March 23, 2011).

140   Nui, Ylan Q., "Recession Set Back Your Wealth by 20 years, Fed Reports," *The Washington Post*, reprinted in *Seattle Times*, June 12, 2012.

141   By the Great Recession I mean the economic downturns experienced globally beginning roughly in 2007. The precise dates of the Recession are a subject of debate among economists.

142   Sylvia A. Allegretto, Economic Policy Institute, *The State of Working America's Wealth, 2011. Through volatility and turmoil, the gap widens. EPA Briefing Paper #292* (March 23, 2011, p. 2.)

143   "Wealth Inequality Fact Sheet." *Inequality.org*, retrieved June 7, 2012.

144   "Interview with Joseph Stiglitz on The Price of Inequality: How Today's Divided Society Endangers our Future," *Democracy Now*, June 6, 2012.

145   Seefeldt et al, School of Public and Environmental Affairs, Indiana University, *At Risk: America's Poor During and After the Great Recession* (2012, p. 5.).

146   Hope Yen, "New Data Place 48% in Poorest Categories, Record 146.4 Million," *Seattle Times*, December 15, 2011.

147   Mattingly et al, Carsey Institute, University of New Hampshire, "One Million Additional Children in Poverty Since 2009," Issue Brief No. 37, Summer 2011, p.1, 2. Nearly 28% of young Southern children were poor in 2010, and nearly 36% of young children were poor in Southern rural areas.

148   As of 2010, 29% of children in central cities, 25% of children in rural areas, and 16 % of children in suburban areas lived in poverty. Regarding children under age six, 31% in central cities, 30% in rural places, and 19% in suburbs were poor. In the South, one in four children lived in poverty. In the rural South, nearly

36% of children were poor. Mattingly et al, Carsey Institute, University of New Hampshire, "One Million Additional Children in Poverty Since 2009," Issue Brief No. 37, Summer 2011, p. 1.

149 Mattingly et al, Carsey Institute, University of New Hampshire, "One Million Additional Children in Poverty Since 2009," Issue Brief No. 37, Summer 2011, p. 2.

150 "Interview with Peter Edelman on Ending U.S. Poverty & Why He Left Clinton Administration over Welfare Law," *Democracy Now*, May 23, 2012.

151 "Income Inequality Fact Sheet," Inequality.org, retrieved June 7, 2012.

152 Charles H. Ferguson, *Predator Nation. Corporate Criminals, Political Corruption, and the Hijacking of America* (2012), p. 313. Between 2001 and 2007, the top 1% households captured half of the U.S. income growth. The top 1%'s share of taxable income including capital gains rose from 10% in 1980 to 23% in 2007, which was comparable to 1928, and three times the share the 1% held in the 1950s and 1960s. The 2008 financial crash reduced the top 1%'s share to "only" 17% in 2009, but it has since risen to about 20% in 2012 (Ferguson, *Predator Nation*, p. 8).

153 Sylvia A. Allegretto, Economic Policy Institute, *The State of Working America's Wealth, 2011. Through Volatility and Turmoil, the Gap Widens. EPA Briefing Paper #292* (March 23, 2011, p. 2.)

154 Sylvia A. Allegretto, Economic Policy Institute, *The State of Working America's Wealth, 2011. Through Volatility and Turmoil, the Gap Widens. EPA Briefing Paper #292* (March 23, 2011.)

155 Sylvia A. Allegretto, Economic Policy Institute, *The State of Working America's Wealth, 2011. Through Volatility and Turmoil, the Gap Widens. EPA Briefing Paper #292* (March 23, 2011.)

156 Hope Yen, "New Data Place 48% in Poorest Categories, Record 146.4 Million," *Seattle Times*, December 15, 2011.

157 Catherine Dodge and Mike Dorning, "Rich-Poor Gap Widens to Most Since 1967 as Income Falls," *Bloomberg News*, Sept. 12, 2012.

158 "Inequality Widened During Post-Recession Period," *Democracy Now*, April 24, 2013.

159 "Income Inequality Fact Sheet," *Inequality.org*, retrieved June 7, 2012.

160 Bill Moyers, quoting economist Dean Baker, in interview with Richard Wolff, Feb. 22, 2013.

161 "Minimum Wage Would Be $21.72 If It Kept Pace with Increases in Productivity: Study," *Huffington Post*, Feb. 13, 2013.

162 "First Survey of U.S. Domestic Workers Reveals Low Pay, Abusive Conditions," *Democracy Now*, Nov. 29, 2012.

163 David Barsamian, "Capitalism and Its Discontents, Richard Wolff on What Went Wrong," *The Sun*, Feb. 2012.

164 Kim Parker and Wendy Wang, "Modern Parenthood, Roles of Moms and Dads Converge as They Balance Work and Family," *Pew Research Social & Demographic Trends*, March 14, 2013

165 Institute for Policy Studies, "Income Inequality Fact Sheet," www.inequality.org, retrieved June 18, 2015.

166 Nathaniel Popper, "C.E.O. Pay Is Rising Despite the Din," *New York Times*, June 16, 2012.

167 "Wage Disparity Between CEO and Workers Continues to Climb," *Democracy Now*, June 18, 2012; Jennifer Liberto, "CEO Pay Is 380 Times Average Worker's –AFL-CIO," *CNNMoney*. This figure was based on preliminary data available on CEO salaries in April 2012 and may understate the size of the gap.

The *average* annual salary of New York bankers, which is now $390,000, stayed approximately constant even after the sector collapsed in 2008. Charles H. Ferguson, *Predator Nation. Corporate Criminals, Political Corruption, and the Hijacking of America* (2012, p. 8).

168 Abby Zimet, "One (Obscenely Profitable) Day in the Life of Big Oil," *Common Dreams*, Aug. 2, 2012.

169 Nelson D. Schwartz, "Recovery in U.S. Is Lifting Profits, But Not Adding Jobs," *New York Times*, Mar. 3, 2013.

170 Catherine Rampell, "Economix. Explaining the Science of Everyday Life; Where Do You Fall on the Income Curve?," *New York Times*, May 24, 2011.

171 Charles H. Ferguson, *Predator Nation. Corporate Criminals, Political Corruption, and the Hijacking of America* (2012, p. 313.)

172 Seefeldt et al, School of Public and Environmental Affairs, Indiana University, *At Risk: America's Poor During and After the Great Recession* (2012, p. 5).

173 Mattingly et al, Carsey Institute, University of New Hampshire, "One Million Additional Children in Poverty Since 2009," Issue Brief No. 37, Summer 2011, p. 2.

174 Charles H. Ferguson., *Predator Nation. Corporate Criminals, Political Corruption, and the Hijacking of America* (2012), p. 6. See also http://portalseven.com/employment/unemployment_rate_u6.jsp. This handy website provides "U6" unemployment stats which encompass not only official unemployment numbers but also discouraged workers who have stopped looking, "marginally attached workers," and people working fewer hours than they want. Note that some of these part-timers may be working as little as one hour a week.

175 "Interview with Paul Krugman, End this Depression Now"; "Paul Krugman Urges Public Spending, Not Deficit Hysteria, to Save Economy," *Democracy Now*, May 17, 2012.

176 Paul Craig Roberts, "The Phony Recovery. No Jobs for Americans," *Counterpunch*, Jan. 13, 2014.

177 Sylvia A. Allegretto, Economic Policy Institute, *The State of Working America's Wealth, 2011. Through Volatility and Turmoil, the Gap Widens. EPA Briefing Paper #292* (March 23, 2011, p. 2.)

178 Sylvia A. Allegretto, Economic Policy Institute, *The State of Working America's Wealth, 2011. Through Volatility and Turmoil, the Gap Widens. EPA Briefing Paper #292* (March 23, 2011, p. 30-31.)

179 Charles H. Ferguson, *Predator Nation. Corporate Criminals, Political Corruption, and the Hijacking of America* (2012, p. 6.)

180 Charles H. Ferguson, *Predator Nation. Corporate Criminals, Political Corruption, and the Hijacking of America*, (2012, p. 6.)

181 "Bloomberg Cuts Threaten Thousands with Eviction as NYC Homeless Population Hits Record 43,000," *Democracy Now*, June 12, 2012. Cites new report issued by the Coalition for the Homeless.

182 Susan Saulny, "After Recession, More Young Adults Are Living on Street," *New York Times*, Dec. 18, 2012.

183 Creditscore.net, "U.S. Consumer Debt in 2011," August 18, 2011; retrieved July 21, 2012.

184 Lawrence Mishel et al, Economic Policy Institute, *The State of Working America* (12th Edition, Wealth, November 2012.)

185 Mishel, *The State of Working America*

186 Mishel, *The State of Working America*

187 "Protests Held Nationwide as Student Debt Hits $1 Trillion," *Democracy Now*, April 26, 2012.

188 Study: Student Debt Reaches Record High with 1 in 5 U.S. Households Affected," *Democracy Now*, Sept. 28, 2012

189 Ylan Q. Mui, "Recession Set Back Your Wealth by 20 Years, Fed Reports," *Washington Post*, reprinted in *Seattle Times* June 12, 2012.

190 Tamar Lewin, "Parents Saddled With College Loans for Their Kids Face Financial Ruin," *Seattle Times*, Nov. 11, 2012.

191 Why So Many Ph.D.s are on Food Stamps," National *Public Radio*, May 15, 2012.

192 Why So Many Ph.D.s are on Food Stamps," *National Public Radio*, May 15, 2012.

193   Charles H. Ferguson, *Predator Nation. Corporate Criminals, Political Corruption, and the Hijacking of America* (2012, p. 6,7).

194   Southern Education Foundation, as cited by *Democracy Now*, Jan. 29, 2015. This was almost twice the number in 2007. More than half of children attending public schools now qualify for federal free or reduced price lunches.

195   "17 Million Suffer 'Very Low Food Security' in U.S.," *Democracy Now*, Sept. 6, 2012.

196   Edward Siedle, "The Greatest Retirement Crisis in American History," *Forbes*, March 20, 2013.

197   Anup Shah, "Poverty Facts and Stats," http://www.globalissues.org/article/26/poverty-facts-and-stats, updated as of September 20, 2010, retrieved June 7, 2012.

198   "Global Inequality Fact Sheet," Inequality.org, retrieved June 7, 2012.

199   Anup Shah, "Poverty Facts and Stats," http://www.globalissues.org/article/26/poverty-facts-and-stats, updated as of September 20, 2010, retrieved June 7, 2012.

200   Anup Shah, "Poverty Facts and Stats," http://www.globalissues.org/article/26/poverty-facts-and-stats, updated as of September 20, 2010, retrieved June 7, 2012, citing World Development Indicators 2008, World Bank, August 2008.

201   Paul Buchheit, "Some Outrageous Facts about Inequality," July 2, 2012, *Common Dreams.*

202   Oxfam, as cited by *Democracy Now*, Jan. 20, 2015.

203   Anup Shah, "Poverty Facts and Stats," http://www.globalissues.org/article/26/poverty-facts-and-stats, updated as of September 20, 2010, retrieved June 7, 2012, citing World Bank analyses.

204   Anup Shah, "Poverty Facts and Stats," http://www.globalissues.org/article/26/poverty-facts-and-stats, updated as of September 20, 2010, retrieved June 7, 2012.

205   Anup Shah, "Poverty Facts and Stats," http://www.globalissues.org/article/26/poverty-facts-and-stats, updated as of September 20, 2010, retrieved June 7, 2012.

206   UNICEF (United Nations Children's Fund), News note, "Tens of Millions of Children Living in Poverty in the World's Richest Countries," May 29, 2012; UNICEF, "Report Card 10, Measuring Child Poverty, New League Tables of Child Poverty in the World's Rich Countries," May 2012.

207   World Hunger Education Service, "Hunger Notes, 2013 World Hunger and Poverty Facts and Statistics"; retrieved July 5, 2013.

208   World Hunger Education Service, "Hunger Notes, 2013 World Hunger and Poverty Facts and Statistics"; retrieved July 5, 2013.

209   Lester Brown, *World on the Edge* (2011, p. 11).

210   Sarah McHaney, "U.S.: High Corn Prices Spread Global Hunger and Instability," *Inter Press Service News Agency*, Oct. 10, 2012.

211 The World Bank, News Release, "World Bank Warns Against Complacency Amid High Food Prices and Hunger," Nov. 29, 2012.

212 "Global Hunger Summit Held in London," *Democracy Now*, August 13, 2012.

213 Charles H. Ferguson, *Predator Nation. Corporate Criminals, Political Corruption, and the Hijacking of America* (2012, p 7.)

214 Control Risks, *Riskmap Report 2013*, p. 27.

215 Sarah Anderson and John Cavanagh, "Top 200: The Rise of Corporate Global Power," Dec. 4, 2000.

216 Charles H. Ferguson, *Predator Nation. Corporate Criminals, Political Corruption, and the Hijacking of America* (2012, p. 8.)

217 George Draffen, *State of Corporate Power 2012*.

218 Nathanial Gronewold, "Exxon Mobil's 4Q Profits Surge Thanks to Gas Production," *E & E*, Jan. 31, 2012.

219 "Energy Transfer Partners to Acquire Sunoco," *OGJ*, April 30, 2012.

220 Abby Zimet, "One (Obscenely Profitable) Day In the Life of Big Oil," August 2, 2012, posted on *Common Dreams*, featuring ThinkProgress data.

221 "These 10 Companies Control Enormous Number of Consumer Brands," *Huffington Post*, April 27, 2012. If you want to focus on just the consolidation of organic corporations, look at the data assembled by Dr. Phil Howard, an Assistant Professor at Michigan State University, available at cornucopia.org. You can also link from there to an animated presentation about who gobbled up whom between 1995 and 2007. The bottom line is that in the food industry, as in business overall, control and wealth are accumulating in fewer and fewer hands as time goes on.

222 Melissa Boteach and Shawn Fremstad, "The Top 3 Things You Need to Know About the 2013 Poverty and Income Data," *Center for American Progress*, September 16, 2014.

223 Latino Hunger Fact Sheet, www.feedingames.org, retrieved Jan. 18, 2014.

224 Neil Shah, "Racial Wealth Gaps: What a Difference 25 Years Doesn't Make, Real Time Economics," Feb. 26, 2015. Shah cites a report by economists at the Federal Reserve Bank of St. Louis that analyzed data from 1989 to 2013.

225 Some researchers use the term "Latino" and others use the term "Hispanic." When I am citing statistics produced by others, I use whichever term they use, in case there are differences with respect to whom they are including.

226 "America's Women and the Wage Gap Fact Sheet," *National Partnership for Women & Families*, Sept. 2014.

227 Ajay Kapur et al, Citigroup, "Equity Strategy. Plutonomy: Buying Luxury, Explaining Global Imbalance," October 16, 2005, p. 1.

228 Citigroup, "Plutonomy: Buying Luxury, Explaining Global Imbalances," Oct. 16, 2005, as cited in "Two Citigroup Plutonomy Memos. Two bombshell documents that Citigroup's lawyers try to suppress, describing in detail the rule of the first 1%" at politcalgates.blogspot.com, December 10, 2011. I was able to view this and other Citigroup memos on this topic cited in this book via Google searches. It took a little patience because Citigroup is aggressively challenging and taking down website postings of its documents on a regular basis. People keep posting the documents, however, and with a little bit of effort, those who wish to see the memos should be able to do so.

229 Ajay Kapur, et al, Citigroup, "Equity Strategy. Plutonomy: Buying Luxury, Explaining Global Imbalance," October 16, 2005, p. 2.

230 Ajay Kapur, Ajay et al, Citigroup, "Equity Strategy. Revisiting Plutonomy: The Rich Getting Richer," March 5, 2006, p. 1, emphasis added.

231 Ajay Kapur et al, Citigroup, "Equity Strategy. Plutonomy: Buying Luxury, Explaining Global Imbalance," October 16, 2005, p. 2

232 Ajay Kapur et al, Citigroup, "Equity Strategy. Plutonomy: Buying Luxury, Explaining Global Imbalance, October 16, 2005, p. 5

233 Ajay Kapur et al, Citigroup, "Equity Strategy. Plutonomy: Buying Luxury, Explaining Global Imbalance," October 16, 2005, p. 11

234 Martin Gilens, "Under the Influence," *Boston Review*, July/August 2012. See also Gilens's book: *Affluence & Influence* (2012).

Chapter 9

235 "I don't take money from oil companies or Washington lobbyists," Obama declared in a 2008 TV ad, for example. His campaign manager enthused early in 2012 that the campaign was raising 98% of its money from small donors and was "building the biggest grassroots campaign in American history." Ari Berman, "The .000063 Percent Election," *The Nation*, February 16, 2012; "Obama Announces Big Fundraising Haul," *CNN*, Jan. 12, 2012.

236 Campaign Finance Institute, News Release: "All CFI Funding Statistics Revised and Updated for the 2008 Presidential Primaries and General Election Candidates," Jan. 8, 2010.

237 Open Secrets.org, www.opensecrets.org/pres12/, retrieved March 2, 2014.

238 www.opensecrets.org.

239 Ken Dilanian, "Obama's Claim of Independence Questioned," *USA Today/ABC News*, April 16, 2008. The Chicago Tribune concluded in July of 2007 that despite the media attention Obama's campaign had enjoyed by having 258,000 donors, including many people of modest means who'd given over the

internet, "a much smaller group of large donors provides most of the funds for the campaign. And those large donors are best tapped through fundraisers who can call on networks of acquaintances and business associates who can easily write big checks." As of that time, 60% of Obama's campaign funds had come from people giving at least $1000, "the kind of donors who are most often recruited by bundlers." Less than 30% of his contributions had come from people giving less than $200. Dorning & McCormick, "Big Fish shadow Obama's small fry," *Chicago Tribune*, July 26, 2007.

240 Opensecrets.org, retrieved March 6, 2015.

241 Opensecrets.org, retrieved March 6, 2015. In 2008, as participants in Obama's fundraising team, two oil company CEOs each pledged to raise at least $50,000. (Ken Dilanian, "Obama's Claim of Independence Questioned," *USA Today/ABC News*, April 16, 2008.)

242 "Top Contributors Barack Obama," opensecrets.org, retrieved March 10, 2015; P. Sainath, "Follow the Money, Find the Leader," *Counterpunch*, Oct. 19-21, 2012; see also, Michael Beckel, "As Presidential Candidates Seek Finance Sector Money, Wall Street Donors Flock Most to Mitt Romney," opensecrets.org, Oct. 17, 2011.

243 Opensecrets.org.

244 Opensecrets.org. Obama's campaign even received major donations from employees of Bain, the private equity firm formerly led by Republican nominee Romney.

245 Peter Nicholas and Daniel Lippman, "Wall Street Is Still Giving to President," *Wall Street Journal*, updated July 3, 2012.

246 Brad Jacobson, "Obama Received $20 Million from Healthcare Industry in 2008 Campaign," *Common Dreams.org*, January 12, 2010.

247 Mosk and MacGillis, "Big Donors Among Obama's Grass Roots," *Washington Post*, April 11, 2008.

248 Opensecrets.org, retrieved March 6, 2015. Obama's campaign not only relied on bundlers from corporations with direct major financial stakes in policies his administration would address, but also from entities like consulting firms that serve those corporations. Deloitte LLP, for example is a huge corporation with multiple subsidiaries that provides consulting and financial services to large corporations. Clients include oil and gas companies, defense corporations, and others. People and political action committees associated with Deloitte historically contributed significantly more money to Republicans than Democrats, but in the 2008 election cycle, its employees and PAC together contributed slightly more to Democrats (Center for Responsive Politics. "Deloitte LLP: Heavy Hitter," opensecrets.org, retrieved 10/2/2012.)

249 Mosk and MacGillis, "Big Donors Among Obama's Grass Roots," *The Washington Post*, April 11, 2008.

250 "Obama's Claim of Independence Questioned," *ABC News and USA Today*, April 16, 2008.

251 Mosk and MacGillis "Big Donors Among Obama's Grass Roots," *The Washington Post*, April 11, 2008.

252 "Obama's Claim of Independence Questioned.," *ABC News* and *USA Today*, April 16, 2008.

253 Kenneth Griffin, who earned $1.5 billion in 2007 and was included on Alpha Magazine's list of the ten top-earning hedge fund managers that year, took Obama under his wing, for example. He invited Obama to speak to employees of his Chicago hedge fund, Citadel Investment Group. In subsequent months, employees and their families donated nearly $200,000 to Obama. Others from Alpha's 2007 list who funded Obama included John Griffen (no relation to Kenneth), founder of Blue Ridge Capital (who made $625 million in 2007); Stephen Mandel Jr. of Lone Pine Capital ($710 million); and George Soros (nearly $3 billion). Obama's national finance chairwoman was Penny Pritzker, a member of an extremely wealthy Chicago family. She bundled $178,782 toward Obama's presidential bid, and was appointed by Obama as Secretary of Commerce in 2013. (See: "Many top hedge fund managers back Obama," *New York Times*, April 22, 2008; and Mosk and MacGillis, "Big Donors Among Obama's Grass Roots," *The Washington Post*, April 11, 2008.)

254 The *Seattle Times* reported on two fundraising dinners near Seattle in late July 2012, for example. "Business leaders, dinner guests pay up to $35,800 for a seat," the subtitle of the article announced. According to the *Times*, the events were expected to raise about $1.75 million for the Obama campaign and affiliated committees. Among the attendees at one of the events were a Costco co-founder, the Gates Foundation's CEO, a former Delta Airlines executive, Microsoft's Executive Vice President, and others (Brian Rosenthall, "Obama Uses Seattle Stop to Raise Cash, Push Vision," *Seattle Times*, July 25, 2012.)

255 Nicholas Confessore, "Obama's Not-So-Hot Date with Wall Street," *New York Times*, May 2, 2012.

256 As yet another example of hob-knobbing with wealthy individuals at high-priced fundraising events, in July of 2012 Obama attended a 60-person, $40,000-a-head dinner that yielded about $2.4 million in one night (Jennifer Epstein, "Obama Rakes in $2.4 million in Brief New York Trip," *Politico*, July 30, 2012.)

257 "A surge in Corporate Donations for Democrats, *The Economist*, Sept. 18, 2008.

258 Campaign Finance Institute, "Heavy Hitters ($250,000 to $3 Million Donors) Supplied 80% of Private Financing for 2008 Party Conventions, Recent Filings Show," Dec. 10, 2008.

259 "This convention is relying on a grassroots network made up of people like you to give small amounts to help make this convention a success," Obama noted in a typical fundraising appeal, for example. Michael Beckel, "Corporate Cash Helps Fuel Democratic Convention Despite Pledges," *Center for Public Integrity*, Sept. 4, 2012.

260 New American City funds were to cover various convention expenses such as salaries for convention workers, promotional materials, overhead, and entertainment for delegates and others. Brody Mullins and Peter Nicholas, "Democrats Fund Taps Corporate Donors for Convention," *Wall Street Journal On-line*, May 11, 2012; according to its filing with the Federal Election Commission, the New American City fund used corporate donations to "defray administrative expenses incurred by the host committee organizations themselves, such as salaries, rent, travel and insurance." The ban on corporate funding only applied to the host committee's main account, which helped stage the nominating process. Common Dreams staff, "Democrats' Fund Taps Corporate Donors for Convention," May 12, 2012, citing *Wall Street Journal* article.

261 Michael Beckel, "Corporate Cash Helps Fuel Democratic Convention Despite Pledges," *The Center for Public Integrity*, Sept. 4, 2012.

262 Hans Nichols and Jonathan Salant, "Companies Pay $20 Million to Fund Democratic Convention," *Bloomberg*, Sept. 4, 2012.

263 "Why Did the Dems Choose Charlotte? Examining Obama's Close Ties to Utility Giant Duke Energy," *Democracy Now*, September 14, 2012.

264 www.conventions2012.com, retrieved Oct. 9, 2012.

265 Janie Lorber, "Conventions 2012 Firm Nears Crunch Time," *Roll Call*, Aug. 23, 2012. Petersen's group and others put on an array of events featuring access to "all the right people". Attendees at the Democratic Convention could attend something called "Gumbo Ya-Ya," for example. This was a private invitation-only event at which attendees could schmooze with members of the U.S. House and Senate Energy and Commerce Committees. One could sponsor the event at different levels: $30,000, $20,000, $10,000, and $5000, receiving various numbers of tickets for each sponsorship level. At a different undisclosed location each night, those with tickets could hang out with members of the House Democratic Caucus, enjoying live music, hors d'oeuvres, and beverages.

"Almost every company I see has some interest pending before the federal government and they want something out of it," said Public Citizen's government affairs lobbyist, regarding corporate convention sponsors in 2012 (Janie Lorber, "Conventions 2012 Firm Nears Crunch Time," *Roll Call*, Aug. 23, 2012). As Coca-Cola spokeswoman Nancy Bailey put it, "[t]he Coca-Cola Company believes we have a role to play in the political process and that includes helping to make the political conventions a success" (Michael Beckel, "Corporate Cash Helps Fuel Democratic Convention Despite Pledges," *The Center for Public Integrity*, Sept. 4, 2012). Coca Cola reportedly planned to send at least three lobbyists from its Washington, D.C., office, as well as several state-based lobbyists, to both conventions. It made a financial commitment to the Democratic convention through New American City, Inc. (Janie Lorber, "Convention Contributions Down and More Discreet," *CQ Weekly—In Focus*, Aug. 31, 2012).

266 Steve Horn, "ExxonMobil Donates $260,000 to Obama Inauguration," *Huffington Post*, Jan. 21, 2013. See also, "Obama Inauguration Sponsors Spent Millions Influencing Government," *Center for Public Integrity*, Jan. 18, 2013.

267 Lee Drutman, "The Political One Percent of the One Percent," *Sunlight Foundation Blog*, Dec. 13, 2011.

268 Ari Berman, "The .000063 Percent Election," *The Nation*, February 16, 2012.

269 Sierra Club, *Beyond Coal, Clean Energy Under Siege, Following the Money Trail Behind the Attack on Renewable Energy*, 2012.

270 Jeffry ErnstFriedman, "Agribusiness Contributions to Members of the House and Senate Agriculture Committees," *Maplight*, November 14, 2011. Similarly, a 2011 analysis by Public Campaign showed that members of the Energy and Power Subcommittee of the U.S. House Energy and Commerce Committee had received $12.2 million in campaign contributions from oil, gas, coal, and electric utilities during their time in Congress. (Adam Smith, "New Report: House Energy Committee's Close Ties to Energy Industry Interests," *Public Campaign*, February 9, 2011.)

271 Citizens for Responsibility and Ethics in Washington (CREW), *Funds for Favors: Exposing Donors' Influence on Committee Leaders*, November 16, 2011. Representative Collin Peterson, a Democrat from Minnesota, for example, received $650,412 from the "agriculture services/products" industry in 2010 as compared to $80,150 in 1998, a change of 711%. Peterson is the ranking minority member of the House Committee on Agriculture. As another example, Representative Frank Lucas, a Republican from Oklahoma, received $444,200 from agriculture industries in 2010, a 531% increase over their contributions to him in 1998 of $70,451. Lucas is chair of the House Committee on Agriculture.

272 An analysis of 15 Democratic and Republican members of the House of Representative who have furthered the interests of the coal industry, for example, reveals major donations from that industry to them (Greenpeace, *Polluting Democracy: Coal Plays Dirty on the Hill*, 2011). As of February 2012, the oil & gas industry had given $238.7 million to gubernatorial and Congressional election campaigns since 1990 (Sharon Guynup, "The Fracking Industry Busy Congress," *Environment News Service*, Feb. 16, 2012). John Kasich, Governor of Ohio, received over $200,000 from the oil and gas industry over a four-year period (Sharon Kelly, "Money to Burn," *Earth Island Institute Journal*, Autumn. 2012). The chemical industry trade group American Chemistry Council spent $648,600 on ads supporting the Republican candidate in the Wisconsin U.S. Senate race (Brendan Fisher, "ALEC Member American Chemistry Council Drops $649K on Wisconsin U.S. Senate Race," *Center for Media & Democracy*, Sept. 6, 2012).

273 At a retreat early in 2012, the billionaire brothers David and Charles Koch and about 250 to 300 other wealthy individuals pledged approximately $100 million to defeat Obama in the election, for example. Charles pledged $40 million and David $20 million ("Koch Brothers, Allies Pledge $100 Million At Private Meeting To Beat Obama," *Huffington Post*, February 3, 2012). In the 2010 elections, as another example, Bob Perry, CEO of Perry Homes, gave $7.3 million to Karl Rove's American Crossroads, which raises money for the Republican Party, and gave $4.4 million to other conservative entities. Fred Eschelman, CEO of Pharmaceutical Product Development, spent $3 million on his own group Right Change, which funds right-wing Republican candidates (Lee Drutman, "The Political One Percent of the One Percent," *Sunlight Foundation Blog*, Dec. 13, 2011.)

274 Mosk and MacGillis, "Big Donors Among Obama's Grass Roots," *The Washington Post*, April 11, 2008.

275 Corrado et al, *Reform in an Age of Networked Campaigns* (2010) pp. 15-16.

276 Kenneth Vogel, "Election 2012: Myth of the Small Donor," *Politico*, August 7, 2012. Obama spent at least $7.3 million on merchandise for his reelection campaign, including top designer items like a Tory Burch tote that sold for $75.

Mark Hertzgaard, *The Eagle's Shadow: Why America Fascinates and Infuriates the World*, 2002, p. 165, excerpted on-line at www.thirdworldtraveler.com. Candidates that want to succeed have to get through the "wealth primary," i.e., the race to prove they have fundraising clout.

As one report looking at opportunities for using the internet and social networking to raise small donations puts it, "The reliance on large contributions during the early phase of the presidential contest is not surprising....Given the financial demands of modern campaigns, candidates—whether seeking the presidency, a congressional seat or state-wide office—face great pressure to raise as much money as possible as quickly as possible. This strategic imperative is a result of both the anticipated costs of a campaign and the widely held perception of fundraising strength as an indicator of a candidate's viability, especially during the early phase of a contest. In other words, the best way for a candidate to generate visibility and be viewed as a major contender is to rank among top fundraisers."

Corrado et al, *Reform in an Age of Networked Campaigns* (2010) p. 18, emphasis added.

277 Scott Helman, "PACs and Lobbyists Aided Obama's Rise," *The Boston Globe*, August 9, 2007.

278 Ken Silverstein, "Barack Obama, Inc. The Birth of a Washington Machine," *Harper's Magazine*, Nov. 2006; Ken Silverstein, "A Bit More on Barack," *Harper's Magazine*, 2006. Silverstein describes, for example, how in 2003 Obama met Vernon Jordan, an investment banking firm senior director and member of the board of several major corporations, including American Express, Xerox, and others. Jordan invited about twenty of his friends to a fund-raiser for Obama at his home. This opened other doors and gave Obama connections that led to more connections.

Valerie Jarrett was another key early Obama promoter. Jarrett's income in 2008 included $300,000 in salary and $550,000 in deferred compensation from a real estate development and management company. It also included $76,000 for services as director of a global consulting group, $146,000 from a building materials corporation, $58,000 for board service with a real estate investment trust, and $34,444 from the Chicago Stock Exchange, which she had chaired. Jarrett ultimately served as one of Obama's senior advisors at the White House, and is sometimes referred to as Obama's Rock.

279 Larry Duncan, a lobbyist for Lockheed Martin, helped organize the Bond Association fundraiser event. Tom Quinn, a senior partner at the law firm Venable that represented Lockheed Martin attended, donated $500, and went on to call people he knew to ask them to donate as well. Robert Harmala, also with Venable, attended, donated $500, and called friends too.

280 Opensecrets.org, "Top 100 Contributions, Barack Obama 2001-2006, and Top Industries, Senator Barack Obama, 2001-2006," retrieved Sept. 28, 2012.

281 Scott Helman, "In Illinois, Obama Dealt with lobbyists, but as Candidate, He Faults Clinton for Ties," *The Boston Globe*, September 23, 2007.

282 Opensecrets.org, Center for Responsive Politics, Top Industries, Senator Barack Obama (Since 1989), retrieved Sept. 28, 2012.

283 Ken Silverstein, "Barack Obama, Inc. The Birth of a Washington Machine," *Harper's Magazine*, November 2006.

284 Mike McIntire, "Nuclear Leaks and Response Tested Obama in Senate," *New York Times*, February 3, 2008. The *Times* also highlighted various other Exelon connections to Obama's campaigns. Two top Exelon officials, Frank M. Clark, executive vice president, and John W. Rogers, Jr., a director, were among his biggest fundraisers. Another Obama donor, John W. Rowe, was not only chair of Exelon, but also chair of the Nuclear Energy Institute, the nuclear power industry's lobbying group based in Washington, D.C. Obama's chief political strategist, David Axelrod, had worked as a consultant to Exelon. Axelrod's company had help Exelon subsidiary, Commonwealth Edison, with communication strategy periodically since 2002.

285 Ken Silverstein, "Barack Obama Inc.: The Birth of a Washington Machine," *Harper's Magazine*, Nov. 2006.

286 Silverstein, "Barack Obama Inc.: The Birth of a Washington Machine."

287 Silverstein, "Barack Obama Inc.: The Birth of a Washington Machine."

288 George Farah interviewed on *Democracy Now*, October 3, 2012: "As Obama, Romney Hold First Debate, Behind the Secret GOP-Dem Effort to Shut Out Third Parties."

289 P. Sainath, "Follow the Money, Find the Leader," *Counterpunch*, Oct. 19-21, 2012.

290 P. Sainath, "Follow the Money, Find the Leader," *Counterpunch*, Oct. 19-21, 2012.

291 Ari Berman, "The .000063 Percent Election," *The Nation*, Feb. 16, 2012; The Campaign Legal Center, A Guide to the Current Rules for Federal Elections, http:..//www.campaignlegalcenter.org, retrieved Sept. 21, 2012.

292 "Outside spending" has allowed wealthy corporations and individuals to influence elections even more than in the past. In the first two quarters of the 2012 election cycle, organizations reported $167.5 million in outside spending, with $12.7 million of that being "secret money" that cannot be traced to its source. Because of gaps in reporting requirements this *reported* data on spending is only part of the picture.

As of June 30, 2012, individuals accounted for 73.8% of Super PAC money in 2012. A whopping 94.1 percent of them gave at least $10,000. That SuperPAC funding came from just 1082 individuals, or 0.00035% of the American population. More than half (57.1 %) of individual Super PAC money came from just 47 people giving at least $1 million. These 47 people accounted for 42.1% of all the money raised by the Super PACs from both individuals and organizations. The average itemized contribution from an individual to a Super PAC in 2012 was $19,944.

Billionaires Sheldon and Miriam Adelson had given $36.3 million to Super PACs as of June 30, 2012. Mr. Adelson has noted that he was willing to spend up to $100 million on the 2012 election. The $36.3 million the Adelsons had given represented only 0.15% of their total wealth—a mere drop in the bucket for them.

The next highest category of funding sources for Super PACs in 2012 was for-profit business. Five hundred and fifteen companies provided $34.2 million as of June 30, or 11.0% of Super PAC funds.

See Blair Bowie and Adam Lioz, *Million-Dollar Megaphones, Super PACs and Unlimited Outside Spending in the 2012 Elections* (2012).

293   Super PAC money only represents part of the money out there, separate from candidates' campaign funds, that is greatly influencing elections. As of April 22, 2012, for example, nonprofit organizations had spent $28.5 million on ads related to the presidential race and had failed to report their funding sources for about 90% of that total (Dan Eggen, "Most Independent Ads for 2012 election Are from Groups That Don't Disclose Donors," *The Washington Post*, April 25, 2012).

294   The U.S. Chamber of Commerce, whose members include major corporations like oil & gas corporations, health insurance companies, Dow Chemical, and others, put big money into the 2010 election cycle. For example, the Chamber reportedly spent nearly $1.5 million on TV ads in New Hampshire attacking the Democratic candidate for U.S. Senate there. In just a single week in 2010, the Chamber spent $10 million on Senate races in nine states and two dozen House races, a fraction of the $50 million to $75 million it intended to spend over the full season. Lipton, Eric, McIntire et al, "Top Corporations Aid U.S. Chamber of Commerce Campaign," *The New York Times*, October 21, 2010. To support these efforts, the Chamber paid its fundraisers well. One fundraiser received $3.7 million in 2008 and had access to a corporate jet and a chauffeur, while another was paid $1.1 million, tax records show.

295   Rt.com, "2012 US Presidential Campaign Cost $7 billion—Election Commission," Feb. 2, 2013.

296   Jay Costa, "What's the Cost of a Seat in Congress," maplight.org, Mar. 10, 2013.

297   Monica Davey, "With Recall Election Near, Walker Raises More Than $5 Million," *The New York Times*, May 29, 2012.

298   Gregory Korte and Fredreka Schouten, "57 Members of Congress Among wealthy 1%," *USA Today*, November 16, 2011.

299   Heidi Przybyla, "Rivals in U.S. House Leadership Also the Wealthiest," *The Seattle Times*, June 15, 2012.

300   Dan Keating, "Members of Congress Trade in Companies While Making Laws That Affect Those Same Firms," *The Washington Post*, June 23, 2012.

Chapter 10

301   The parent company Dow Chemical spent $10,565,000 and the subsidiary Dow AgroSciences spent $1,005,000.

302   Eric Lipton et al, "Top Corporations Aid U.S. Chamber of Commerce Campaign," *New York Times*, Oct. 21, 2010.

303   Kate Sheppard, "Chamber Calls Obama's Clean Energy Plan 'Ridiculously Premature,'" *MotherJones.com*, February 1, 2011. Early in 2011, for example, the Chamber's Institute for 21st Century Energy held a press conference unveiling its energy plans for the year. The Institute opposed setting a clean energy standard, called for increased industry access to land for oil and gas drilling, advocated the streamlining of environmental reviews, and otherwise championed the oil and gas industry's agenda.

304   Unless otherwise noted, source is opensecrets.org, Center for Responsive Politics.

305   Joshua Kennon, "The Net Worth and Stockholdings Disclosure of Each Member of the United States Congress," Sept. 23, 2012.

306   http://www.alec.org/about-alec/, retrieved October, 11, 2012.

307   Bill Moyers, *United States of ALEC*, Sept. 28, 2012. Information about ALEC is from this report unless otherwise noted.

308   Common Cause, http://www.commoncause.org/site/pp.asp?c=dkLNK1MQI wG&b=8078765, retrieved October 11, 2012.

309   "Washington State Vote to Label GM Food Defeated by Corporations' 'Sophisticated Propaganda Machine,'" *Democracy Now*, Nov. 8, 2013.

Chapter 11

310   Wendy Wagner et al, "Rulemaking in the Shade: An Empirical Study of EPA's Air Toxic Regulations," *Arizona Legal Studies Discussion Paper No. 10-01*, December 2010, p. 24.

311   There are almost no nonprofit public interest reps. One of the few is NRDC, which has been identified by Controlling Risk, a consulting firm for the shale oil and gas industry, as likely to support fracking. The NRDC staff scientist included on lists of participants I reviewed is Briana Mordick. Her bio notes that she worked for Anadarko Petroleum for six years as a petroleum geologist on projects that included shale gas, tight gas sands, and $CO2$ enhanced

oil recovery. U.S. EPA, lists of fracking technical roundtable and workshop participants in 2012 and 2013, at http://www.epa.gov/hfstudy/techwork12. html, updated as of Jan. 29, 2013, retrieved Feb. 13, 2013.

312 The Letter: http://www.peer.org/docs/epa/06_25_5_union_ltr.pdf. The News Release about it: http://www.peer.org/news/news_id.php?row_id=691.

313 A University of California analysis provides a rare review of the actual impacts of so-called "collaborative" processes on environmental justice communities, i.e., communities of color and low-income populations that bear disproportionate environmental burdens compared to the rest of society. The researchers reviewed California water issue discussions that were supposedly inclusive and empowering, and concluded that these "systematically marginalized the role of environmental justice in California's water policy." Historical power dynamics, how issues were framed, lack of resources for environmental justice issue research and discussion, and other factors all came into play. (Fraser M. Shilling et al, *Marginalization by Collaboration: Environmental Justice as a Third Party in and Beyond CALFED,* 2009 Elsevier Ltd., May 9, 2009.)

314 Jennifer Sass and Daniel Rosenberg, NRDC, *The Delay Game. How the Chemical Industry Ducks Regulation of the Most Toxic Substances* (Oct. 2011.)

315 Rena Steinzor et al, Center for Progressive Reform, *Behind Closed Doors at the White House: How Politics Trumps Protection of Public Health, Worker Safety, and the Environment* (November 2011.)

316 Steinzor, *Behind Closed Doors at the White House.*

317 Center for Progressive Reform, "Obama White House Changes More Agency Regulations in Backroom Process than Bush Administration Did, Says New CPR Report," News Release, Nov. 28, 2011.

318 Rena Steinzor el, Center for Progressive Reform, *Behind Closed Doors at the White House. How Politics Trumps Protection of Public Health, Worker Safety and the Environment* (November 2011.)

319 Steinzor, *Behind Closed Doors at the White House.*

320 As we've seen, regulated industries dominate rulemakings and block meaningful regulatory action. Nonetheless, well-funded PR strategies paint big corporations as the victims of aggressive governmental regulatory action, a claim that turns reality on its head. In October of 2012, for example, Republicans on the Senate Environment and Public Works Committee issued a report accusing the Obama Administration of planning to issue strong rules after the presidential election and delaying issuance until then to avoid voter backlash. One would have no idea from this report that regulated industries had successful derailed and gutted key regulations for the past four years, and that there are no indications of things changing any time soon. Emily Yehle,

"EPA: Inhofe says Obama plans post-election 'regulatory onslaught,'" *E&E News*, Oct. 18, 2012. Similarly, in the 2012 presidential campaign, Republican candidate Mitt Romney accused Obama's EPA of being the "most active regulator" even in the face of "our economic travails." ("Industry assesses effect of US elections," *ChemicalWatch*, Oct. 16, 2012.)

321 Ismael Hossein-Zadeh, "Inside Obamanomics," February 2011, published in *Hopeless*, edited by Jeffrey St. Clair & Joshua Frank, 2012. An Op-Ed by Obama appeared in the *Wall Street Journal* the same day claiming that sometimes "rules have gotten out of balance, placing unreasonable burdens on business—burdens that have stifled innovation and have had a chilling effect on growth and jobs." Obama said his Administration was "seeking more affordable, less intrusive means to achieve the same ends—giving careful consideration to benefits and costs."

322 Ben Geman, "Chemicals Lobbying Group Presses White House On Reg Review," *The Hill*, Jan. 19, 2011.

323 Sources: Rena Steinzor et al, Center for Progressive Reform, *Behind Closed Doors at the White House: How Politics Trumps Protection of Public Health, Worker Safety, and the Environment* (November 2011); John Broder, "Re-election Strategy Is Tied to a Shift on Smog," *New York Times*, Nov. 17, 2011. At this writing, EPA is making noises about tightening the ozone/smog rule. We'll see where that goes. Those sickened and killed by over six years of Bush-era smog standards under Obama will not regain what they have lost in any case.

324 Eric Lipton, "Ties to Obama Aided in Access for Big Utility," *New York Times*, August 22, 2012.

325 Ed Lasky, "The President's Utility: Crony Capitalism Turns 'Green' into Greenbacks," *Capital Research Center Green Watch*, September 2013.

326 Eric Lipton, "Ties to Obama Aided in Access for Big Utility," *New York Times*, August 22, 2012.

327 Jeremy P. Jacobs, "EPA: Lax State Oversight Has Led to 'Weak And Inconsistent' Enforcement," *IG, Greenwire*, Dec. 13, 2011.

328 Lisa Sumi, "Breaking the Rules. The Crisis in Oil & Gas Regulatory Enforcement. States Are Betraying the Public by Failing to Enforce Oil and Gas Development Rules," *Earthworks*, Sept. 2012.

329 In 2010, Pennsylvania and Colorado collected $1 million each in total penalties, while Ohio, New York, and New Mexico each collected $200,000. Data for Texas in 2010 was not available, but the state's total 2009 penalties were more than $2 million. These penalties sound big when added together, until you think about the money to be made on the wells in question. The value of the gas from one average Marcellus shale gas well is $2.9 million. So, the

value of the gas in one well is greater than the total penalties collected by any studied state in 2010.

330   Lise Olsen, "Drilling Boom, Deadly Legacy," *Houston Chronicle*, Feb. 22, 2014.

331   *Democracy Now* headlines and stories, Jan. 13, 14, and 23, 2014.

332   Sharon Kelly, "Money to Burn, Oil and Gas Interests Are Spending Big to Keep Their Allies in Office," *Earth Island Journal*, Sept. 2012.

333   Emily Yehle, "EPA: Agency plans to drastically scale back enforcement," *E&E News*, Dec. 9, 2013. EPA estimated that it would clean up less than 2 billion pounds of waste each year via enforcement cases, a number that was down 4.4 billion pounds compared to 2012, and 6.5 billion pounds as compared to 2008. For water pollutants, EPA's goal was to require treatment for about 220 million pounds each year, down from 320 million pounds per year previously.

334   Graham Kates, "Environmental Crime: The Prosecution Gap," *The Crime Report*, July 14, 2014.

Chapter 12

335   Thomas McDonagh, "Unfair, Unsustainable, and Under the Radar. How Corporations Use Global Investment Rules to Undermine a Sustainable Future," *Democracy Center*, 2013.

336   "Corporation Uses NAFTA to Sue Canada for $250 Million Over Fracking Ban," *Common Dreams*, Nov. 27, 2012.

337   "Corporation Uses NAFTA to Sue Canada for $250 Million Over Fracking Ban," *Common Dreams*, Nov. 27, 2012.

338   "Presidential Candidates' Key Proposals on Health Care and Climate Will Require WTO Modifications," *Public Citizen*, February 2008.

339   Americans for Financial Reform, Citizens Trade Campaign, Consumer Watchdog, Public Citizen, U.S. Public Interest Research Group, "Joint Letter to Deputy U.S. Trade Representative Michael Punke," April 11, 2011.

340   Josiane Georges, Trade and the Disappearance of Haitian Rice, Ted Case Studies Number 725, June 2004.

341   "We Made a Devil's Bargain": Former President Clinton Apologizes for Trade Policies that Destroyed Haitian Rice Farming," Democracy Now, April 1, 2010, retrieved from democracynow.org on February 20, 2012.

342   Trade Stories Project, http://www.tradestories.org/Mexico.html, retrieved Feb. 21, 2012. Over 11 million undocumented immigrants as well as large numbers of "legal" immigrants in the U.S. have not yet been granted citizenship. They work hard, often in vital jobs like growing food, enduring taxation without representation in a land founded on the principle that such an arrangement is despicable.

343 Robert Scott, Environmental Policy Institute, *Heading South. U.S.-Mexico Trade and Job Displacement After NAFTA* (May 3, 2011). Visit TradeWatch.org to pull up certified trade-agreement-related job loss data for your state or city.

344 Thomas McDonagh, Democracy Center, *Unfair, Unsustainable and Under the Radar. How Corporations Use Global Investment Rules to Undermine a Sustainable Future* (2013).

345 Lori Wallach, "NAFTA on Steroids," *The Nation*, June 27, 2012; Citizens Trade Campaign, "The Trans-Pacific Partnership (TPP) Fact Sheet," www.citizen-strade.org, retrieved October 25, 2012. See also, "Obama & McConnell Pledge Cooperation; Will Fast-Tracking Secretive TPP Trade Deal Top Their Agenda?" *Democracy Now*, Nov. 6, 2013. In March of 2013, Japan announced its intention to enter the TPP. One of the reasons it may be interested in joining the trade pact is that participating countries will likely get automatic access to U.S. natural gas. The Department of Energy usually is required to examine whether exporting U.S. natural gas is in the public interest before approving exports, but that requirement may be waived for those who sign the TPP agreement. This means that even if exporting natural gas is shown to harm the public interest, the U.S. could still be forced to send natural gas overseas to Japan and other TPP countries without any review or delay. On top of that more than 6000 Japanese corporations have operations in the U.S., including many in oil, gas, and mining industries. One or more of these corporations could use the TPP agreement to drag governments in the U.S. who attempt to regulate fracking before a private trade tribunal seeking unlimited cash compensation for alleged financial losses associated with those regulations. The TPP deal affects nearly 40% of the global economy.

346 See Alison Rose Levy, "Obama's Trade Deals Could Overturn New York's Fracking Ban and Accelerate Climate Change," *EcoWatch*, March 26, 2015; and Food Democracy Now! Team, message to supporters, May 13, 2015, citing language from leaked TPP documents.

347 CropLife, "America and European Crop Association Discuss Joint Proposal During TTIP Negotiations," March 14, 2014.

348 Center for International Environmental Law, "Chemical Industry Secretly Manipulating US-EU Trade Negotiations (TTIP)," News Release, March 10, 2014. The joint proposal was prepared by the American Chemistry Council and the European Chemical Industry Council. The leaked document gave members of the public a glimpse of what is going on behind closed doors. It is the subject of a report by Center for International Environmental Law and ClientEarth entitled "Toxic Partnership. A Critique of the ACC-CEFIC Proposal for Trans-Atlantic Cooperation on Chemicals."

349 Charles Riley, "Obama, Hu meet American CEOs," *CNN Money*, Jan. 19, 2011.

350 Kavitha Rao, "Inside Indian Business Culture," *Executive Travel Magazine*, Sep. 2011.

351 Michael Snyder, "Even the CEOs on Obama's Job Creation Panel Are Shipping Jobs Out of the United States," Oct. 11, 2011.

352 Michael Snyder, "Even the CEOs on Obama's Job Creation Panel Are Shipping Jobs Out of the United States," Oct. 11, 2011, citing Professor Alan Blinder of Princeton University.

353 Dow Chemical bought Union Carbide, the corporation responsible for the Bhopal disaster. That disaster took place in 1984 when Union Carbide's pesticide factory leaked methyl isocyanate (MIC), immediately killing thousands of people. Hundreds of thousands more were injured, including thousands who died later, and thousands who were severely permanently disabled.

354 "America linked Bhopal to aid," *videowired.com*, Aug. 18, 2010.

355 "Drilling and Killing," *Democracy Now*, documentary, aired Friday, July 11, 2003.

356 Cables from U.S. embassies in Ecuador, Slovakia, Argentina, India, France, and Thailand report on embassy efforts to promote GMOs. There are undoubtedly many others. Cable from Quito Embassy, sent Jan. 15, 2010, source http://wikileaks.org/cable/2010/01/10QUIT)54.html; cable from U.S. Embassy in Bratislava, Nov. 8, 2007, source: http://wikileaks.org/cable/2007/11/07/BRATISLAVA605.htm; cable from U.S. Embassy in Buenos Aires, Aug. 15, 2008, source: http:// wikileaks.org/cable/2008/08/08BUENOSAIRES1153.html; cable from U.S. Embassy in New Delhi, Feb 11, 2010, source: http://wikileaks.org/cable/2010/02/10NEWDELHI275.html; cable from Chiang Ma, Thailand, Sept. 24, 2007, source: http://wikileaks.org/cable/2007/09/07CHIANGMAI155.html; cable from Chiang Ma, Thailand, Sept. 24, 2007, source: http://wikileaks.org/cable/2007/09/07CHIANGMAI155.html; cable from Bangkok, Thailand, Jan. 14, 2010, source: http://wikileaks.org/cable/2010/1/10BANGKOK111.html.

357 Cable from Paris, France, Dec. 14, 2007, source: http://wikileaks.org/cable/2007/12/07PARIS4723.html. See also cables: http://wikileaks.org/cable/2007/10/07/STATE150199.html; http://wikileaks.org/cable for Paris dated Oct. 30, 2007, and for April 15, 2008, and http://wikileaks.org/cable/2008/04/08PARIS614.html.

358 Paris cables mentioned in the endnote above refer to attacks on France's precautionary principle, for example. In attacking precaution in France, U.S. diplomats acknowledge that the French Constitution mandates precaution as if that doesn't matter.

359 A cable from the U.S. Embassy in Budapest in 2010, for example, reports on Hungary's overall status in terms of foreign corporations investing in the country. (Cable from Budapest, Hungary, Jan. 27, 2010, source: http://wikileaks.org/cable/2010/01/10BUDAPEST43.html.) According to the cable, "[o]f the U.S.'s 50 largest multinationals, 40 are present in Hungary." Examples listed include GE, Coca-Cola, Citibank, ExxonMobil, McDonalds, Dow Chemical, Pfizer, Monsanto and others. These sorts of discussions, exposing the plans of multinationals to expand their holdings in and control over countries around the world, appear in cable after cable. (Mike Ludwig, "US to Vatican: Genetically Modified Food Is a 'Moral Imperative'", *Truthout*, Dec. 29, 2010.)

360 Ajay Kapur et al, Citigroup, "Equity Strategy. Plutonomy: Buying Luxury, Explaining Global Imbalance," October 16, 2005, p. 2.

Chapter 13

361 See chapter 2 for the story of how that program was undercut after it supported air monitoring.

362 "Nuclear Agencies Are Wholly Controlled by (and Serve) the Nuclear Industry.... Just Like the Fed is Owned By (And Serves) Its Member Banks," *WashingtonsBlog*, Dec. 11, 2011; "EXPOSED: US Nuclear Regulatory Commission Covers Up Risk of Fukushima Like Disaster in the USA," *NSNB*, Mar 10, 2014; "Nuclear regulators misled the media after Fukushima, emails show," *RT.com*, Mar 10, 2014. The U.S. Nuclear Regulatory Commission is the same Commission that candidate Barack Obama denounced as a "moribund agency that....has become captive of the industries that it regulates" in 2008.

363 When I recently attempted to make sure that an "internal wood stabilizer" product was truly environmentally benign, for example, the manufacturer refused to disclose the ingredients. This was especially frustrating because I wanted to confirm that treating wood for raised garden beds in my yard would not interfere with obtaining organic certification down the road. As state certification staff were not familiar with the product, I was told that the only option was to build the beds, apply for certification, and hope for the best. Once an application was received, *the state* could obtain the list of ingredients from the manufacturer and make a determination after the fact. Even then, I would not be allowed to know what was in the product.

364 "Washington State Vote to Label GM Food Defeated by Corporations' 'Sophisticated Propaganda Machine,'" *Democracy Now*, Nov. 8, 2013.

365 Alicia Gallegos, "Doctors Fight 'Gag Orders' Over Fracking Chemicals," *amednews.com*, Aug. 27, 2012.

366 Jill Richardson, "Monsanto's College Stranglehold," *Salon.com*, May 14, 2012.

367 Food & Water Watch, *Public Research, Private Gain* (April 2012, p. 4.)

368 David McNeill, "Concerns Over Measurement of Fukushima Fallout," *New York Times*, Mar 1, 2014.

369 David Michaels, "It's Not the Answers That Are Biased, It's the Question," *The Washington Post*, July 15, 2008.

370 F. Vom Saal and W. Welshons, "Large Effects from Small Exposures. II. The Importance of Positive Controls in Low-Dose Research on Bisphenol A," *Environmental Research*, 100: 50-76; (2006) as quoted and summarized at www. ourstolenfuture.org.

371 Lenard I. Lesser et al, "Relationship Between Funding Source and Conclusion Among Nutrition-Related Scientific Articles," *PLoS Medicine*, January 2007, Vol. 4, Issue 1.

372 The Lesser study begins by citing studies reviewing heavy reliance on pharmaceutical firms for biomedical research and finding significant associations between industry sponsorship and pro-industry conclusions, for example.

373 Lesser et al, "Relationship Between Funding Source and Conclusion Among Nutrition-Related Scientific Articles," *PLoS Medicine*, Jan. 2007.

374 Richard Smith, "Medical Journals Are an Extension of the Marketing Arm of Pharmaceutical Companies," *PLOS Medicine*, May 7, 2005; See also David Michaels, "It's Not the Answers That Are Biased, It's the Questions," *The Washington Post*, July 15, 2008.

375 Eval Pressl and Jennifer Washburn, "The Kept University," *Atlantic Magazine*, March 2000, p. 7.

376 *Food & Water Watch*, "Public Research, Private Gain," April 2012, p. 8

377 F. Vom Saal and W. Welshons, "Large Effects from Small Exposures. II. The Importance of Positive Controls in Low-Dose Research on Bisphenol A," *Environmental Research* 100: 50-76 (2006) as quoted and summarized at www. ourstolenfuture.org.

378 www.ourstolenfuture.org, summary of F. Vom Saal and W. Welshons, "Large Effects from Small Exposures. II. The Importance of Positive Controls in Low-Dose Research on Bisphenol A." *Environmental Research* 100: 5-76 (2006).

379 *Food & Water Watch*, "Public Research, Private Gain," April 2012, p. 8.

380 *Food & Water Watch*, "Public Research, Private Gain," April 2012, p 8, 9.

381 *Food & Water Watch*, "Public Research, Private Gain," April 2012, p. 10.

382 Docket: EPA-HQ-OPP-2008-0836, "Evaluation of the Resistance Risks from Using a Seed Mix Refuge with Pioneer's Optimum AcreMax 1 Coren Rootworm-Protected Corn"; Comment Document #: EPA-HQ-OPP-2008-0836-0043.

383 A "genome" is the complete set of genetic material for an organism.

384 Michael Specter, "Can We Patent Life?," *The New Yorker*, April 2, 2013.

385 Sharon Levy, "Our Shared Code: The Myriad Decision and the Future of Genetic Research," *Environ Health Perspect*, Doi: 10:1289/ehp 121-A250, (2013). The Court ruled that "a naturally occurring DNA segment is a product of nature and not patent eligible, merely because it has been isolated." In other words, genetic materials and discoveries that involve more than mere "isolation" will still be patentable. This fact will continue to stymie research by non-patent holders.

386 Eval Press and Jennifer Washburn, "The Kept University," *Atlantic Magazine*, March 2000, p. 6.

387 Press and Washburn, "The Kept University," 6.

388 As discussed in an earlier chapter, research for this book revealed that scientists studying farm worker family pesticide exposures also treated research related to organic agriculture's ability to reduce exposures as off-limits. This stance served the interests of pesticide manufacturers, sellers, and users.

389 Food & Water Watch, *Public Research, Private Gain*, April 2012, p. 7. Jill Richardson, "Monsanto's College Stranglehold," *Salon.com*, May 14, 2012.

Chapter 14

390 "Outside Groups Influence Congressional Races," *Bloomberg.com*, Sept. 6, 2012.

391 Elizabeth Wilner, "Toothpaste vs. Candidates: Why the Mad Men Approach Doesn't Work in Politics," *AdAge*, August 9, 2012.

392 Jeremy Jacobs, "Biotech: Dow Rolls Out PR Campaign as USDA Weighs Herbicide-Resistant Corn Seed," *E&E*, May 8, 2012.

393 "War on Truth, the Secret Battle for the American Mind, An Interview with John Stauber," http://www.ratical.org/ratville/PRcorrupt.txt.

394 Thomas Edsall, "The Lobbyist in the Gray Flannel Suit," *New York Times*, May 14, 2012.

395 Dow Enlist PR video as linked to by Jeremy Jacobs, "Biotech: Dow Rolls Out PR Campaign as USDA Weighs Herbicide-Resistant Corn Seed," *E&E*, May 8, 2012.

396 Fred Wilcox, "Agent Orange is Still Killing People in Vietnam and America," *History News Network*, Jan. 2, 2012.

397 Deloitte, *Gaining Ground in the Sands 2012. A Deeper Look at Major Trends and Opportunities in the Oil Sands Sector* (2012, p. 24.) This particular page is signed by Chris Lee, National Industry Leader, Energy & Resources, Deloitte.

398 Deloitte, *Gaining Ground in the Sands 2012. A Deeper Look at Major Trends and Opportunities in the Oil Sands Sector* (2012, p. 3.)

399 Paula Crossfield, "UN: Eco-Farming Feeds the World," *Huffington Post*, March 9, 2011.

400 Angela Gadino, Tree Fruit Research and Extension Center, Washington State University, "Summary Audience 'Clicker' Surveys, Perspectives of North Central Washington Apple Growers and Consultants. Reporting results of Surveys Conducted in the Winter of 2011-2012".

401 The quoted representative worked for Winfield, which sells products made by Monsanto, Syngenta, and others. The company provides information to growers throughout the year through its "Interactive Answer Plot Knowledge Event program," which "builds the trust that leads to a smoother sales road." Winfield "pairs up the retailer and the grower throughout the season, and integrates crop protection [pesticides] and fertilizer with seed selection to more closely align the agronomist with cropping decisions all along the way." "Selling Seeds With Knowledge," *Croplife.com*, retrieved June 3, 2011.

402 Comments of Alan Miller, Philip Morris Incorporated, Workshop—Dealing with the Issues Indirectly: Constituencies, at 1984 Corporate Affairs World Conference, Rye Brook, New York, Sept. 13, 1984, p. 5-6.

403 Comments of George Woodward, Workshop—Dealing with the Issues Indirectly: Constituencies, at 1984 Corporate Affairs World Conference, Rye Brook, New York, Sept. 13, 1984, p. 26.

404 See *Chicago Tribune* series May 2012: Callahan and Roe, "Fear Fans Flames for Chemical Makers," May 6, 2012; Callahan and Roe, "Big Tobacco Wins Fire Marshals as Allies in Flame Retardant Push," May 8, 2012; Roe & Callahan, "Distorting Sciences," May 9, 2012; Michael Hawthorne, "Toxic Roulette," May 10, 2012.

405 These toxic chemicals migrate from furniture into house dust and human beings. They are linked to serious health problems, and there is mounting evidence that they are not even effective at preventing or minimizing fires. Yet health advocates have faced an uphill battle encouraging safer, more effective alternatives in part because of the testimony of seemingly independent experts who are anything but independent.

406 The President of the Professional Fire Fighters of Vermont has expressed outrage at Citizens for Fire Safety's "dirty tactics" in his state, for example. "Citizens for Fire Safety did everything they could to portray themselves as firefighters, as Vermont citizens for fire safety, when it really wasn't Vermont citizens for fire safety at all," he said.

407 There are also other flame retardant front groups beyond Citizens for Fire Safety. The PR firm Burson-Marstller helps run the Bromine Science and Environmental Forum based in Brussels, for example. It was founded and funded

by four chemical manufacturers to influence the debate about flame retardants made with bromine. Burson-Marsteller also helps run the Alliance for Consumer Fire Safety in Europe, funded by a flame retardant manufacturers' association.

408 Cornucopia Institute, "CMD Unveils Documents Detailing Insidious PR Campaign to 'Greenwash' Weed-Killer Polluting Drinking Water Across the Country," Feb. 7, 2012. An ACSH letter addressed to "Dear Syngenta Friends" seeks funds for preparing a report on atrazine, "consumerizing" it in a consumer booklet, and distributing the report to reporters and via Op-eds, letters to the editor, media appearances, etc. "This is separate and distinct from general operating support Syngenta has been so generously providing over the years, which we request to continue at current or increased levels," the letter says. "Such general operating support is the lifeblood of a small non-profit like ours, and is both deeply appreciated and much needed."

409 "Syngenta Confidential Request for Proposal," available via Center for Media and Democracy website.

410 Alexis Bade-Mayer and Ronnie Cummins, "Meet the Corporate Front Groups Fighting to Make Sure You Can't Know What's in Your Food," *Alternet.org*; May 31, 2012.

411 Geoff Dembicki, "How Big Oil and Canada Thwarted US Carbon Standards," *The Tyee*, Dec. 15, 201. CEA has used its ample funding to run slick radio and TV ads claiming that low carbon fuel laws "threaten thousands of American jobs" and "would be disastrous for American consumers." CEA's work is part of a larger strategy in which energy consumer groups dependent on oil (e.g., truckers and highway users) are mobilized to denounce low carbon fuels, and other "third party" advocates also advance the oil industry's cause. As the result of these efforts low carbon fuel bills in various states and in Congress don't survive

412 Take Energy In Depth (EID), for example. Visitors to its website will see small independent oil and gas associations mentioned, but not big corporations. A memorandum sent in 2009 by the Independent Petroleum Association of America to its members, however, unequivocally states that EID would not have been possible without early financial commitments from Occidental Petroleum, BP, Chevron, Shell, Halliburton, Marathon, and other big oil and gas corporations. Barry Russell, Independent Petroleum Association of America, letter to members announcing formation of Energy in Depth.org, "a state of the art online resource center to combat new environmental regulations especially with regard to hydraulic fracturing," June 5, 2009.

 With a staff of 15 in their Washington, D.C., office, EID has been prolific. It has churned out articles, fact sheets, videos, charts and graphs, and other materials. It has also helped churn out bodies for public meetings. In early October of 2012, for example, EID posted an article publicizing an October 15th pro-fracking rally in Albany, NY. The article and the official poster for the rally referred people to Landowner Advocates of New York, for information and to sign up (Fred Peckham, "Rally for Truth and Energy, Rally for Natural Gas in Albany, October 15," EID website, Oct. 4, 2012).

One thousand people attended the October 15th rally. Many wore red T-shirts with the word "JOBs" emblazoned on them. The *Times Herald-Record* reported that the T-shirts had been provided by the American Petroleum Institute (API). API was included in a long list of rally "participants" in Landowner Advocates' press release about the rally (Steve Israel, "1,000 Rally Against Moratorium," *Times Herald-Record*, Oct. 16, 2012). This article notes that a woman quoted "was wearing a red T-shirt that said "JOBS" provided by *the rally's organizer*, the American Petroleum Institute" (emphasis added). .

The amazing thing is that Landowner Advocates of NY had only been in existence a few weeks when it somehow pulled off this impressive rally. An article both announcing that the organization had been formed and calling on people to attend the rally had appeared on the EID website on October 3rd, only 12 days before the rally. Despite being brand new, the organization clearly did not lack for resources. Its website emphasized that it was providing "FREE, COMFORTABLE, bus transportation from a broad range of locations." The *Times Union* newspaper reported that 16 buses transported people to the rally from all over the state. In short, the whole thing smacks of Astroturf.

The consistent message permeating the rally and publicity for it bore all the signs of a carefully crafted PR communications strategy on behalf of the oil and gas industry. "Third-party" speakers talked about jobs, declared fracking to be safe, and called for NY to not take time to examine environmental risks before approving fracking. The sea of red T-shirts with the word "Jobs" on them emphasized the jobs message.

EID serves as a central hub for various landowner groups. The characterization of Landowners Advocates as "a front group for a front group" likely hits the nail right on the head. (Steve Horn, "New Gas Industry Astroturf: Landowner Advocates of NY Buses Activists to Albany Pro-Fracking Rally," *DeSmog Blog*, Oct. 16, 2012.)

413 Memo from Joe Walker, American Petroleum Institute to "Global Climate Science Team," Subject: Draft Global Climate Science Communication plan, April 1998.

414 Union of Concerned Scientists, *A Climate of Corporate Control. How Corporations Have Influenced the U.S. Dialogue on Climate Science and Policy* (May 2012).

415 Corporations were affecting climate change perceptions and policies through memberships in, board seats on, and contributions to other organizations. These organizations included trade groups such as the U.S. Chamber of Commerce, think tanks, and other entities. Often industry organizations concealed the funding they got from corporations, thus hiding the agenda of those corporations. The UCS report identified the Heartland Institute, George C. Marshall Institute, and Competitive Enterprise Institute as examples of think tanks funded, mainly by industry, to oppose climate and other science-based regulations.

The UCS report only covered publicly traded corporations, noting that privately held corporations play even bigger roles influencing climate policy. Since 1997, the Koch Foundation, for example, had given more than $55 million to groups that misrepresent climate science or oppose climate policies, including the Heritage Foundation and several Koch organizations: Americans for Prosperity, Freedom Works, and the Cato Institute.

416 Naomi Klein, "Capitalism vs. the Climate," *The Nation*, Nov. 9, 2011.

417 Tom Clynes, "The Battle," *Popular Science*, July 2012, p. 39.

418 Tom Clynes, "The Battle," *Popular Science*, July 2012, p. 40

419 Clare Howard, "Special Report: Syngenta's campaign to protect atrazine, discredit critics," *Environmental Health News*, June 17, 2013; "100 Reporters Syngenta Clare Howard Investigation EXHIBIT 19"; Rachel Aviv, "A Valuable Reputation," *The New Yorker*, Feb. 10, 2014.

420 Rachel Aviv, "A Valuable Reputation," *The New Yorker*, Feb. 10, 2014, p. 7.

421 Rachel Aviv, "A Valuable Reputation," *The New Yorker*, Feb. 10, 2014.

422 Nicole Casal Moore, University of Michigan Office of the Vice President for Global Communications, "U-M researchers receive share of $250 million from Dow Chemical Co.," Oct. 28, 2011.

423 UC Berkeley College of Chemistry, "College of Chemistry Receives $3.5 Million Gift from Dow to Develop Sustainable Chemistry Education." "Together we will facilitate enhancements to both the curriculum and the learning environment..." said Dow CEO Liveris. Thanking Dow, College of Chemistry Dean Richard A. Mathies said "[t]he impact of this gift is huge because these courses serve thousands of students every year."

424 Praising the new award, Craig J. Hawker, the director of UCSB's Materials Research Lab, said "the questions that Dow will allow us to ask based on their experience" are very valuable. He was probably using the verb "allow" to mean that Dow's money make it possible to ask those questions. But in a very real sense, by holding the purse strings, Dow gains the ability to greatly shape what questions

are asked. What gets asked and what does not get asked are very important aspects of scientific research.

425 Food & Water Watch, *Public Research, Private Gain. Corporate Influence Over University Agricultural Research*, April 2012.

426 Food & Water Watch, *Public Research, Private Gain. Corporate Influence Over University Agricultural Research*, April 2012.

427 Association of University Technology Managers, http://www.autm.net/Bayh_Dole_Act1.htm.

428 Food & Water Watch, *Public Research, Private Gain*, April 2012, p. 1.

429 Food & Water Watch, *Public Research, Private Gain*, April 2012, p. 5-7.

430 Food & Water Watch, *Public Research, Private Gain*, April 2012, p. 7.

431 Food & Water Watch, *Public Research, Private Gain*, April 2012, p. 7.

432 Public Accountability Initiative, "Contaminated Inquiry. How a University of Texas Fracking Study Led by a Gas Industry Insider Spun the Facts and Misled the Public," July 2012; Jim Efstathio Jr., "Frackers Fund University Research That Proves Their Case," *Bloomberg*, July 23, 2012; Forest Wilder, "At Universities, Fracking Research Funded by Oil and Gas Companies," *Common Dreams*, Sept. 9, 2012. More specifically, Groat served on the board of an oil and gas company involved in fracking, and had received more than $1.5 million in cash and stock since 2007.

433 University of Texas at Austin, Statement from The University of Texas System: "University of Texas Accepts Findings on Shale Gas Development Report," Dec. 6, 2012.

434 Forest Wilder, "At Universities, Fracking Research Funded by Oil and Gas Companies," *Common Dreams*, Sept. 9, 2012.

435 Dow UM Announcement, "Dow and U-M Launch Innovative Program to Develop Sustainability Leaders," March 12, 2012.

436 Eval Press and Jennifer Washburn, "The Kept University," *Atlantic Magazine*, March 2000.

437 James Boyle, as quoted in Eval Press and Jennifer Washburn, "The Kept University," *The Atlantic* 2000, p. 12.

438 Joe Walker, American Petroleum Institute, "Memo to Global Climate Science Team, Global Climate Science Communication Action Plan," April 1998.

439 www.exxonmobil.com, various pages.

440 http://www.kidsgardening.org/node/13384, retrieved Nov. 8, 2012.

441 Syngenta website pages on Environmental Stewardship, retrieved Nov. 9, 2012.

442 "Syngenta to Help Fund New Agriculture Education Program," *PR Newswire*, July 26, 2002.

443   www.ffaconvention.com/2012/10/25/Syngenta-celebrates-50-years-of-sponsorship.

444   "America's Farmers Grow Rural Education[SM] Launches for Second Year," *Monsanto.com*, Jan. 10, 2013.

445   "Bayer Celebrates 15 Years of Helping Kids Experience the Wonders of Science," *Corporate Social Responsibility Newswire,* Sept. 10, 2010.

446   So pleased is Bayer with its image as an educator that it has published a compendium of "best practices" for K-12 STEM Education. Bayer Corp., *A Compendium of Best Practice K-12 STEM Education Programs* (updated 2010.)

447   "Choose Your Challenge," essay contest web pages, *Dupont.com*, retrieved Jan. 15, 2013.

448   According to the Keystone Center's website its mission is "bringing together today's leaders to create solutions to society's most pressing challenges." The Center takes an "independent, collaborative approach to problem solving". The Board of Trustees Executive Committee includes representatives of Monsanto, Pacific Gas & Electric, and The Nature Conservancy, among others. The full board includes Dow, DuPont, Duke Energy, Coca-Cola, the Natural Resources Defense Council, and others.

449   Similarly, Dow's curriculum has students take sides on this whopper: "Dihydrogen oxide should be banned in public places." Dihydrogen oxide is, of course, water, and Dow's subtle lesson is again that activists concerned about toxic chemicals don't know what we're talking about

450   Sara Bernard, "Can Corporate Funding Boost STEM Education?," *Mindshift*, Feb. 28, 2011.

451   "Syngenta to Help Fund New Agriculture Education Program," *PRNewswire*, July 24, 2002.

452   Bayer Corp., *A Compendium of Best Practice K-12 STEM Education Programs* (updated 2010, p. 7).

453   Education Commission of the States.

454   Jennifer Levitz and Stephanie Simon, "A School Prays for Help. Towns Tap Businesses, Churches to Shore Up Budgets," *Wall Street Journal*, June 14, 2010.

455   Patrick Morrison, *Media Monopoly Revisited, Fairness & Accuracy in Reporting* (October 2011). Examining only the types of media addressed by the 1983 analysis, the update concluded that the number of corporations dominating the media had dropped to 15. Adding in newer media technologies like the internet, cable television, and satellite radio, however, brought the number back up to 20.

456 Fairness & Accuracy in Reporting, Interlocking Directories, www.fair.org, retrieved Nov. 9, 2012.

457 Robert McChesney, Statements made in an interview on Democracy Now: "How the Washington Post's New Owner Aided the CIA, Blocked Wikileaks & Decimated the Book Industry," *Democracy Now*, August 7, 2013.

458 Robert McChesney, statements made in an interview on Democracy Now, "How the Washington Post's New Owner Aided the CIA, Blocked Wikileaks & Decimated the Book Industry," *Democracy Now*, August 7, 2013.

459 Jack Mirkinson, "Koch Brothers Not Buying Tribune Company Newspapers," *The Huffington Post*, August 22, 2013.

460 Amy Chozick, "Conservative Koch Brothers Turning Focus to Newspapers," *The New York Times*, April 20, 2013.

461 Amy Chozick, "Conservative Koch Brothers Turning Focus to Newspapers," *The New York Times*, April 20, 2013.

462 Fairness & Accuracy in Reporting, "What's Wrong With the News," www.fair.org, retrieved Nov. 9, 2012.

463 John Sullivan, "PR Industry Fills Vacuum Left by Shrinking Newsrooms," *ProPublica*, May 1, 2011.

464 John Sullivan, "PR Industry Fills Vacuum Left by Shrinking Newsrooms," *ProPublica*, May 1, 2011.

465 Jon Queally, Common Dreams.org, citing Inside Climate News, Jan. 11, 2013

466 John Sullivan, "PR Industry Fills Vacuum Left by Shrinking Newsrooms," *ProPublica*, May 1, 2011.

467 John Sullivan, "PR Industry Fills Vacuum Left by Shrinking Newsrooms," *ProPublica*, May 1, 2011.

468 UCS surveyed climate and energy stories run in 2011 and 2012 by eight major news organizations such as the *Washington Post*, the *New York Times*, *USA Today*, and NPR. It examined whether the stories reported funding sources for eight prominent entities that dispute climate science, such as Americans for Prosperity, the Heritage Foundation, and the American Enterprise Institute. All eight received funding from fossil fuel industry benefactors such as ExxonMobil, the American Petroleum Institute, and Koch Brother foundations.

469 Ellin Negin, "U.S. News Media Help Koch Brothers and ExxonMobil Spread Climate Disinformation, UCS Investigation Finds. Top News Outlets Failed to Cite Think Tank Funding in Two-Thirds of Climate and Energy Stories in 2011 and 2012," *Union of Concerned Scientists*, May 13, 2013.

470 "Dow Chemical Reaps Rewards by Funding PBS' 'American Revealed'," *Common Dreams*, April 23, 2012

471 Fairness & Accuracy in Reporting, Issue Area: Official Agenda, www.fair.org, retrieved Nov. 9, 2012.

472 Matthew Creamer, "Obama Wins!...Ad Age's Marketer of the Year," *Adage.com*, Oct. 17, 2008.

473 James Ledbetter, "Obama: the Pepsi Candidate," *Slate*, Aug. 21, 2008.

Chapter 15

474 For example, EME Homer city Generation, a coal-burning power plant owned by General Electric, filed a suit that struck down EPA's cross-state air pollution rule in 2012 (*Democracy Now*, August 22, 2012). Dow and other pesticide corporations challenged the National Marine Fisheries Service's biological opinion instructing EPA to not allow spraying close to waterways in order to protect salmon. (Mateusz Perkowski, "Pesticide makers ask court to overturn restrictions," *Capital Press*, Nov. 2012.) Oil and gas corporations have sued to overturn moratoriums on fracking. (Paula Dittrick, "Lenape files NY lawsuit to overturn fracking moratorium," *OGJ*, Dec. 3, 2012.)

475 "Slap Back," *NPR*, April 2, 2010.

476 Center for Food Safety, *Save Our Seeds, Seed Giants vs. U.S. Farmers* (2013, p. 6).

477 "Why Does Monsanto Sue Farmers Who Save Seeds?," www.monsanto.com, retrieved May 21, 2013.

478 Quoted in Gary Ruskin, *Spooky Business: Corporate Espionage Against Nonprofit Organizations* (2013, p. 8).

479 Gary Ruskin, *Spooky Business: Corporate Espionage Against Nonprofit Organizations* (2013, p. 5).

480 Ruskin, *Spooky Business*, 7.

481 Mary Cuddehe, "A Spy in the Jungle," *The Atlantic*, Aug. 2, 2010.

482 Gary Ruskin, *Spooky Business: Corporate Espionage Against Nonprofit Organizations* (2013).

483 Beau Hodai, *Dissent or Terror: How the Nation's Counter Terrorism Apparatus, in Partnership with Corporate America Turned on Occupy Wall Street*, (Center for Media and Democracy, DBA Press, 2013); "Dissent or Terror: New Report Details How Counter Terrorism Apparatus Was Used to Monitor Occupy Movement Nationwide," *PR Watch News Release*, May 20, 2013.

484 Beau Hodai, *Dissent or Terror: How the Nation's Counter Terrorism Apparatus, in Partnership with Corporate America Turned on Occupy Wall Street* (Center for Media and Democracy, DBA Press, 2013); "Dissent or Terror: New Report Details How Counter Terrorism Apparatus Was Used to Monitor Occupy Movement Nationwide," *PR Watch News Release*, May 20, 2013.

485   Beau Hodai, *Dissent or Terror: How the Nation's Counter Terrorism Apparatus, in Partnership with Corporate America Turned on Occupy Wall Street*, (Center for Media and Democracy, DBA Press, 2013); "Dissent or Terror: New Report Details How Counter Terrorism Apparatus Was Used to Monitor Occupy Movement Nationwide," *PR Watch News Release,*, May 20, 2013.

486   Glenn Greenwald, "How Covert Agents Infiltrate the Internet to Manipulate, Deceive, and Destroy Reputations," *The Intercept*, Feb. 24, 2014.

487   "'It was Time to Do More Than Protest': Activists Admit to 1971 Burglary That Exposed COINTELPRO," *Democracy Now*, Jan. 8, 2014.   Cointelpro stands for COunter INTELligence PROgram,

488   "Spies of Mississippi: New Film on the State-Sponsored Campaign to Defeat the Civil Rights Movement,", *Democracy Now*, Feb. 25, 2014.

489   See graphs showing increasing defense industry profits since the U.S. "war on terror" began in Glenn Greenwald's article "Key Democrats Led by Hillary Clinton Leave No Doubt that Endless War is Official U.S. Doctrine," *The Intercept*, Oct. 7, 2014. Note that the Obama Administration adopted a policy in early 2015 allowing foreign allies to purchase U.S.-made armed drones, *Democracy Now*, Feb. 18, 2015.

490   Tom Bawden, Intervention in Civil Wars far More Likely in Oil-Rich Nations, *Independent*, Jan. 28, 2015.

491   See documents at http://www.fuelonthefire.com/index.php?page=documents, retrieved Jan. 23, 2013.

492   See for example," Meeting of Michael Arthur (Head of Economic Policy, FCO) with Richard Paniguian (Group Vice President for Russia, the Caspian, Middle East and Asia)," November 6, 2002, Document 3: http://www.fuelonthefire.com/index.php?page=documents, retrieved Jan. 23, 2013.

493   : "Meeting of Edward Chaplin (Middle East Director, Foreign & Commonwealth Office) with Tony Wildig, Senior Vice President for New Business in Middle East, Shell)," Oct. 2, 2002, Subject Header: IRAQ – VIEWS OF UK BUSINESS, Importance: Document 1 at http://www.fuelonthefire.com/index.php?page=documents, retrieved on Jan. 23, 2013.

494   "Meeting of Baroness Liz Symons (Trade Minister) with representatives of BP, Shell, and BG, October 2002," Document 2 at http://www.fuelonthefire.com/index.php?page=documents, retrieved. Jan 23, 2013.

495   "Meeting of Baroness Symons with Richard Paniguian and Tony Renton (Commercial Director Middle East, BP) December 4, 2002"; Document 4 at http://www.fuelonthefire.com/index.php?page=documents, retrieved January 23, 2013.

496 The British Ambassador to Iraq lobbied for BP to be awarded a study contract, which was likely instrumental in the corporation winning a 20-year contract for that oil field in 2009, for example. BP not only won that contract, but it also was able to renegotiate almost immediately, greatly improving the terms for BP. Other foreign corporations got contracts in 2009, as well.

497 Jim Michaels, "Iraq Buys U.S. Drones to Protect Oil," *USA Today*, May 20, 2012.

Chapter 16

498 Jennifer Bjorhus, "Hot Money Turns from Stocks to Farmland," *StarTribune*, June 24, 2012.

499 Stock Whiz, "Resilient Recessionary Hedge: 18 Companies With Large Farmland Holdings," April 30, 2012, http://seekingalpha.com/article/540891-resilient-recessionary-hedge-18-companies-with-large-farmland-holdings?source=feed, retrieved Jan. 29, 2013.

500 Carey L. Biron, "Private Equity Predators and the Great American Farm Grab," *Common Dreams*, Feb. 19, 2014.

501 Biron, "Private Equity Predators and the Great American Farm Grab."

502 Steve Savage, "Who Owns America's Farmland," *sustainablog*, Nov. 29, 2011.

503 Loma Salzman and Bernardo Issel, "Natural Resources Defense Council: Eco-logic or Eco-sell-out?," http://www.lornasalzman.com, 2002.

504 American Farmland Trust, "Threatened Farmland: What's Happening to Our Farmland?," www.farmland.org/resourcs/fote/default.asp, retrieved Jan. 29, 2013.

505 GRAIN, "Hungry for Land; Small Farmers Feed the World With Less Than a Quarter of All Farmland," May 28, 2014.

506 Nick Olle, "Occupy Brazil: The Landless Dig In (And Ditch the Pesticides)," *The Global Mail*, Sept. 20, 2012.

507 "US Farmers Scramble to Buy Brazil's Farmland," *Aljazeera*, Sept. 29, 2012.

508 Carey L. Biron, "Private Equity Predators and the Great American Farm Grab," *Common Dreams*, Feb. 19, 2014.

509 Jeff Goodell, "The Big Fracking Bubble: The Scam Behind the Gas Boom," *Rolling Stone*, March 15, 2012.

510 U.S. General Accounting Office, Management of Federal Oil and Gas Resources, http://www.gao.gov/highrisk/risks/efficiency-effectiveness/management_federal_oil_gas.php, retrieved Jan. 30, 2013.

511 "Global 500 list," *CNNMoney*, http://money.cnn.com/magazines/fortune/global500/2012/full_list/index.html, retrieved Jan. 29, 2013.

512 Sylvia A. Allegretto, "The State of Working America's Wealth, 2011. Through volatility and turmoil, the gap widens. EPI Briefing Paper #292," *Economic Policy Institute*, March 23, 2011, p. 2.

513 See Jennifer Franco and Kay Sylvia, Transnational Institute, Water Justice, "The Global Water Grab: A Primer," http://www.tni.org/primer/global-water-grab-primer, March 13, 2012, retrieved Jan. 30, 2013, and Shirley Varghese, "The Global Water Grab," *Institute for Agriculture and Trade Policy*, Jan. 18, 2013, http://www.iatp.org/blog/201301/the-global-water-grab.

514 Barton Brooke, "Can Top Corporations Develop Needed Water Solutions?", *Greenbiz.com*, Feb. 26, 2013.

515 Gus Lubin, "Map of the Day: The World Water Crisis," *Business Insider*, Mar. 22, 2011.

516 Heather Pilatic, "What Do GMO Seeds Have to Do With Bee Die-Offs in the Corn Belt?," *Common Dreams*, May 16, 2012.

517 Cary Gillam, "Pesticide Use Ramping Up as GMO Crop Technology Backfires: Study"; *Reuters*, Oct. 1, 2012.

518 See Center for Food Safety & Save Our Seeds, *Seed Giants vs. U.S. Farmers* (2013).

519 Dominic Gates, "Boeing's Wish List for 777X Asks for 'No Cost' Site," *Seattle Times*, Dec. 5, 2013.

520 Jim Levitt, "What's the Point of a Labor Union? Boeing Machinists Narrowly Approve End to Pensions," *Common Dreams*, Jan. 7, 2014.

521 Steven Mufson, "Shale May Bail Out Ohio, for a Price," *The Washington Post*, March 11, 2012, as reprinted in the *Seattle Times*.

522 John A. Miller, "A Town Embraces Its Explosive Past. A Chemical Once Made in Nitro, W. Wa., Is Behind Health Problems, Lawsuits Allege, But Many Residents Want the Industry Back." *Wall Street Journal*, March 1, 2012.

523 Democracy Now Headlines, Oct. 10, 2012.

524 Graham Kates, "Environmental Crime: The Prosecution Gap," *The Crime Report*, July 14, 2014.

525 Workers in Freeport, Illinois, publicly begged Mitt Romney to intervene and stop the dismantling and shipping overseas of their jobs by Sensata Technology, for example. Their pleas didn't work. Thus, after decades of serving the corporation and its precursor, workers in their 50s faced bleak futures without decent jobs and the benefits that come with them. Sensata bought the business, dismantled it, and shipped it overseas to take advantage of higher profit margins there. Romney was petitioned because of his ties to Bain Capital, which owned Sensata. ("Workers at Bain-Owned Illinois Factory Bring Fight to Save Their Outsourced Jobs to Romney and RNC," *Democracy Now*, Aug. 28, 2012).

526   Working America & AFL-CIO, *Outsourced. Sending Jobs Overseas: The Cost to America's Economy and Working Families* (2010); Alex Lach, "Facts About Overseas Outsourcing," *Center for American Progress,* July 9, 2012.

527   Jim Tankersley, "As Manufacturing Bounces Back From Recession, Unions Are Left Behind," *The Washington Post,* Jan. 16, 2013.

528   Bonnie Kavoussi, "Low-Wage Jobs Replace Middle-Income Work, Study Finds," *The Huffington Post,* Jan. 29, 2013.

529   A cable from the U.S. Embassy in Argentina, for example, lists things corporate representatives want changed in Argentina to facilitate their investments there. They don't like "controversial" taxation measures, lack of enforcement of intellectual property laws, and strong unions demanding regular cost of living wage increases. Teletech, Staples, and Prudential all cite labor issues as a constraint on their growth. (Embassy Cable, Argentina: "American Chamber Describes Investment Challenges, Opportunities to Wha Das McMullen," Oct. 17, 2008. Obtained via http://wikileaks.org/cble/2008/10/08BUENOSAIRES1427.html).

The cable mentions that Exxon-Mobil's Esso Argentina had been considering leaving Argentina only six months earlier "due to its frustration with an over-regulated energy market." It goes on to share this news: "However, thanks in part to US Embassy assistance, Esso is better able to deal with Argentina's challenging investment environment and will soon be talking to the GOA [Government of Argentina] about the possibility of expanding its upstream investments in Neuquen province." (Embassy Cable, "Argentina: American Chamber Describes Investment Challenges, Opportunities to WHA Das McMullen," Oct. 17, 2008. Obtained via http://wikileaks.org/cble/2008/10/08BUENOSAIRES1427.html).

A cable from the U.S. Embassy in Thailand notes that Monsanto finds northern Thailand "an advantageous location for low-cost production of hybrid corn seeds for domestic and export markets....For Monsanto, the big money—and thus potential big investment—hinges on whether the Royal Thai Government (RTG) lifts its moratorium on biotech crop field trials..." (Embassy Cable, Thailand, Sept 24, 2007, http://wikileaks.org/cable/2007/09/07CHIANGMAI155.html.)

A U.S. Embassy cable from Brazil notes that, "Monsanto officials echo many of the complaints of other foreign investors doing business in Brazil..." They want various things changed, such as the country's commitment to protecting intellectual property rights. "Were the Brazilian government to take steps to improve the investment climate...Monsanto would be disposed to pour billions into the country...," the cable notes. (Embassy Cable, Brazil, Nov. 16, 2005, http://wikileaks.org/cable/2005/11/05/BRASILIA3026.html.)

Part IV Introduction

530 According to one source, when you count all the different aspects of environmental activism ranging from land conservation and preservation groups to wildlife management organizations to environmental health groups, there are over 6500 national and some 20,000 local environmental organizations in the United States. Together these organizations have an estimated 20-30 million members. Robert Brulle, "Chapter 21: Politics and the Environment," *Handbook of Politics: State and Society in Global Perspective* (2010). Environmental nonprofits range from tiny ones with very limited resources that are not registered with the federal government to giant organizations like World Wildlife Fund with total assets of over $377 million. National Center for Charitable Statistics, ncccsweb. urban.org, retrieved Feb. 11, 2013.

531 National Center for Charitable Statistics, *The Nonprofit Sector in Brief: Public Charities, Giving and Volunteering* (2011).

Chapter 18

532 Private foundations generally are created by a single individual, family, or corporation. This figure does not include "community foundations," which collect money from many different sources to create a pool of money for grantmaking.

533 Mafruza Kahn, Environmental Grantmakers Association, in an interview with Worldwide Initiatives for Grantmaker Support, Jan. 18, 2013, reposted from May 2012.

534 See for example, Bullard et al, *Toxic Wastes and Race at Twenty 1987-2007* (March 2007); Pollution Watch, *An Examination of Pollution and Poverty in the Great Lakes Basin* (Nov. 2008).

535 Corporations, governments, and consultants are much more careful about how they word things now, but a report prepared by Cerrell Associates in 1984 for the California Waste Management Board provides a glimpse of how this disproportionate reality came to be. Hired to help the Board overcome opposition to the siting of solid waste incinerators, Cerrell Associates offered this eye-opening advice:

> "Certain types of people are likely to participate in politics, either by virtue of their issue awareness or their financial resources, or both. Members of middle or higher-socioeconomic strata (a composite index of level of education, occupational prestige, and income) are more likely to organize into effective groups to express their political interests and views. **All socioeconomic groupings tend to resent the nearby siting**

of major facilities, but the middle and upper-socioeconomic strata possess better resources to affectuate their opposition. Middle
and higher-socioeconomic strata neighborhoods should not fall at
least within the one-mile and five-mile radii of the proposed site."
(Emphasis added.)

536 Michael Barker, "An Interview with Daniel Farber, Foundations and the
Environmental Movement," *Counterpunch*, Sept. 13, 2010. Only two-tenths
of one percent of all foundation grant dollars go to the environmental justice
movement.

537 EJ groups are excluded from foundation funding through a variety of mechanisms. They may not have the resources to apply for grants at all, and foundations fail to proactively seek them out. EJ communities that do apply for
grants face multiple Catch-22s in the criteria generally used to screen applications. To receive grants, organizations usually need to already have money
in hand, fundraising staff and strategies, experience as nonprofits, and access
to money. They need to have staff dominated by "professionals" as opposed
to community members who don't have professional degrees. Asked whether
grants always go to the communities with the greatest need, many funders
openly acknowledge that this is not the case. "We give money to the strongest people and the strongest program—not necessarily the one that is in
the lowest-income area," a nonprofit advice book quotes a funder as saying.
Excluded from funding for decades while wrestling with not only severe environmental problems but also other challenges that come with poverty and
racism, EJ groups are unlikely to appear "strong" to foundation funders. See
Ellen Karsh and Arlen Sue Fox, *The Only Grant-Writing Book You'll Ever Need*
(Third Edition, 2009, p. 214, 217, 247).

538 Michael Barker, "An Interview with Daniel Faber, Foundations and the
Environmental Movement," *Counterpunch*, Sept. 13, 2010, citing Brulle and
Jenkins. See also, Robert Brulle," Chapter 21: Politics and the Environment,"
Handbook of Politics: State and Society in Global Perspective (2010).

539 Michael Barker, "An Interview with Daniel Faber, Foundations and the
Environmental Movement," *Counterpunch*, Sept. 13, 2010.

540 Ellen Karsh and Arlen Sue Fox, *The Only Grant-Writing Book You'll Ever Need*
(Third Edition, 2009, p. 112.)

541 Michael Barker, "An Interview with Daniel Faber, Foundations and the
Environmental Movement," *Counterpunch*, Sept. 13, 2010.

542 Ellen Karsh and Arlen Sue Fox, *The Only Grant-Writing Book You'll Ever Need*
(Third Edition, 2009, p. 44.)

543 Ellen Karsh and Arlen Sue Fox, *The Only Grant-Writing Book You'll Ever Need* (Third Edition, 2009, p. xxix.)

544 Michael Barker, "An Interview with Daniel Faber, Foundations and the Environmental Movement," *Counterpunch*, Sept. 13, 2010.

545 Ellen Karsh and Arlen Sue Fox, *The Only Grant-Writing Book You'll Ever Need* (Third Edition, 2009, p. 259).

546 Ellen Karsh and Arlen Sue Fox, *The Only Grant-Writing Book You'll Ever Need* (Third Edition, 2009, pp 217, 258.)

547 Ellen Karsh and Arlen Sue Fox, *The Only Grant-Writing Book You'll Ever Need* (Third Edition, 2009, p. 259.)

548 In 2012, the Cummings Foundation invited activists to a briefing on the State of the Union address in advance of that address, for example. The foundation also invited activists to participate in a phone call with the Director of the National Economic Council during which we would be briefed and we could pose questions.

549 Bill & Melinda Gates Foundation, 990 tax form for 2010; available on-line via the National Center for Charitable Statistics, www.nccsdataweb.urban; Bill & Melinda Gates Foundation, *Building Better Lives Together 2011 Annual Report*; see also, Claudio Schuftan, "The New Philanthropies in World Health Affairs," *World Public Health Nutrition Association*, www.wphna.org, September 2011, retrieved Feb. 5, 2013.

550 Bill & Melinda Gates Foundation, *Building Better Lives Together 2011 Annual Report*.

551 Bill & Melinda Gates Foundation, 990 tax form for 2010; available online via the National Center for Charitable Statistics, www.nccsdataweb.urban.

552 Bill & Melinda Gates Foundation, *Building Better Lives Together, 2011 Annual Report*.

553 Sign-on letter to the Gates Foundation sponsored by GRA Watch/Community Alliance for Global Justice & La Via Capesina of North American, Dec. 7, 2010.

554 Bill & Melinda Gates Foundation, *Building Better Lives Together, 2011 Annual Report*.

555 See for example, Tom Philpott, "Gates Foundation Throws Its Lot With Agribusiness," *grist.org*, Jan 9, 2010, and Community Alliance for Global Justice, "Gates Foundation Invests in Monsanto," http://www.infowars.com/gates-foundation-invests-in-monsanto/, Aug. 27, 2010.

556 Bill & Melinda Gates Foundation, 990 tax form for 2010; available online via the National Center for Charitable Statistics, www.nccsdataweb.urban; Bill & Melinda Gates Foundation, *Building Better Lives Together 2011 Annual Report*; see also, Claudio Schuftan, "The New Philanthropies in World Health Affairs,"

World Public Health Nutrition Association, www.wphna.org, September 2011, retrieved Feb. 5, 2013.

557 Bill Gates, 2012, "Annual Letter from Bill Gates," at www.gates.foundation.org.

558 Caroline Preston, "Confronting the Gates Foundation's 'Brass Knuckle' Dominance," *The Chronicle of Philanthropy*, Dec. 7, 2011.

559 Activists have long expressed frustration at the power exerted by the Pew Foundation, for example, which has been funding environmental groups since the early 1990s. (See Dru Oja Jay, "Can Pew's Charity be Trusted," *The Dominion*, Nov. 25, 2007.) It has been accused of putting together coalitions of groups who support compromises that give very modest gains to environmentalists in exchange for capitulation on more important matters. As one example of the kind of money Pew can spread around that heavily influences outcomes on environmental issues, the Foundation spent approximately $41 million on Canadian boreal forest programs between 2003 and 2007. "In the 1970s and 1980s a vibrant, truly grassroots public land protection movement emerged," an Oregon old growth forest activist recalls. "During the 1990s Pew, with support from other foundations, moved decisively to control this movement."

Late author and activist Alex Cockburn said that in its initial National Forest Campaign, "Pew demanded that recipients of grant money agree to focus their attention on government actions; corporate wrongdoers were not to be named. This extreme plan was modified after some recipients balked." Another critic of Pew said, "[t]he Pew Charitable Trusts have consistently set up front groups" that act as a drag on overall demands of environmental groups. The approach supported by the foundation is one in which selected environmentalists meet with industry and other stakeholders to work out agreements. In other words, by definition, the groups will not win anything the corporations do not want.

560 Julie Lloyd, "Philanthropy Is a Four-Letter Word: Suggestions for Real CSR," www.triplepundit.com, Oct. 2, 2009, retrieved Feb. 11, 2013.

561 Committee Encouraging Corporate Philanthropy & The Conference Board, *Giving In Numbers* (2012 Edition.)

562 Health, education and community and economic development were the top recipients of aid in 2011. Allocations to environmental organizations comprised 4% of that total.

563 Exxon Mobil Corporation, "2011 Worldwide Contributions and Community Investments: Public Information and Policy Research," www.exxonmobil.com/.

564 Exxon Mobil Corporation, 2011 Worldwide Contributions and Community Investments: Public Information and Policy Research, www.exxonmobil.com/.

565 Christine MacDonald, Green, Inc., *An Environmental Insider Reveals How a Good Cause Has Gone Bad* (The Lyons Press, 2008, p. 25).

566 Alliance of Nonprofits, *Washington State Nonprofit Sector Economic Impact Report 2010.*

567 Johann Hari, "The Wrong Kind of Green," *Common Dreams*, Mar 6, 2010.

568 Louis Sahagun, "Sierra Club Leader Departs Amid Discontent Over Group's Direction," *Los Angeles Times*, Nov. 19, 2011.

569 Brian Walsh, "Exclusive: How the Sierra Club Took Millions From the Natural Gas Industry—and Why They Stopped," *Time*, Feb. 2, 2012; Felicity Barringer, "Answering for Taking a Driller's Cash," *The New York Times*, Feb. 13, 2012; see Sandra Steingraber, "Breaking Up with the Sierra Club," an open letter, March 23, 2012, for a discussion of how the Sierra Club took and hid fracking money and why she no longer supports the Club.

570 "Conservation Groups Debate Their Ties to Gas Drilling," *AP*, Nov. 24, 2012, http://www.dailylocal.com/article/20121123/NEWS/121129839/conservation-groups-debate-their-ties-to-gas-drilling.

571 John Stauber, "Endangered Wildlife Friends Are Here!," *PR Watch*, Third Quarter 2001, Vol. 8, No. 3.

572 See for example: Associated Press, "Shell, Environmentalists Team Up to Save Texas Land," *Dallas News*, Feb. 28, 2012.

573 TNC and Dow announced a "breakthrough collaboration" in 2011, for example, involving a $10 million commitment from Dow to develop tools and demonstrate models for valuing nature in business decisions. By that point, Dow had already given lots of funding to TNC, including $1.5 million in 2008 for rainforest restoration in Brazil. ("Working with Companies. Dow Announces Business Strategy for Conservation," TNC website article, retrieved Feb. 8, 2013. See also GreenBiz Staff, "Dow Commits $10M in Partnership to Put Business Value on Ecosystems," *GreenBiz*, Jan. 24, 2011.)

Dow's corporate giving extends well beyond TNC, of course. Community organizations can apply for local grants in areas where Dow has facilities, for example, and proposals related to "sustainability" are encouraged. (See http://www.dow.com/michigan/contrib/dowgives/communityGrant.htm regarding giving in Michigan, for example. See Dow website pages related to grant program in Texas as another example.) Dow grant recipients include food pantries, bird observatories, fire departments, boy scout troops, summer camps, and suicide support groups ("Texas Nonprofits, Groups to Benefit from Dow grants," *tsnp.org*, July 2009).

574 *Greenwash, Getting Environmentalists on side*, http://www.uow.edu.au/~sharonb/STS218/greenwash/opponents/cooption.html, retrieved Oct. 26, 2012, citing Rauber,

1994, "Beyond Greenwash: An Insider's Guide to Duping the Public," *Sierra*, Vol. 79, No. 4:47-50.

575 "Philanthro Craft, Why Corporate Social Responsibility Is So Important in 2013," *Truist Blog*, Feb. 4, 2013.

576 Brian Walsh, "Exclusive: How the Sierra Club Took Millions From the Natural Gas Industry—and Why They Stopped," *Time*, Feb. 2, 2012.

577 Sierra Club and Beyond Coal, *Clean Energy Under Siege. Following the Money Trail Behind the Attack on Renewable Energy* (August 2012.)

578 Kim Klein, "Chapter One: Philanthropy in America," *Fundraising for Social Change* (5ᵗʰ edition, 2007). More specifically, consistently over time seven out of ten adults in the U.S. and Canada have donated money, with middle- and low-er-income individuals giving between 50 and 80% of overall individual funds. Most people who give money give to at least five different organizations and up to fifteen. About 20% of people on welfare give money.

Chapter 20

579 Sierra Club, News Release, "Sierra Club Endorses Move to Amend," Jan. 27, 2012.

580 Thomas McLaughlin, "Your Nonprofit Business Model: Is it Really Healthy?, Member Update," *Alliance for Nonprofits Washington*, Jan. 2012.

581 As foundations replace multi-year grants with single year grants that means more frequent final reports and proposals for grantees. Some foundations now ask for mid-year reports as well. Ellen Karsh and Arlen Sue Fox, *The Only Grant-Writing Book You'll Ever Need* (Third Edition, 2009).

582 John Mutz and Katherine Murray, *Fundraising for Dummies* (2010).

583 Ellen Karsh and Arlen Sue Fox, *The Only Grant-Writing Book You'll Ever Need* (Third Edition, 2009, p. 278)

584 Brian Rosenthal, "'Green' Strategists Hired by Coal Companies to Push Train Proposals, *Seattle Times*, Feb. 26, 2013.

585 Joel Makower, "Mark Tercek in Conversation With Joel Makower," *GreenBiz.com*, May 13, 2013.

586 John Mutz and Katherine Murray, *Fundraising for Dummies* (2010, p. 112.)

587 John Mutz and Katherine Murray, *Fundraising for Dummies* (2010, p. 129-131.)

588 John Mutz and Katherine Murray, *Fundraising for Dummies* (2010, 138-139.)

589 GuideStar email message, sent on behalf of The Not for Profit Group, April 3, 2012, and www.notforprofitgroupvt.com/pricing, retrieved April 3, 2012.

590 Gary Jones, email, "Wealth Screened Decision Makers Email Database (Blowout Promotion)," April 30, 2012. As another example, Elect Strategies said it could provide mailing addresses and phone numbers for the entire country, email

addresses for a significant segment of the U.S. population, and data related to age, race, religion, education level, and income level, all at a 20% price break. (Stephen Molldrem, email "Data Price-Breaks for the New Year," Jan. 5, 2012.)

591   Previously we discussed foundation pressure on grantees to elect such board members. Advisors to nonprofits exert the same pressure. The book *Fundraising for Dummies*, for example, encourages groups to insist upon a 100% giving board, with each board member being asked to give generously as a model for others; John Mutz and Katherine Murray, *Fundraising for Dummies* (2010, p. 69.) This approach assumes that either the community affected by an environmental issue has lots of money to donate (which is not the case in environmental justice communities) and/or that it is okay to put individuals who are not from affected communities in a position of power over environmental organizations.

592   John Mutz and Katherine Murray, *Fundraising for Dummies* (2010, 20-21.)

593   John Mutz and Katherine Murray, *Fundraising for Dummies* (2010, p. 107.)

594   John Mutz and Katherine Murray, *Fundraising for Dummies* (2010, p. 324-325.)

595   John Mutz and Katherine Murray, *Fundraising for Dummies* (2010, p. 326-327).

596   Ellen Karsh and Sue Arlen Fox, *The Only Grant-Writing Book You'll Ever Need* (Third Edition, 2009, p. 182-183.)

597   Leslie R. Crutchfield and Heather McLeod Grant, *Forces for Good. The Six Practices of High Impact Nonprofit* (2008, p. 75.)

598   Thomas McLaughlin, "Your Nonprofit Business Model: Is it Really Healthy?, Member Update," *Alliance for Nonprofits Washington*, Jan. 2012.

599   Joanne Fritz, "5 Steps to Defining Your Nonprofit's Brand," *nonprofit.about. com*, retrieved July 17, 2013, drawing from Larry Checco, *Branding for Success: A Roadmap for Raising the Visibility and Value of Your Nonprofit Organization* (2005).

600   Leslie R. Crutchfield and Heather McLeod Grant, *Forces for Good. The Six Practices of High Impact Nonprofits* (2008, p. vii).

601   Leslie R. Crutchfield and Heather McLeod Grant, *Forces for Good. The Six Practices of High Impact Nonprofits* (2008, p. 72). We will see "increased cooperation and a blurring of the lines between" nonprofit and for-profit ventures, *Fundraising for Dummies* predicts. John Mutz and Katherine Murray, *Fundraising for Dummies* (2010, p. 345-346.)

Chapter 21

602   Stephanie Clifford, "Unexpected Ally Helps Wal-Mart Cut Waste," *The New York Times*, April 13, 2012. EDF's Executive Director and Walmart's CEO have reportedly hung out together in a cabin discussing environmental issues. EDF opened an office in Bentonville, Arkansas, to have direct access to Walmart headquarters.

603   Stacey Mitchell, "EDF Sells Greencred to Walmart for the Low, Low Price of $66 Million," *grist.org*, Nov. 6, 2013; "EDF Applauds New Walmart Policy That Promises Safer Products for Consumers," EDF News Release, Sept. 12, 2013.

604   Stephanie Clifford, "Unexpected Ally Helps Wal-Mart Cut Waste," *The New York Times*, April 13, 2012.

605   Tara Lohan, "Wal-Mart Accused of consumer fraud," *Alternet*, Jan. 22, 2007.

606   Stephanie Clifford, "Unexpected Ally Helps Wal-Mart Cut Waste," *The New York Times*, April 13, 2012.

607   "Walmart on Bangladesh: We're Open to Improving Worker Safety Conditions," *Huffington Post Business*, May 2, 2013.

608   Stacey Mitchell, "EDF Sells Greencred to Walmart for the Low, Low Price of $66 Million," *grist.org*, Nov. 6, 2013. The Walton foundation ramped up its funding on environmental causes as it launched and developed its sustainability campaign. In 2011 it gave $71 million to environmental organizations, with the biggest grants going to groups that collaborate with Walmart. In addition to EDF, Conservation International, which has a corporate partnership with Walmart, is a big recipient, as is the Marine Stewardship Council. MSC started getting money the same year it agreed to certify and provide an eco-label for some of the seafood Walmart sells. These three organizations received 46% of the foundation's environmental funding in 2011 (Stacey Mitchell, "Walmart Heirs Quietly Fund Walmart's Environmental Allies," *Grist*, May 10, 2012.)

609   As quoted in John Stauber, *Toxic Sludge is Good for You* (1995, p. 76.)

610   Heather Rogers, *Green Gone Wrong. How Our Economy is Undermining the Environmental Revolution* (2010, p. 191.)

611   Gar Lipow, "Emissions Trading: A Mixed Record, With Plenty of Failures," *Grist*, Feb. 20, 2007.

612   Heather Rogers, *Green Gone Wrong. How Our Economy is Undermining the Environmental Revolution* (2010, Chapter 6.)

613   Johann Hari, "The Wrong Kind of Green," *The Nation*, March 6, 2010.

614   Elisabeth Rosenthal and Andrew Lehren, "Profits on Carbon Credits Drive Output of a Harmful Gas," *New York Times*, Aug. 8, 2012.

615   Rosenthal and Lehren, "Profits on Carbon Credits Drive Output of a Harmful Gas."

616   Gar Lipow, "Emissions Trading: A Mixed Record, With Plenty of Failures," *Grist*, Feb. 20, 2007.

617   Lipow, "Emissions Trading: A Mixed Record, With Plenty of Failures."

618   "EJ Matters Fact Sheet, 2009, Factsheet—Debunking the Myths of Cap-and-Trade," www.ejmatters.org; "Debunking the Myths of Cap-and-Trade," citing Jim Downing, "Green Rice on Menu," *Sacramento Bee*, Feb. 17. 2008.

619 Elisabeth Rosenthal and Andrew Lehren, "Profits on Carbon Credits Drive Output of a Harmful Gas," *New York Times*, Aug. 8, 2012.

620 The Sierra Club sent emails to supporters in January of 2013, for example, urging each to "complete five green actions in 2013—anything from bringing a reusable bag to the grocery store to installing rooftop solar panels to taking action against dirty energy companies." The Club offered to keep track of people's goals for them and to remind them periodically throughout the year about those goals (Sarah Hodgdon, Sierra Club, Email, "Thank You Carol," Jan. 1, 2013). As a second example, Northwest Coalition for Alternatives to Pesticides (NCAP) has asked me to pledge to not use pesticides in my home, yard, and garden, and to encourage local businesses to make the same pledge. These actions are identified as "an important step" in an email alert focused on the pollinator die-off problem. The email notes that my pledge will be added to a U.S.-wide pesticide-free places map. As a final example, my former organization, the Washington Toxics Coalition, produces reports and fact sheets evaluating products based on their toxicity and it answer people's questions related to these matters. I've used this great service often myself just as I've used the Seattle Tilth hotline about how to garden organically, as well as the services of other nonprofits helping people understand the environmental impacts of personal choices.

621 Ronnie Cummins, "Open Letter to the Organic Community: The California Ballot Initiative to Label GMOs," *Common Dreams*.org, Aug. 2, 2012.

622 Stephen Cogswell, info@greenbiz.com, email invitation to conference on ecolabels, Dec. 11, 2012.

Take one mother's experience trying to buy an environmentally safe and sustainably produced baby crib mattress as an example of the utter confusion that awaits a consumer striving to buy green. According to a news article, New Yorker Bobbi Chase Wilding found that manufacturers of more than half of about 190 crib mattresses sold in the U.S. make environmental or health claims about those mattresses. These were often backed by at least one official-sounding certification. Thirty-nine of the ones making green claims used potentially dangerous chemicals. Some mattresses claimed to have foam made of soy, but soy was a minor ingredient, and the product still relied on petrochemicals. The Federal Trade Commission has issued new guidelines in response to the "tsunami of environmental marketing" that is going on. But consumers are still basically on their own trying to figure out what is what. (Brian Nearing, "Digging up the dirt on 'greenwashing,'" *Times Union*, Oct. 14, 2012.)

623 Sheltongrp.com, retrieved April 23, 2013.

624 Toby Webb, "The Ethical Consumer at Scale Myth: Why Do We Persist in Believing We Can Buy Our Way Out of Trouble," *Smarter Business Blog*, Jan. 30, 2012.

625 Mark Gunther, "The Elusive Green Consumer," www.marcgunther.com, Feb. 12, 2012.

Writing in 2013, Makower said that his annual sampling of environmental opinion data "doesn't offer much reason for optimism." He quotes an opinion survey group that reported that "[d]espite the belief that the Millennial generation is particularly passionate about environmental issues, there are few, if any, differences in their level of concern about the environment or the importance they place on responsible behavior versus the Boomer generation." Joel Makower, "Two Steps Back: Earth Day and the Polling of America, 2013," *greenbiz.com*, April 22, 2013.

Makower identifies the dismal economy as a top reason for Americans' actions not reflecting environmental concerns as much as he would like. It is interesting to revisit the leaked Citigroup memo discussed earlier in the book. The dismal economic situation for vast numbers of people is why Citigroup advised investors to put their money into corporations providing goods and services for the wealthy few. The "non-rich," as the leaked Citigroup memo labels most people in the world today, just don't have much purchasing power.

Journalist Mark Gunther puts it this way: Twenty years after the book *The Green Consumer* came out, "American homes, cars and bellies have all grown bigger faster than the much-touted LOHAS (Lifestyles of Health and Sustainability) market."

626 I've also received various invitations to trainings on how to pressure corporations. A Greenpeace Social Mobilisation promised to discuss tactics groups can use to hold companies accountable via social media like Facebook, Twitter, and videos, for example.

627 "NewsFlash: P&G taking carcinogens out of Tide," *As You Sow*.

628 "De-Gassing the Soft Drink Biz," *Sierra Club Insider*, May 14, 2013. See also Sierra Club website page on their Future Fleet campaign, retrieved May 15, 2013.

629 "NewsFlash: P&G taking carcinogens out of Tide," *As You Sow*.

630 "Pepsi Pulls Gatorade Ingredient After Online Campaign," *Democracy Now*, Feb. 1, 2013.

631 Joel Schectman, "San Francisco Officials Plan to Block Apple Procurement," *Wall Street Journal CIO Journal*, July 10, 2012.

632 Heidi Welsh and Michael Passoff, "Helping Shareholders Vote Their Values," *proxypreview 2013*, p. 5.

633 "Investors Challenge Natural Gas Companies to Increase Transparency, Reduce Risks to Public Health and the Environment From Fracking Operations," *Investor Environmental Health Network*, News Release, Feb. 8, 2012.

634 A self-congratulatory announcement in April of 2014 from "As You Sow," an organization that files shareholder resolutions, was typical. After half a decade of

effort, their big victory was this: Exxon had agreed to "provide increased transparency about how it manages the environmental and community impacts of its fracking operations. We believe companies that disclose risk and address shareholder concerns openly "will perform better than those that lack transparency" As You Sow said hopefully. That vague hope is meaningless. What we really need is for oil and gas companies to stop extracting oil and gas from the ground, something they clearly don't plan on doing. In fact, the announcement mentions Exxon's recent assessment that a low-carbon future is "highly unlikely."

635 "Historic Shareholder Agreement Reached with McDonald's on Pesticide Use Reduction," *Investor Environmental Health Network*, Press Release, March 31, 2009.

636 Metam sodium use had actually increased from 20,823,000 pounds in 2005 to 33,264,000 in 2010, with 26 percent of potato acres treated with this pesticide in 2010 as compared to 16 percent in 2005. The volumes and percent of use in my own state of Washington remained at 9.7 million pounds applied in 2010 on 46 percent of the potato acres as compared to 10.8 million pounds applied in 2005 on 45% of the potato acres.

637 Sachie Hopkins-Hayakawa, Sally Bunner, and Lauren Ressler, "Students for Climate Justice: We're Not a Single-Issue Movement," *YES! Magazine*, March 7, 2013, as reprinted on *Common Dreams.org*.

638 Sachie Hopkins-Hayakawa, "Students to Colleges: Take Our Money Out of Dirty Energy," *YES! Magazine*, Jan. 31, 2013, as reprinted by *Common Dreams. org*; Sachie Hopkins-Hayakawa, Sally Bunner, and Lauren Ressler, "Students for Climate Justice: We're Not a Single-Issue Movement," *YES! Magazine*, March 7, 2013, as reprinted on *Common Dreams.org*.

639 Chuck Collins, "11 Reasons to Divest from the Fossil Fuel Industry," *Common Dreams.org*, July 23, 2013, citing Wen Stephenson, "The New Abolitionists," *The Boston Phoenix*, Mar. 12, 2013.

640 Sachie Hopkins-Hayakawa, Sally Bunner, and Lauren Ressler, "Students for Climate Justice: We're Not a Single-Issue Movement," *YES! Magazine*, March 7, 2013, as reprinted on *Common Dreams.org*.

641 Sierra Club, "A Major Fracking Victory," *Sierra Club Insider*, April 16, 2013.

642 There were demonstrations around the country at the same time as the protest on the mall, including one in Seattle that I attended.

643 James Gerken, "'Forward on Climate' Rally Brings Climate Change Activists to National Mall in Washington, D.C.," *The Huffington Post*, Feb. 17, 2013.

644 Jeffrey St. Clair, "The Mirage of an Opposition. Designer Protests and Vanity Arrests in DC," *Counterpunch*, April 12-14, 2013; "Activist Malpractice: the Celebrity

Catch-and-Release Movement," *Wrong Kind of Green blog*, Feb. 16, 2013; Michael Donnelly "Tweeting as the World Burns," *Counterpunch*, Feb. 15-17, 2013.

Chapter 22

645 The Citizens Trade Campaign that *opposed* NAFTA included about 300 national and grassroots organizations. By some estimates this represented almost three times as many people as the Environmental Coalition *for* NAFTA. But Clinton was able to point to the latter coalition, claiming that environmentalists were for NAFTA. "Katie McGintie, director of Clinton's Council for Environmental Quality, noted that "the leading environmental groups in the United States... joined the president in support of NAFTA." Loma Salzman and Bernardo Issel, "Natural Resources Defense Council: Eco-logic or Eco-sell-out?" http://www.lornasalzman.com/collectedwritings/nrdc.html, 2002.

646 Peter Montague. "Big-Picture Organizing, Part 5: A 'Movement' in Disarray," *Rachel's Environment & Health Weekly #425*, Jan. 19, 1995.

647 Montague, "Big-Picture Organizing, Part 5: A 'Movement' in Disarray."

648 EDF, for example, has been pushing for more disclosure of chemicals used in fracking, regulations to improve fracking safety, and the like. A senior EDF policy adviser was featured in a *Wall Street Journal* article claiming that ground water pollution incidents had been caused by well construction problems, not by the process of fracking itself. (Russell Gold, "Faulty Wells, Not Fracking, Blamed for Water Pollution," *Wall Street Journal*, March 12, 2012 and updated March 25, 2012.) EDF says it supports renewable energy and does not see natural gas as a real solution, but the work it is doing will be used to claim that fracking should continue and expand. You can't simultaneously prepare for fracking and prevent it. News articles have noted that "[e]nvironmentalists and the energy industry appear to be edging towards a consensus that would permit a big expansion in hydraulic fracturing for oil and gas in exchange for stricter rules on engineering procedures such as well casing and cementing." (John Kemp, "Fracking Safely and Responsibly," *Reuters*, March 13, 2012.)

Similarly, the Natural Resources Defense Council writes compellingly about the threat posed by fracking, noting for example, that millions of acres of land in the U.S.—more acreage than California and Florida combined—are already leased to oil and gas companies, with 85 to 90% of oil and gas development reportedly done by fracking. But what are NRDC's solutions? Maximize renewable energy development. Tighten existing rules and issue new ones. Make some of the "most sensitive lands" off limits for fracking. And give local communities authority to restrict fracking. While the last suggested solution and the most-sensitive land exclusion hint at actual prohibitions, overall NRDC's position allows fracking to continue, putting faith in regulations despite the inherent limitations of those regulations and the likelihood of inadequate implementation and enforcement. (Amy Mall, "NRDC Fact Sheet, Spreading Like Wildfire: Oil and Gas Leases Mean That Fracking Could Occur on Tens of Millions of Acres of U.S. Land," Feb. 2013.)

649   "President Obama to Nominate Gina McCarthy as EPA Administrator; Ernest Moniz as Energy Secretary," *Natural Resource Defense Council*, News Release, March 4, 2013. Moniz also supports nuclear energy.

650   In 2009, over 150 environmental justice and social justice organizations and individuals issued a news release denouncing "corporate environmentalism and their proposal to establish a national carbon trading scheme." The letter named EDF, NRDC, The Nature Conservancy, and others as undercutting environmental justice and solutions to global warming. ("Environmental Groups Blast Corporate Environmentalism and Their Proposal to Establish a National Carbon Trading Scheme," *Physicians for Social Responsibility—Los Angeles*, News Release, Jan. 15, 2009.)

651   Colin Sullivan, "EDF Chief: 'Shrillness' of Greens Contributed to Climate Bill's Failure in Washington," the *New York Times*, April 5, 2011.

652   Center for Media and Democracy, SourceWatch, Global Climate Coalition, http://www.sourcewatch.org/index.php/Global_Climate_Coalition.

653   Duchin's presentation as quoted in Environmental Research Foundation, Rachel's Hazardous Waste News #361, Oct. 28, 1993. The speech was delivered to the National Cattleman's Association.

654   David McCumber, "Questions Raised on Authorship of Chemicals Bill," *San Francisco Gate*, sfgate.com, Mar. 16, 2015; Jenna McLaughlin, "His Chemical Romance: Tom Udall Teams Up With the Chemical Industry, With Explosive Results," *Mother Jones*, Mar. 23, 2015.

655   Fred Krupp, Environmental Defense Fund, "Sen. Udall Is a True Champion for Environment," *abqjournal*, Mar. 23, 2015.

656   Richard Denison, EDF, "Reality Check on TSCA Reform Legislation," June 5, 2013; Richard Denison, EDF, "A Pivotal Moment for TSCA reform," July 24, 2012.

657   Center for Progressive Reform, *Behind Closed Doors at the White House, How Politics Trumps Protection of Public Health, Worker Safety and the Environment* (Nov. 2011).

658   Union of Concerned Scientists, *A Climate of Corporate Control* (May 2012).

Chapter 23

659 Elizabeth Keating, "WA Climate Action Bill Passes State Legislature," Cascade Sierra Club article, 2013.

660 Lisa Remlinger, Environmental Priorities Coalition, May 3, 2013 announcement.

661 Aaron Ostrom, Fuse Washington, email solicitation, Dec. 28, 2012.

662 Hodgdon, Sierra Club, Email message, "Thank you Carol," Jan. 1, 2013; Sierra Club 2012 Success Video.

663 John Mutz and Katherine Murray, *Fundraising for Dummies* (2010, p. 16-17.)

664 David Doniger, "The Copenhagen Accord: A Big Step Forward," *Huffington Post*, Dec. 23, 2009

665 Johann Hari, "The Wrong Kind of Green," *The Nation*, March 6, 2010.

Chapter 24

666 I refer to "Demophilia" with a capital D rather than demophilia with a small d, as the latter means "a love of crowds or people."

667 CropLife America represents companies that develop, manufacture, formulate, and distribute pesticides in the United States. It has more than 60 members including Dow, Syngenta, Monsanto, Bayer, and DuPont.

668 Moniz was on British Petroleum's Technology Advisory Council between 2005 and 2011, receiving a stipend for that work. BP provided $50 million in funding to Moniz's MIT Energy Initiative. From 2002 to 2004, Moniz sat on the strategic advisory council of USEC, a company that provides enriched uranium to nuclear power plants, for which he was paid. USEC has been seeking a $2 billion loan guarantee from the Energy Department.

Moniz was also on the board of directors of the Electric Power Research Institute, which does research for industry, and which paid Moniz $8000 between 2009 and 2011. He is a trustee of the King Abdullah Petroleum Studies and Research Center, a Saudi Aramco-backed organization (Justin Elliott, "Drilling Deeper: The Wealth of Business Connections for Obama's Energy Pick," *Propublica*, Mar. 20, 2013).

At this writing, Moniz is on the board of ICF International a company that receives consulting contracts from the Energy Department. As a board member, Moniz received $158,000 in cash and stock in 2011, according to the company's annual report. He is also on the strategic advisory council of NGP Energy Technology Partners, a firm that invests in fossil fuel and alternative energy companies.

669 Organic Consumers Association, "Six Reasons Why Obama Appointing Monsanto's Buddy, Former Iowa Governor Vilsack, for USDA Head Would Be a Terrible Idea," Nov. 12, 2008; as USDA Secretary, Vilsack has aggressively advanced the agenda of the biotech industry, deregulating genetically modified alfalfa and sugar beet seed in 2011, for example. (Ari LeVaux, "Monsanto Wins, for Now," *High Country News*, Feb. 16, 2011.) At this writing, Obama's USDA under Vilsack is moving to greatly weaken organic standards, prompting outrage among supporters of organic agriculture. According to Food Democracy Now, USDA is engaged in "one of the biggest assaults on the integrity of organic foods ever conceived, with high-level Obama political appointees working behind the scenes with giant corporate organics to gut 20 years of precedent in the congressionally-mandated National Organic Standards Board, a citizen oversight board." Food Democracy Now, email letter to supporters, May 1, 2014.

670 John M. Broder, "Environmentalists Wary of Obama's Interior Pick," *The New York Times*, Dec. 18, 2008. At a press conference in December of 2008 after Obama had announced his decision to nominate him, Salazar emphasized his support for continued domestic development of coal, oil, and natural gas, which contribute to global warming. The executive director of the Independent Petroleum Association of Mountain States issued a statement praising Salazar's desire to make use of all domestic energy sources, including those found on and under public lands. Environmentalists spoke out against Salazar, to no avail. "Salazar has a disturbingly weak conservation record, particularly on energy development, global warming, endangered wildlife and protecting scientific integrity," said the director of Public Employees for Environmental Responsibility. "It's no surprise oil and gas, mining, agribusiness and other polluting industries that have dominated Interior are supporting rancher Salazar—he's their friend."

671 Isabella Kenfield, "The Return of Michael Taylor, Monsanto's Man in the Obama Administration," Counterpunch, August 14-16, 2009; Frederick Ravid, Letter to Obama objecting to appointment of Taylor which was circulated as a petition for sign-ons via a MoveOn.org Feb. 6, 2012 email to MoveOn's list.

672 "Choices for Cass Sunstein," *ProgressiveReform.org*, 2013. Sunstein had suggested that it "might be better" to help future generations deal with global warming by doing things "that make posterity richer and better able to adapt" as opposed to reducing greenhouse gas emissions. As co-chair of the American Enterprise Institute Center for Regulatory and Market Studies advisory board, he had worked for one of the country's most influential anti-regulatory think tanks. See Frank O'Donnell, President of Clean Air Watch, "How Anti-Regulation is Obama's New Regulatory Czar?," *ThinkProgress.org*, Jan. 10, 2009; Frank

O'Donnell, President of Clean Air Watch, "Cass Sunstein's Appalling Anti-Regulatory Reign," *ThinkProgress.org*, Dec. 2, 2011.

673 Darren Samuelshohn, "Energy Sector Donations Fuel Obama Campaign," Politico, May 14, 2012.

674 Barack Obama, Remarks by the President on Energy, March 22, 2012, delivered in Maljamar, New Mexico, and in Cushing, Oklahoma.

675 Abrahm Lustgarten, *Run to Failure. BP and the Making of the Deepwater Horizon Disaster* (2012).

676 Stanley Reed, "Ban Lifted, BP Bids $42 Million to Win Gulf Oil Leases in U.S. Auction," *New York Times*, March 19, 2014.

677 Barack Obama, Remarks by the President on Energy, March 22, 2012, delivered in Maljamar, New Mexico.

678 Donations came from a mix of employees and BP's political action committees, with $2.89 million flowing to campaigns from the BP-related PACs and about $638,000 from individuals. During his time in the U.S. Senate and while running for president, Obama received over $77,000 from the oil giant and was the top recipient of BP PAC and individual money over those 20 years (Erika Lovley, "Obama Biggest Recipient of BP Cash," *Politico*, May 5, 2010).

679 Abrahm Lustgarten, *Run to Failure. BP and the Making of the Deepwater Horizon Disaster* (2012).

680 Sean Cockerham, "Feds Favor Use of Air-Gun Blasts to Track Oil, Gas in Atlantic," *The Seattle Times*, Feb. 27, 2014.

681 Sarah Lazare, "Cries of Betrayal, Calls to Organize as Obama Approves Arctic Drilling," *Common Dream*, July 22, 2015.

682 John Broder and Clifford Krauss, "New and Frozen Frontier Awaits Offshore Oil Drilling," *The New York Times*, May 23, 2012; Nafeez Ahmed, "Obama's Arctic Strategy Sets Off a Climate Time Bomb," *The Guardian*, May 17, 2013; Abrahm Lustgarten, *Run to Failure. BP and the Making of the Deepwater Horizon* Disaster (2012).

683 Brad Plumer, "As Fracking Booms, the EPA Leads Cautiously," *washingtonpost. com*, April 18, 2012.

684 Fiona Harvey, "Natural gas is no climate change 'panacea', warns IEA. Reliance on gas would lead the world to a 3.5C temperature rise, and out-of-control global warming, says new research," *The Guardian*, June 6, 2011; MCARICAR. "Switching From Coal to Natural Gas Would Do Little for Global Climate, Study Indicates," *Atmos*, Sept. 8, 2011; Joe Romm, "Natural Gas Bombshell: Switching from Coal to Gas *Increases* Warming for Decades, Has Minimal Benefit Even in 2100," *ClimateProgress*, Sept. 9. 2011.

685 Neela Banerjee, "EPA Drastically Underestimates Methane Released at Drilling Sites," *Los Angeles Times*, April 14, 2014.

686 The rule was a long time in the making. It was about to be issued in April of 2013, for example, but was held back due to industry concerns. John Broder, "E.P.A. Will Delay Rule Limiting Carbon Emissions at New Power Plants," *New York Times*, April 12, 2013; Joshua Frank, "Obama's Environmental 'Victory' Was a Huge Win for Frackers," *Counterpunch*, Nov. 16-18, 2012.

687 In 2005 1.13 billon tons of coal was mined in the U.S. with 49.9 million tons of that exported. In 2012, the figures were 1.01 billion tons and 125.7 million tons, respectively. As discussed earlier in the book, the coal industry is seeking permits to build coal export stations. Source: National Mining Association. Most Requested Statistics U.S. Coal Industry, www.nma.org/pdf/c_most_requested.pdf.

688 Jack Tuholske and Rachel Stevens, "Powder River Basin's Abundance of Coal at the Epicenter of Energy Development," *Vermont Law Top 10 Environmental Watch List 2014.*

689 Michael Brune, "Obama Oversees Big Coal Giveaway," *ecopolitology.org*, March. 25, 2011.

690 Hannah Levintova, "The Little Office Behind Obama's Big Enviro Flops," *Mother Jones.com*, Dec. 1, 2011; Rena Steinzor, and Michael Patoka, "Mounting Coal Ash Spills Will Be OIRA's Legacy," *Center for Progressive Reform*, Feb. 19, 2014; Rena Steinzor, "North Carolina's Coal Ash Spills: A Glimpse of the Future under OIRA's Weak Option," *Center for Progressive Reform*, Feb. 20, 2014; Katie Greenhaw, "Coal Ash Waste Standards Inch Forward, But Industry Opposition," *Center for Effective Government*, Nov. 19, 2013; "Duke Energy Urged to Move Coal Ash Away from Water Sources After North Carolina Spill," *Democracy Now*, Feb. 11, 2014.

   In the absence of tougher regulations, another huge coal ash spill occurred in February of 2014. Duke Energy spilled tens of thousands of tons of coal ash and millions of gallons of polluted water into a North Carolina river. Duke Energy, as discussed earlier, was a sponsor of the Democratic Party's nominating convention in North Carolina in 2012. The official host committee for the Convention was co-chaired by Duke Energy's CEO.

691 Juliet Eilperin and Steven Mufson, "Obama Rejects Keystone XL project, Citing U.S. Climate Leadership," *The Washington Post*, Nov. 6, 2015. "America's now a global leader when it comes to taking serious action to fight climate change," Obama asserted.

692 Ibid.

693   "Utah's Carbon Bomb," State Plots Massive Tar Sands & Oil Shale Projects Despite Climate Concerns," *Democracy Now*, Mar. 14, 2014.

694   "TTIP Can Be Forged by End of 2015, Greatest Benefit in Energy, Merkel Says," *Bloomberg BNA*, May 6, 2014.

695   Damian Carrington, "Tar Sands Exploitation Would Mean Game Over for Climate, Warns Leading Scientist," *The Guardian*, May 19, 2013.

696   See for example, the *U.S. News* article "State of the Union: Has Obama Kept His Promises on Energy and the Environment?" Jan. 27, 2014, and the slippery definitions discussed in the paper's analysis. See also Daphne Wysham, "Inside Obama's Energy and Environment Budget," *Counterpunch*, Feb. 17-19, 2012.

697   As another example, $6.1 billion in proposed loans for rural electric cooperatives and utilities for "renewable" energy development lumped "advanced biofuels" in with "renewable energy." But increasing these fuels is not carbon neutral. Moreover, using land for fuel pulls it away from food production, contributing to higher food prices and creating major problems for the poor.

698   Sierra Club, *Clean Energy Under Siege. Following the Money Trail Behind the Attack on Renewable Energy* (August 2012).

699   Ehren Goossens, "Clean Energy Support Falls Again to $254 Billion in 2013," *Bloomberg News*, Jan. 15, 2014.

700   "Shale Boom Reduces Producers' Profits, Kills Alternative Energy Projects," *Bloomberg/Greenwire*, Jan. 18, 2012.

701   Fiona Harvey, "Natural Gas Is No Climate Change 'Panacea', Warns IEA," *The Guardian*, June 6, 2014.

702   Remarks by the president on American-Made Energy, March 22, 2012, Cushing, Oklahoma.

703   Mark Z. Jacobson and Mark A. Delucchi, "Providing All Global Energy With Wind, Water and Solar Power, PART I: Technologies, Energy Resources, Quantities and Areas of Infrastructure, and Materials," *Energy Policy* 39 (2011) 1154-1169; Mark A. Delucchi and Mark Z. Jacobson, "Providing All Global Energy With Wind, Water and Solar Power, Part II: Reliability, System and Transmission Costs, and Policies," *Energy Policy* 39 (2011) 1170-1190.

704   Robert Krupp, "Climate Change Outpacing Green Investment, Report Shows," *Greenbiz.com*, Feb. 13, 2013.

705   Joel Makower and the editors of GreenBiz.com, *State of Green Business 2012* (Jan. 2012).

706   Vera Pardee, "New Mileage Standards Out of Step With Worsening Climate Crisis," *Center for Biological Diversity*, News Release, Aug. 28, 2012.

707 Jessica Goad, "Carbon Catastrophe: Obama Administration To Sell 316 Million Tons of Coal," *ClimateProgress*, Aug. 21, 2013. At this writing, successful bids had not yet been received, but with time, they likely will be. My point is that the Obama Administration is working hard to facilitate global warming pollution from fossil fuels. The impacts of these fossil-fuel-promoting actions dwarf token subsidies and encouragement for renewables.

708 350.org and many other organizations, Letter to Interior Secretary Sally Jewell, April 15, 2013.

709 See for example Chris Busby, "Fukushima Fallout Damaged the Thyroids of California Babies," *Counterpunch*, Nov. 19, 2013.

710 Elliott Negin, Union of Concerned Scientists, "The Unclear Nuclear Revival," *Huffington Post*, Feb. 17, 2012; Mariah Blake, "The Bailout Goes Nuclear," *Mother Jones*, Dec. 10, 2009.

711 Sources for this section include EPA's Carbon Pollution Standards and Clean Power Plan Proposed Rule documents released June 2, 2014, including Clean Power Plan Proposed Rule Federal Register Notice and EPA Fact Sheets: Overview of the Clean Power Plan—Cutting Carbon Pollution from Power Plants; Flexible Approach to Cutting Carbon Pollution; National Framework for States; Setting State Goals to Cut Carbon Pollution; and The Role of States—States Decide How They Will Cut Carbon Pollution. Sources also include: Coral Davenport and Peter Baker, "Taking Page from Health Care Act, Obama Climate Plan Relies on States," *International New York Times*, June 2, 2014.

712 Ben Spencer, "The World Must Shift to Solar and Wind Power Rapidly to Avoid Catastrophic Global Warming, Say UN scientists in Major Report," *MailOnline*, April 12, 2014.

713 Mark Schwartz, "Stanford Scientist Unveils 50-State Plan to Transform U.S. to Renewable Energy," Feb. 26, 2014.

714 U.S. EPA, Clean Power Plan Proposed Rule, June 2, 2014, pp 152, 214-219, 284-285; "EPA's Proposed Carbon Rules Provide Subsidies to Uneconomic, Aging, Dangerous Nuclear Reactors," *GreenWorld*, June 2, 2014.

715 New York Governor Cuomo has banned fracking, for example. This welcome step was forced by activists' hard work. Meanwhile, however, the state Energy Planning Board, composed primarily of Democratic Governor Cuomo's appointees, has produced a draft state energy plan that relies heavily on coal, oil, gas, and nuclear power, including new natural gas pipelines and infrastructure and increased reliance on natural gas. There are some good recommendations in the plan, but these lack detail and measurable goals. Even though Stanford scientists laid out a pathway that swiftly moves New York to a fossil-fuel-free

and nuclear-free future, the state's draft plan is the same old same old. Howie Hawkins and Steve Breyman, "What's Wrong With Cuomo's Energy Plan?," *Counterpunch*, June 2, 2014.

716 Darren Samuelson and Darren Goode, "Sierra Club, Big Green Groups to Endorse Obama," *Politico* April 17, 2012.

717 Sierra Club, LCV, Clean Water Action, Environment America, News Release: "National Environmental Groups Endorse President Obama," April 18, 2012.

718 Sierra Club, Sierra Club Insider email, Sept. 4, 2012. See also Mary Anne Hitt, Sierra Club, "Why the Sierra Club is Endorsing President Obama," *Huffington Post*, April 18, 2012.

719 Michael Marx, Sierra Club, "Great News" email to supporters, Aug 28, 2012.

720 David Foster, Executive Director Blue-Green Alliance, Testimony on Greenhouse Gas Emissions and Corporate Average Fuel Economy Standards at a joint EPA-NHTSA hearing in Detroit, Jan. 17, 2012.

721 Mary Anne Hitt, Sierra Club, "Why the Sierra Club Is Endorsing President Obama," *Huffington Post*, April 18, 2012.

722 Michael Brune, Sierra Club, email to supporters, "Go Time, Carol!" Oct. 28, 2012; and Cathy Duvall, Sierra Club, email message to supporters, "Two Visions," Nov. 6, 2012 (election day.)

723 Michael Brune, Sierra Club, email message, "What This Means," Nov. 7, 2012; Hodgdon, Sierra Club, broadcast email, "Time to Lead on Climate," Nov. 15, 2012.

724 Jeremy Jacobs, "Enviros Claim Election Results Boost Green Issues," *E& E*, Nov. 7, 2012.

725 Miles Grant, "Inauguration Renews Hope for Secure Climate Future," *National Wildlife Federation blog*, Jan. 21, 2013.

726 Amy Harder et al, "EPA to Seek 30% Cut in Emissions at Power Plants," *Wall Street Journal*, June 1, 2014.

727 Anna Galland, MoveOn.org, "Should We Do This?" Email to members, June 5, 2014.

728 Ben Adler, "The Politics of Climate, Energy, and Cities," *grist.org*, June 5, 2014.

729 The *New York Times* reported that the plan was "[l]argely welcomed by environmentalists" while it "generated a torrent of criticism from industry, coal-state lawmakers from both parties, and Republican leaders, Coral Davenport and Peter Baker, "Taking Page From Health Care Act, Obama Plan Relies on States," *New York Times*, June 2, 2014.

730 Hannah Levintova, "The Little Office Behind Obama's Big Enviro Flops," *Mother Jones*, Dec. 1, 2011; links to Tim McDonnell, "Clogged! Obama Delays Keystone XL Pipeline," Nov. 20, 2011.

731   This missive from the Sierra Club is one of many from not only the Club but also other groups expressing outrage at the developments on the fossil-fuel front, without ever pointing a finger at Obama. This is the year that Obama will stand for the Arctic if he hears from me, I am told, for instance, as if Obama were not leading the charge against the Arctic! See for example: Sierra Club, email to supporters, July 5, 2012; Sierra Club, email to supporters, "Drilling in the Polar Bear Seas?" July 29, 2012; Michael Brune, Sierra Club, broadcast email, "Not If, But When," April 14, 2013; Alaska Wilderness League, Funding appeal, April 2012.

732   Jim Hightower solicitation letter 2012.

733   Frank O'Donnell, "How Anti-Regulation Is Obama's New Regulatory Czar?" *ThinkProgress*, Jan. 10, 2009.

734   Michael Brune, Sierra Club, "Congress' Gift to Big Oil for Earth Day," April 8, 2013.

735   Elana Schor, "Campaign 2012: Enviro's Public Health Pivot Hitting Red States Too," *E&E*, Feb. 1, 2011.

736   Here's another example of this Demophilial behavior. MoveOn.org sent an alert in June of 2015 warning that "House Republicans" were pushing Fast Track approval for the latest trade agreement that is, like its predecessors, a massive corporate power grab. MoveOn studiously avoided mentioning the fact that the agreement itself is the handiwork of President Barack Obama, whom they endorsed and campaigned for. Nor do they mention that it is Obama who is twisting arms to secure fast track approval. (MoveOn.org message to supporters: "Last Day to Stop a Very Bad Thing," June 11, 2015.)

737   Suzanne Goldenberg, "Revealed: The Day Obama Chose a Strategy of Silence on Climate Change," *The Guardian*, Nov. 1, 2012.

738   Goldenberg, "Revealed: The Day Obama Chose a Strategy of Silence on Climate Change."

739   Patrick Rucker, "Obama Gives Unexpected Nod to Climate as Second Term Priority," *Reuters*.com, Jan. 21, 2013.

740   Fred Krupp, Environmental Defense Fund, "The President Takes the Lead on Climate Change," EDF Voices, June 25, 2013.

741   "2 Million Submit Objections as Keystone Comment Period Closes," *Democracy Now*, March 10, 2014.

742   Bill Moyers interview with McKibben, Feb. 7, 2014, "Bill McKibben to Obama: Say No to Big Oil."

743   "XL Dissent: 398 Youth Arrested at Anti-Keystone XL Pipeline Protest at White House," *Democracy Now*, March 3, 2014.

744 Richard Matthews, "Keystone XL Protest Ends in Washington," *GreenConduct. com*, September 5, 2011.

745 Obama's supposed "legacy" and the need to protect it are common themes in environmental organizations' statements. Decrying Obama's approval of Arctic oil drilling, Friends of the Earth climate campaigner Marissa Knodel declared that he was "threatening both the resilience of the American arctic Ocean and his climate legacy." This statement bizarrely implied that Obama's record was one of fighting fossil fuels when he has aggressively promoted them. (Sarah Lazare, "Cries of Betrayal, Calls to Organize as Obama Approves Arctic Drilling," *Common Dreams*, July 22, 2015.)

746 "'We Need to End the Fossil Fuel Age': Music Legend Neil Young Protests Keystone XL Oil Pipeline," *Democracy Now,*, April 28, 2014. In a speech in Washington D.C., Neil Young urged Obama to reject the pipeline: "This is your defining moment in the history of the world. Make your statement. ...Why not stand up and put America on the right side of history?" he said.

747 Bill McKibben, "Obama and Climate Change: The Real Story," *Rolling Stone*, Dec. 17, 2013.

748 Frank O'Donnell, "How Anti-Regulation is Obama's New Regulatory Czar?," *ThinkProgress*, Jan. 10, 2009.

Chapter 25

749 Kay Lehman Schlozman, "Response: The Role of Interest Groups," *Boston Review*, July/August 2012; see also, Schlozman et al, *The Unheavenly Chorus. Unequal Political Voice and the Broken Promise of American Democracy* (2012).

750 There have been at least eight polls showing support at 60% or higher. (Andy Coates, M.D., "Two-thirds of Americans support Medicare-for-all," Physicians for a National Health Plan, Single Payer FAQ, Dec. 9, 2009, www.pnhp.org, retrieved June 18, 2014.) Polls also make it clear that the more information people have about single payer, the more they like it. A strong majority of doctors also support single payer.

751 The U.S. spends more than twice as much per person on health care than other industrialized countries. Private insurance corporations eat 31 cents out of every health care dollar on non-medical costs. Physicians for a National Health Plan, Single-Payer National Health Insurance, www.pnhp.org.

752 Christopher Murray, MD et al, "Ranking 37th—Measuring the Performance of the U.S. Health Care System," *New England Journal of Medicine* 2010, 362-98-99, Jan. 14, 2010; Committee on Population at the National Research Council, The National Academies, *U.S. Health on International Perspective: Shorter Lives,*

Poorer Health, Report Brief (Jan. 2013). A longstanding pattern of poorer health has been "strikingly consistent and pervasive over the life course—at birth, during childhood and adolescence, for young and middle-aged adults, and for older adults," according to the National Research Council. In 2006, the United States was number 1 in the world in terms of spending on health care per capita, but it was number 39 for infant mortality, 43 for adult female mortality, 42 for adult male mortality, and 36 for life expectancy.

753 Sabrina Tavernise and Robert Gebeloff, "Millions of Poor Are Left Uncovered by Health Law," *The New York Times*, Oct. 2, 2013. These states are home to about half of the country's population; about 68% of poor, uninsured blacks and single mothers; and about 60% of the U.S.'s uninsured working poor. An estimated 4.8 million people in those 26 states are too poor to qualify for subsidies but will not be eligible for Medicaid.

754 Congressional Budget Office, Joint Committee on Taxation, "Estimates for the Insurance Coverage Provisions of the Affordable Care Act Updated for the Recent Supreme Court Decision," July 2012.

755 Paul Craig Roberts, "Obamacare: A Deception," *Counterpunch*, Feb. 5, 2013.

756 In Washington State, for example, in 2014, a 56-year-old woman earning $21,000 (pre-tax) could pay $113.75 per month ($1365 per year) on premiums for a "silver" plan after receiving a subsidy of $333.02 per month. The more affordable "bronze" plan was only $6.08 per month ($72.96 per year) but had a deductible of $6000 and an out-of-pocket maximum of $6350. If the 56-year-old earned $30,000 a year she could pay $171.54 per month ($2058 per year) for the cheapest silver plan with a deductible of $1750, or $59.06 per month ($708 per year) for the cheapest bronze plan with a $6000 deductible.

Meanwhile, in Arizona a 30-year-old earning $30,000 per year—the average salary of a pre-school teacher—could pay $2772 per year on premiums for a median-priced higher quality plan with a $5000 deductible in 2014. In Illinois, this same 30-year-old would need to spend $4092 for the same plan.

According to the Kaiser Commission on Medicaid, the national average premium was $270 per month for a silver plan and $224 for a bronze plan for a 40-year-old buying insurance through the ObamaCare "Marketplace" as of early 2014.

How are people supposed to afford high premiums and/or high deductibles and co-insurance? In Seattle, average rent alone is $1284 per month, which adds up to $15,408 per year. What should people give up to fork over money to insurance companies and/or to deal with big medical bills? Saving for retirement or college? Making payments on debts? Food?

See also, Lisa Stiffler, "Affordable Care Act Premiums Out of Reach for Many in State," *Seattle Times*, Feb.13, 2015.

757 ObamaCare places caps on out-of-pocket maximums in insurance policies, but those caps are typically quite high. Even for folks well above the Federal Poverty Line, $6350 for an individual and over $12,000 for a family can spell disaster. For people closer to the poverty line, lower caps remain daunting. Caps don't apply to premiums and care provided by out-of-network providers. Moreover, when people are sick or injured they may lose income because they can't work and they have extra costs like those associated with traveling to treatment centers.

758 Ricardo Alonso-Zaldivar and Jennifer Agiesta, "Poll: Many Insured Struggle With Medical Bills," *Seattle Times*, Oct. 13, 2014; Lisa Stiffler, "Skipped Care a Side Effect of High-Deductible Health Plans," *Seattle Times*, Dec. 27, 2014.

759 Morgan Blake via Change.org, "My Brother Isn't 'Sick Enough'?" Sent September 25, 2012.

760 Murray Waas, "WellPoint Routinely Targets Breast Cancer Patients," *Reuters. com*, April 23, 2010. WellPoint has not been alone in its "rescission" activities, i.e., kicking needy people off their plans. Assurant Health reportedly similarly targeted HIV-positive policyholders for rescission, a problem that also became public because of Reuters investigations.

761 Del Beccaro explained that "[t]he narrow networks are threatening the access to care at both Seattle Children's and Mary Bridge [in Tacoma]." According to Del Beccaro, Children's Hospital has spent an inordinate amount of time appealing on behalf of children whose insurers have denied coverage for care at Children's. Similarly, as of late April 2014, 114 cancer patients had told the Seattle Cancer Care Alliance that its center was now out-of-network for their insurers. (Carol Ostrom, "Insurers, Hospitals Complain to Kreidler About New Rule," *The Seattle Times*, April 22, 2014.)

762 Tara Siegel Bernard, "Out of Network, Not by Choice, and Facing Huge Health Bills," *The New York Times*, Oct. 18, 2013.

763 In Massachusetts, the percentage of personal bankruptcies linked to medical bills or illness changed little, and the absolute number actually increased after RomneyCare was implemented. (RomneyCare is the model for ObamaCare.) A comparison of RomneyCare plans and ObamaCare plans during the brief time they were concurrently searchable online found that ObamaCare plans tend to have higher out-of-pocket risks than RomneyCare plans (Himmelstein et al, "Medical Bankruptcy in Massachusetts Has Health Reform Made a Difference?," *The American Journal of Medicine* (2011)124,

224-228, Himmelstein et al, News Release, "Massachusetts Reform Hasn't Stopped Medical Bankruptcies: Harvard Study," March 8, 2011.) See also: KS LaVida, "Romneycare and NoCare Give Way to Obamacare; How Do They Compare?," *Dailykos.com*, Oct. 1, 2013.

Medical debt has been the biggest cause of bankruptcies in the United States for a while, and the ranks of those filing for bankruptcies have included vast numbers of people who have insurance. There is every reason to expect that medical bills will continue to trigger bankruptcies under ObamaCare (John Walker, "Actually Obama, Your Health Care Law Will Not Stop Medical Bankruptcy," *firedoglake.com*, April 30, 2014; Dan Mangan, "Medical Bills Are the Biggest Cause of US Bankruptcies: Study," *CNBC*, June 25, 2013; Christina LaMontagen, "NerdWallet Health finds Medical Bankruptcy Accounts for Majority of Personal Bankruptcies," wwww.nerdwallet.com, March 26, 2014; Himmelstein et al, "Medical Bankruptcy in the United States, 2007: Results of a National Study," *The American Journal of Medicine* (2009). A study of bankruptcies in the U.S. in 2007 found that 62.1 percent had a medical cause, and three-quarters of medical debtors had health insurance.

764 As just one example, ObamaCare also imposes a hefty tax on so-called Cadillac plans provided by employers—in other words plans that do a better job of covering people's medical expenses. The tax creates incentives for employers to reduce the quality of the plans they provide.

765 We wrestle with tough choices about which unacceptable financial burdens and risks to take on. Those living on the line between Medicaid-eligibility and ineligibility may bounce back and forth between Medicaid and some private insurance policy. As we shift between insurers, our choice of doctors also changes. If we end up making more money than projected, we owe a nasty bill at the end of the year to repay our subsidies.

766 Barack Obama, speaking to the Illinois AFL-CIO, June 30, 2003.

767 When Democratic Congressman John Conyers, a sponsor of HR 676, asked Obama to invite him and Drs. Marcia Angell and Quentin Young, single-payer supporters, to a big health care summit planned for the White House, he was turned down. No single-payer supporter was invited to participate in that pivotal meeting (Corporate Crime Reporter, "Obama to Single Payer Advocates: Drop Dead," *Common Dreams*, March 3, 2009); when six physicians from Oregon, with 191 years of combined medical experience among them, drove across the U.S. in a tour called "Mad as Hell Doctors" and asked Obama for a meeting to discuss single payer, they were turned down (Ralph Nader, "The Drive for Single Payer," *Common Dreams*, Sept. 1, 2009).

768 See YouTube videos of the "Baucus Eight" such as this one: http://www.youtube. com/watch?v=ncb58qnDyxs.

769 Ralph Nader, "The Drive for Single Payer," *CommonDreams.org*, Sept. 1, 2009.

770 Elizabeth Fowler worked for Senate Finance Committee Chair Baucus and was then hired as Vice President for Public Policy and External Affairs at WellPoint, a huge health insurance provider. Fowler then returned to Baucus's staff as his point person on the health care bill, where she was a lead drafter of ObamaCare. (Meanwhile former Baucus health issue counselor Michelle Easton lobbied for Wellpoint as a principal at Tarplin, Downs, and Young.) In 2010 Fowler moved to the U.S. Department of Health and Human Services to help implement ObamaCare. And then once again Fowler went back to working for a private industry benefited by ObamaCare, this time the pharmaceutical industry. Fowler runs global health policy for Johnson & Johnson, a pharmaceutical giant that strongly supported the ObamaCare bill that Fowler drafted. (Stolberg, Sheryl Gay, "Reaping Profits After Assisting on Health Law," *New York Times*, Sept. 17, 2013.)

771 One of the reasons Democrats give for not advancing public-interest legislation even when they control both houses of Congress is that irrational undemocratic rules govern the Senate. Under those rules, a senator or series of senators can block a majority-supported bill from coming to a vote through obstructionist tactics such as speaking for as long as they wish. Three-fifths of the Senate— usually 60 votes—are needed to end such a filibuster. Thus those in the minority can block legislation supported by a majority of senators. The Supreme Court has ruled that the Senate can change its rules by a simple majority vote, but Democrats have failed to do so. Then they complain about Republicans blocking majority-supported bills. Senator Dianne Feinstein worked against meaningful filibuster reform and then bemoaned the sorry state of things when a gun control bill amendment she wanted failed despite yes votes from 54 senators, for example. "Everything needs 60 votes today. This is supposed to be a majority body," Feinstein said. See: "Dianne Feinstein Whines About Filibuster Rules She Voted for," *Daily Kos*, April 18, 2013; Carolyn Lockhead, "Feinstein Assault-Weapons Ban Defeated," *San Francisco Chronicle*, April 18, 2013; Chris Miles, "Dianne Feinstein: Doesn't Want Huge Filibuster Reform Because It Will Hurt Dems Later," www.policymic, Jan. 3, 2013.

Note also that the Democrats had a filibuster-proof 60 votes in the Senate prior to Senator Kennedy's death. For an analysis of why their claim that they couldn't pass a strong bill with "only" 59 votes (a clear majority of the Senate) was a hoax, see Glenn Greenwald, "The Democratic Party's Deceitful Game," *Salon. com*, Feb. 23, 2010.

772 Supporters included Republican Senators Orrin Hatch, Charles Grassley, and Congressman Newt Gingrich.

773 It was surreal to watch Romney criticize ObamaCare in the presidential debates in 2012, in an attempt to differentiate himself from Obama.

774 For details, see Physicians for a National Health Program, "The Massachusetts Plan: A Failed Model for Reform." Problems include, for example, large numbers still uninsured, high plan prices and out-of-pocket costs for those insured creating ongoing financial insecurity, vulnerability for those who lose coverage by losing jobs, decimation of the state's safety net, very high numbers exempted from the mandate due to unaffordability, and unsustainability of the plan.

775 Brad Jacobson, "The Raw Story, Obama Received $20 Million from Healthcare Industry in 2008 Campaign," Jan. 12, 2010. The article is based on results of a custom research request performed by the Center for Responsive Politics, which pulled together contributions data from various relevant sectors such as pharmaceuticals, health services/HMOs, hospitals/nursing homes, etc. Totals for each industrial sector include PAC contributions and those from individuals and immediate family members who work for the industry, usually at top levels. Bundling of contributions is one of the ways corporations influence elections while adhering to campaign finance law limits on direct contributions.

776 Opensecrets.org, retrieved March 24, 2015. These contributions were apparently made to Senate race coffers for these candidates, which could be tapped for presidential activities (email communication with Center for Responsible Politics, March 24, 2015); see also, Lynn Sweet, "Money Obama Now Spurns Helped Launch White House Bid," *Chicago Sun Times*, Nov. 20, 2013.)

777 Opensecrets.org. Data retrieved June 15, 2014.

778 Opensecrets.org. Data retrieved June 15, 2014.

779 Bill Moyers, Journal, Oct. 9, 2009.

780 Dan Eggen and Kimberly Kindy, "Familiar Players in Health Bill Lobbying," *Washington Post*, July 6, 2009.

781 Opensecrets.org, data retrieved June 15, 2014.

782 Opensecrets.org, data retrieved June 16, 2014.

783 Kevin Zeese and Margaret Flowers, "Obamacare: The Biggest Insurance Scam in History," Oct. 30, 2013.

784 One HCAN TV ad, for example, showed various people asking questions and then shaking a Magic Eight Ball for answers that were invariably negative. "Will they pay for his inhaler?" a mother asks as her young son sits by her side. "Not likely," the Eight Ball says. After various people in the ad get similarly frustrating

answers, an off-screen voice intones "We can't trust insurance companies to fix the health care mess. If you're ready to demand quality affordable health care now, join us" (HCAN ad, July 2008). And yet ObamaCare leaves insurance corporations in charge, funnels taxpayer money to them, and forces people to buy their policies.

785 Looking back on the health care debate, single-payer activist Stuart Bramhall described the dynamics of new health care groups popping up and how they changed the terms of the debate. Single-payer activists in Washington State "quickly discovered that single payer activists in Ohio, Oregon and California were experiencing the exact same problems as we were," Bramhall wrote. He also wrote:

> As in our state, short-lived 'parallel' single payer organizations were being created by brand new left think tanks of left leaning foundations that claimed to support single payer health care—but disagreed with grassroots organizing to mobilize public support for it. Despite their nominal support for nationalizing health care, their newsletters, brochures, and public forums almost exclusively focused on arguments against lobbying for single payer health care. What was even more uncanny was that the language articulated by the staff employed by these parallel organizations was virtually identical in state after state. All their arguments boiled down to the 'political climate' and 'politically timing' being wrong for single payer and accusations about grassroots single payer activists being 'inexperienced', 'reckless' and 'wrong-headed' to aggressively push for it. In some cases these parallel organizations also launched competing proposals based on the private health insurance model.

Bramhall details some of the groups that undercut single-payer advocacy. For example, a group called Code Blue Now was "supposedly formed to develop 'public consensus' on the best way to reform health care (despite polling showing that 60% of Washington voters supported a single, publicly financed system," he wrote. (Stuart Bramhall, "Infiltrating the Single Payer Movement," stuartbramhall.aegauthorblogs.com, April 21, 2011.)

786 Rose Ann DeMoro, "Why is Health Care for America Now Giving Up on Real Reform?," *Huffington Post*, July 18, 2008.

787 Nyceve, "Has MoveOn Lost Its Mind?" *DailyKos*, July 10, 2008.

788 Dr. David Himmelstein, Radio debate with Richard Kirsch, "Progressives Disagree on Healthcare Reform," *Uprising Radio*, July 10, 2008.

789 Ralph Nader, "The Single-Payer Taboo," *Counterpunch*, May 11, 2009.

790 For example, he assured the American Medical Association of this in a speech in June of 2009, which can be viewed via YouTube.

791 As I urged people to not be diverted from fighting for single payer, I was amazed at how angry they got at me. There was real pressure to stop being "unrealistic" and to get with the program, which was public option, public option, public option. Others have commented on this animosity directed towards those who maintained a clear stance in favor of single payer (Kevin Zeese and Margaret Flowers, "Obamacare: The Biggest Insurance Scam in History," Oct 30, 2013).

792 David D. Kirkpatrick, "Obama Is Taking an Active Role in Talks on Health Care Plan," *The New York Times*, Aug. 13, 2009; Glenn Greenwald, "Truth About the Public Option Momentarily Emerges, Quickly Scampers Back into Hiding," *Salon.com*, Oct. 5, 2010; Igor Volsky, "Daschle: Public Option 'Taken Off the Table' in July Due to Understanding People Had With Hospitals," *ThinkProgress*, Oct. 5, 2010.

According to a book by Senator Majority Leader Tom Daschle and interviews with those privy to negotiations, for-profit hospital lobbyists obtained Obama's promise to drop the public option early on. Even as they encouraged people to focus on fighting for the public option, Obama and other Democratic Party leaders knew it was a goner. Public option proponent Senator Russ Feingold aptly acknowledged that the public-option-less bill that ended up moving forward appeared "to be legislation that the president wanted in the first place..." (Glenn Greenwald, "White House as Helpless Victim on Healthcare," *salon.com*, Dec. 16, 2009).

793 Victoria Kaplan, "Provin' 'Em Wrong: College Students and Young People Buck GOP, Get Health Coverage," *MoveOn.org*, Oct. 2, 2013.

794 Abby Goodnough, "Next Challenge for the Health Law: Getting the Public to Buy in," *The New York Times*, Dec. 19, 2013.

795 Goodnough, "Next Challenge for the Health Law: Getting the Public to Buy in."

796 Wendell Potter, "Skyrocketing Salaries for Health Insurance CEOs," *Truthout*, June 10, 2014.

797 Potter, "Skyrocketing Salaries for Health Insurance CEOs."

798 Robert Reich, "Obamacare Is a Republican Construct (So Why Are They So Upset?)," *Common Dreams*, Oct. 27, 2013.

799 Since 1933, Glass-Steagall had mandated the separation of commercial and investment banking to protect depositors from risky investments and speculation. Its repeal is largely understood to be a major factor leading to the financial meltdown of 2007-2008. The law repealing Glass-Steagall passed the Senate with 38 of the 45 Democratic Senators voting Yes. It passed the House with 138 Democrats supporting it, as compared to only 69 opposing it. Clinton signed it into law (William Kaufman, "Shattering the Glass-Steagall Act," *Counterpunch*,

Sept. 19-21, 2008; "The Price of Inequality: How Today's Divided Society Endangers Our Future," *Democracy Now*, featuring Joseph Stiglitz, June 6, 2012.)

800 See discussion of campaign contributions in chapter 9 for more information.

801 The day after his election in 2008, Obama announced a transition team, with an inner circle dominated by Citigroup executive Michael Froman, who led the search for Obama's economic team even as Citigroup received a second massive bailout. (Matt Taibbi, "Obama's Big Sellout," *Rolling Stone*, Dec. 9, 2009.) Examples of Obama's stunningly inappropriate Wall-Street-serving appointments include Timothy Geithner, Larry Summers, Bill Daley, Jack Lew, Mary Jo White, Gary Gensler, Eric Holder, Lanny Breuer, and Penny Pritzker.

802 Financial institutions that were failing as the result of their own irresponsible behaviors got publicly announced gigantic taxpayer-funded bailouts. Hundreds of billions of dollars were given to Bank of America, JPMorgan Chase, Citigroup, Goldman Sachs, AIG, and other banks and financial firms. Obama voted for bailouts as a senator and pressured his colleagues to do so as well. Then as president he implemented remaining disbursements and new bailout programs.

The Bush and Obama Administrations also carried out a huge *secret* bailout that dwarfed the publicly reported ones. Without telling Congress or the American public, the Federal Reserve gave out massive very low-interest loans to banks in trouble. According to an analysis by *Bloomberg Markets Magazine*, the Fed had committed $7.7 trillion as of March 2009, more than half of the value of everything produced in the U.S. that year. The secret loans enabled banks to look healthier than they really were to investors and to Congress as it approved publicly visible bailouts. They enabled banks to reap an estimated $13 billion or more in income. The six biggest U.S. banks borrowed as much as $460 billion from the Fed, even as they received $160 billion of Troubled Asset Relief Program (TARP) funds. (Ivry et al, "Secret Fed Loans Gave Banks $13 Billion Undisclosed to Congress," *Bloomberg Markets Magazine*, Nov. 27, 2011.) The six biggest banks were JPMorgan, Bank of America, Citigroup Inc, Wells Fargo & Co., Goldman Sachs Group, Inc, and Morgan Stanley. Later analyses by the Government Accountable Office and others indicate that the amount of secret low interest loans may be considerably higher than $7.7 trillion.

803 The Wall Street Reform and Consumer Protection Act of 2010, better known as the Dodd-Frank Act, was narrow and weak. JPMorgan Chase spent $14 million on lobbying during the 2009-2010 election cycle, while Goldman Sachs spent $7 million. There were 3000 lobbyists involved in the legislation, more than five per

member of Congress. A few were public-interest representatives, but Wall Street outspent them by 100 to 1 or more.

(Gary Rivlin, "The Billion-Dollar Bank Heist," *Newsweek*, July 13, 2011.) The Act left an extraordinary number of critical details to rulemaking. Since Wall Street representatives served in high places in the Obama Administration, the law was weakened even further via rulemaking. (Wayne Abernathy, "Dodd-Frank Act Implementation: Well Into It and No Further Ahead," *chicagofed.org, Economic Perspectives*, 3Q/2012; CFO Journal.) The financial industry then used its ample resources to file lawsuits challenging any rule provisions they didn't like. (For an in-depth play-by-play, see Matt Taibbi's article "Politics: How Wall Street Killed Financial Reform," *Rolling Stone*, May 10, 2012. See also, Daniel Indiviglioi, "5 Ways Lobbyists Influenced the Dodd-Frank Bill," *The Atlantic*, July 5, 2010; gjohnsit, "The Failures of Dodd-Frank," *Daily Kos*, April 28, 2014; Gary Rivlin, "The Billion-Dollar Bank Heist," *Newsweek*, July 13, 2011; Marcus Stanley, and Rebecca Thiess, "Years Late and Many Dollars Short," *US News & World Report*, April 23, 2014; and JP Sottile, "US Plutocracy and the Dodd-Frank Sausage Machine," *Truth-Out*, April 27, 2014.)

804 The Bush tax cuts battle focused on reductions in taxes on earnings above $200,000 for individuals and $250,000 for couples put in place during the George W. Bush years. They were set to expire, and the debate was over whether or not to make them permanent instead. Obama declared he would never support anything that maintained the tax cuts above $200,000 and $250,000, but he joined with other Democrats and Republicans in allowing the cuts to continue except for incomes of $400,000 and above for individuals and $450,000 and above for couples. So the "big victory" for regular Americans was that this particular cut for very high incomes was allowed to expire for those with extremely high incomes, though not for those with very high incomes.

Let's look at this victory in context. When Obama was still insisting that the cuts would be allowed to expire at the $200,000/$250,000 level, Citizens for Tax Justice, analyzed the impacts of this approach as compared to the Congressional Republicans approach which would have let the cuts continue even for incomes above the $400,000/$450,000 level. Under the Obama proposal, taxes for the richest 1% of Americans would have been cut by $20,130 on average in 2013, as compared to $70,790 under the Republican proposal. Wealthy individuals and couples still enjoyed tax savings under either party's proposal because everyone, including the 1%, would still receive tax cuts for their first $200,000/$250,000 of income. The poorest fifth of Americans would have saved $270 on average under Obama's proposal, and $120 under the Republicans'. (Citizens for Tax Justice, "U.S. Taxpayers and the Bush Tax Cuts, Obama's Approach vs. Congressional GOP's Approach," June 20, 2012.) Commentator David Sirota pointed out that the wealthiest households would only be able to cover the cost of *one* butler under Obama's approach, while they could afford *three* butlers under the Republican approach. (David Sirota, "More Butlers for the 1 Percent," *The Seattle Times*, July 21, 2012.) Remember also that the Citizens for Tax Justice analysis assumed that Obama would keep his commitment to the lower cutoff. With the cutoff ultimately being $400,000/$450,000 instead, the difference between the Democratic and Republican policies was even less significant.

805   At the end of World War II, "for every $1 Washington raised in taxes on individuals, it raised $1.50 in taxes on business profits. In contrast, today, for every dollar Washington gets in taxes on individuals, it gets 25 cents in taxes on businesses." (Karl Grossman, "Tax the Rich, Then Tax Them Again," *Counterpunch*, Dec. 7-9, 2012.). The Obama Administration has proposed cutting corporate taxes from 35 percent to 28 percent. (Jim Kuhnhenn, "Obama Administration to Propose Cutting Corporate Tax Rate From 35 Percent to 28 Percent," *Huffington Post*, Feb. 22, 2012.)

806   The tax rate for dividends, capital gains income, and "carried interest" is only 15%.

807   Citizens for Tax Justice and the Institute on Taxation and Economic Policy published a major study in the fall of 2011 that reviewed taxes paid and not paid by 280 big and profitable Fortune 500 companies. Among other things, the report found that 30 companies paid no net federal income tax from 2008 through 2010. An update in 2012 revealed that 26 of those 30 companies continued to enjoy negative federal income tax rates. That means they still made more money after taxes than before taxes over the four years of 2008 to 2011. (Citizens for Tax Justice, *Big No-Tax Corps Just Keep on Dodging*, April 9, 2012.)

Of the remaining four companies, three paid four-year effective tax rates of less than 4%. One company paid a tax rate of 10.9% for 2008-2011. In total, federal income taxes for the 30 companies remained negative, despite $205 billion in pretax U.S. profits. Overall, their average effective federal income tax rate was 3.1 percent over the four years.

808   Dave Lindorff, "Audit the Rich!" *Counterpunch*, April 8, 2013. A *Wall Street Journal* analysis of 60 major U.S. companies found they squirreled away a total of $166 billion offshore in 2012. This reportedly shielded more than 40% of their annual profits from U.S. taxes. ("U.S. Firms Stashed $166 Billion Offshore in 2012, Shielding 40% of Annual Profits," *Democracy Now*, March 12, 2013.)

Similarly, a bipartisan Senate committee issued a report indicating that Apple avoided paying U.S. taxes on $44 billion in income between 2009 and 2012. The report described a huge web of affiliates spanning several continents, including subsidiaries hiding Apple profits even in countries without Apple employees. ("Senate Report Says Apple Avoids Billions in Taxes," *Democracy Now*, May 21, 2013.)

According to Senator Bernie Sanders, corporations that received bailouts have been among those using offshore tax havens and other methods to get out paying taxes. Bank of America set up more than 200 subsidiaries in the Cayman Islands in 2010, paying no taxes and even receiving a rebate worth $1.9 billion from the IRS, according to Sanders, as just one example. (Sanders, Bernie, "A Choice For Corporate America: Are You With America Or the Cayman Islands," *Common Dreams*, Feb. 9, 2013.)

809   Dave Lindorff, "Audit the Rich!," *Counterpunch*, April 8, 2013.

810   We were told that government actions would solve the problem of financial institutions being "too-big-to-fail" and "too-big-to-prosecute," and so big that they can drag us all down in an instant when things go wrong. But giant banks have gotten *bigger*, not smaller, as a result of government policies. They have used publicly known bailouts and secret federal loans to solidify their positions. They've enjoyed the false reputation of being healthy because bailout money was only supposed to go to viable entities. And they've benefited from the implicit guarantee that the federal government will bail them out again in the future if they run into trouble. (Ivry et al, "Secret Fed Loans Gave Banks $13 Billion Undisclosed to Congress," *Bloomberg Markets Magazine*, Nov. 27, 2011.) Examples of how giant banks have gotten bigger include the deals that created Chase-Bear Stearns and Wells Fargo-Wachovia and Bank of America's acquisition of Merrill Lynch. America's six largest banks—Bank of America, JPMorgan Chase, Citigroup, Wells Fargo, Goldman Sachs, and Morgan Stanley—now have 14,420 subsidiaries among them.

811   Bailouts were supposed to lead to substantial help for individuals with burdensome mortgages and to increased lending, which would put people back to work. Instead banks have been sitting on money instead of loaning it, and aid to mortgage holders has been a tiny sliver of what was promised. In 2013, investigative journalist Matt Taibbi pointed out the irony that bailed out banks were earning $3.6 billion per year on money just sitting in accounts, which was the equivalent of the total spent on homeowner relief over the course of four years. While $50 billion had originally been earmarked for Home Affordable Modification Program, that amount was cut to $30 billion in 2010, but as of

November 2012, only $4 billion total had been used for loan modifications and other homeowner aid. The inspector general for the bailout found that lending among the nine biggest recipients of TARP aid "did not, in fact, increase." (Matt Taibbi, "Secrets and Lies of the Wall Street Bailout," *Rolling Stone*, Jan. 8, 2013.)

812   In 2010, Obama created a bipartisan Commission to explore ways to reduce the deficit and appointed as its co-chairs Alan Simpson, the former Republican Senator from Wyoming, and Erskine Bowles, who tried to privatize Social Security as Clinton's Chief of Staff. Both were well known to favor cuts to Social Security.

813   Obama has perpetuated and expanded U.S. military involvements.   Dave Lindorff, "Obama the War President," *Counterpunch*, Feb. 10, 2015; Phyllis Bennis, "As Obama Hails 'Turning Page' on Wars, U.S. Drone Strikes Continue Across Globe," *Democracy Now*, Jan. 21, 2015.

814   "New York Hedge Funds Pour Millions of Dollars into Cuomo-Led Bid to Expand Charter Schools," *Democracy Now*, Mar. 11, 2015.

Chapter 26

815   Justin Ruben, email message: "Obama's Heartbreaking Social Security Cuts," Dec. 21, 2012.

816   Bill McKibben, "Winter Heat Wave Underscores Need for Obama to Reject, Not Fast-Track, Keystone XL," *Democracy Now*, Mar 22, 2012.

817   "Tens of Thousands Rally to Stop Keystone XL Pipeline, Urge Obama to Move 'Forward on Climate,' *Democracy Now*, Feb. 18, 2013.

818   Martin Gilens, "Lead Essay: Under the Influence," *Boston Review*, July/August 2012. See also Gilens book: *Affluence & Influence*, 2012.

Chapter 27

819   Note also that under capitalism, never-ending growth is imperative. Economic soundness is determined by whether more and more products and services are being produced as compared to earlier time periods. This conflicts with an environmentally sustainable model in which we minimize consumption, energy use, and waste.

820   Here are two other examples of the laws of supply and demand undermining environmental protection:

  *   As discussed earlier, people who are supposed to be promoting organic agriculture in Washington State instead advocate capping organic acreage to

keep crop prices higher for existing organic growers. The realities of supply and demand won't let organic agriculture expand, they say. It's not that we *can't* grow more organic food, reducing our dependence on highly toxic pesticides and petroleum-based fertilizers. It's not that we *want* organic food to be expensive. It's that our market-based economy won't let us grow more apples sustainably.

※ Three wind-rich states—North Dakota, Kansas, and Texas—could satisfy the electrical needs of the entire U.S. by harnessing the wind. Why is this not happening? One reason is that we don't have the necessary grid infrastructure in place for this amount of wind power. With wealthy corporations and individuals appropriating the profits our labor generates, little is left in public coffers for such work. Widespread fracking is another factor undercutting wind power. It has driven down the price of natural gas, spurring investors to drop wind investments. In other words, capitalism is leading to investments in fossil fuel at the very time we need to keep those fuels in the ground to prevent climate catastrophe. The problem is not that we can't generate enough wind power for our needs. It's that capitalism undermines that outcome.

821 Ellen Schrecker, *Many Are the Crimes. McCarthyism in America* (1998).

822 Thomas Ahern, "Constitutional Law—Cole v. Richardson—Another Look at State Loyalty Oaths," *DePaul Law Review*, Vol. 22, Issue 4, Summer 1973.

823 Lewis F. Powell, Jr., "Confidential Memo. Attack on American Free Enterprise System," Memo to Eugene B. Sydnor, Jr., Chairman, Education Committee, U.S. Chamber of Commerce, August 23, 1971.

824 Powell was deeply concerned about the voices "joining the chorus of criticism" of free enterprise that came "from perfectly respectable elements of society: from the college campus, the pulpit, the media, the intellectual and literary journals, the arts and sciences, and from politicians."

825 Charlie Cray, *The Lewis Powell Memo—Corporate Blueprint to Dominate Democracy*, Aug. 23, 2011, www.greenpeace.org.usa.

826 See *Democracy Now* interview with David Talbot, author of "The Devil's Chessboard, Allen Dulles, the CIA, and the Rise of America's Secret Government," October 14, 2015.

827 Richard D. Wolff, "The Wages of Capitalism," Dec. 8, 2014; Richard D. Wolff, "Capitalism Hits the Fan," *www.rdwolff.net/sites/default/files/attachment/4/03Wolff.pdf.*

828 Leon Trotsky, *The Revolution Betrayed* (1937).

829   Leon Trotsky, *The Revolution Betrayed* (1937); Richard Wolff, *Economic Update*, October 16, 2015.

830   Kate L. Roeger et al, "The Nonprofit Sector in Brief. Public Charities, Giving and Volunteering," 2011.

831   Darlene Superville, "Obama praises HW Bush for volunteer initiative," *AP U.S. & World News*, July 15, 2013.

832   Robert Reich, *Saving Capitalism. For the Many, Not the Few* (2015.)

833   Food & Water Watch, *Public Research, Private Gain* (April 2012.)

834   Sharon Levy, "Our Shared Code: The *Myriad* Decision and the Future of Genetic Research," *Environ Health Perspect*, DOI: 10.1289/ehp 121-A250.

835   Ed Rampell, *Cooperatives and Workers' Self-Directed Enterprises. An Interview with Richard Wolff on Counterpunch*, April 6, 2013.

836   Kshama Sawant, Statement at *The Climate Crisis: Which Way Out? Forum*, New York City, September 20, 2014.

837   Citizens United v. Federal Election Commission, 558 U.S. 310. The case involved a film documentary entitled "Hillary: The Movie" which was highly critical of then-Senator and presidential candidate Hillary Clinton. Citizens United, the nonprofit corporation that made the film, sought to run TV commercials early in 2008 promoting it on DirecTV. The U.S. District Court said that the commercials violated a provision of the Bipartisan Campaign Act of 2002, better known as the McCain-Feingold campaign finance law. The provision in question prohibited corporations and unions from using money in their general treasuries to fund "electioneering communications"—broadcast advertisements mentioning a candidate—within 30 days before a primary or 60 days before a general election. The Supreme Court ruled that corporations and labor unions can spend their own money to support or oppose political candidates through independent communications like television advertisements.

The decision is widely described as having "opened the floodgates," allowing wealthy individuals to pour unlimited funds into elections, inundating the public with their views about those running for office. It is true that very large sums of money were pumped into federal races as a result of the decision, but it is wrong to imply that elections were not already unduly influenced by big money prior to the decision, as chapter 9 makes clear.

838   Move to Amend, Constitutional Amendment Introduced in Congress Ensuring Rights for People, not Corporations, Feb. 11, 2013; Move to Amend website, retrieved Aug. 13, 2013.

839   See Matt Bai, "How Much Has Citizens United Changed the Political Game?" *The New York Times*, July 17, 2012; Irene Kan, "Soft Money Makes a Comeback at the Conventions," OpenSecretsblog, June 13, 2008; Bradley A. Smith, "The Myth of Campaign Finance Reform," *National Affairs*, Winter 2010.   In the early 1900s, the first federal campaign finance law banned corporate campaign contributions, but corporations just started having their executives deliver the money and spending money *on behalf* of candidates instead of handing it to them directly.   Other reforms prompted corporations to establish Political Action Committees (PACs) that collected money from members, shareholders, and others involved with the corporation.

In the 1970s Congress passed a major campaign finance law that established all sorts of regulations, including limits on contributions from individuals and PACs, while maintaining the ban on corporate campaign contributions.   The law created the Federal Election Commission to keep an eye on things.   But Big Money continued to pour its cash into elections.   In particular, would-be mega donors and the political parties discovered "soft money," unregulated cash that could be handed over to the political parties for things like "party-building."   The parties ran "issues ads" which clearly promoted their candidates, but stopped short of expressly urging viewers and readers to vote one way or another.

In 2002 the McCain-Feingold Act ended "soft money" donations to the parties.   But still Big Money flowed.   Organizations arose that served as "shadow parties," with their own voter turnout and advertising capabilities.   These organizations could not engage in "express advocacy," i.e., overtly calling for support or opposition of candidates.   Nor could they use corporate money for "electioneering communications" (i.e., radio or TV ads) that even mentioned candidates within 30 days of primaries and 60 days of general elections.   A lot can be done to influence elections even within these confines.   In addition, wealthy interests used other loopholes to throw their monetary weight around, such as funding the Democratic and Republican Conventions.   See chapter 9 to see a few of the techniques in Big Money's bag of tricks for heavily influencing elections, despite campaign finance laws on the books.

840   Agribusiness interests have already secured passage of "food disparagement" laws in numerous states that make it easier for growers and others to charge critics with defamation (http://cspinet.org/foodspeak/laws/existlaw.htm).   Organizations sued under these statutes can at least defend themselves by proving that what they said was true.   If the First Amendment no longer applies to corporations and other "artificial entities," lawmakers might be able to directly bar them from publicly expressing concerns, regardless of veracity.

841   Ira Glasser, "Testimony of Executive Director Ira Glasser on Campaign Finance Reform Legislation Before the Senate Committee on Rules and Administration," Before the U.S. Senate Committee on Rules and Administration, Mar. 22, 2000.

Chapter 28

842   World Hunger Services, 2012 World Hunger and Poverty Facts and Statistics, retrieved June 7, 2012, p. 2; FAO, Reducing Poverty and Hunger: The Critical Role of Financing for Food, Agriculture and Rural Development, February 2002, p. 9.

843   Joyce Nelson, "A Real and Ready Solution for Climate Change, *Counterpunch,* July 21, 2015, citing Rodale Institute, *Regenerative Organic Agriculture and Climate Change,* October 2014.

844   Paul Buchheit, "Some Outrageous Facts About inequality," *Common Dreams,* July 2, 2012.

845   Adolpho Alvarez, an orchardist who was active with Farm Worker Pesticide Project, is one example. See: NRCS, "Conservation Showcase: A Passion for fruit: Organic grower finds niche farming with nature," 2008.

846   Unite National Human Rights, Office of the High Commissioner, "Eco-Farming Can Double Food Production in 10 Years, Says New UN Report," March 8, 2011; "Hungry for Land: Small Farmers Feed the World With Less Than a Quarter of All Farmland," *Grain,* May 30, 2014; College of Natural Resources, Berkeley, *The Agroecological Revolution,* 2011.

847   Rodale Institute, *Regenerative Organic Agriculture and Climate Change* (October 2014.)

848   Water includes things like wave and tidal technologies as well as hydroelectricity from dams.

849   Mark Z. Jacobson and Mark A. Delucchi, "Providing All Global Energy With Wind, Water and Solar Power, Part I: Technologies, Energy Resources, Quantities and Areas of Infrastructure, and Materials," *Energy Policy* 39 (2011) 1154-1169; Mark A. Delucchi and Mark Z. Jacobson, "Providing All Global Energy With Wind, Water and Solar Power, Part II: Reliability, System and Transmission Costs, and Policies," *Energy Policy* 39 (2011) 1170-1190.   Drs. Jacobson and Delucchi are by no means alone in their analyses. A report by Synapse Energy Economics released in April of 2013, for example, projects mixes of *existing* technologies and practices, concluding that the energy grid is capable of balancing projected load "for each region, in nearly every hour of every season of the year." It finds that "strategies to address one of the most pressing challenges faced by our species and our planet are already not only achievable,

but cost-effective."(Vitolo et al, "Meeting Load with a Resource Mix Beyond Business as Usual," April 2013.)

850 Drs. Jacobson and Delucchi's energy plan for New York State was published in 2013. They concluded that all of the State's energy for electricity, transportation, and heating and cooling could come from renewable energy sources by 2050. By 2030, New York's power could be provided by 10% onshore wind, 40% offshore wind, 10% concentrated solar, 10% solar PV plants, 6% residential rooftop PV, 12% commercial/governmental rooftop PV, 1% tidal, and 5.5% hydroelectric. The conversion to renewables would create more jobs than those lost. (Jacobson et al, "Examining the feasibility of converting New York State's all-purposed energy infrastructure to one using wind, water and sunlight," *Energy Policy*, 2013.)

851 Robert Hunziker, "The Holy Grail of Energy?" *Counterpunch*, Jan 24-26, 2014.

852 Wenonh Hauter, "Memo to Fracking Apologists: You're Hurting Renewables (and You're Greenwashing, Too)," *Commondreams.org;* Sept. 20, 2012.

853 Center for Food Safety, *Soil and Carbon. Soil Solutions to Climate Problems* (April 2015.) See also, Ronnie Cummins, "World Food Day: Cook Organic, Not the Planet," *Common Dreams*, Oct. 16, 2013.

854 Rodale Institute, *Regenerative Organic Agriculture and Climate Change* (Oct. 2014.)

855 Richard Fenning, Control Risks, Riskmap Report 2013, p. 27.

856 Less than 1% of what the world spends on weapons each year could have put every child into school by 2000, but that didn't happen. Anup Shah, Poverty Facts and Stats, http://www.globalissues.org/article/26/poverty-facts-and-stats, updated as of Sept. 20, 2010, retrieved June 7, 2012, citing State of the World, Issue 287, Feb. 1997, New Internationalist.

857 Center for Budget and Policy Priorities, "Policy Basics: Where Do Our Federal Tax Dollars Go?" March 31, 2014.

858 Frontline workers hold non-managerial positions. Examples include cashiers, cooks, custodians, and greeters.

859 Allegretto et al, *Fast Food, Poverty Wages. The Public Cost of Low-Wage Jobs in the Fast-Food Industry* (Oct. 15, 2013).

860 At the time of this writing, the average sales associate hourly wage at Walmart's Sam's Club stores is slightly over $10.30.

861 Democratic staff of the U.S. House Committee on Education and the Workforce, *The Low-Wage Drag on Our Economy: Wal-Mart's Low Wages and Their Effect on Taxpayers and Economic Growth* (May 2013); The six Walton family heirs to the Walmart Empire have a combined wealth of $69.7 billion, the equivalent to that owned by the entire bottom 30% of the U.S. population. "Interview with Joseph

Stiglitz on the Price of Inequality: How Today's Divided Society Endangers our Future," *Democracy Now*, June 6, 2012, p. 2.

862 Kevin Zeese and Margaret Flowers, "Obamacare: The Biggest Insurance Scam in History," *Truthout*, Oct. 30, 2013.

863 Kim Klein, *Fundraising for Social Change* (2011.)

864 Robert Brulle, Chapter 21: Politics and the Environment, Handbook *of Politics: State and Society in Global Perspective* (2010.)

865 Adam Ruben, MoveOn, letter to members dated September 10, 2012.

866 Kate L. Roeger et al, "The Nonprofit Sector in Brief. Public Charities, Giving and Volunteering" (2011). See also, John Mutz and Katherine Murray, *Fundraising for Dummies* (2010.) Mutz and Murray reported that between September 2007 and September 2008 more than 61 million adults (26.2 percent of the population 16 and over) volunteered. Volunteers donated 8.1 billion hours of service to nonprofit organizations. The average amount of volunteer time offered was 52 hours per year. Seniors (over age 65) offered the greatest amount of time at 96 hours per year.

867 Center for Responsive Politics, "Heavy Hitters, Top All-Time Donors, 1989-2010," *OpenSecrets.org*, retrieved March 10, 2011.

868 The Mellman Group, results of public opinion research, September 2010.

869 "Are Millennials Really 'Greener' than Boomers?" *DDB Worldwide*, *Blog*, 2013.

870 League of United Latin American Citizens, League of Women Voters, and Natural Resources Defense Council, "National Poll Shows Strong Disapproval for President Obama's SmogRule Delay, Unfavorable Ratings for Congress' Assault on Clean Air Act," Oct. 13, 2011.

871 Jean Chemnick, "Air Pollution: Poll Shows Voter Support for EPA Rules," *E&E News*, Oct. 13, 2011.

872 Sierra Club, *Clean Energy Under Siege. Following the Money Trail Behind the Attack on Renewable Energy* (August 2012.)

873 Chris Williams, "How to Fight Climate Change and Rebuild a Stricken City," *Counterpunch*, Nov 2-4, 2012.

874 Ruy Teixeira, "Public Opinion Snapshot: Americans Are Concerned About Outsourcing," www.americanprogress.org, July 2, 2012.

875 Medicare for All, Chart of Americans' Support, retrieved Sept. 17, 2013. The polls were conducted by AP LA Times/Bloomberg, CBS News, CNN/Opinion Research, the *New York Times*, and others.

876 Harris International, "PACs, Big Companies, Lobbyists, and Banks and Financial Institutions Seen by Strong Majorities as Having Too Much Power and Influence in DC," Harris Poll results discussion, May 29, 2012.

877 Harris International, "PACs, Big Companies, Lobbyists, and Banks and Financial Institutions Seen by Strong Majorities as Having Too Much Power and Influence in DC," Harris Poll results discussion, May 29, 2012.

878 Pew Research Center, "Little Change in Public's Response to 'Capitalism,' 'Socialism,'" Dec. 28, 2011.

879 Justin McCarthy, "In U.S., Socialist Presidential Candidates Least Appealing," June 22, 2015, http://www.gallup.com/poll/183713/socialist-presidential-candidates-least-appealing.aspx.

880 "World's Faith in Capitalism Erodes as Financial Crisis Continues: Survey," *Common Dreams*, July 13, 2012.

881 Pew Research Center, "Frustration with Congress Could Hurt Republican Incumbents," Dec. 15, 2011.

882 Tribune Washington Bureau and The Associated Press, "Poll: Partisan Divide Grows; Affiliation with Parties Erodes," *Seattle Times*, June 5, 2012.

883 David Ferry, "Election Total Likely Tops $3 Million," *RichmondConfidential*, Nov. 16, 2010; and private communication from environmental justice network leader working with EJ groups in the Richmond area, Nov. 4, 2010.

884 AMP Agency Inc, and Cone, Inc., "The Millennial Generation: Pro-Social and Empowered to Change the World," www.greenbook.org, 2013.

885 Richard Fenning, Control Risks, Riskmap Report 2013, p. 2

886 http://www.democracyatwork.info/; http://www.toolboxfored.org/project/own-the-change/. The free TESA/GRIFtv video *Own the Change* offers how-to information for people curious about starting co-ops, for example. Listen to the Economic Update podcast produced by Democracy At Work dated Oct. 16, 2015 for a discussion of WSDEs.

887 E. Scott Reckard and Jim Puzzanghera, "Consumers Flock to Credit Unions as Bank Fees Rise," *Los Angeles Times* as printed in the *Seattle Times*, March 21, 2012.

888 For example, fast-food workers staged a one-day strike in at least 150 U.S. cities and 30 countries on May 15, 2014 (*Democracy Now*, May 15, 2014.) In August of 2013, as part of a national strike, workers walked off the job in Detroit, St. Louis, Chicago, Kansas City, and Flint, Michigan (*Democracy Now*, Aug. 1, 2013). In May of 2014, a crowd of up to 2000 protested outside of McDonald's Illinois headquarters. The crowd included hundreds of McDonald's employees in uniform. It marched on McDonald's "Hamburger University" campus near Chicago. One hundred people were arrested (*Democracy Now*, May 22, 2014.)

889 The people's mic was popularized by Occupy Wall Street but was used at prior protests as well, such as the WTO protests and nuclear protests. It is used as a substitute for an electronic microphone, which may require a permit. To

start using the "people's mic" a person shouts "mic check." Others repeat "mic check." Then the person offers his or her statement phrase by phrase, with each utterance echoed back by the nearby crowd so that those farther away can hear the message.

890 "'We Have to Stop This Inequality': Fast-Food Worker Strike Spreads to Dozens of Cities," *Democracy Now*, May 15, 2014.

891 Lynn Thompson and Amy Martinez, "Seattle City Council Approves Historic $15 Minimum Wage," *Seattle Times*, June 2, 2014.

892 Kevin Zeese and Margaret Flowers, "Major Social Transformation Is a Lot Closer Than You May Realize—How Do We Finish the Job?," *Alternet*, Dec. 30, 2013.; Max Fisher, "Peaceful Protest Is Much More Effective Than Violence for Toppling Dictators," *Washington Post*, Nov. 5, 2013.

Chapter 29

893 For an example of a broader agenda, see Bruce Lesnick, "Top Secret: A Practical Plan to Save the World," *truthout*, Dec.15, 2014, http://www.truth-out.org/speakout/item/28016-top-secret-a-practical-plan-to-save-the-world.

Chapter 30

894 Richard Wolff, Democracy at Work, Discussion of Worker Self-Directed Enterprises (WSDEs), "Economic Update," Oct. 16, 2015.

895 At this writing, the organization Socialist Alternative is very active in the fight for a $15 minimum wage and for rent control, for example. Socialist Alternative works throughout the U.S. and is affiliated with the Committee on Workers International, a worldwide socialist organization in 47 countries on every continent. Socialist Alternative runs candidates for office, and succeeded in putting Kshama Sawant on the Seattle City Council, focusing on minimum wage, rent control, and related issues.

896 At this writing U.S. Senator Bernie Sanders, a self-proclaimed socialist, is running for President. Unfortunately, Sanders is not actually a socialist. He supports reforms that keep capitalism in place. Moreover, he is running as a Democrat and has pledged to support whatever candidate is nominated by the Democratic Party.

Chapter 31

897 Martin Luther King, *I See the Promised Land*, April 3, 1968.

898 Naomi Wolf, "Revealed: How the FBI Coordinated the Crackdown on Occupy," *The Guardian*, Dec. 29, 2012; The Partnership for Civil Justice

Fund, "FBI Documents Reveal Secret Nationwide Occupy Monitoring," Dec. 22, 2012.

899   Historically, there is ample documentation of infiltration in other social justice movements, and the documents obtained by the Partnership for Civil Justice Fund, though heavily redacted, hint strongly that infiltrators attended Occupy meetings.

900   Sam Geduldig et al, "Clark, Lytle, Geduldig Cranford Memo to American Bankers Association, Proposal: Occupy Wall Street Response," Nov. 24, 2011; "Leaked Memo Plans Occupy Wall Street Destruction," *Whiteoutpress*, Nov. 19, 2011.

901   Charles M. Young, "Yes, the 99% Spring Is a Fraud," *Counterpunch*, April 13-15, 2012.

902   "Two Years After Occupy Wall Street, a Network of Offshoots Continue Activism for the 99%," *Democracy Now*, Sept. 19, 2013.

Chapter 32

903   Public Outreach Fundraising, job posting, idealist.org, Feb. 18, 2012.

904   Brian Rosenthal, "'Green' Strategists Hired by Coal Companies to Push Train Proposals," *Seattle Times*, Feb. 23, 2013.

905   Allegretto et al, *Fast Food, Poverty Wages. The Public Cost of Low-Wage Jobs in the Fast-Food Industry* (Oct. 15, 2013.)

906   National Employment Law Project, *The Low-Wage Recovery: Industry Employment and Wages Four Years into the Recovery* (April 2014.)

907   Timothy Cama, "Oil Industry Launches New Recruiting Campaign," *The Hill*, June 12, 2014.

908   Pete Seeger, "My Rainbow Race", © Figs. D Music (BMI) obo itself and Sanga Music, Inc. (BMI) c/o The Bicycle Music Company, All Rights Reserved. Used by Permission.

Index

• • •

Made in the USA
Middletown, DE
28 May 2019